THE COLLECTED POEMS OF
PHILIP WHALEN

Wesleyan Poetry

THE COLLECTED POEMS OF
PHILIP WHALEN

EDITED BY MICHAEL ROTHENBERG

WESLEYAN UNIVERSITY PRESS

MIDDLETOWN, CONNECTICUT

Wesleyan University Press

Published by University Press of New England,

One Court Street, Lebanon, NH 03766

www.upne.com

Designed by James Brissam

© 2007 by Brandeis University Press

Printed in the United States of America

5 4 3 2 1

LIBRARY OF CONGRESS CATALOGING-IN-PUBLICATION DATA

Whalen, Philip.

The collected poems of Philip Whalen / edited by Michael Rothenberg.

   p.   cm. — (Wesleyan poetry)

Includes bibliographical references and index.

ISBN–13: 978–0–8195–6859–5 (alk. paper)

ISBN–10: 0–8195–6859–7 (alk. paper)

I. Rothenberg, Michael. II. Title.

PS3545.H117A6 2007

811'.54—dc22   2007016905

The publisher and editor gratefully acknowledge reprint of Gary Snyder's Foreword from *Shambala Sun and Continuous Flame,* as well as previous publication of Philip Whalen's *Meditation and writing peace (Fish Drum).*

CONTENTS

Appendixes

EDITOR'S NOTE AND ACKNOWLEDGMENTS

The Collected Poems of Philip Whalen contains all of the poems from Philip Whalen's poetry collections, his uncollected poems published in small press magazines and anthologies, and *Calendar,* his graduate thesis from Reed College which Whalen considered his first "completed" book of poems. (Whalen's "Notes and Appendices" to *Calendar* appear in the appendixes to this volume). The poems gathered here are organized chronologically by date of completion, according to the dates Whalen gave them. He used many different formats for noting the date, and I have preserved these variations here.

Although Philip Whalen talked about his poetry as a "picture or graph of the mind moving," I believe his heart is what moved him to record the "nerve movie" in his mind. This is the poetry of a body, speech, and mind consciousness that exceeds all expectations, hinged to humor and playfulness. The love and respect felt for Philip Whalen by friends and students remains with us still, in our thoughts and in our writing.

Whalen's book *Highgrade* is made up of pieces often referred to as "doodle poems" or "visual poems." The intended titles of these pieces are not always clear. Within this book, I have chosen to use dates (when available) and/or prominent lines for titles. I have bracketed these titles in the table of contents to indicate that they are my approximations and should not be considered Whalen's choice.

Although it is always important to know when a poem was completed and published, it is also interesting to know how poems are organized into manuscripts. I have included the original table of contents from each of Philip Whalen's major books to provide additional insight and show his compositional and organizational perspective and aesthetic.

However, sometimes Philip Whalen's "creative process" was simply to allow a publisher or editor to make their own organizational choices. For example, when I asked PW why the poems in *On Bear's Head* were not organized chronologically, he told me he had no idea, "It just came from the publisher that way."

✲

Special thanks to Terri Carrion, Nancy Victoria Davis, Joanne Kyger, Norman Fischer, Jane Falk, Clark Coolidge, Pat Nolan, Leslie Scalapino, Gary Snyder, and Larry Keenan. I am also grateful to James Koller, Keith Abbott, Bill Berkson, Jennifer Birkett, Mairead Byrne, Diane di Prima, Larry Fagin, Hammond Guthrie, Gary Gach, Stephan Hyner, Alastair Johnston, Michael McClure, William Mohr, Jonathan Penton, Jerome Rothenberg, Ron Silliman, Dale Smith, Dave Vandeveer, Jr., Joel Weishaus, and Suzi Winson for their consultations.

I would also like to acknowledge Gay Walker and Mark Kuestner, Special Collections, Philip Whalen Archive, Eric V. Hauser Memorial Library, Reed College, Portland, Oregon; Yvonne Schofer, Humanities Bibliographer (English) at Memorial Library, University of Wisconsin-Madison; Tony Bliss and David Kessler and the University Archives of The Bancroft Library, University of California, Berkeley; Columbia University, Rare Book and Manuscript Library; Columbia University, Rare Book and Manuscript Library; Geoff Smith and "The Rare Books and Manuscripts Library of The Ohio State University Libraries"; and the Literary Estate of Philip Whalen for their cooperation and assistance with this project.

My thanks to Suzanna Tamminen, Leslie Starr, Eric Levy, and Stephanie Elliot at Wesleyan University Press. Most importantly, my deepest appreciation goes to Wesleyan University Press for giving us this opportunity to celebrate Philip Whalen's work.

FOREWORD

gary snyder

HIGHEST AND DRIEST
For Philip Zenshin's Poetic Drama/Dharma

I first saw Philip from the wings back stage, he was out front in a rehearsal, directing some point with the actors. His confidence and clarity impressed me, a freshman at seventeen, naïve and new.

Philip as director and actor for some student production—I heard soon, though, that he wrote poetry and then in conversation later, I was delighted by his erudition and searching wit. We became friends.

Philip had grown up in The Dalles—up the Columbia gorge and at the beginning of the dry side of the ranges. He had been in the Air Force, and had already read much philosophy, literature, and history. Being part of Phil's circle was like being in an additional class—having an extra (intimately friendly) instructor, one with nutty humor and more frankly expressed opinions. He extended us into areas not much handled by the college classes of those days, such as Indian and Chinese philosophy. I had done some reading in the *Upanishads,* had ventured into the *Tao Te Ching* and the Confucian Classics, and was just beginning to read Warren's translations from Pali Buddhist texts. Philip led the way in making conversation possible, and then making poetry out of the territory of those readings. His own poetry circled around and into it a bit, with a dimension that was not quite present in our official modernist mentors Yeats, Pound, Eliot, Williams, and Stevens. (My other close new poet friend in this loose group was Lew

Welch.) Philip had an elegant style of speaking with intonations, phrases, and subtle linguistic mannerisms that lightly affected many.

The Chinese-American World War II veteran Charles Leong, brilliant student and expert calligrapher, plus Lloyd Reynolds who taught printing, calligraphy, art, creative writing, William Blake's poetry, and much else—moved in and out of these conversations as well. In some odd way there was already a Pacific Rim post-industrial consciousness in the air then, right in the sleepy backward old Pacific Northwest where the restaurants were either Swedish smorgasbord or things like "The Oyster House." The memories of W.W. I were not totally dried up either; same with the memories of the big old time logging camps and the extravagant earlier salmon runs.

I wasn't writing much poetry yet—but Lew and Phil were, and we all admired it. I didn't begin to write poems that I could relate to until I was in my mid-20s. By that time I'd been briefly in Indiana for graduate school and then back to the Bay Area to live and work on the docks of San Francisco. Philip and I shared an apartment on Montgomery Street, and began to move in cosmopolitan circles of writers and artists of the whole Bay Area: Robert Duncan, Jean Varda, Jack Spicer, Michael McClure, and many more. We got to know Alan Watts, met Claude Dalenberg and the McCorkle brothers; and attended the Berkeley Buddhist Church's Friday night study group meetings. (Jodo Shin was our first contact with a living Buddhist practice.)

Philip and I would go our separate ways to job opportunities here or there, up and down the whole West Coast, but we would always end up back in San Francisco at some convenient meeting place like Cafe Trieste, or a little later, Kenneth Rexroth's Friday evening salon. Chinese poetics, the flow of Indian Sanskrit poetry, Pound's line, Blake quoted by heart, Gertrude Stein avidly read aloud, Lew Welch singing Shakespeare songs to his own melodies, all led the way toward whatever it was we did next. Like taking up the study and practice of Mah Jong and the I Ching, or cross-town walks to the beach and the Legion of Honor. Philip was always writing, always reading, and whenever possible playing music. At one time he went to considerable trouble to get an old pump organ into our apartment, to play Bach on.

Allen Ginsberg and Jack Kerouac came to town, and catalyzed the energy already fully present into a more public poetics and politics. I left for my long residence in Japan. For some years I sent Philip the news of the Capital, until he came there. Once in Kyoto, Philip seemed instantly intimate with the sites of literature and history, commenting that "*here* was where Lady Murasaki had that little altercation with the other lady over which carriage should go first" or some Buddhist temple that had been built on an old palace foundation. Then he began to be drawn more and more to the message of the big Buddhist temples, and the lessons of impermanence their vast graveyards out back provide: thousands of little stupas for the priests of the past, thus moving from the seductive cultural fascinations of old Japan to a deeply realized *samsaric* awareness. Note well his poetry and prose from the Old Capital. Once back on the West Coast it was not long before he made the step into full Zen practice.

Once a priest, it was clear that this was Philip's true vocation. He had the dignity, the learning, the spiritual penetration, and the playfulness of the archetypal Man of the Cloth, of any tradition, and yet was not in the least tempted by hierarchy or power. Philip never left his poetry, his wit, or his critical intelligence behind; his way of poetry is a main part of his teaching. His quirks became his pointers, and his frailties his teaching method. Philip was always the purest, the highest, the most dry, and oddly cosmic, of the Dharma-poets we've known—we are all greatly karmically lucky to have known him. And we are very fortunate to have this volume of his collected verse, which will keep his voice alive for everyone and help secure his legacy as one of our greatest poets.

leslie scalapino

LANGUAGE AS TRANSIENT ACT, THE POETRY OF PHILIP WHALEN

A characteristic of all avant garde movements has been to change the way of seeing in a time by removing or breaking down the barrier between the spectator/reader and their *being* that present-time (also being *in* that present): To remove the barrier so that the spectator can no longer be separate from their present, from their being phenomena. This puncturing of time as space, in the conceptual space of poetry or theater, can also operate to dismantle social structuring.

The Beat movement was particularly American as literary, visual art, and cultural phenomena: a populist avant garde. (While the term "avant garde" commonly implies 'elite,' in contrast to 'populist,' the term means "vanguard" denoting the new, a change of the language and perception.)

While removal of the barrier between the spectator (participant as reader, listener) and (their) present-time, being what *is* the present, is akin to Gertrude Stein (a grandmother of the Beats), it was also compatible with Buddhist philosophy and practice—and it has intrinsic political meaning. Dismantling social structuring on an overt level was evident in the Beat movement as history of activism. Anti-war activism and writings, and expressions of sexual freedom were characteristic of the Beats (as cited in, for example, the famous censorship trials of Allen Ginsberg's *Howl* and Michael McClure's play, *The Beard,* for their explicit sexuality).

Extending on their Modernist basis to include Asian sources (differently from Pound's use of these), some Beats also incorporated Western visionary traditions. Ginsberg's range included W. C. Williams and William Blake, yoga practice, use of hallucinogens, and Tibetan Buddhism. McClure's influences were Blake and Shelley,

Pound, Williams, Olson, biology and physics, peyote, and later Zen Buddhism. Gary Snyder is a Zen monk. Burroughs' texts drew on the use of drugs and the method of cut-ups from other sources as a way of bypassing the controls implicit in intuitive, psychological self-expression.

Philip Whalen, a Zen monk, a voluminous reader learned in Asian as well as European and American texts of philosophy and literature, who could quote and cite sources from memory even blind at the end of his life, was influenced early-on by Williams, whom he met when Williams visited Reed College where Whalen was a student with Gary Snyder and Lew Welch. Whalen described (to me in conversation) his discovery of Williams' poetry: It opened for him the possibility of freedom from an 'academy' notion of a poem, which he viewed as being narration of subject matter in a preconceived ordering, bound up. Rather, he realized that a reordering of every level can take place in the line and in the sound structure of the language itself. Whalen was also influenced by Stein and Pound. He made the distinction to me that his direction was more the phenomenological undertaking of Stein than the visionary direction suggested by Blake that was taken up by Ginsberg.

The relation the Beats created between Modernism and Asian thought and Buddhist practice was that of making a phenomenological relation in the language: Breaking down the U.S. cultural convention of mind-body split, language is brought to bear as physically as mind phenomena itself.

The freedom that Whalen took from Williams' poetic line, for example, as (in Williams) only its own sound/shape (rather than being "about" something else, a subject) is applied in Whalen to an examination of mind itself as shape and movement itself, or stillness, even extending that movement or shape to see the mind as inseparable from history (from being phenomena 'outside')—while history's inseparability undoes dichotomy of 'outside' and 'inside.'

The poem "In the Night," for example, is a series of lines that are comparisons between dissimilarities, sounds Whalen hears at night, which include demons and ghosts, Whalen running, an elephant, a hen, the Japanese wars of Onan:

"I FUCKING RAN"

❁

"elephant and sunset"

❁

"huge hen"

❁

Lots of speed makes the surfboard slicker
Falling upward. . .
         ONIN-NO-RAN (1467–1475)
Lots of speed. I fucking ran.
Civil wars more interesting than any other kind
      America

(p. 690)

The relation in this night space to (its) events and sights, real and imagined, is 'actually' only sound (such as a Japanese war, "ONIN-NO-RAN," and "I fucking ran"). Everything that is left out, infinite numbers of sounds, also creates that space, of 'actual' referenced history and of night perceived by Philip Whalen. His only editorial remark in the poem is that, "The world is larger / More complicated than we can remember / And so we fall upward / Into a fake superiority." That is, we order falsely when we summarize and explain, a hierarchical construct that conceals relation. So Whalen playfully orders on the basis of sound (similarity/dissimilarity at once), condensing to be only a view in history at once an observation *on* history.

In some poems Whalen used the structure of the fugue, the form of which is variations returning to a theme that's a basis, his measure being invention that becomes a way of seeing the separation of (his/reader's) mind from events outside when 'applied' in a structure, the structure being his comparison of events from different periods chosen by their intuitively derived contrast or similarity (such as, again, the similarity of the sound of the language rather than the content).

In "Occasional Dilemmas," Whalen says "I applied the gentle but determined pressure of my right/forefinger," as if physical pressure applied to words (such as "DUCKRABBIT," "BLUE," and "NIGHT-JAR"), and equates the pressure applied to words to "the marvelously double vision: total security is the same as total surveillance and repression." He concludes "Occasional Dilemmas" with what I take to be a humorous but clear statement of his poetic purpose and method:

> Olson told us that history was ended.
> A.—"O.K. What is it you think you're doing?"
> B.—"I'm trying to wreck your mind, that's all."
>   (p. 685)

Whalen is proposing to use language—which by omitting consecutive steps at his will (while acknowledging the total surveillance and repression of will, his or any) not only ends history in the sense of that which is conventionally presented *to* us, but ends history in the sense of anyone's own re-creation of any event—while his movement in a poem is a series of leaps each leading to more than one event or "result" at the same time. He prolongs the "pressure" (sometimes by his producing a stream of fictions in a poem) until the writer/reader can reach a state of giving up on constructing and on figuring out. The poems are modes of freedom from security. Security is a state of curtailment.

The Beats altered use of image to incorporate relativity. Ginsberg's description in his *Indian Journals* of viewing the fire inflamed corpses burning on the ghats on the Ganges is concentration on the disintegrating self as no entity of being, reflecting Hindu and Tibetan meditation methods. That is, his intention is not vivid image (is not fixation on the image as such) but rather language as transgression of the barrier between flesh (regarded as not an entity of self, there being none) and the filter of 'our seeing,' customary social behavior compartmentalizing experience. Ginsberg is breaking down the separation between optical seeing and (language which is to be) 'seeing' as changing conceiving. He used chanting (physical, hearing) to break down compartmentalizing of experience (such as customary description as subject). Sound in Ginsberg's poetry gives an incantory, visionary frame.

In Michael McClure's poems, the language shapes are both his mind's activity as imagination (or image as 'vision,' at once optical and visionary) in the instant of writing—and are a poem's language investigating shape made by its movement as such. Using the separation, the fact that language can't ever be the same as the object (words can't be the object "black lily"), McClure breaks down the distinction between text as object and the phenomenal object of "black lilies" (only words), and physical sensation (of the 'speaker' or reader). As image, the distinction between material phenomena and intuitive apprehension is broken down—or between that which is 'visual' and (that as) language.

In comparison to McClure or Ginsberg, Whalen's writing, not image-based and dismantling its own frames, is sound schemes, frequently the leaps and omissions of conversational exchange whose space and process are active mind phenomena. Conversation implies more than one voice, also implies the mind creating self, and simulation of history, the inside and the outside together. For Whalen, sound as mind phenomena is not only memory, fantasy, and sound of speaking in conversation, but these as transient, relative history itself *only* 'taking place' as being apprehended in the process of readers' minds making relations in reading and speaking as the writing. His drawings that were maps or graphs figured into this as both making and seeing connections *then,* at once. Reading's apprehension is actively constructing the text.

Whalen thus decreases the distance between us as spectators (readers) and phenomena by breaking down the separation one continually makes of oneself as ideas (one being outside phenomena) rather than being one's actions that are also continual and simultaneous with one's idea of these. As in the poem "The Same Old Jazz," he's making a structure that's itself an illusion seen outside ("OK, it's imperishable or a world as Will / & Idea, a Hindu illusion that our habits continuously / Create"): until that illusion is exactly what is created 'inside' as the poem at the same time going on at once (by the reader reading): "And it all snaps into focus / The world inside my head & the cat outside the window / A one-to-one relationship / While I imagine whatever I imagine." That is, his language both *is,* and also breaks down, the illusion of causation as a one-to-one relation of inside and outside—and breaks down the illusion of their separation, of one being outside this process, is both at once.

As causation and illusion of such simultaneously, Whalen frequently created a compression of all times onto one in a poem while keeping each historical time or reference distinct and dropping the consecutive steps of mind process forming connections. The conceptual space as the space of the text is a series of leaps, yet such a 'leap' (just as occurs in a joke, for example) is not a subject, connection, or sensation. As if there were points "A" and "B" in which the 'leap between' has no explicit expression that is a particular, rational 'result' that we could label "C"—nor is the place between stemming from either "A" or "B"—in reading there is the impression of all points, as if on all of space, producing each other at once. Yet one point is not movement between them, either. Short poems in *The Kindness of Strangers* are indicative of this method: which is to create a present-time that is only disjunctive (therefore is not time as such, though for description, I'm characterizing it as "times"), allowing the mind to be nowhere in formation. The 'times' (such as "I fucking ran" and "elephant and sunset") are occurring separately and at the same time (as taken in at once by the reader). So the present is only empty there (has no nature as itself, is words), and the future and past being a series of such presents-without-entity *appear* to rise from each other. Similar to Japanese Zen master Dōgen's articulation of being as time, in Whalen's use of line (or one stanza, which may be two or more times superimposed on each other), past, future, and present are going on separately and at once and not excluding each other. That is, everything as poetic line and the use Whalen makes of sound scheme arises in relation to everything else.

I asked Whalen if his writing was the same as meditation: that is, if his writing was doing the same thing as the process of meditation as the 'disjunctive present' which is no-separation of self and outside, and does not form these (self or outside) either. He answered no, that writing is writing and meditation is itself. I take that to mean: Language is always an ordering device. Language can't be the same as a state that does not rely upon any device and creates no entity, can't be a state that hasn't even language to rely upon (which is the characteristic of meditation). If the *subject* of writing is 'being only a disjunctive present,' the writing is not doing that, it would merely re-produce subject matter and division from it. Yet I think Whalen was using language to make being outside even what language is, let alone its conventional usage, while his poetry is based in language's daily usage as speaking, thinking and fantasizing. The Beats as a movement were undertaking to undo the convention of U.S. 'seeing' that continually reproduces 'being' divided from subject matter *as* subject matter. Whalen undertook that 'undoing' as the process of the language itself.

Language as Transient Act: Whalen's poems being imitation of mind phenomena akin to one speaking to others (to him—his writing is much like his own intonation was, his syntax and vocabulary in speaking in conversation), this 'speaking' is also akin to one speaking to oneself as if rehearsing and making-up scenes that thus create the future and past. These have no other existence than performance (no other existence than reading and speaking).

He was writing as reading, an activity as if inside each present instant of one's mind process unfolding, active reading that's transformative by being a continuous nerve movie, simulation of already existing interior and outside as these are at once (rather than writing being simply entertainment which we view from outside). He described the result as "A continuous fabric (nerve movie?) exactly as wide as these lines—'continuous' within a certain time-limit, say a few hours of total attention and pleasure: to move smoothly past the reader's eyes, across his brain: the moving sheet has shaped holes in it."

The sense of the continuous nerve movie is particularly applicable to what I'm calling his 'history poems,' his time-simulations that may be many times at once stacked as a continuous present. One such is the poem "Life in the City, In Memoriam Edward Gibbon: (HB, p. 13) which is four times at once: the time of the Victorian who was Edward Gibbon, but synonymous with Whalen writing the poem, the times of the Roman Empire whose rise and fall Gibbon wrote, and the immediate (in the poem) present time of Heian Japanese life (black lacquer hats and ox-drawn carriages for people in the Middle Ages). A Whalen time experiment may be a dream, one time period of dreaming (though the dream may reproduce several times 'of its own' at once) retaining only the original dream order, statement of its motions as the state of mind in that exact instance unrelated to composing or representing anything (such as "Dream."). He asks whether the poem (these relations) is the only occurrence of a time that also changes time: "What if I never told any of this?" Thus the poem is different from the dream.

The longer poems such as "Scenes of Life at the Capital" or "Birthday Poem" were written by hand in a notebook over extended periods of time. Eventually, Whalen would type up the entirety, cut apart the phrases placing these on the floor, and place phrases together depending on the intuitive leap made by their juxtaposition as active choice of the instant of compilation. The 'comparison' (of two passages or phrases chosen from 'random' times) both *is,* and is outside of, the close-up of whatever particular historical instant in which the separate phrases were written *or* juxtaposed. Any event, once an aspect of Whalen's view or psychology, is only itself, a relation to its context. The 'history poem,' as simulation of present-time continually, is only a present illusion superimposed (as play, memory, and separate current present) on a past illusion that is action *then* (the text as real-time past and present). Thus action is going on in all times at once, these elements brought to be simultaneous by the factor that the language itself, by being chosen as random times, not related in the sense of a purpose for narrative, is outside of conscious shaping, even as Whalen cites in the poems the constant effect of his own determining; "I've run so far in one circle I'm visible now."

Whalen extends that freedom to a conceptually spatial range, his texts broaching the possibility of, or being, free-fall not bound by preconceived boundaries of ordering (arbitrary definitions or boundaries in the sense of the relation being merely assigned, customary labels), and sometimes not bound by even sound comparisons or narrating emphasis (these would also be hierarchical structuring). To say that it is not bound or determined even by sound is to say that he sometimes drops even the use of a sound scheme that would supply cohesion. That is, he is not manufacturing resonance or any means of 'applying' union or resolution as if from the outside. The text is allowed possibly to 'fall' as in movement, as if a waterfall. The poem may risk even inertia, or may be attentive staying at a line, by virtue of its own workings. His works were thus a mind experiment of reality equivalent to the Buddhist concept of free-fall, which recognizes all supposition, perception, and phenomena as having no actual order of occurrence except that imposed by the mind as its own context. All perception as events are temporary states: "What are you doing right this minute? / What shall you do one second from now? / . . . Feather spins as it falls / Even if you did it better, who would care?" Whalen was proposing the possibility that all of this order, constructed, and the entire fabric of constructed order could be dropped. I asked Whalen whether the intention in his poems was to drop all structuring either as use of sound or time (similar to the Zen conception of language as itself phenomena: that words are merely labels of entities and all labeled entities are a giant web where the only reality is the imposed inter-relatedness of the entities). As to whether his poetry was an intentional breakdown and therefore investigation as mind free-fall, Whalen replied that this interpretation was interesting, implying by his tone that he did not disagree, also that this was not necessarily his preconceived plan, he was experimenting, which is what gesture as investigation *is*.

He was the first American poet to propose or work within this terrain of free-fall in the Buddhist sense (but which is also akin, for example, to Wittgenstein's writings, seminal for many contemporary poets, as some Language poets) of words being merely labels, language itself as the material of investigation.

All of Whalen's poems were originally composed in notebooks like illuminated manuscripts, notebooks in which he included color drawings, some like maps of the poems placed beside poems but maps that are unlike the poems. The drawings are a different space. They may be within the text, possibly a translation of it or related, or not. These doodles with hand-drawn text tend to have multiple readings that are possibilities as reading order in which none of the sections or stanzas of handwritten text are foremost (that is, there is no hierarchy of interpretation in reading). Also, the drawings in color are a space that can't be translated, the poems printed later are suppressing material from the hand-drawn version of the text, which, however, remains in the text as a shadow. When I remarked to him that the sense of this translation is that there is no original (not even the hand-drawn journals), therefore no privileging of one view or strata over another, Whalen agreed.

The influence of Pound's *Cantos* is present in some of the time experiments in which Whalen superimposes historical events separated in time (thus effectively being: at the same time), inserting drawings that are a different space within the poem (as Pound inserted Chinese characters, for example). The comparison to Pound, however, demonstrates a notable difference: Pound's model was authoritarian, a few who have knowledge are the top of a pyramid, disseminating knowledge downward by teaching. Pound urges the reader of the *Cantos* to know excellent models in order to learn: The sight-at-once of ideograms is predicated on deciphering sources from lines of traditions. Learning a language, which is a composite of centuries of tradition, is also the *goal* in reading the ideograms. Equally learned, Whalen, however, was writing a poetic structure that is non-hierarchical, in that activity is occurring everywhere (throughout a poem) in each line and in the relation between two lines: in the activity in reading, in Whalen's text the outside and the inside occurring at once. Whalen's structure is as if 'the opposite' of Pound's, reversing its implications, while incorporating an imprint of it.

Thus Whalen's structure is non-hierarchical in the action of dropping narrating organizing principles, all being authoritarian. Activity of his text (reading) is everywhere not operated upon by only one— in the sense that the reader participating as in conversation, and like being inside one's own mind movement, is in the activity of reading in the same way as the author writing. By undergoing the same mind movements as the author (rather than 'identifying with' him psychologically or looking upon him as an expert and teacher), the reader is on the same level, is 'in the place of,' is an equal as an occurrence in the text.

Whalen's mode, in which reading is seeing constructing of history occurring from oneself/the reader by (and) also occurring outside of oneself, implies that the dropping of that construct would create a different history. Compression in Whalen's poetry, for example, is the activity of compassion—which is "just seeing" throughout clearly, the effect of which alters occurrence. Not sentiment or 'expression,' compassion in a Buddhist sense is not about feeling, is not a summary or expression of how one feels at some time about something, it's (as in Whalen's writing) a transpiration 'taking place' as the action of the text itself.

While my description of Whalen's influences and inventions is an attempt to suggest aspects of reading the poems, Whalen many times stressed that he didn't write to teach or reform, he wrote for pleasure and curiosity. He had the view that if there was no pleasure for reader and poet, there was no reason to do it. His poems in their playfulness are sometimes jolly, gentle pinpricks as mock-ups of history in free-wheeling menageries. *The Collected* is a vast terrain that's a clear, compassionate mind-revelation in which the reader can bask.

THE COLLECTED POEMS OF
PHILIP WHALEN

IV

Slightly indistinct about the edges
and rather humming
She
surrounded by an incandescent dust of moments
descends staircases of years (many of which
are quite disputable)
into the present now
which is practically deaf
to her song of eons
to record us who become her song

[Winter 1947]

VIII

Moon under a screen
of telegraph wires
Moon under no screen but the wind
Moon under the sea
and no spray but self
wandering

[Winter 1947]

1

XVIII

Lined with lines of lines
and solitary
Not unsurrounded but solitary
Standing as far as I know
as it was when I left and looked over
my shoulder for the last time
not without a certain remorse

[Winter 1947]

Three Desert Poems

THE GREAT AMERICAN DESERT

Planar miles sun-fused beyond sterility
Into sun-resistant efflorescence—fierce
Dry life—green thorn, zig-zag scale,
Orange beaded poison.
These seared and calcined form thin humus
Through the bright dead sands.

Wind wrinkles dust over new earth exhuming
    old
Chance-planted seeds.
Watered by passing jacks or unusual weather
Sprout thorn, shade beaded poison
Hide scales, stymie dunes.

SAGUARO

Rock's memory of the sun warms desert nights
Sand's recollection is shorter
Soon cools to a cloudy mirror for stars
Mice and lizards print fern patterns on the restless
      dunes.

Walking to enjoy the stars and mountains
I find a saguaro still blooming at midnight
Transient perennial beauty remembers the sun
Through a whole year of darkness.

NEW CANAAN

Sand grains, spikey greens.
These forbid the casual
Assure the certain traveler
For whom the day is as imperative
As parting the earth to sun thorns
Or splitting the air to scare stars.
Earth here bears only mountains,

[8:i:48]

from THE TEMPTATION OF ST. ANTHONY

I

Housed in pseudo-Tudor brick they sit
Pouring brilliant sand over languid hands
Whose disinterested fingers let the crystals
Fall.

3

Eyes intolerant of seasonal change
Gaze out through limestone oriels
Across calm lawns embalmed in tepid rains
Evergreen trees and shrubs that guarantee
A reassuring landscape throughout the winter.
Lives intolerant of living need heavy insulation
Ivy over brick walls
The laws of Relativity and Individuation.

Hands are real. Sand sticks to them
Gets under fingernails, lodges
In the tiny creases of the skin
Is never really brushed away.
I have filled the pockets of my clothes
But the weight is slowing down my progress
Through a world where speedy walking is success.

Alone beside the college lake
Sifting an ounce or two of sand from hand to hand
Anthony recalled the sun
Perpendicular above the desert
Only monumental things or deep-rooted plants
Can endure the constant weight of light—
(There is no real night where there are
So many stars)

Here light is muted green and grey
Pervasive stench of decomposing words
Constant noise of nervous laughter
And a feeling of insecurity in the region
Of the genitals. Digestion is poor,
Breath bad. No amount of O-dor-ono
Can disguise our fear of tasting
The undiluted product.

He paused to empty out his pockets
Shining stream of sand among soaked twigs
Black leaves. Water skippers dodged
Plenty was left in the seams and linings
Ballast for a journey.

II

At the station time is traded in for motion
A forty-hour day from familiar bed to hotel rack
A thousand miles away begins.
Immersion in a book, hiding from the smelly
Squall of children
And the passage of a once-loved landscape.

Constant eating at too high a price
Attendant constipation, cleaving of the gut
To the last native meal, inherent dread of approaching
Drive-ins.
Unwilling consignment to an early tomb with
Boring books, no pipe, and the worries of the man
In the upper berth returning to a wife he doesn't want
To see.
Sailors in the day-coach sleep in the complaisant,
Padded arm of railroad whores.
(This Pullman was a big mistake—
Should I have come at all?)

Yesterday's companion replaced by billowy lady
Wooly child: Continuous circuit over reading shins
From water tap to ladies' room, demanding
     explanations
Yes, the man is that color all over
I don't know what town it is look at the sign
Hush the gentleman is reading

5

Speed across unhurried earth
Down the coveted Valley in the sun
Then motion passes on, the journey ends
At the foot of a butte topped with granite boulders
House high. Anthony sat down to contemplate
The miles of heat and space nobody wanted
Protected from destructive hands by inutility
And gauche, un-Academic color. My refuge from
Desolation
Geographical circumcision.

III

At night the desert is safe for walking
Snakes and lizards wake only in heat,
Die with the sun. Meek mice and owls inherit
The sand after dark.

Walking alone when weirdly enveloped
In light out of air, surrounded by circular
Marching of dodos, gross beaks and fat plumes
And a concentric ring of great auks, penguin-marked
All marching and singing

Ho ho Antonio
You'll be the last to know
Tee hee Anthony
Soon you'll be extinct as we
Dead buried and forgotten
Only a dictionary definition

Anthony replied
My presence proves you wrong
Somebody changed and I am here
Someone survived the Lisbon quake
Noah's flood, Chicago's fire
(Delenda est Carthago!)

Decline and fall of Everybody's Empire
And the Hanging Gardens
(By the rivers of which they sat down)
They came through, I am here
Father of those who can learn.
Your lives are their lesson
Depart with my blessing.

Ascent in an echoing wail
Shuffling of feathers, chink
Of bird feet among stones
Anthony alone.

Destruction is an inconclusive thing
Something always manages to live
If only an amphora or a ring of crystal beads
Crying Caveat! History is there to know.

IV

Saw ivory bitches pumped with gold
Whelping rubies on the crumpled ground
Breasts squirting silver
Sparrows dropping dimes on platinum curbs
Chirping pearls

Weeping women stringing their tears and
Monthly drops on silver wire
Coral and diamonds for neck and ears
(Normal breasts yield two full pints
Red or white wine, left or right.)
Virgin wombs await your coming
To beget only females like themselves.

"I'm not in the market for buying or selling
No wife to bejewel, no hunger
For maidenheads. I only give and receive
Real goods, no luxurious minerals
Where could I spend all those dimes in this desert?
(I could use the wine, but the bottles distract)
Besides, too eager to trade you've scared me away."

The other sighed, thoughtfully furrowing sand
With the point of his tail. "Won't you take these
On trial?
"No sale."
Then packed up his pitch and departed.

A solitary ruby lay at Anthony's feet
In his palm it smouldered a moment,
Searing the skin before he could pitch it away
Over the rim of a dry water-course.
Geologists will be pained, but
The pleasures of explaining ought to soothe 'em.

He climbed back up the mesa to sit near his fire
By the rocks, watching the sky in the false-dawn
Then the real light transmuting the granite western
        ranges
From onyx to rose, topaze to amethyst,
Then warmth out of night, and space out of
Limiting darkness.
Drug on the market.

[Feb. 1949]

8

The Plaster Muse:
6 Poems in the Classic Mode

FOR DONALD MACRAE

I. MOSHE SUR L'EAU

Anon a swanflight
Schoenheit
Deliberation among the bull rushes
And the infant Moses presently embarks
For the arms of Pharaoh's daughter
And desert Sinai
Ducks among the reeds
Sang all night long
To hush the noisy pyramids
Bellering at the moon

※

II. ODE

Muted harps and ostrich tails
Flail peacock shaded air
Several generations of felahin
Gather at the river witnessing
The descent of beauty

Cleopatra (bare) don't give a damn
"Get up another plate of them
Pickled alligator toes
And tell them Niggers to get

9

The lead out of their oars
I got a heavy date in Cairo
(Powder my neck again, dearie
I'm sweating like a pig.")

✻

III. LEDA

You walked alone beside the pool
Looking for love, daring the god
Hearing the thunder, lured it ashore
With a scatter of crumbs (withholding the loaf)
You waited for lightning to flash
From the beady bird eye
Then won your swan—
Trapped God in an egg.
Loosed him to fly.

✻

IV. THURSDAY IN BYZANTIUM

Today is the queen of heaven
Eleven new jewels dwelling in her crown
Demand admiration
Singing seven gay notes
Announcing replevin.

✻

V. "A L'OMBRE DES JEUNES FILLES . . ."

Delight detains me not
Neither admiration
For your subtle brain nor pretty wit
Nor long legs nor furry Place
Only the recollection of the
Pleasure
And the odor of the tiny wrinkles
Underneath your breasts

☼

VI. SONNET FOR VALENTINE'S DAY

Time lived then in a clock of ice
Chimed hours on gelid bells
Cold weights drove glassy wheels around
Love was nowhere to be found
So I sat underneath a tree
Til love found me.
Heart's heat melted Time away
Then love fell into a snit and died
Winter descended and froze all my tears
Into delicate gears.   Time took them aside
And built a new home:
Now tears tick
And will dim the eyes
That shed them.

☼

[Summer 1949]

ADVENT

Unaccompanied by crowned or numbered monsters
Or lewd bejeweled Babylon
But in the dead of night
And through the bloody door.

Returned obscurely
But in complete accordance with the laws
Expounded on the occasion
Of his last recorded visit

To make the necessary simplification
Of all the orthodox confusions
So elaborately wrought
In our bereaved seclusion

The seven seals remain unbroken
The vials of wrath unopened
The trumpet still unsounded
Yet he has come again.

[19:ix:49]

"A COUNTRY WITHOUT RUINS"

His kids
Raising hell in the grape arbor
Throwing all they don't eat

"Where can you find images enough?
I could never . . ."

And around the house again,
"IO PAEAN!   IO!
(Crash!
Rattle!)
Brass and wood echoing
(*Krotales*)
Whoops

"This country is too big
For anyone to see it all;
Not enough human associations."

Where has not Artemis danced?

[?]

IN THE PALACE OF THE HEART

A shining tear of the sun
Enclosed
By thin bone plates
A lantern for a guide.

[?]

INVOCATION TO THE MUSE

Green eyes, you always change
A rose-bed complete with briars
Making liars of angels
Cats-meat of gods
Boxers into queens.

Let down that golden ladder
                one more time
I'll shinny up and make a song or two
Before the withered hand
                clips those locks
And tumbles me among the thorns.

NOVEMBER FIRST

At the bus stop
I saw two crisp spiders,
Each clamped onto his own slowly warming stones.
Black stars in the unexpected sunlight.

In the yard behind me
A mother called her son, "Come back."
"Don't have to." (But he came
And she began to beat him angrily)
"Don't tell *me* you don't have to
When *I* tell you!"

The child on the porch covered his eyes
Leaned his head on his knees
"I want daddy."
Working again but unrelenting
"I'd hide *my* face too!"

Small radial holes through the stones
—or channels of crystal through them?

Bright sunlight's out of place in November.

[1950]

14

AN ELEGY UPON THE

UNTIMELY DEATH OF MRS. W. F.

She salted roses in a Chinese jar
Kept curtains drawn to cover up the sea
While great shells listened eagerly
Upon the marble shelf. She painted
Portraits of herself and friends
From memory.

She chided us for the naked mirror
Which betrayed the correspondence from our friend—
The one to whom she never would be introduced—
The traitor glass that showed us in our pointed shoes
Privately happy in the garden
While she must sit inside,
Piled with unwelcome revelations
By a suite of garrulous furniture.

She took her hat and stick
And the soundest fragments
Of a tender mind for a walk
Beside the River Ouse.
Seeing these reflected in a world
Of perpetually silent, ordered motion
She chose then to become her own
Reflection. "Here at last I can ignore
The ocean's importunity."

[Feb. 1950]

THE ROAD-RUNNER

Thin long bird
    with a taste for snakes' eyes
Frayed tail, wildcat claws
His pinions are bludgeons

Few brains, topped
By a crown—
And a flair for swift in-fighting—
Try to take it from him.

[23:iii:50]

THREE ORMOLU PIECES FOR STANLEY MOORE

Primavera

With a delicacy profound as light
Passionate, inviolate,
She comes:
Untempted by quotidian blandishments
She passes on,
Craving none.

Diana Bathing

No matter how remote the view
It still can satisfy the avid,
Ever-searching eye
Bring moisture to the eager mouth
Of hot and lustful youth or old
Satiety.
Frosted glass alone can screen
The intimate from being seen.

16

Artemidora Dead

Restore the lilies to her tomb
Conceal the profligate growth
Of impudent moss
Drag a moment of surety
From those marble blooms

[Oct. 1950]

SONG

O there was lightning in my room
The walls glowed
The closed piano sang to the thunder
Hail Mary,
House of gold!

Lightning and the sound of wings
As a coronal of doves came down
In their midst, a bead of flame

And I divided myself into love
        and lover
After the manner that I know

Hagia Sophia!

The same day I planted a tree
To mark the corner of a new garden.

[13:x:50]

APOSTROPHE TO A BORROWED TIGER

The recollection of a song
And of a fire mirrored by cliffs onto the sea
Disturbs your gnawing,
Turns a tiny, scratchy wheel
Behind those glowing eyes,
Fakes a sea-scent among the Himalayan jungles
Where you terrorize with silence and great claws.

Recall that a leopard lies dried and frozen
Near the western summit of The House of God
(No one has explained what the leopard
Was seeking at that altitude).
Forget that salty singing
And seek a striped mate
Among the hot dry grasses
Not too far from the trees—

That Mermaid's on some other beach
And besides,
The sea is dead.

[Nov. 1950]

THE SEALION

Barging along
Not twenty feet from the brilliant shore
Great swells arching over him
His shadow soundless,
Slow
Across the roller-polished sand

Two with rifles
Wheezed up to the cliff-edge:
"kill it for the bounty."

18

"Dive in with a lance
Where he'd maul you for missing—
I want no guns here."

Their boot-prints marred the beach
　　　for six hours.

[16:xi:50]

THEORY

"Where were you when the lights went out?
Where were you when the shit struck the fan?
There must be a complete, exact, scientific
Analysis and description of the whole occurrence.
There must be an end made to all shoddy thinking:
Facile explanations must be ruled out—
I want profundity, and that on many levels."

Certainly the Zodiac cannot be held responsible—
The poison in the Scorpion's tail
The Water-Bearer's laughter

"Who's in charge here? Who said that?
I want the name of every man typed up in duplicate.
Nobody will leave until I know who's responsible:
Everybody's got to suffer because one is too yellow
To step out like a man."

Whoever said what everyone thought
Must be defended. We shall suffer together,
Hate the man in charge.

"Someone must retain a position of responsibility—
A reliable person who believes in the position
And in order, direction, responsibility—
Without these, an undisciplined mob."

(We of course are unfit. Statistics show
That we fingered Milly's vulva
In a dark closet *dans l'an dixième de nos âges* —
Numbers and their curved analysis among the squares—
No facile explanations)

Whether down in the cellar eating sauerkraut
Or squatting ignorantly above the fan
Relieved at last
Officially we renounce all shoddy thinking
Bid facility goodbye and lay in a stock of graph-paper
To plot the way towards profundity,
Content with a written description of the other stars

Out of the depths we shall sing a new song.

[20:xi:50]

"OF COURSE," SHE SAID

and impaled the kitchen spider
        on a darning-needle
Stuck the point through a small clay ball—
A heavy world to ride
        to the bottom of her glass

"I hate waiting for people."

[7:xii:50]

20

THREE SATIRES

I. In the Museum Basement

Dawdling among the plaster Greeks
"They didn't have very big dicks then,
        did they?"

"They had lots of other muscles:
The main idea was quality—
'You can't never tell
The depth of the well
By the length
Of the handle
On the pump.'"

II. To the Poets Who
Insist on a University Job

The peacock roams the pleasure-ground
Stuffing his craw with poisons
        that color his plumes;
Immune as Mithradates—
A penetrating voice
And no humility.

The parrot earns a cracker
By remembering—
Sings any song you want to hear
And loudly.

Envy of the peacock dyes his wings.

III. "Tradition and the
Individual Talent"

A jade bell
Priceless
A round bronze mirror
See it
A bath-tub sagely inscribed

(Hear it?
A discrete sound
Something massive
Breaking
    under its own weight)

"Every day a clean start"

      Do not leave papers on the floor
      in B. Room. *Please* be neat and
      help keep Bath Room *clean.*
      Thank You.

The rest is either lost
    or forgotten

"Nous sommes très pauvre dans cette maison."

                              [26:xi:50–?51]

THE ENGINEER

"Out on the ranch you can run
    and holler all you please . . ."

But not in the presence of expensive animals
Nor through fields of nervous oats

Plows and harrows
Dangerous,
The creek, barn-fouled,
Not for amusement—

Upstream
Past the hundred-acre field
(One corner devoted to neurasthenic hogs)
The water lay dull beside oaks and alders

Pocketfuls of rock—robbing the driveway—
Mud, sticks: a weir—
Tearing the water, forcing it
To sound
If only temporarily

". . . and Aunty loves you
Like her very own."

[6:ii:51]

THE GREAT INSTAURATION

Weakened by winter
Indigent age and puny youth
Decline and die
Having survived one crisis
Salute Persephone returning
As they go to her place
Among the shades

Others
Hounded by a nervous wife
To be shot by the burglar
        in the pantry

Or freeze beside a mud-clogged jeep
Or other piece of expensive junk
Contrived most prayerfully
To civilize the League
      of the Militant Godless.

II

Those remarkable breasts
And her thighs
Boas and Jachin
Splendidly wrought

Castalian spring
Urn of memory
The portal of the years

III

Lettuce for lunch
In honor of Aphrodite
Delicate green

And my head between your breasts
Their mantic music
One to lip and one to ear—
A telephone!

(Distant thunder)

Lettuce to keep the spirit high
Some parsley, celery
A few sea-urchins
My own globe humming
And on that lovely telephone a lovely
Boom
The music of the spheres

IV

Sun in the bamboos
Beside the lake
The ducks behaving
Scandalously

V

Spring so loud and tender
Two sophomores rough-house
    in the college entrance
Hug and pound arms about the weather—
Not pansies but spring
Why fight it?

The regulars are flying high enough
The army and navy kindly absorbing the surplus
And it can be spring at sea

A phenomenon!

Thick in the air
Around the dormitories
The gymnasium reeking with attempts
    at converting it all into sweat

Why fight it?

VI

There can't be too much love.
I have known many varieties of selfishness
Mistaken for it
Was once rendered celibate by pride
Learned you must rub someone else
Squeeze
Pretend you're off in Beulah Land

(This is as close as you'll ever be)
Stroke
Titter together
Get too tired sometimes—
Even that sadness
A pleasure.

A nuisance in summer—
Sliding in sweat is only pleasant once
Like the time in the shower.

Hate a little, late in winter
But in spring there can't be too much love:
An orgy by preference
A righteous excess.

[21:ii:51]

THE ROSE FESTIVAL PARADE

HERE:
A Pegasus laboriously constructed
Chicken-wire and red carnations
Mount for a blonde
        (gold bathing-suit)
Brandishing a trophy—
The sweepstakes!

[1:iv:51]

META

Line
From sun to stone to eye
Splits the year
Edge of the new dominion
Parting royalty from the flesh:
A lustrum

II

Dissolved in mead
Bound with willows to the oak
Twelve stones circling
Beat him to sleep.

The golden blade shears manhood from him
Divides him for the diners,
Re-christened in his blood.
The eye of the year
Mistletoe-blinded

III

Balls and all in a boat of alder
Long gone down the river
The rest sizzling on the fire
To redeem the tribe.
(Publish it not in the streets
      of Askelon
Lest the uncircumcised ignorantly rejoice)

[5:iv:51]

"THE SHOCK OF RECOGNITION"

Through the stone gate
Blinking in the weak light
Only seven have returned
        from the whirling tower
        behind the star

Striding antlered among the bare
        new trees
"There you are. Why did you run?
These arrows aren't for you."

Slipping the mended collar
        round his neck
Silver, with seven-score knobs.

[11:iv:51]

TWO MIRACLES

I

Dark sleep lighted by a nasty voice:
"Now who in Christ's name's that?"

"There seems to be some confusion,
Eight-Eyes
(Don't bother the snake,
He's one of the family)
You've skipped a breath somewhere"

WHEN
        it sprouted right out of the water
Slick hard and throbbing
Pricking straight upwards

The Gander soared up,
Boar diving for those unbelievable loins.
Where dive and flight met,
The smaller central column burst into speech:
"Gander the right pillar,
Boar to the left and myself
The hollow, binding center
The tunnel of love
Corridor of the generations"

Twirling the hand-drum
He stepped out to dance
        the circle of fire

II

"Every time I carry you this way . . ."
God's voice from the Boar's face
And she young as ever
Clinging to the tusk,
        "I suppose the mask gets him—
        But those bristles!
        I always fall for his slick suit
            and that line
        Then he gets possessive."

Coil after coil of snakeskin
Small sharp hooves tromping them into place
(A noise of many waters)
Then the flower
Re-set above them.

                    [11:iv:51]

29

THE FIVE QUEENS

I   V.R.

Magna Mater
Swathed in shawls
Unamused by her children's gifts
The ivory, silk and glass all stored away.
She rules us yet from Windsor
Protecting us from every moral pang
The conscientious mother of the world.

II   S. Catherine

"The scent of lemon-groves
Then no street before the door
A walled garden
Far sounds of jubilation
And he gave me a ring
The fire-circle to which I was faithful"

III   Theodora

Out of the bear-garden
Into the whorehouse
And straight to the throne

With too rigorous a moral code
To suit the happy Byzantines

A supple queen
Great Babylon reformed

IV Aega

Shield us
An idiot sun burns brains away
Its power and precision
Cooking eyes
Roasting tongues

Arm us
Before ignorance kills us

V Artemisia

"He was successful, but he died"
Leaving her to stack up marble
High as a kite
Making the city splendid with his name.

[14–16:iv:51]

HOMAGE TO LUCRETIUS

It all depends on how fast you're going
Tending towards light, sound
Or the quiet of mere polarity

Objects: Slowness

Screen
        A walking sieve
Wide-open and nowhere
The mountains themselves
Sucked up into turnips, trees
Wander as bones, nails, horns

And we want crystals,
Given a handful of mercury
    (Which can be frozen into a pattern vulnerable to body heat)

The notion intimidates us
We can't easily imagine another world
This one being barely
Visible:
        We lined up and pissed in a snowbank
        A slight thaw would expose
        Three tubes of yellow ice

And so on . . .
A world not entirely new
But realized,
The process clarified
Bless your little pointed head!

1952

A NEW VOYAGE

    They worship mice.
    Cats are hanged and eaten by priests
    Who interpret the roars from a college
    Of deified imbeciles;
    There is no written law.
    Among them
    The sun is an image of fear.

[28:xii:52]

32

SCHOLIAST

Regards the chrysanthemums
Stalks flat on the ground
Flowers twisting the tips
Past the roof shadow

A honeycomb
A hornet's nest
Significant once, as a pattern—
But a theory of progress?

A constant explosion produces all shapes
Quiet fringed yellow
Burning—and the bush
Utterly consumed!

Venice 4:xi:51
San Francisco 4:ii:53

OUT OF IT

What's it to me? The telephone
Rings only when I'm not home
The biggest knockers in the world
On television; I have no set

We never see you; what do you do?

I sun myself in the agora
Watch periwinkles on the rocks
Below the Palace of the Legion of Honor
Record the fishes' comments on the children
Outside the tank (the aquarium is wired)

33

You inhabit public buildings?

A taste for marble in a wooden age
A weakness for the epic that betrays
A twiddly mind.

8:iv:53

TELL ME MORE

Not a word
Not for love or money
Not a single word from me, nor music
    (these are not words but signs
    they carry no charge)
Make your own speech
You'll get none of mine
Not a consenting silence
Not withdrawal
The continuation in another mode
      A finger pointing at the moon
All the rest is for you
You name it
And welcome

11:i:54

"PLUS ÇA CHANGE ..."

What are you doing?

I am coldly calculating.

I didn't ask for a characterization.
Tell me what we're going to do.

    That's what I'm coldly calculating.

You had better say "plotting" or "scheming"
You never could calculate without a machine.

    Then I'm brooding. Presently
    A plot will hatch.

Who are you trying to kid?

    Be nice.

(SILENCE)

Listen. Whatever we do from here on out
Let's for God's sake not look at each other
Keep our eyes shut and the lights turned off—
We won't mind touching if we don't have to see.

    I'll ignore those preposterous feathers.

Say what you please, we brought it all on ourselves
But nobody's going out of his way to look.

    Who'd recognize us now?

We'll just pretend we're used to it.
(Watch out with that goddamned tail!)
Pull the shades down. Turn off the lights.
Shut your eyes.

(SILENCE)

There is no satisfactory explanation.
You can talk until you're blue

35

Just how much bluer can I get?

Well, save breath you need to cool

Will you please shove the cuttlebone a little closer?

All right, until the perfumes of Arabia

Grow cold. Ah! Sunflower seeds!

Will you listen, please? I'm trying to make
A rational suggestion. Do you mind?

Certainly not. Just what *shall* we tell the children?

28:ix:53
1:ii:55

MARTYRDOM OF TWO PAGANS

Out on a limb and frantically sawing
The saw teeth go dull and at last
Wear smooth
Leaving us here, still throned in the air
   Like the sage in the basket
   And the one in the jar
Either branch or tree will fall
Or we'll both drop, sleeping
A heavenly meal for the animal saints
Who march continuously round the bole

A distinction or a difference, I said
Either one a horn on Io's head
A giddy heifer chased by bees
All are immortal
Laugh and lie down

Discriminate or perish, he replied
    While all with one voice (about
        the space of two hours) cried out
    Great is Diana of the Ephesians!
Stay awake, he said, sleep is confusion
    My eyelids have grown tea-leaves for the pot
Brew it strong
Defy illusion
The weakened branch snaps off
We join the company of saints
Remaining conscious—
                        though dismembered
To the last.

The sacred beasts all ate
And marched and sang:
    'Love is better than hate
    Love is better than hate
Love is better than hate
        and stronger than hell'
        For we took our shoes off
        As we fell.

Seattle, 18–24:iii:55

IF YOU'RE SO SMART, WHY AIN'T YOU RICH?

I need everything else
Anything else
        Desperately
But I have nothing
Shall have nothing
        but this
Immediate, inescapable
        and invaluable

No one can afford
        THIS
Being made here and now

        (Seattle, Washington
                17 May, 1955)

        MARIGOLDS

Concise (wooden)
        Orange.
Behind them, the garage door
        Pink
(Paint sold under a fatuous name:
"Old Rose"
        which brings a war to mind)

And the mind slides over the fence again
Orange against pink and green
Uncontrollable!

Returned of its own accord
It can explain nothing
Give no account

What good? What worth?

        Dying!

You have less than a second
        To live
To try to explain:
Say that light
        in particular wave-lengths
        or bundles wobbling at a given speed
Produces the experience
Orange against pink

Better than a sirloin steak?
A screen by Korin?

The effect of this, taken internally
The effect
       of beauty
            on the mind

There is no equivalent, least of all
These objects
Which ought to manifest
A surface disorientation, pitting
Or striae
Admitting *some* plausible interpretation

But the cost
Can't be expressed in numbers
Dodging between
      a vagrancy rap
      and the newest electrical brain-curette
Eating what the rich are bullied into giving
Or the poor willingly share
Depriving themselves

More expensive than ambergris
    Although the stink
        isn't as loud. (A few
Wise men have said,
    "Produced the same way . . .
    Vomited out by sick whales.")
Valuable for the same qualities
    Staying-power and penetration
I've squandered every crying dime.

Seattle 17–18:v:55

SOURDOUGH MOUNTAIN LOOKOUT

Tsung Ping (375–443): "Now I am old and infirm. I fear I shall no more be able to roam among the beautiful mountains. Clarifying my mind, I meditate on the mountain trails and wander about only in dreams."

—in *The Spirit of the Brush*, tr. by Shio Sakanishi, p. 34.

FOR KENNETH REXROTH

I always say I won't go back to the mountains
I am too old and fat there are bugs mean mules
And pancakes every morning of the world

Mr. Edward Wyman (63)
Steams along the trail ahead of us all
Moaning, "My poor old feet ache, my back
Is tired and I've got a stiff prick"
Uprooting alder shoots in the rain

Then I'm alone in a glass house on a ridge
Encircled by chiming mountains
With one sun roaring through the house all day
& the others crashing through the glass all night
Conscious even while sleeping

  Morning fog in the southern gorge
  Gleaming foam restoring the old sea-level
  The lakes in two lights green soap and indigo
  The high cirque-lake black half-open eye

Ptarmigan hunt for bugs in the snow
Bear peers through the wall at noon
Deer crowd up to see the lamp
A mouse nearly drowns in the honey
I see my bootprints mingle with deer-foot
Bear-paw mule-shoe in the dusty path to the privy

40

Much later I write down:
      "raging. Viking sunrise
      The gorgeous death of summer in the east"
(Influence of a Byronic landscape—
Bent pages exhibiting depravity of style.)

Outside the lookout I lay nude on the granite
Mountain hot September sun but inside my head
Calm dark night with all the other stars

HERACLITUS: "The waking have one common world
But the sleeping turn aside
Each into a world of his own."

I keep telling myself what I really like
Are music, books, certain land and sea-scapes
The way light falls across them, diffusion of
Light through agate, light itself . . . I suppose
I'm still afraid of the dark

            "Remember smart-guy there's something
            Bigger something smarter than you."
            Ireland's fear of unknown holies drives
            My father's voice (a country neither he
            Nor his great-grandfather ever saw)

            A sparkly tomb a plated grave
            A holy thumb beneath a wave

Everything else they hauled across Atlantic
Scattered and lost in the buffalo plains
Among these trees and mountains

From Duns Scotus to this page
A thousand years

("... a dog walking on his hind legs—
not that he does it well but that he
does it at all.")

Virtually a blank except for the hypothesis
That there is more to a man
Than the contents of his jock-strap

EMPEDOCLES: "At one time all the limbs
Which are the body's portion are brought together
By Love in blooming life's high season; at another
Severed by cruel Strife, they wander each alone
By the breakers of life's sea."

Fire and pressure from the sun bear down
Bear down centipede shadow of palm-frond
A limestone lithograph—oysters and clams of stone
Half a black rock bomb displaying brilliant crystals
Fire and pressure Love and Strife bear down
Brontosaurus, look away

My sweat runs down the rock

HERACLITUS: "The transformations of fire
are, first of all, sea; and half of the sea
is earth, half whirlwind. . . .
It scatters and it gathers; it advances
and retires."

I move out of a sweaty pool
        (The sea!)
And sit up higher on the rock

Is anything burning?

The sun itself! Dying

Pooping out, exhausted
Having produced brontosaurus, Heraclitus
This rock, me,
To no purpose
I tell you anyway (as a kind of loving) . . .
Flies & other insects come from miles around
To listen
I also address the rock, the heather,
The alpine fir

BUDDHA: "All the constituents of being are
Transitory: Work out your salvation with diligence."

(And everything, as one eminent disciple of that master
Pointed out, has been tediously complex ever since.)

There was a bird
Lived in an egg
And by ingenious chemistry
Wrought molecules of albumen
To beak and eye
Gizzard and craw
Feather and claw

My grandmother said:
"Look at them poor bed-
raggled pigeons!"

And the sign in McAlister Street:

"IF YOU CAN'T COME IN
SMILE AS YOU GO BY
L♡VE
THE BUTCHER

I destroy myself, the universe (an egg)
And time—to get an answer:
There are a smiler, a sleeper and a dancer

We repeat our conversation in the glittering dark
Floating beside the sleeper.
The child remarks, "You knew it all the time."
I: "I keep forgetting that the smiler is
Sleeping; the sleeper, dancing."

From Sauk Lookout two years before
Some of the view was down the Skagit
To Puget Sound: From above the lower ranges,
Deep in forest—lighthouses on clear nights.

This year's rock is a spur from the main range
Cuts the valley in two and is broken
By the river; Ross Dam repairs the break,
Makes trolley buses run
Through the streets of dim Seattle far away.

I'm surrounded by mountains here
A circle of 108 beads, originally seeds
    of *ficus religiosa*
        Bo-Tree
A circle, continuous, one odd bead
Larger than the rest and bearing
A tassel (hair-tuft) (the man who sat
        under the tree)
In the center of the circle,
A void, an empty figure containing
All that's multiplied;
Each bead a repetition, a world
Of ignorance and sleep.

Today is the day the goose gets cooked
Day of liberation for the crumbling flower
Knobcone pinecone in the flames
Brandy in the sun

Which, as I said, will disappear
Anyway it'll be invisible soon
Exchanging places with stars now in my head
To be growing rice in China through the night.
Magnetic storms across the solar plains
Make Aurora Borealis shimmy bright
Beyond the mountains to the north.

Closing the lookout in the morning
Thick ice on the shutters
Coyote almost whistling on a nearby ridge
The mountain is THERE (between two lakes)
I brought back a piece of its rock
Heavy dark-honey color
With a seam of crystal, some of the quartz
Stained by its matrix
Practically indestructible
A shift from opacity to brilliance
(The Zenbos say, "Lightning-flash & flint-spark")
Like the mountains where it was made

What we see of the world is the mind's
Invention and the mind
Though stained by it, becoming
Rivers, sun, mule-dung, flies—
Can shift instantly
A dirty bird in a square time

Gone
Gone
REALLY gone
Into the cool
O MAMA!

Like they say, "Four times up,
Three times down." I'm still on the mountain.

Sourdough Mountain 15:viii:55
                                      Berkeley 27–28:viii:56

NOTE: The quotes of Empedocles and Heraclitus are from John
Burnet's *Early Greek Philosophy*, Meridian Books, New York.

from THREE VARIATIONS, ALL ABOUT LOVE

I

So much to tell you
Not just that I love
There is so much more
You must hear and see

If I came to explain
It would do no good
Wordlessly nibbling your ear
Burying my face in your belly

All I would tell is you
And love; I must tell
Me, that I am a world
Containing more than love

Holding you and all your other
Lovers wherein you
And I are free from each other
A world that anyone can walk alone
Music, coathangers, the sea
Mountains, ink, trashy novels
Trees, pancakes, *The Tokaido Road*
The desert—it is yours

46

Refuse to see me!
Don't answer the door or the telephone
Fly off in a dragon-chariot
Forget you ever knew me

But wherever you are
Is a corner of me, San Juan Letrán
Or Montreal, Brooklyn
Or the Lion Gate

Under my skin at the Potala
Behind my eyes at Benares
Far in my shoulder at Port-au-Prince
Lifted in my palm among stars

Anywhere you must be you
Drugged, drunk or mad
As old, as young, whatever you are
Living or dying the place will be me

And I alone the car that carries you away.

III

(*Big High Song for Somebody*)

F
Train
Absolutely stoned
Rocking bug-eyed billboards WAFF!
No more bridge than Adam's
   off ox
     Pouring over 16⅔ds MPH sodium-

Vapor light yellow light

LOVE YOU!

Got *you* on
    like a coat of paint
Steamy girder tile

LOVE YOU!

Cutting-out blues
    (Tlaxcala) left me
   like stoned on the F-train
whole week's load ready
   for that long stretch ahead
    Prisoners jailed
      SHBAM
Train chained to this train
   boring through diamonds
     SQUALL

LOVE YOU!

Barreling zero up Balcony Street
   Leaning from ladders
    Same angle of lean; different cars
The Route of the PHOEBE SNOW

LOVE YOU!

Blue-black baby
   16-foot gold buddha in your arms
  Taking you with me!
    Straight up Shattuck Avenue
Hay-burning train, bull-chariot
  With bliss bestowing hands

LOVE YOU!

And I'm the laughing man
  with a load of goodies for all

Bridge still stands, bulls may safely graze,
Bee-birds in the frangipani
clock

LOVE YOU!

Berkeley 28–31:x:55
17:xi:55

SAUCED

I go reeling down the hall
into the leaves!
Tree of Heaven balcony door is open
A Trio for Jaybird, Telephone & Trombone
Jay
Jay
Trambone! poo-poo-poo POO!
Jay
Telephone
Poo jay telebone
Tram Sunday poo

The landlady explains the vacant room across the hall:
"Very quiet."

Gold squirrel!
in pear tree
Surgeons the stem & (Campanile 5 P.M.)
pear wobbling in his no-chin-space
Leaps into Heaven tree
The neighbors' pears

Jay Jay
( )

49

F train horn
Wren
airplanes in the eves like hornets
Notably drunken Berkeley Sunday 6 November '55

UNFINISHED, 3:xii:55

We have so much
That contemplating it
We never learn the use—

Poisoning ourselves with food, with books
    with sleep

Ignorance quicker than cyanide
Cuts us down

No lack of opportunity to learn;
Flat-footed refusal! Call it
Perversion, abuse, bullheadedness
It is rejection of all we know

A single waking moment destroys us
And we cannot live without
Ourselves

You come to me for an answer? I
Invented it all, I
Am your tormentor, there is no
Escape, no redress

You are powerless against me: You
Must suffer agonies until you know
You are suffering;

Work on that.

DENUNCIATION, OR, UNFROCK'D AGAIN

The trouble with you is
That sitting on a bench in the back yard
You see an old plank in the fence become
A jeweled honeycomb of golden wires
Discoursing music, etc.

The trouble is aggravated by the grass
Flashing alternately green and invisible
Green and non-existent
While the piano in the house plays
The Stars & Stripes Forever

The landlady's son has a tin ear

"The trouble with you is you keep acting
Like a genius: Now you're not a genius
You're nothing but a prick . . . in fact you're
Not even that, you're nothing but a son-of-a-bitch

GET OUT OF MY HOUSE!"

"There you are, sitting in the sun too . . .
Have you noticed all the flowers? There
Is an iris; there are hyacinths; these
Are tulip buds. I thought that was
A peach tree in the neighbor's yard; the
Landlady says it is an almond,
But the almond is always the first to flower."

The trouble with you is
You neither take it nor leave it alone.

What plant puts out those
Tall thin stiff green leaves? Lines
Drawn from the tip of each one

Would describe the surface of what
Regular solid polyhedron?

You don't dare invent a name;
Nameless, it threatens you with destruction.
To hell with it. It's a subtropical lily.

The trouble with you is that you're backed up
Against a wall
Convinced that any instant
You will fall right through it.
The real trouble with you really is
That you don't think,
You simply worry.

I sat down in my house and ate a carrot.

11:iii:56

HOMAGE TO ROBERT CREELEY

What I thought
  was a fly on the window was
A knot on the branch outside

Near it a real fly sat
Quiet in the sun

Wind rocked all the branches the fly
  sat still

25:v:56

INVOCATION & DARK SAYINGS,
IN THE TIBETAN STYLE

1.

The biggest problem in the world:

    "Where are you?"

And the second:

    To persuade you that I truly
    Want you here. I mean goddamit
That since you removed that celestial
      SNATCH
From these now desolated regions

    Nothing.
    Blank.

Vaseline,
Soap,
Hand-lotion,
Cold-cream,
Baby-oil,
Raw eggs,
Butter,
One pound of raw liver (delicately oven warmed),
One canteloupe   ("   "   "   ),
Several chickens,
One heifer,
Half a dozen assorted trulls,
A versatile but rather confused young man: : : :

Double-blank equaling
Half-nothing
With which I'm supposed to be content while you
Retain the only delectable sparkling furry magical

WHEN ARE YOU COMING HOME?

2.

MESSAGE: To the Reader
    ½ of me is asleep
When it wakes up
       EVERYTHING
Will be destroyed
Or transmogrified.

    (Have you got a hard-on?
     I've got a hard-on.)

You will never know what I think
Because I'm not saying.

    "This is a picture of a man.
     The man is hiding something.
     Try to guess what it is.
     If you guess wrong . . ."

Look at that old thing stand up there!

A midge crosses the page
Slowly
Then feels his way (wings balancing)
Along the edge and falls
On his head.
When he wakes up,
Watch out!
I mean like

"Look where it comes again!"

      (You dirty bastard, where did you ever get
      Such a filthy mind?

      My daddy lay on a sunny stone
      Fiddling with his cock
      The sun shone hot, the sun yelled
              "Sam!"
      My daddy went home
      But here I am.)

"Knowledge cannot be transmitted.
You can recount your own experiences
And a person who has had similar experiences
MIGHT know what you meant. Perhaps
That is communication. However . . ."

      You will never know what I think.
      What you see
      Is a dead idea.
      Now I'm thinking of
      Something else:

I can't tell it fast enough.

                           9–10:viii:56

THE SLOP BARREL:

Slices of the Paideuma for All Sentient Beings

NOTE: "Slices" was suggested as a title by Mike McClure. The
anecdote of the bicycle's demise is the original property of
Mr. Grover Grauman Sales, Jr., of Louisville and San
Francisco & used with his kind permission.

I

We must see, we must know
What's the name of that star?
How that ship got inside the bottle
Is it true your father was a swan?
What do you look like without any clothes?

> My daddy was a steamboat man
> His name was Lohengrin, his ship
> *The Swan,* a stern-wheeler—
> Cargoes of oil and wheat between Umatilla
> And The Dalles before the dam was built

I want to look at you all over
I want to feel every part of you

So we compare our moles and hair

> You have as many scars as my brother, Polydeuces
> That's the only mole I've got
> Don't look at it. I worry sometimes it will
> Turn into cancer. Is that the mark of Asia
> On your body? It is different from my husband's.

It was done when I was born
A minor sacrifice to Astarte (the priests
Lose everything)
A barbarous practice, I suppose.

      Gods demand a great deal. This coming war
      Nothing will be saved; they claim
      It will rid the earth of human wickedness . . .

Nevertheless when we are vaporized
To descend as rain across strange countries
That we will never see
The roses will row human ears for petals
To hear the savoy cabbages philosophize.

II

You say you're all right
Everything's all right
Am I supposed to be content with that?

      If I told you everything
      You'd have nothing to say
      If I fell to pieces you'd walk away flat
      (A weather-vane)

Suppose we were the first to begin
Living forever. Let's start
Right now.

Do you want this peach?
It's immortal.

      Both my watches are busted.

Meanwhile, back at the ranch
Pao Pu-tzu ("in the latter years
Of a long lifetime")
Is making those pills . . . ("the size of a hemp-seed")

    (I would prefer the hemp, myself
    Since *Sa majesté impériale*
    "took a red pill . . . and was not."
    None of them artificial kicks for me.)

to show up later
Riding a Bengal tiger
Both man and beast gassed out of their minds
Laughing and scratching
Pockets and saddlebags full of those pills:
"Come on, man, have a jellybean!"

The business of this world
Is to deceive but *it*
Is never deceived. *Maya Desnudata*
And the *Duchess:* the same woman. Admire her.
Nevertheless she is somebody else's
Wife. I don't mean unavailable
I mean preoccupied.

You and me
We make out, the question is
How to avoid future hang-ups, and/or
Is this one of them now?
We could take a decent time
Figuring out how to avoid repeating
Ourselves

    I know where I'm going
    I been there before
    I know when I get there
    I'll travel no more

Do you?
Are you still all right?
I don't want you to freeze.

I guess my troubles are pride
And doubt. You *are*
All right.

Have a jellybean . . .
Here comes a tiger.

III

By standing on the rim of the slop barrel
We could look right into the birds' nest.
Thelma, too little, insisted on seeing
We boosted her up
                    and over the edge
Head first among the slops in her best Sunday dress
Now let's regret things for a while
That you can't read music
That I never learned Classical languages
That we never grew up, never learned to behave
But devoted ourselves to magic:

Creature, you are a cow
Come when I call you and be milked.
Creature, you are a lion. Be so kind
As to eat something other than my cow or me.
Object, you are a tree, to go or stay
At my bidding . . .

Or more simply still, tree, you are lumber
Top-grade Douglas fir
At so many bucks per thousand board-feet
A given amount of credit in the bank
So that beyond a certain number of trees

59

Or volume of credit you don't have to know or see
Nothing

Nevertheless we look
And seeing, love.
From loving we learn
And knowingly choose:
Greasy wisdom is better than clothes.

I mean I love those trees
And the printing that goes on them
A forest of words and music
You do the translations, I can sing.

IV

Between water and ice
(Fluid and crystal)
A single chance

Helen, Blodeuwedd manufactured
Entirely of flowers
or flames
A trilium for every step
White trifolium, purple-veined
(Later completely purple)

> The heavy folds of your brocade
> Black waves of your hair
> Spilled across the *tatami*
> Black water smashed white at Suma
> "No permanent home"

I just don't understand you, I'm really stumped

Petal from the prune tree
Spins on a spider web

Slung between leaves
A flash in the sun

Baby scrooches around on the rug trying
To pick up the design

PAY NO ATTENTION TO ME

The pen forms the letters
Their shape is in the muscles
Of my hand and arm

Bells in the air!

At this distance the overtone
Fourth above the fundamental
Carries louder
Distorting the melody just enough
To make it unrecognizable

YOU DON'T LOVE ME LIKE YOU USED TO
YOU DON'T LOVE ME ANY MORE.

The sun has failed entirely
Mountains no longer convince
The technician asks me every morning
"Whattaya know?" and I am
Froze.
Unless I ask I am not alive
Until I find out who is asking
I am only half alive and there is only

WU!

(An ingrown toenail?)

WU!

(A harvest of bats??)

    WU!

A row of pink potted geraniums///???)

                                  smashed flat!!!
The tonga-walla swerved, the cyclist leapt and
The bicycle folded under the wheels before they stopped
The tonga-walla cursing in Bengali while the outraged
Cyclist sullenly repeats:
You *knows* you got to *pay* for the motherfucker
You knows you *got* to pay for the motherfucker

The bells have stopped
Flash in the wind
Dog in the pond.

                                        Berkeley 5:iii:56
                                          11:viii:56

SMALL TANTRIC SERMON

The release itself—
The comfort of your body—
Our freedom together and more, a
Revelation
Of myself as father, as a landscape as a universe
Being. . . .

This breaks down,
Here, on paper, although I am free
To spread these words, putting them
Where I want them (something of a release
In itself)

All they can say is
       Your foot
       Braced against the table-leg beside the bed
       Springing your hips to admit
       My gross weight, the other foot
       Stroking the small of my back:
A salacious picture of a man and a woman
Making out together
Or ingenuous autobiography—
"Memoirs of a Fat & Silly Poet"—
It might as well show them gathering tulips
Or playing cards

To say concisely
That the man in the picture
Really made it out through the roof
Or clear through the floor, the ground itself
Into free space beyond direction—

Impossible gibberish no one
Can understand, let alone believe;
Still, I try, I insist I can
Say it and persuade you
That the knowledge is there that the revelation
Is yours.

Berkeley 17:ix:56

FURTHER NOTICE

I can't live in this world
And I refuse to kill myself
Or let you kill me.

63

The dill plant lives, the airplane
My alarm clock, this ink
I won't go away

I shall be myself—
Free, a genius, an embarrassment
Like the Indian, the buffalo

Like Yellowstone National Park.

22:ix:56

I GIVE UP

I hate the morning, I hate the night
Lie down and die, tell me some more
Don't go to sleep, don't leave me alone

The dreams: of changes, suffocation
Loss of speech, pursuit by monsters
Or of endless logical argument

Awake and watching you sleep is worse
The stores are closed, no buses run
Homicidal maniacs prowl the suburbs

And the happy phantom of my greatness
Wakes and grasps this pen, leaving
A heap of used-up words to read

After a morning dream of music.

22:ix:56

THE FIRST DAY OF NOVEMBER

I'll walk to the postoffice & then to work
Seeing hot cinnabar geraniums green circular leaves
Dry heads and drying stalks of yarrow

Hearing in my head   *"Ist das nicht ein' schöne Welt?*
                          . . . schöne Welt?
                Schöne Welt! Und nimmer,
Mahler!   *Nimmer. . . ."*

Don't see that wren I hear

No rain after all
Though the air is heavy
                 and the war is on again
    (caused by my own carelessness, goofing)
Sphinx will have another medal on her chest

And the postoffice is closed
In commemoration of the Feast of St. Fellation

The same sad war, the universal drag, I lost
Four teeth in the service
            "Schöne Welt!"
I must have been bored without knowing it
And now the rain comes down.

FICHE-MOI LA PAIX!

                                                 1:xi:56

ESPRIT D'ESCALIER RANT,

Directed at Dr. P.'s class in English 106-B

You didn't see me, you didn't hear me, I said
The theory comes in later, a frame,
And even then the picture juts
Past it, down or sometimes through the wall.

Me, I don't understand counterpoint
But playing Bach on the piano
I really pick up and fly with him. The shapes
The figures are on the page

My eyes are fingers and ears
They work a design, a real
Imaginary pattern in the mind
That feels rough or buttered, like Dante said.

Triangle to Bach
Is triangle to me—*and*
A clown's hat and a lovely hair pie
(Turn it over in your heads.)

Like I mean you
Aren't questions, each of you
Is an answer.
But you'd gone, all of you afraid

Of mistaking CAT for "cat," a merry-go-round
For a gift-horse with a smile. Not, damn it, I SAID *NOT*
A private world,
Nor off a Georgian platter;

And when the dish I did use broke
I hope to God some
Of the contents splashed on everybody's clothes. You
May not call it love, but that's what it is.

9:i:57

THE SAME OLD JAZZ

OK, it's imperishable or a world as Will
& Idea, a Hindu illusion that our habits continuously
Create. Whatever I think, it
Keeps changing from bright to dark, from clear
To colored: thus before I began to think and
So after I've stopped, as if it were real & I
Were its illusion.

But as Jaime de Angulo said, "What's wrong with two?"

So Sunday morning I'm in bed with Cleo
She wants to sleep & I get up naked at the table
Writing
And it all snaps into focus
The world inside my head & the cat outside the window
A one-to-one relationship
While I imagine whatever I imagine

     Weed
   dry stalks of yarrow,
   repeated Y-branching V's, a multiplication

Of antelope, deer-horns? Umbels
Hairy brown stars at the tip of brown wires
A *menorah,* or, more learnedly, "hand" written in Great Seal Script

Almost against the window, horns again
Reindeer colored (in the sun) branching
Bare young loquat tree

Next door on the right the neighbors are building
Something in the garage, sawing & whirly-grinding
On wood. Models of the NIÑA, the PINTA & the SANTA MARIA
Life-size with television sails

Bright sky & airplanes & bugs mixed with
Flying paper ashes, the lid's off somebody's incinerator

There all that is & the reflection of *tatami*-color
In the silver bowl of my hanging lamp.

What if I never told any of this?

White cat
Spooked in the grass, alert against the satyrs
That pursue, she's full of kittens already
     . . . gone under the steps, under the porch

Cleo rises to bathe
& closes the bathroom door
My own bathtub becomes a mystery

Now that cat's on the window-ledge
Propped against the green sash, whiter
In the creamy light reflected off the kitchen door

What if I never said?

Singing & splashing in the bathtub
A mystery, a transformation, a different woman
Will emerge

     The birds have been pleased to show up
Bugs in the air won't last

And the chief satyr cat arrives
Ignores the birds, ascends the back stairs to spray the newel-post
A Message To The White Queen:
      "Sweet Papa is here."

He disappears and immediately
There she is, delicate pink nose reading:
      "Sweet Papa! The same old jazz."

Water glugs in the drain
A strange girl scours herself with my tired old towels
I think of her body & stop writing
To admire my own, some of her beauty rubbed off on me
Now some of my ugliness, some of my age
Whirls down the bathroom drain.

She'll go away. I'll go away. The world will go away.
    ("The idea of emptiness engenders compassion
      Compassion does away with the distinction
            between Self & Other . . .")
But through her everything else is real to me & I have
No other self.
"What's wrong with two?"

Berkeley 27:i:57–6:ii:57

ANCHOR STEAM BEER, FOR MICHAEL MCCLURE

I am here,
I like this

That is there
The sign says "Dinner?"
While underneath the picture changes
From Lobster Thermidor

69

(How did the French Revolution
                get in among the crustacea?)

       To Oysters Rockefeller
       I think of the 1900 nickle on my desk at home
       And it is there
       I like it

                                                          [9:ii:57]

SOUFFLÉ

TAKE I   Carol said, "I looked at all my cells today
              Blood & smear samples from all over me.
              They were all individuals, all different shapes
              Doing whatever they were supposed to
              And all seeming so far away, some other world
              Being I."

TAKE II   How do you feel?
              Me? Oh, I feel all right, but sometimes
              I feel like a motherless child.
              I feel like walking out of here & spending
                    vast sums of money. How do you
              Feel? I feel with my.

TAKE III   The wind increases as the sun goes down
              The weight of that star pulling air after it
              Naturally the prune trees blossom now
              And some kind of bush with pink trumpet flowers
              All the other trees except acacias have quit

TAKE IV   High strato-cumulus clouds and a
              Light north-easterly wind (possibly
              Two m.p.h. on the Beaufort Scale)

"What ever became of old Whatch-callum,
Old what's his name,
Old . . . you know, the old fellow
Who had that little ranch out by Mt. Pisgah,
Out by the Pisgah Home? Had that
Eight-finger Chinese cook & everything
    tasted like kerosene,
We went out there once & put up blackberries."

"Why, Dell, I don't remember . . .
He was a friend of yours."

TAKE V   How do I feel? I'm under it
Way under but I'm
Coming out, working out
The weight, the pressure
Piles of detritus already removed
The weight of half the earth, slowly
You can hear me underneath it all
Breathing, a faint
Scraping, a sifting rattle
Falling away below
Back towards the hollow center.
A little more
And I peer out

TAKE VI   Intolerable
You don't accept or reject it
You see it and know.
There is a difference.
    "You got to wash them dishes
        (pronounced "deeshes")
    And hesh that clattering tongue!
    Lolly-too dum, too-dum, &c."
No particular reply because the question
Isn't a question at all, it's the presence
Or absence of light
        among those trees.

TAKE VII   Nowhere, this is getting us no-
                where
         And we need a place to do it.

TAKE VIII I drank myself into a crying jag face down
         On Ginsberg's woolly green rug
         Roaring, "Gone, everything gone,
         Cold, cold, cold, cold, cold!"

         A nearly perfect vacuum at minus 278 degrees
              Absolute
         H O R R E U R D U V I D E

         The Messrs. Ginsberg & Kerouac, also juiced,
         Wrapped me in blankets while I froze & squalled

TAKE IX   "I want you to go out & amount to something;
         I don't want you to be an old ditch-digger all your life
         Work with your head if you can, let other people
              use their hands"

TAKE X   Can you look at a bug without squashing it?
         Can you look into a glass without hate, without
         Love, without murder?

         We have nothing but thoughts of murder, i.e.
         Complete ignorance of the world's own nature; or
         Where there's no sense there's no feeling.
         As for myself, I'm a genuine thug, I believe
            in Kali the Black, the horrific aspect
            the total power of Siva
            absolute destruction
         BUT it don't mean
         What it looks like
              and the description misleads.

TAKE XI   Bud-clusters hang straight down from the sharplycrooked
Geranium stem like strawberries, the wild mountain kind
These flowers almost as wild right here
Barbarous thick-jointed tangle, waist-high
Escaped once for all from the green-houses of the north
A weed, its heavy stalks jointing upwards & winding out
In all directions, too heavy to stand straight
The neighbors clipped some out of their yard
The stalks lay in the gutter & grew for days
In the rain water, flowering red
Ignorant of their disconnection

TAKE XII   I shall be in LA
    La Puebla de Nuestra Señora la Reina de los Angeles
On Palm Sunday
        a necklace of skulls & fingers,
         her belt dangling human arms, legs & heads
        her several hands brandishing
           the noose
           the sword
           the axe
           the skull-cup of blood
           the *dorje* (double lightning-bolt)
           Fire
           Drum
           Rosary
Having (*DV*) arrived by streamline train
    "Coast Daylight"
"in a throng of happy apprehensions"

TAKE XIII Don't you ever get tired
of your own sunny disposition?

TAKE XIV   I know perfectly well what became of old Mr. Daigler
            Greatly advanced in years he removed from Mt. Pisgah
            To the Odd-Fellows Home in Portland where he died
            Of malnutrition and the radio.

TAKE XV   The whole point of it is,
            When I saw that her necklace was made of my own
            Severed fingers, that I'd only just combed the hair
                        on that skull
                  (now containing lots of my blood
                        & her wasting it, slopping it
                        All down one of her arms)
            She was mine & we made it together
            The Island Of Jewels
            On a tiger-skin rug

            The Sun & Moon shining together.

TAKE XVI   It was so noisy in my head a rush of lights & motion
            And music & now the type lies on the page
            Perfectly silent, perfectly static, perfect
            The same temperature as the space between

                  Minus 278 ABSOLUTE

                  radio frequencies in the ten-meter band
                  from the direction of the constellation
                  Herakles

                  Light

                  Hard radiation (cosmic particles, beta
                        & gamma rays)

                  A few vagrant atoms of hydrogen, scatterings
                  of metallic &/or mineral dust shoved along
                  by the pressure of the

Light

Absolute

○

Berkeley, The Anchor Inn, 23:ii:57
8:iv:57

TAKEOUT, 15:IV:57

To have something fall is bad
To fall and break   worse.

fruitful ape
wiggy porcupine

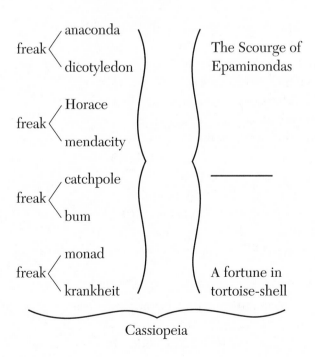

anaconda
freak
dicotyledon

Horace
freak
mendacity

catchpole
freak
bum

monad
freak
krankheit

The Scourge of
Epaminondas

A fortune in
tortoise-shell

Cassiopeia

We must learn to make mistakes gracefully;
However, all the fun resides in trying to be right
every time

Suppose it had floated in mid-air
That heavy solid porcelain teacup?

TERROR

The contravention of seemliness, abrogation
of all that is, &c.

("&c." equaling "if p, then q; if not p,
then x, solve for x," a simple quadratic) let it

Go.

FOR C.

I wanted to bring you this Jap iris
Orchid-white with yellow blazons
But I couldn't face carrying it down the street
Afraid everyone would laugh
And now they're dying of my cowardice.

Abstract beauty in the garden
In my hand, in the street it is a sign
A whole procession of ithyphallic satyrs
Through a town whose people like to believe:
"I was made like Jesus, out of Love; my daddy was a spook."

The upright flower would scare them. "What's shot,"
they think, "from the big flesh cannon will decay."
Not being there I can't say that being born is a chance
To learn, to love and to save each other from ourselves:
Live ignorance rots us worse than any grave.

And lacking the courage to tell you, "I'm here,
Such as I am; I need you and you need me"
Planning to give you this flower instead—
Intending it to mean "This is really I, tall, slender,
Perfectly formed"—is uglier than their holy fantasies,

Worse to look at than my own gross shape.
After all this fuss about flowers I walked out
Just to walk, not going to see you (I had nothing to bring—
This poem wasn't finished, didn't say
What was on my mind; I'd given up)

I saw bushes of crimson rhododendron, sparkling wet
Beside the hospital walk—I had to see you.
If you were out, I'd leave these flowers.
Even if I couldn't write or speak
At least I broke and stole that branch with love.

Berkeley 16:iv:57

A DIM VIEW OF BERKELEY IN THE SPRING

A graduated row of children, the biggest
Old enough to feel the boredom
Leading the rest, tearing up flowers in the driveway

The boredom, the tension

Fraternity men crowded into the wire cage—
A volley-ball court—jumping, hollering, laughing
        (only one is headed down the hill with his books
        to the campus, smoothing his crewed-down hair)
Too loud,

TENSION: The flying ball an indeterminate
Future, the Army? The Navy? Marriage before
Or later?

Leap, shout, a pattern of release that actually comes
Much later in some parked car
Trying to make out with some chick who
WON'T, she wants a home of her own to do it in
　　(Who can blame her?)
Then going back to the house with a stone-ache
Or gooey underwear, the tension
Relieved so they can sleep or built high enough
To be dreamed off or jacked away in the shower at 3 A.M.

Where's the action? What's going on?

The Suez is not at home to anyone.
Mr. Dullness says, 'War is no longer profitable.'
Daddy Warbucks in the White House says
'Everything is going to be just dandy.'

What are we going to do?

In Hungary they had a good idea
They all got together to kill the government
But the government mowed them down . . . who cares
About revolutions, the old corpses in the street routine?
Who cares?

Several hundred of us crowded in to watch a student
Gassed to death at Q
Later, a lot of other students went to peek at the body
Preserved in the basement of the University
　　THE MURDERER ON ICE
So we all saved the trouble and expense of a trip
To Central Europe

Charley Olson told me, '"Intolerable" is all right, a very
Dramatic word, but that isn't it at all.'
What I mean is, nobody
Can stand it, the tension, the boredom, whatever . . .
Mama and Papa scream at each other about the new deep-freeze,

('. . . and sometimes I just turn the TV off & go
do something else, I get so tired of it.'—that

Was the egg-lady speaking) and
The children continue destroying the flowers,
Being too young to go to the show at night alone.

[Winter 1957]

LITERARY LIFE IN THE GOLDEN WEST

A BIRTHDAY POEM FOR (&/OR ABOUT)
MR. J-L. K., 20:V:57

✺

Now we are thirty-five we no longer enjoy red neon
(MILNER HOTEL)
We don't know what to do except
Stand on our head four minutes a day
To adjust our metabolism and feel a physical
Ecstasy when we stand up & the blood
Rushes down from our head

It is impossible to write in the big front room
The space, the high ceiling scares us
In the kitchen we write:

"I have nothing to write about,
no work to do—I made a pastel picture of the backyard
I'm reading *Swann's Way,* I talk to my mother & go see
my friends, they are dull and vaguely busy suffering
from metabolic disturbances (they don't stand on their
heads) I just finished writing a book 1000 pages long,
I'm going away to—or am going to have to manufacture—
another world, this one is all worn out, Buddha is much
more interesting than fucking, eating or writing, my
mother is happy, now I can die next week."

None of our serious friends approve of this
Routine they write articles against us in all
The liberal magazines, the young hitch-hike from New York
And Alabama with their poems, we sit together in Portsmouth
Plaza
Drinking muscatel and swapping stories
Until the buttons drive us home.

TAKE # 4, 15:VIII:57

FOR N.

You say, "I want you to kiss me" and you being
Beautiful I comply becoming right then
Beautiful and universally loved, like I don't know what
Year it is or come away with me into the lush life

Which is this,
Sitting in the dark by the radio jazz writing in the light
From the bathroom, one cat already stone out on the floor
The tradition of this place
You never saw such a pad all the wine all the ones
Who made it here the poems proliferating from this point

THE MUSES HELICON

I know what I want I want you and all this
Which is impossible . . . what can I

    Not just the most the best I want the superb
    With hot and cold running water unimaginable nothing
    Else will do, in the center of an impenetrable wilderness
    Square miles of it you couldn't guess that . . . or that I've
    Had it and it's not enough . . . what can I

        With my last paycheck buy a new suit & a pair of sox
        And a good paying job to keep you?

We are nowhere and nothing ever started

I guess you wanted a point of reference, right then
To locate yourself, OK? But I've been further than you
And back again, it's the same at both ends: You're looking
At two sides, your own and one that's different and scary

    (I have an argument with X . . . who keeps talking about
    "Low Life," "I keep wanting to do a novel about Low Life,
    Like I knew a lady boxer, I was crazy about her, she had
    A beautiful body, I used to strap her into her iron brassiere
    She was a gorgeous woman . . . and absolutely queer.")

It's an imaginary choice between two imaginary worlds
Here I am high as a kite writing or trying to spell properly
The Tearful Tragedy of the Minotaur in Love or, *The Bull-Headed
Monster* (as Picasso draws him, although I don't have as good a
build) . . . the body of a man
but alien
Non-human from the neck up
Most Notable Monster

Our children would have the heads of angels
And the bodies of cows

☼

☼

All that's the honest picture of a cheating mind
I mean hogwash—I didn't have or want anything—
I needed you and didn't know it
I hung the monster mask on you and ran away
Imagining scenes of you asleep at nine and I
Standing by the bed at two A.M. trying to waken you

 "Come outside, the stars are falling,
 I've found a caterpillar that glows in the dark!"

For all I know, I'm the biggest prize there is
Certainly you are
& maybe you would like to starve with me
& if I had you what would I care about food or the telephone bill?

But I never asked you
Supposing that I knew all the answers. . . .

What else is there to find out?
It's all very simple, it's all like this,
We are 750 miles apart.

I stand here in my underwear wondering what to do
What was I going to do. . . .
      clean these pipes,
Illuminate all these worlds. . . .
        I'll eat breakfast

Attentively as possible
Thinking of you.

AGAINST THE MAGIC WAR:

AN OPEN LETTER TO ROBERT DUNCAN

Dear Robert, for whatever reason, you sent this dream against me:
A lady brought me over in a boat with several kinds of bread.
She says, "You ought to see him singing hymns and wheedling
around, "Won't any of you buy yourselves a bridge game?""

I paid several times to get in and out of the amusement park.
I showed all my mis-marked identification & all the children
laughed and shot hot sparks at me. I should have busted their
space helmets!

Then my father said, "I could take you to India," and I
cried then because I'm sorry he's old & I haven't done any-
thing about it & he said, "That don't mean anything, all that
bawling around, you're only feeling sorry for yourself, just
like Jack tells me (he's been crying, too, at his father—he
says, "There's too much furniture in my apartment"—we've
had a lot of long talks lately)"

A double rebounding track of lightning. Victory to salute
and Salute to Victory

and I awoke with eye-pains, conscious of swift lights and motions
through the room and your name & I exorcised the shade, the
emanation of Robert Duncan from this room with magical imple-
ments and music, spells of magic so profound I am ashamed of
having used them. Later, you caused your demons to laugh outside
my house at four in the morning—I know they were yours, your
name was on them, it shone through the walls. I invited them in
for gasoline, lit fires to warm them, keep up their strength. One
had a sore: I poulticed it with tabasco sauce and sandpaper & in
gratitude he became a horde of pride-spiders that swarmed over
me, biting & singing:

> "Temperance, Fortitude & Justice
> The pen is mightier than the sword
> Celibacy, poverty, obedience—
> Virtue always gets its own reward."

I hid them in the oven when the sun came up. I'll send them home tonight with cookies & milk for you and all your friends.

O Robert, all of us are bound by hate & power—all we know is misery and self-indulgence—why this battle among enchanters?
> Blind power the sightless crown the enchained sword
> A tyranny of magic in the sun
> Hitting out on all sides to defend an empty center
> The raving Face of Glory whirling, raining down
> Flooding with fire

If it were as splendid as all that
If the destruction were total
If it took that single hair out of my soup
Then yes, I praise it, I consent, I worship
But it does everything else. The hair remains,
The nature of soup admitting a possible hair
Or somebody's thumb

LIST OF POSITIVE THINGS TO DO

1) Wash the dishes.
2) Wear a hair-net while cooking.
3) Keep the cat out of the kitchen, the diningroom.
4) Serve the soup in a dish with a wide brim—or
   don't fill the rimless dish too full.

With many blessings,
P.

23:vii:57

84

HARANGUE FROM NEWPORT,

TO JOHN WIENERS, 21:IX:57

What if I never told you
What if I never said what I'm trying
To say now?

A long time ago I thought it would be better
If I hadn't been born
But since I had been it might save trouble
To minimize the whole thing:
Play it not only cool but invisible

That doesn't work any more, everybody
Asks: "What's the matter"   "Are you mad about something?"
            "What's worrying you now?"

Well, what . . .
        I just saw my landlord go by
                the great carbuncle on his nose
                a sea anemone at low tide, petals retracted
                center full of sand, the circulation
                in his legs is bad so his feet hurt & he has
                dizzy spells because he won't stop eating
                fried fish
                        (athero- or arteriosclerosis,
                        anyway, too much cholesterol)
                being some sort of Swede
Now what?
        My hernia has skidded again
    More:
        I found a couple chunks of jasper-agate on the beach
        and one entire family (7 or 8 of them) jumping about
        in the surf with all their clothes on
        being some sort of Dukhobors-in-reverse?
    More?

I should burn the garbage and wash the frying pan
I should write you something that would
Scare you, make you laugh
Or generally turn you on
WHAT
    I'm doing now: Trying hard to be visible, to be
    Totally conscious of this time and place,
                of you
    And every sentient being

    I'm stacking bb's day & night
    Working miracles left & right

    (Log-truck poops by in the street while I'm writing—I
changed it into gold: perfect wisdom, perfect compassion,
perfect freedom. . . . Texas-boot red shirt sideburns bodhisattva
                                    driver
instantly swung out of the cab to render his bows and performs
his circumambulations)

NOTICE,
    That the landlord still has his carbuncle
    That the family who frolicked in the waves have wet sandy
        clothes which chafe them
    That the frying pan remains unwashed
    That the log truck must go live at Ft. Knox
    And that nobody can see me, I've closed all the blinds
        it being night outside
    But everybody knows I'm here
        the light's turned on
Notice also that you not only see me clearly

    (A MIRACLE!)

You understand everything I say.

10:X:57, 45 YEARS SINCE
THE FALL OF THE CH'ING DYNASTY

The Summer Palace burnt, the Winter Palace, wherever it was
"Ordre, ordre, Je suis une maniaque pour l'ordre!"
(Meaning that all those sheets are promptly sent to the wooden
Laundries of the Seine,
That all the shoes and sox are lined up in rows
That the words follow each other in ecstatic parentheses, NOT
That you and me are lined up against the innocent wall, torn
By the bullets of righteousness)

I am hid, as William Blake puts it, where nobody can see me not
Even those sad angels who busted the slippery membrane across
My stifled face so I could breathe the incense coming in
From the pavilion under Coal Hill my brocade sleeves raveling
Among the chips of jade and the withered peony blossoms and
The night of the boat-light Dragonboat orgies on the River
In pious memory of whosis that first made the water scene
with an ingenious system of *canali* and Nationally Federated Dams
    Where nobody can see me
        I read all about Jimmy Dean with 16 photographs
        and more than a hundred pages of vulgar prose

Nobody can find me I came here with that purpose of being alone
    (R. . . . says we have all these self-destructive impulses and it
    BUGS him, like he went to the neighborhood soda-fountain
    For a coca-cola and everybody/all these monster teen-age hoods/
    Jumped on him at once)

Not unlike the United States Marines building teakwood campfires
Out of the Empress's bedroom furniture on the Phoenix-Viewing
Terrace roasting their wienies.

APEDEATH

Today I found record of a dream: the marble rotunda
Virtuous bronze & the dying hairy ancestor

The marble paternal dome empty without my double and me
I cannot save the ancestor totem-beast
Which dies & I am pursued as his killer

Through the Dutch wooden store (a thief & no thief but afraid)
To the river/canal bank—safety in the white house
Impossible to reach

Escape up the wooden ramp to bridge
Into Seattle/Portland foggy rain

I wake up in a strange house, looking at a familiar chair
& a door that doesn't belong & wake dying
My own cottage floor bed facing the bookcase Berkeley summer
                night.

11:xi:57

IN MEMORY OF A STATESMAN

What's become of my brains, my eyes?
I had them here a minute ago,
Now I can't find them anywhere . . .
        THE CHILDREN!
                arranging them in saucepans? the toy stove?
Bring them back immediately!
Carefully, clumsily ladling, a few hasty stitches
        (the dolly sewing machine)
Now listen!
The children wildly protest their future good behaviour

88

Return their attention to Baby
& I am free to continue:

> After the opening of the Crimean war it became evident
> that the tensile strength of a single hair from a sea-otter
> pelt (one which later became part of the great cape of
> that fur presented to the Empress Catherine of Russia)
> was found to be just ⅔ds that of beryllium. . . .

MY DEARS!
Daddy is sorry that he has had forcibly to detain you at the very
beginning of what in prospect appeared to be a highly interest-
ing & instructive expedition into the never so dim & expensive
interior of the television receiver and it is my duty to express
the most profound regrets of my Government concerning the
untoward incident which so recently disturbed the equanimity
of your Government's Minister Plenipotentiary during his late
visit to Chagrin Falls.

If I give you one cooky you must drink a full glass of milk
And a full glass of milk with each succeeding cooky.
Do you understand?

27:xii:57

LETTER, TO MME. E. T. S., 2:I:58

                        so T. comes on with the usual
"Come, tell me how you live" routine & I:
            "Like a pope, on indulgences; like the king
                        on benevolences."

        Poor little fly ain't got no home

89

Nor the seagulls outside, dining—
     an abundance of Pacific decapods
       (copepods?)

T: "But what can you *do* there? Noplace to go,
     you don't see anybody . . ."
I: "I have a part-time job;
  I read and write."

       & everyone marvels at my Devotion to Literature
       Or figures I'm coming on too innocent, I must be
         Up to Something
       (T. imagines, "Some chick is on the scene"
       & L., "Or an infallible connection . . . ?")

All day Christmas the sea whirled this tangle—
Spruce logs, redwood stumps, fishboxes and lightglobes—
A big eddy at the creek mouth
Carting several tons of debris back & forth across a hundred
                 feet of beach

In water maybe a foot & ½ in depth

As the tide went out a gull rode a heavy smooth-swimming log
Perfectly flat-footed, no trouble balancing
Nothing to hang on to
Nothing to hang on with, raining like hell
   Poor little seagull got no home
Riding just now for the fun of it
In a generally Japanese direction

       I think of children in a department store
       Playing on the escalators, kings and queens
       In magic palaces where the stairs walk up & down
       Whether you move your feet or not
       Hop to the stationary (moving) floor
       Then sink through it & soar out of the ceiling

An angel in lights and music floating down
Just above Mama's head among the yard-goods
& costume jewelry

Poor little fly ain't got no clothes

Even to me this looks fishy, all
I get out of it is these idiot routines about seagulls—
the astrologers and palm-readers insist I have
Great Executive Ability a head for business
       & organization
(You can imagine the opinion
Of "eminent medical authorities,"
Not to mention the police)

L. (at the end of a letter) "What are *you*
      doing?"

& most of the time I'm not even writing this
Wishing I'd get started
& having started . . .

      THE DISCOVERY,

That it's sheerest self-indulgence
Just like the Pope building bridges to heaven
   (I presume that's the point of the *Pontifex Maximus* jazz)
Whether you move your feet or not

Laid end for end this poem is exactly
   a foot & ½ in depth
   Try to buy it

      BOOK DEPT. . . . . 6th Floor
Children Not Allowed On Escalators Unaccompanied By Adults

FOR MY FATHER

Being a modest man, you wanted
Expected an ordinary child
And here's this large, inscrutable object

ME

(Buddha's mother only dreamed
        of a white elephant;
    my mother . . .)

Cross between a TV camera and a rotary press
Busy turning itself into many printed pages
Heavy, a dust-collector, almost impossible
        to get off your hands, out of your house
Whatever it was, not an actual child

You recognize parts of the works, ones you first donated
But what are they doing—the flywheel horizontal
Spinning two directions at once
A walking-beam connected to a gear train turning camshafts—
Which produces material like this
Sometimes worth money to folks in New York
Or not, nobody knows why.

                                                    3:i:58

"WHILE THE PATIENT SLEPT"

Why inquire into the astrolabe?
What use the quincunx now?
Unicorn.
            TROY IS DOWN
Stubborn

92

> Thebes in all her glory
> Great Babylon
> fol-de-rol
> I live in a different town.

Spring 1958

TRANSLATION OF A LOST PLAY BY M. M.

Maurice.   O, Ferdinand, listen!
What is that noise there, that tiny
Sound issuing from that place there? Do you
Hear that sound? What can be producing
That so dolorous as if weeping baby?

Ferdinand.   That? Ah that, dear Maurice, that is
The infantine Moses child weeping there amidst
The bullrushes beside the dark river's edge making
That sound there.

Maurice.   Why is it that he weeps there in that unique position?
Ferdinand.   He weeps there for that he is already a prophet.
Maurice.   Ah, glorious wretched little!

desunt ceterae

19:iii:58

SENSELESS COMMENTARIES ON CHAO-CHOU

The One is reduced to assorted shoes in the closet
Nobody here but these shoes
People come in and name them "his", "yours"
They are actually shoes

And these naturally words
Product of certain active chunks of protein
i. e., MEAT pleased to suppose itself "I" and "Mine"
Capable of reproducing itself
Over and over again.

Shoes are made of its skin.
Cloth is made of its fur.
Most of the rest is used for food
      on which it feeds,
The orts, offals, manures make plants grow and
      it eats them, too.

Plum tree moonlight crocodile soap:
Which one is my name?

Kangaroo:
Where's my history?

Crying Fern-Women:
Who's hungry?

        "Sergeant, what's going on in here?"
        "War-dance down at the cuckoo-house,
               Sir!"

LET UP!   LET UP!   LET UP!

LAY OFF ME, WILL YA?

How come I
　　　always have to lose?

Turtle-back, how come?
It's the shape of mountains
Turning rivers—
A ginkgo leaf
When?
Snail plague time in Berkeley.

Newport
23:iii:58

SINCERITY SHOT

My hair is itchy, my wandering shorts
Provoke fantasies of sexual congress
& having removed them I have this to say:

　　　I'm drinking sweet Italian vermouth with ice in it
　　　No more visions, only sensations of general contentment
　　　& a certain smug self-righteousness
　　　　　　　about my present continence

& " 'a babbled o' green fields" (cheating already! A quote.)
　　　　　　&
This vermouth tastes like shaving-soap

　　　(Eating a dish of ginger beef,
　　　The Judge: "I don't like it."
　　　I: "It's good; it tastes like Cashmere Bouquet."
　　　The Judge: "Some people *like* to eat soap.")

More cheating, that was memory
& not what I have to say, which is:
   My nose itches, a prognostication
     a) I shall presently kiss a fool
        or
     b) Someone is coming to visit me,
   . . . but a lying prophecy, it being 12:35 A.M.
   & I don't know nobody to kiss in this town,

               23:iii:58

METAPHYSICAL INSOMNIA JAZZ. MUMONKAN XXIX.

            Of
Course I could go to sleep right here
With all the lights on & the radio going

(April is behind the refrigerator)

      Far from the wicked city
      Far from the virtuous town
      I met my fragile Kitty
      In her greeny silken gown

  fairly near the summit of Nanga Parbat & back again, the wind
     flapping the prayer-flags

"IT IS THE WIND MOVING."
———————————
"IT IS THE FLAG MOVING."

Hypnotized by the windshield swipes, Mr. Harold Wood:
    "Back & forth; back & forth."

We walked beside the moony lake
Eating dried apricots
Lemons bananas & bright wedding cake
& benefits forgot

"IT IS THE MIND MOVING."

& now I'm in my bed alone
Wide awake as any stone

7:iv:58

LETTER TO CHARLES OLSON

This surface (which grows increasingly Riemannian)

 how's your topology now? When you turn this over
 do you have a right- or a left-hand glove?

(A WALL)

Right now is just fine, don't monkey with the postoffice
It's shut for the night:
I won't be able to buy a stamp for this until after 9 A.M.
No matter what I do, no matter how hard I try.

(A WALL)

So here we are, sweet Indolence and I and middling Luxury

(NO WALL)

And at last I can hear the radio say:
    "It is 29 minutes past 3 A.M."
Without flipping into a spin about being on time in the "morning"
Because I shall . . .
                                    No strain
But—can I turn off Brahms' *Tragic Overture*
    now? Put out my pipe and go to bed?
Not until
    (ouch! a pain in the skull!)
I've said this
    (and in the left eye, the frontal sinus
    breaking down.)

                (A WALL)

I guess it's tragic if he said so, incidental music
For some Shakespearian or Goethean tragedy, I forget
    although I read about it ONCE

No, I'll get up . . .

Well, go on, let Brahms take over with plenty of tremolo,
e.g.:
    I will collapse time, it is 4 A.M.
    And this is the Berkeley cottage, I've been drinking
    Wine with Allen & Jack, I must be at my sink at 8
    ON TIME, as I was the morning before, after a similar
    4 A.M. wine & goof-balls

            (AN ARTIFICIAL PARTITION)

    TIME IS RELATIVE/ or irrelevant; it is space, the surface
    Which makes the distinction?

        (& of course Rexroth has the last word,
            it is the PERSON)
Or more nearly canonical, Epictetus: "Not events
But the judgment of men . . ."

("all that learning so gratuitously hurled at us—
　　　　why don't he (i.e., PW) get a job in a college?")
Dryden sang, ". . . Jealousy, that Tyrant of the mind"
As if the mind weren't tyrannical enough
　　　　　　　　　　　　　　　　　　on its own hook

　　　(Very beautiful lady on a visit to apartment inhabited
　　　　　by Snyder & me, years ago . . . she views a hunk of my
　　　　　library:
　　　　　"Did you take English 1109 at Cal.?"
　　　　　"No."
　　　　　"But you have all the *books!*"

(A WALL . . . OF BOOKS)

Lacking either space or time
Here we sit between Planck's Constant & the Speed of Light (*c*)
Theoretically discontinuous & haunted by an antique radio voice
(Mr. Jack Pearl in the character of "Baron Munchausen":
　　　　　"Was you there, Charlie?")
The whole world looking at its hand,
Betelgeuse at or near the eighteenth turning of whose particular
Small intestine? (Cf. a cartoon by Mr. George Gamow)
　　　　　(our editor writes me,
　　　　　"You are *not* interested in geometry!")
　　　"the judgment of men"
　　　the postoffice: Closed
　　　the time: Well, my watch is wrong
　　　but now is more or less six days since the first line.
　　　The library is in storage. Leave it there.

(A WALL . . . OF BOOKS)

People is a door, particularly for me, ladies I have loved
And the mind a Moebius-strip, a single surface
Turned through itself—or better, a sphere inside a sphere
That can be a torus (like the body) without losing anything
No wasted material.

Wall certainly is here, ⅝ths Philippine mahogany
Peachy-painted plaster for the rest.
There is a top and a bottom and two ends—
And another side! which is yellow, a DISCONTINUITY
Like radiation (Planck again)

> "each radiator emitting energy in equal amounts
> termed *quanta*, the value of which depend on a universal
> constant (A WALL) and the frequency of the vibration
> of the radiators"

I said LEAVE IT THERE!
The song tells it best:

> *So high you can't get over it;*
> *So low you can't get under it;*
> *So wide you can't get around it—*
> *Got to come in by the door.*

  which is what don't exist, although the wall does
(Notice the absence of "Therefore, etc.")

FOR REFERENCE ONLY

Wm. Shakespeare: *A Midsummer Night's Dream,*
Act V, Sc I, ll. 161–162:
Wall. "This loam, this roughcast, and this stone doth show
That I am that same wall. The truth is so."

TORUS: looks like a smooth & perfect doughnut. It will bear
only 7 contiguous areas of differently colored paints
without the repetition of a color. Turning itself through
itself it becomes a sphere with a sphere inside itself.
Which way is up? Charles is in Gloucester. I am here.

Newport 23:iv:58

UNSUCCESSFUL SPRING POEM

Warm night/morning walking
I'm looking for anything

Beside a white wall: Soft ponderous callas, white against white
Nothing can move them in this heavy moon & streetlight

_____SUDDEN ANTIQUE VISION OF MAY_____

when no one shall marry

women clean house, bank all fires, a white cone of ashes
the coals deep inside
girls & their marble images bathe in the sea

men & boys keep to the rivers, fish for spring salmon
(Stay away from the ocean!)
after steam-baths & fasting, eat dream-journey medicine
gathering   power

_____

Although completely open, perfectly formed, white
Nothing will move these massive lilies until June

3:v:58

CORVALLIS DOWN THE ROAD

Where does the weather turn off for Elk City?

18:v:58

TRYING TOO HARD TO WRITE A POEM
SITTING ON THE BEACH

Planted among driftwood
I watch the tide go out
It pulls the sundown with it
& across this scene & against the wind
Man on a motorbike white crash-helmet
His young son rides the gas tank before him
Slows down for the creek mouth
& not too fast up the beach north

Flat dull whistle buoy heard again
and though the wind is right the bell buoy is inaudible

Fat seagull picks at a new hake skeleton
Choosily—not hungry walks away
Returns a moment later,
Room for a few more bites inside

Here comes a family of five
Man prodding with a stick whatever the children test
                    with their fingers
Mama is bundled up naturally cold & yellow plastic bucket
Complaining a little ". . . kind of a long way from the car . . ."

The children explore ahead the beach goes on forever & they
Will see it all this evening they aren't tired

Motorbike man coming back slows down for them
            & for the creek mouth

Fog joined into fat clouds cover the sun
Move south stretching rivers & islands of blue
Fine moving sheets & shafts of light on the water horizon

I'm not making it, I'm cold, I go into the house.

12:vii:58

102

20:VII:58, ON WHICH I RENOUNCE
THE NOTION OF SOCIAL RESPONSIBILITY

The minute I'm out of town
My friends get sick, go back on the sauce
Engage in unhappy love affairs
They write me letters & I worry

Am I their brains, their better sense?

All of us want something to do.

    I am breathing. I am not asleep.

    In this context: Fenellosa translated *No* (Japanese word)
        as "accomplishment"

                (a pun for the hip?)

Something to do

        "I will drag you there by the hair of your head!"
        & he began doing just that to his beautiful wife
        Until their neighbors (having nothing better to do)
        Broke it up

If nothing else we must submit ourselves
To the charitable impulses of our friends
Give them a crack at being bodhisattvas
    (although their benevolence is a heavy weight on my head
    their good intentions an act of aggression)

Motion of shadows where there's neither light nor eye to see
Mind a revolving door
My head a falling star

7:v–20:vii:58

103

NEWPORT NORTH-WINDOW VIEW

FOR BRUCE MCGAW

Graveled vacant lot
Left corner breaks into blackberry gulch

Straight ahead, spruce and jackpine grove
A set-up for Sesshu, the jackpines good as his
Sitka spruce behind them, stiff ragged feather wall

(Marred, I thought at first, by these trashy little shacks:

> Left-hand cabin partly dropped in the gully, its base
> > battered a little outward, a single row of windows
> > under the roof-line, not badly proportioned,
> > a jackpine leans toward its left back corner and up
> > then my direction; hazelbush hides front corner

> A pile of stovewood
> High square end of a blue bus (truck? trailer?)
> Half round-top cabin, a government colored, up on blocks
> > portable office for a construction boss
> Square gray house, white trim, its corner facing me, its
> > back against two pines)

Yesterday early evening fog dissolved the shacks into the scene
An occasional plane edge or corner, two or three steady lights
While up above, black tree earth air water transmutations

> Cloud becomes mountain
> Tree becomes beast
> Beast into cloud

Now in full sunlight
Trunks and branches carve black space out of walls and roofs
Which become flat irregular plane surfaces of light
    floating among the trees;
jumbled apricot pyramid woodpile blazes on the tawny ground.

27:vii:58

FROM AN ENVELOPE ADDRESSED TO CHARLES OLSON

Zucchini rollers
Summer-squash crown gears
Innocent vegetable machine
Illegal thousand-dollar cabbage leaves
New Jersey Mafia salad contemplation

3:vii:58

HYMNUS AD PATREM SINENSIS

I praise those ancient Chinamen
Who left me a few words,
Usually a pointless joke or a silly question
A line of poetry drunkenly scrawled on the margin of a quick
            splashed picture—bug, leaf,
                caricature of Teacher
        on paper held together now by little more than ink
        & their own strength brushed momentarily over it

Their world & several others since
Gone to hell in a handbasket, they knew it—
Cheered as it whizzed by—
& conked out among the busted spring rain cherryblossom winejars
Happy to have saved us all.

31:viii:58

COMPLAINT: TO THE MUSE

You do understand I've waited long enough
There's nobody else that interests me more than a minute
I've got no more ambition to shop around for poems or love
Come back!
        or at least answer your telephone
I'm nowhere without you

    This is the greatest possible drag
    Slower than the speed of light or always
    A little less than critical mass

    The energy the steam the poop is here
    Everything is (by Nature) Energy, I myself
    A natural thing & certainly massive enough

    A block of lead (the end of all radiation)
    I don't even reflect much daylight, not to speak of
        glowing in the dark
    I'll never get it off the ground

This room is full of 1 fly & an alarmclock
It is uninhabitable

If I wasn't drunk & blowing wine-fumes & peanut breath in your face
Maybe you'd be nice to me.

You do understand
I'd much rather listen, Lady
Than go on babbling this way, O rare gentle
& wise, it isn't enough that your face, your body
Are uniquely beautiful—I must hear you tell me
                    about the weather
We might even quarrel if nothing else

You know the answer & don't, won't quit kidding me along
Hanging me up like Sir John Suckling
                    in a tag of lace or muslin

I can see right through all those veils
But you can run fast & I've got a bum knee

& you been a long time gone

11–12:ix:58

PROSE TAKE-OUT, PORTLAND 13:IX:58

I shall know better next time than to drink with any but certified
drunks (or drinker) that is to say like J-L. K. who don't fade away
with the first false showing of dawn through the Doug-fir & hem
lock now here Cornell Road First of Autumn Festival
    a mosquito-hawk awakened by my borrowed kitchen light
    scrabbles at the cupboard door
& the rain (this is Portland) all over the outdoor scene—let it—
I'm all in favor of whatever the nowhere grey overhead sends—
which used (so much, so thoroughly) to bug me

Let it (Shakespeare) come down
      & thanks to Paul Bowles for
reminding me)
there it rains & here—long after rain has stopped—continues from
the sodden branch needles—to rain, equated, identified with no-
where self indulgence drip off the eaves onto stone drizzle mist
among fern puddles—so in a manner of speaking (Henry James
tells us)   "There we are."
the booze (except for a hidden inch or so of rosé in the kitchen
jug) gone & the cigarets few—I mean where IS everybody & they
are (indisputably) very sensibly abed & asleep—
      one car slops by fast on overhead Cornell Road the
fireplace pops I wouldn't have anything else just now except the
rest of the wine & what am I trying to prove & of course nothing
but the sounds of water & fire & refusing to surrender to uncon-
sciousness as if that were the END of everything—Goodbye, good-
bye, at last I'm tired of this & leave you wondering why anybody
has bothered to say "The sun is rising" when there's a solar ephem-
eris newly printed, it makes no difference—but you will be less
than nowhere without this pleasurable & instructive guide.

13:ix:58

SELF-PORTRAIT SAD 22:IX:58

At last I realize my true position: hovering face down above the world
(At this point the Pacific Coast of The United States)
The lights of the cities & my lives & times there
A second rate well finished nothing too much wrong with it but not too
                 interesting
Piece of music—think of De Falla's *Nights in the*
        Gardens of Spain:
Very like that—mildly extravagant, vaguely romantic
Some overtones of a home grown exoticism

Trying to break this all up I meditate a while
Walk on the beach to look at the moon (some sort of festival moon surely
First full moon after Autumn Equinox)

Sudden seabird exclamations very loud just over my head invisible

Broken tooth. Shrouded typewriter. Noisy clock. Poorly tuned radio.
Sick refrigerator in the next apartment.
I know exactly what I'm doing
& after sleeping and waking again the rest of this day will be wonderful

(DREAM PANTOMIME)

Stacked high around us while we practice unspeakable vices
Bones of Senacherib his victims
O Babylon, dear Babylon all drowned!

The irresponsible waves & fickle winds
    (Great Atlantis!)
Flying fish & giant cephalopods
Poison floating dumpling Portuguese man o'war
    (O Camoens!)
& immoral Plotinian nautilus high above the temple courts

Alas dainty Belshazar!   Divine Exogamite!
            Perished!

Folie de grandeur: horror & degradation is my name

Another damned lie, my name is I
Which is a habit of dreaming & carelessness
            no nearer the real truth of any matter
In any direction myself bound & divided by notions

ACT!   MOVE!   SPEAK!

Forgetting last night's moon & paying no attention now
To the sunlight in these pines

Deer Demon & Yak Demon stir my brains
Mouth grows tinier, belly
Huge—I'm a *preta,* starving ghost
Self-devoured

PARALYZED   AGAIN!

(O rage, O désespoire, &c.)

Swinging in the same eccentric orbit from depression
To mania—imbecility to genius

Unlike Tobit I'm awake but the seagulls mute
            dung as warm as sparrows
                    per usual

& I'm tired of being tired of it
A simply switch from hating to loving
That's not enough, walking from one end of a teeter-board
                    to the other
Go sit under a chestnut tree & contemplate the schoolhouse
You won't believe that its thin tall red brick
Peaked roof & elegant cupola with bell
Narrow high green-trim crumble-sill windows (& this
            is the NEW side, the 1910 Union St. facade
            the Court St. front is 1897 its great solid doubledoors
            Sealed)

& now the tree's cut down
            Oh, well
            I was never good at throwing rocks to knock down
            Pods from it anyway, horsechestnuts
            Cold calsomine smell, solid chunks of brown watered-
                    silk inside
            To contemplate
                    or decorate with a pocket knife

DOTE   DOTE   DOTE

Suppose (unbelievably) you were fat & forty for the last 20 years
With sporadic fits of low-frequency radiation
Lots of side-bands, poor modulation, the oscillator
                Unstable

        DOTE   DOTE

(PLEASE REPLACE YOUR OLD TANK WITH A ((PIEZO-
ELECTRIC)) CRYSTAL!   —Yours truly, F.C.C.)

Useless for any practical purpose
i.e. unemployable for clear transmission

  So it was the wrong tree; the school remains
                                          &

There's a library not far away
Also brick but under vines with slick blueblack poison berries
A mansard roof thanks to Mr. Carnegie

  Mama said: "You don't HAVE to believe EVERYTHING they
             tell you in school—think for yourself a little bit!"

The library: A house of correction
                      There is a boardinghouse
                      Far far away
                      Where they serve hash & beans
                      Every Saturday
Intermezzo
                      O how those boarders yell
                      When they hear that dinnerbell
                      O how the boarders yell
                      Far far away

Teeter-totter   Contemplate the schoolhouse
Bread & water   Look at the library

chestnuts

DOTE

I go home again all the time
It nearly drives me dotty but I go & will go again

. . . Far away

& it's as real as anything else
However changed in many particulars—specifically
The love & hate gone out of it leaving what the Friends call
"A concern"
        (is it properly "compassion"?)

DOTE

    I forget how Tobit saw again
          neither school nor library
          not that kind of ignorance
    He had to bring some story
    Tell the truth on at least one
    Occasion or subject
    He had to DO
                something first & then the Angels
                The Archangel Raphael, I think?
                brought him eye-cups

    Telling you I'm paralyzed—
    Inside a thin cast of seagull lime—
    None of that was true for more than a minute (vile hyperbole!)
    You are the ones walking around inside your shells, I soar
    Face down high above the shore & sea
                Ho ho, *skreak*, &c.
        Come live on salmon & grow wise!

22:ix–23:ix:58

I THINK OF MOUNTAINS

I keep thinking of Matlock Lake, nobody can live there
Not for Long, it's Government land over two miles high
Not enough air (which gives you notions, "This is real, this is true")
University Peak stands/falls just overhead, the mistaken idea
"Of mountains he is Sumeru," a little over 13000 feet

Wednesday morning's "test-shot" from Nevada, I figured
"The mountain has split, the Goddess has appeared!"

They've had these thoughts in India thousands of years
& every minute millions die of them—
Radiation sickness from the mountains

It is only a question of balance—
Power and knowledge their proper economy
Are we stuck at last with Aristotle?

When I came down to Berkeley my cottage was a birdhouse
I had to crawl in the door on my hands and knees I was immense!
What was I doing there? What was the ceiling for? The walls?

I NO LONGER HAD TO BREATHE

Nobody could live there, town of perpetual childhood
Babyland the wrong door of the time-machine
No changes except the buildings and trees no future
Except Five o'clock or the week-end about to happen
                    (Life stops at midnight Sunday)

To D O anything (consciously) N O W
A problem, paradox, quandary.
The disciples, the hearers listen in silence
The inside boys don't crack a smile
The Big Wheel hollers "Turtle eggs!"

113

The difference between wisdom and ignorance
The potential between them
A current of human misery (freedom and slavery) which
Can be accurately measured

The mountain a lump of granite in my skull
My mouth filled with Indian corpse meat

28:x:58

FOND FAREWELL TO THE CHICAGO REVIEW

All these demands for my voice, my voice
Wrapped up in a ball rolled under the bureau

Retrieved with the help of the vacuum-cleaner
It just won't work any more

I whack it with a hammer & all it says is

> Plato
> Plautus
> Pliny
> Plotinus
> Plutarch

> before it falls apart

In the garbagecan the pieces hum vague fitful music in the dark.

From now on it's the Harpo Marx routine for me:
Creating wordless havoc in pursuit of blondes.

Newport i.xi.58

FROM A LETTER TO RON LOEWINSOHN, 19:XI:58

Well, love, sure, love, ok, love if
(As it is) penultimate to action, the ultimate being
    compassion
    (a detached interest)
& some sort of understanding in between the letters

  "PRETTY IS AS PRETTY DOES"

  (What are you doing with your hand between my legs?
  (
  (Why don't we just go down to the corner for a chocolate malt?
  (
  (& 2 straws & Norman Rockwell to draw it?

Anyway, you've seen these people, the one trying desperately
To Make It & I mean on a strictly H E R E hardup basis

& the other WONT (stand/sit/lay) still for it
Because it might complicate things (or any other REASON)
IT IS PRIDE: A false humility, we put ourselves down
None of us believes
    "I am a prize package"
    that we aren't idly chosen

  (Darwin is all about South American bugs)

  or that our own taste in lovers
    is infallible

           19:xi:58

DELIGHTS OF WINTER AT THE SHORE

A little sauce having unglued me from my book
I take the present (Ernest Bloch on the phonograph)
I salute the fire in the fireplace
The red sectional settee
All the potted plants I moved onto the diningroom table
        so they could get more light
And beyond the window North Pacific Ocean

An editor writes to me, "Takes, takes, all the time takes . . . what
        are you scared of, nobody's trying to cut your throat . . .
        Why don't you just sit down & write a novel?"

& wild with energy & power I'm curled up in the grey reclining chair
Carefully writing one letter at a time

                Check the barometer . . . . falling
                Check the swiss steak in the oven . . . . .
                      . . . . turn up the heat

It goes like that, all the "talent," the "promise"
My mortgage very nearly foreclosed
My light going out

      X. keeps telling me how sad everything is
           (he cries all the time)
      Maybe he's right, but I don't *see* sad
      & the pursuit of happiness around a square track

How loyal have I been to myself?
How far do I trust . . . . anything?
I wonder "self-confidence" *vs.* years of self-indulgence
        (am I feeling guilty?)
How would anything get done if I quit? Stopped
      whatever it is you choose to call it?

Put it as fancy & complicated as possible:
Here I sit drunk beside the biggest ocean in the world
Tosca destroying me on the phonograph
Everybody else in the world dying of starvation, cruelty
                lack of my love

No amount of promise or talent about to do anything to fix that.
It was 20 years ago they worried about what I might do
Now everybody can see what I've done, what I'm doing

                Everybody starves
                Everybody is a huge (biological) success
                Everybody's maybe like me: perpetually scared
                        & not giving a shit
                                As long as there's beef in the oven
                                Out of jail
                                Drunk

Everybody says Horace was a two-bit snob, writing
                "Odi profanum vulgis"
Maybe he meant he hated himself for being lazy, preferring old wine
Pretty girls & sunshine
To the dignity & usefulness of public office?

Now the Second Act of *Tosca:*
Big party downstairs, the cantata going on
Police interrogation upstairs, Cavaradossi on the rack
(These *palazzi*—a real idea of splendor)
& topping it all off, as if it explained E V E R Y T H I N G

                "Vissi d'arte, vissi d'amore . . ." I've lived for Art,
                        I've lived for love . . ."
                                (incontinently stabbing the villain)

DIE!   DIE!   DIE!

I eat an olive out of my glass

TOSCA: "...*tutta Roma!*"

                    & 1 is left

Some psychiatrist says "Quotation, a relaxation for, an evasion by
the *id.*"

I eat the second final olive & pretend to hurl my glass
            into the fireplace
I don't actually throw it, the glass isn't mine & there's a screen
            in front of the fireplace

                        ✳
                        ✳

24 hours later, not drunk but dissociated completely from past
            & present (absolute rejection of any future)
3 severed heads are staring at me through the windows above the door
A large patient hungry monster breathes once a minute at the keyhole
All violence has returned to sit on my chest, slide into my armpits
The whole works only part of this particular link of a heavy gold
            suspended chain circle
                    the chain is also manifest as music

I try to decide if it's light on dark
Or dark on a light ground . . . intensely occupied with this . . .

& start again: Air is colder than ice
Interstellar space is (a few parsecs from a star)
Colder than air, *et cetera*

The way I'm sitting now is the past, the way my fingers hold this pen

The letters themselves
2 minutes from now I'll do something equally characteristic
Something I've lived, survived 35 years in order to accomplish

Viz., Laid aside the pen, took off my glasses & rubbed my eyes
Considering the idea of staying up until daylight

Everything between time
Crazy as a peach-orchard bull . . .
                        I turn my head
Expecting the ocean to be empty & black;

                there are tiers of lights
Apparition of downtown office building standing on the waves

            GANDHARVA CITY!

A Swede boat bound for China

17, 18, 19:xii:58

SOMETHING NICE ABOUT MYSELF

Lots of people who no longer love each other
Keep on loving me
& I

I make myself rarely available.

19:xii:58

31.IV.59

The end, of a month of Sundays
Hurrah for the church

Loud Music Now BIG GOOFING RUIN

Down
down
DOWN

NO LIMIT
NO LOWER LIMIT

feature that!
{if you will.}

BODHISATTVA IN BEAR WORLD

Philip Whalen

Mr. R: Whereabouts in the Waldport area do you live?

Mrs. H: About five miles south of Waldport on Highway 101.

Mr. R: Down towards Yachats?

Mrs. H: You know where the whale skeleton is? Tilly the Whale?

Mr. R: Yes.

Mrs. H: Right near there.

✿

Later. The court reporter sits at her machine, apparently asleep. From where I sit I can see her fingers working the keys, but it seems that the lawyers can't. One of them asks, severely, "Did you get that, Miss Reporter?" The reporter opens her eyes, looks surprised and says, "Yes I did." The lawyer asks her to read the last question and answer. She begins turning loops of paper tape from behind her machine, peering at them, mumbling and moaning like the Pythian priestess, then suddenly articulates the question very clearly, and its answer as well. She added, "I've got you in there all the way through, Mr. Co-counselor." The judge said, "Well, let's proceed."

29:i:59

1:II:59   a very complicated way of saying "appearances deceive"?

Subjects

Ⓐ
1. I see a bird
2. Some birds are good to eat
3. Birds' eggs are good to eat
4. Bird feathers make good pillows
5. Bird-dung is hard to remove from automobiles & buildings
6. My Grandmother kept canaries
7. I can take birds or leave them alone

Ⓑ
1. I see a bird.
2. I hate birds
3. What if it bit me?
4. I'm going to hit that bird with a rock.
5. What if it got loose inside the house? TERROR
6. Uncle Lester's parrot bit me.
7. The world without birds would be better.

Ⓕ
1. Walking thing goes away quick in the air. Where? How? BAW!

Ⓔ
1. I see a bird.
2. The bird is a thrush, mistakenly called "robin" in the U.S.A, "Turdus migratorius"
3. Habitat: spring to autumn US winter: south America
4. Diet: bugs & worms 5. Call: "peeowoopoo"
6. Many feathers. 7. Fits an ecological niche

Ⓒ
1. I see a bird
2. I love birds
3. All birds are beautiful & free
4. Birds ought not to be kept in cages.
5. People ought not to shoot birds.
6. Poor bird, starving in the snow!
7. Dear birds!

Ⓓ
1. Bird
2. No bird
3. Bird

BLOCK

4. I'm not a bird. ?
5. Bird's name is Sam.
6. If Subject Ⓑ kills Sam with a rock, that will be hard luck for both Ⓓ and Sam; however it is Ⓑ's nature to kill birds – he'll have to figure it out.
7. Ⓑ & Sam & me —? Subject? object?

122

4:2:59 TAKE 1

What I need is lots of money
No
What I need is somebody to love with unparalleled energy
     and devotion for 24 hours and then goodbye

I can escape too easily from this time & this place
That isn't the reason I'm here

What I need is where am I

Sometimes a bed of nails is really necessary to any man
Or a wall (Olson, in conversation, "That wall, it *has* to be there!")

Where are my hands.
Where are my lungs.
All the lights are on in here I don't see nothing.

I don't admit that this is personality disintegration
My personality has a half-life of 10^∞ years; besides

I can put my toe in my mouth
If (CENSORED), then (CENSORED), something like
Plato his vision of the archetypal human being

Or the Gnostic Worm.

People see me; they like that . . .
I try to warn them that it's really me

They don't listen; afterwards they complain
About how I had no right to be really just that:
Invisible & in complete control of everything.

SELF-PORTRAIT, FROM ANOTHER DIRECTION

Tuned in on my own frequency
I watch myself looking
Lying abed late in the morning
With music, thinking of Y.
Salal manzanita ferns grasses & grey sky block the window
Mossy ground

I think what is thinking
What is that use or motion of the mind that compares with
A wink, the motion of the belly

              Beside the highway
              Young bullock savages the lower branches
                            of a big cedar tree

A Journey,
              Lownsdale Square
To The City   Huge seagull on rump of bronze elk
              Looking the other way

              Wm Jennyns Baker (getting breakfast for his
                  family & me):
              "Count your blessings
              Name them one by one
              You will be surprised
              What the L O R D hath done!"

            THOUGHT IS NOT SWIFT!
perhaps the mind is slower than this pencil, its rate of motion
nearer that of the heartbeat—
moving slower than the head which turns
    not as quick as a wink

Pieces broken off a sandstone cliff
Grass & salal bushes still growing on it, roots exposed
I said a new landslide; the Judge: "It fell off two years ago"

POSSIBLE TRUE STATEMENTS ABOUT A REAL PIECE
OF SANDSTONE

Now it is here.
Now it is falling.
Now it is there.
              which we agree upon . . .

What comes next?

The landslide has revealed
The bones of Adam protruding from the soil
A bronze door into Magic Land
Z. really *was* sore at me seven years ago in
Hollywood, which is the reason Sandra never
returned my umbrella,—I see it all now . . .

Any of these things?

      "wasn't built in a day"

Considerably faster, the Basilica of St Peter
A momentary flash, a brainstorm, an internal shifting
Nothing to do with time-keeping or spending, the rules of the
                              stonemason's guild
Maybe a headache between the hours of 1 & 10 P.M.
Walking the street alone

   I said leave it the hell alone now or you'll have the whole thing
                    all gee-hawed up

   Quicker than dammit

Rain/wind bulging the window
An Absolute, i.e. what we think of as
      "an Absolute," "Force," "NATURE"
   know nothing of my love, my mind
Looking into a mirror, shaving, is I?
& I told Q., "the toes, knee-caps *et cetera*
All thinking"   or this

Lights on or off
The kitchen is the same
Tuesday or Wednesday

2 Reedies cross-legged on Taylor Street sidewalk
Beards   *Another*
Waiting for the campus bus   *Journey*
                                                 To The
On Broadway another one gets off a trolley   *Same City*
Full pack & walking-shoes dangling

Moral: Not all the younger generation going to hell

                              to bed & all my nerves
woke up to sing & dance I got up & dressed made a pot of tea lit a pipe &
sat patiently watching them hop, flashing red, blue, etc. random motion
through a number of dimensions &/or continua—fascinating but completely
exhausting to watch, to be

                    (*2 lines canceled*)

Climb on & ride—
                    progress by explosion
All the elements analyzed out & recombined

                    /with your finger on the throttle
                    & your foot upon the treadle of the clutch

an open eye neither *oculus Dei* nor yet the sun
"*omicron*" the lesser "o"

                    (*2 lines canceled*)

Any word you see here defies all fear doubt destruction ignorance &
        hatefulness
All the impossibilities unfavorable chance or luck
It will have overcome all my strength (the total power of a raging maniac
        self-hypnotized berserk missing one arm part of the entrails exposed

        running with incredible speed)
Superhuman force,   an exorbitance—
               slingstone hurled at a tangent to the circle
               in which it lately whirled
               zipping off in high-speed parabola

Into the mirror (NOW showing many men) all of them "I"

11:ii:59

I RETURN TO SAN FRANCISCO

Scared?

M.M. says, I just found out what's wrong with me
        is fear & it scares the shit out of me

Jo B.,   Intellectual comics, they've taken EVERYTHING
          there's nothing left—jokes about Proust, Joyce, Zen
          Buddhism, it's the end of culture, the world . . .

And J.W., What are we going to do?

        I said, I'm going home & start typing
        I'm tired of nothing happening

✻

CONTINUATION, IN ANOTHER KEY

E N O U G H , I'm tired of sound & silence, the alternation of opposites
The weak middle sagging between both
                    ALL RHYTHMS
There must be an eruption, a boil, an imposthumation
            Come to a head

    Horace Walpole writes to one of his boyfriends, "at least
    write & tell me that you have nothing to write me about"

So I take off down the street with my bed on my back
        easy as not

The time element is the least important:
        Strobe-light photograph shows a one-drop milk-splash

    A solid coronet shape, the walls faithfully reflecting the light
            which was faster than the crown-world's history . . .
    How long did it take to build that circular wall of milk
        its pointed towers
                & each of them transforming into a satellite droplet
                heading out to make smaller, briefer crowns?

Our notion of time, of history . . . what's wrong?

Figuring it all out again
                A, B, C . . .
                1, 2, 3 . . .
We don't really GET what it is, looking at it drives it
        someplace else (consider the eye in the act of looking;
        can we see it?)
Only fair-sized lumps make any sense at all—
        (the idea of "critical mass")
Form patterns that suggest a moral, with fright, sleep, the skin
        as LIMIT?

Too hot this evening, I whistle for a wind
   hilltop bayview bridgewink Golden Gate
& breeze from the South green marble apartmenthouse lobby wall

✻

CLT,   A lovely day
      Rain has washed the car all beautifully clean
      & the battery is completely dead

✻

Something on this page about waterlilies
& how these lines are distant mountain ridges seen
From across the desert, the old *"horreur du vide"* routine

✻

While I wait, a shining beige/brown chevron clothes-moth
        settles on the bedspread
Eyebrow-hair antennae heavy beads under the lens
Moves now to the wall

          this would happen easier if I got laid oftener
          stayed away from crowds
          worked very hard at it

Long hair from my left eyebrow just fell out
      One inch long
I hate putting it in the ashtray

          or maybe I'm trying to tell about it without looking at it
          remembering it all wrong or some doctored cut version

    I saw a butterfly set in clear unbreakable plastic block
    I start out with a rubber balloon & a live bug
    Blow up the balloon & this bug
          flies around outside . . .

Something entirely different, a failure, a mistake . . .
What I want you to see is yet another lovely
          & inexplicable thing

☼

something complicated going on in the kitchen
turn off the gas & the stove (cooling)
exchanges heat for noise & motion

☼

RIGHT NOW
If I had a pet rabbit right now
I'd pinch it & make it squeak
NOBODY pays any attention to me & I really need LOTS
          of loving

☼

Since you won't come to me
I'll think about mountain cypress trees
Something has taken the bark away the wood weathers orange & twisty

☼

While I'm looking for sleep
Bright shapes of day bedevil my eyes
          identification with one's own "good" qualities
          and vice-versa—where does that put you?
          identification with neither—what you call that?
          or with both?
          With ANYTHING ELSE . . . shape, form, quality, mode
          what then?
"What was your original face, before you were conceived?"

☼

same routine as above, with respect to our *common*
          space/time continuum?

＊

IDENTIFICATIONS : : : : RESONANCES. . . . ? (*vide* Erwin
Schroedinger)

＊

while I'm looking for sleep's bright devils the day of the fly the
morning's blank dissociations cannons & waterclocks sunny towered
fugal castles torrents of malicious corn & fleet shadows of a dear
remembrance falling by

＊

Naturally there's no recollection of your low forehead peculiar
Cheekbones & curious nose
    in the silk-paintings from Tun Huang
    the rock-sculptures at Ellura

The complications of living with love
& without it—an absolutely even balance?

Spending more hours asleep than awake, happy than unhappy
Talking more than listening

Do we breathe in one more time than we breathe out?

Julian Huxley is worried about the population explosion
If he understood what I'm saying here
He'd come at me personally, a pair of shears held low

WHAT *IS* (properly) THE QUESTION?

a false proposition (?):   All any of us wants is a simple life;
               A simple mind invents a complicated life.

＊

BIRD WORLD

> J.M., A bird's head (while it sits on a perch) stays
> in one place its body
> moves from side to side, up & down, conditioned
> (ORIENTED) to operate in 4-dimensional space

CARNELIAN MARABOU EYE

> Something will happen if we let it
> Everything happens no matter what we decide

✿

Now dreams are nearer, brighter, louder & sleep a progression of paralyses difficult pose/gestures (infinitely long-lasting) with waking breaks between them recalling summer in lookout as in poem, "conscious even while sleeping"—& after waking the dream continues somewhere "underneath" my present "consciousness"?

I keep getting takes on the stone face with live glass eyes—from 1) statue at Jo B.'s house, & 2) dream wherein it was a significant figure, 30:III:59

20:iii:59–15:iv:59

TAKE, 25:III:59

> I've run so far in one circle I'm visible now
> only from the chest upwards
> Any poet who's really any good
> Dances a complicated maze on top of the ground
> scarcely wearing out the grass

A REPLY

You ask, "a flash in the pan?" (i.e. can you
            dismiss us?)
I say, "No.
No torches, no beacons—
            FLASHES OF MEN IN TIME: rare,
            discontinuous, an after-image
Remains, a retinal overcharge (& add:
            persistence of vision)
EFFECT AN AMBIENCE OF LIGHT

                                        4:iv:59

FOR A PICTURE BY MIKE NATHAN

Two surgeons tired waiting—break
            between operations
Their baffled faces knowing, they imagine
            life and death are private secrets
Tiny balances, thin alterations between "me"
            and "meat" insulate
            isolate from the rest of us . . .

Frightened, they must depend (like us)
            on "the doctor," one of themselves
They know in the end they'll be yelling
            SAVE ME!   SAVE ME!   I AM A MAN!
                INFINITELY VALUABLE!
Knowing the doctor might be nervous or unstable
            on just that particular day

We must pretend to respect their mystery
Uninitiated as they are to ours, tolerate
Their damned insulting manners, their open sadism
They are lonely and they need our help.

4:iv:59

A DISTRACTION FIT

I walk around town with my baby
While I'm sound asleep the middle of a nervous breakdown

Big pieces of the world break off
       Slowly
      sleeping
          she didn't know the right way home, I lead the way
              with my eyes closed

Pieces of myself plaster & stucco walls
         Potemkin facades
      drifting away

Lungs breathe me out
Heart circulates me through pipes & tubing
Brains imagine something walking
      asleep

She holds this man by the arm it stretches
        across the world
Hand in his pocket
Dream of love in 2 houses
      asleep
She breathes me in

4:v:59

WITH COMPLIMENTS TO E. H.

a target

a crooked arrow

an asymptote

a balance, an
anomaly

a dissonance, an intentional
asymmetry

Sound B & B-flat together (in the bass) & hear
yet another: "beat frequency"

Light through a diffraction-grating projects rings
of darkness (a silence)
"cancellation"

Paradigms, correspondences i.e. inverse proportions

_____

_____

_____ A mutual confusion
or mine alone?

_____

_____   _____

a confutation of Hermes Trismegistus

I think mostly I remember, am remembered
By my own brains muscle skin
which never sleep
An imaginary difference of frequency between them
speaks here?

✵

(interrupted by a poet:
>   "Going to work as an airline purser
>   all my friends will forget me
>   I'll be up in the air
>
>   . . . .
>
>   I'll see you again before the world blows up."

>   I: "That's a solipsist view."
>   He: "What do I know about New York?"

✿

A TARGET
A CROOKED ARROW
AN ASYMPTOTE
"You hit the nail right on the thumb!"

A false note between "The Real" &
>   "The Illusory"

HONK

>   "I don't think you want to talk to me"
>   (this is another, earlier poet)
>   "Why don't you just tell me to go home?"

The brain
>   actually T H E R E 1 minute
>   out of any waking hour
>   busy between whiles talking & listening
>   in cahoots with skin & bones to make a raft
>   sentient beings without number

136

NOT A DECISION OR A CHOICE:

DISCOVERY

sidewheel steamboat carried
Grandpa Kelly from San Francisco to Portland
sank on the return trip, all hands lost

✵

✵

"... no permanent home ..."

CHAO-CHOU SAYS "WOOF!"
"Open Scandal," Mumon Decl
NORTH-SOUTH ZEN RIFT WIDENS
Jiriki or *Tariki?*

(P H O T O)

Mr. A. C. PILLSBURY

Flour Magnate Says, "Eventually . . . why not now?"

Accused of Southern Sympathy

PALACE SOURCES MUM

so he says gimmee the coat & I says
it's yours if you're man enough to pick
it up so he grunts & strains & say I
magicked it so he couldn't & wants me to
teach him how, I told him it wasn't me,
the boss didn't want it to go no further
& it wasn't any good to me neither & if

anybody hexed it it was him the Old Man
No. 5, I said I'll tell you all I know about
it but you'll have to figure it out for
yourself

Intentionally out of whack
The bow-string, the bent bow

DISTORTION

Power, to kink space (distance)
    the target impaled on the arrow!
The bow-string hauling the target
    to where I stand
Snaps back

THWUNK!

7/8:v:59

ADDENDA

HERAKLEITOS OF EPHESOS, Frs. 45 & 66 (John Burnet
translation):

"(45) Men do not know how what is at variance agrees with itself.
It is an attunement of opposite tensions, like that of the bow and
the lyre.

(66) The bow (Βιòς) is called life (Βίος), but its work is death."

    "Love is a law, a discord of such force,
      That 'twixt our sense and reason makes divorce;"

          —Anon., from *The Thracian Wonder,* 1661

6:v–8:v:59

Awake a moment
Mind dreams again
Red roses black-edged petals

8:v:59

I AM KING GIANT DRAGON SUN

F a d i n g

you're sitting (Baby) on my toe
& your arm on some kind of nerve-center
            my trembly hand
my liver singing anthems
            (Have you been eating roses?)
cotton eyes calm sea belly

                (LACUNA)

        . . . flat out, much speed high above the vacant page
        & no connection. The Daly City Turnoff
        Submergence
                    as under molten metal pouring into a cast
                    a form incomprehensible from the outside. . . .

                (LACUNA)

I pretend my life stops & after my exit the whole continuum
Snaps back into its own shape after my passing
An ordinary sequence, ice to water to steam
Carbon cycle in a star a sun
King as king (not OF anything or place)
Crown, robe, sceptre and orb, complete royalty
No power problem, the powers completely known & understood

139

a chess king, a star of the Main Sequence
i.e. a predictable life-cycle blue white yellow orange red
& the attendant internal sub-atomic shifts between too hot
too compressed to be thought of as "substance"
& existence under some other name

"Our "space" has the property of being distorted
by electromagnetic waves."—A. Einstein (we do not know
why the radio works, a mystery no matter how inane its
                                              conversation
a guillotine for shelling peas)

Please don't cut off my circulation

         to wake up embarrassed
                          half soaked into this oriental rug

You got that pearl-chain Byzantine look again
Chiafu's calligraphy on the wall:

                    MOUNTAIN
                    Eye/walk
                    gate/heart ("mind," "*l'esprit,*" &c.)

its characters either most eccentric or very live
         I can't tell which

Portrait of Han Shan and his broom, by an unknown hand
                    (Liang Kai?)
Not immediately decipherable either
                              if at all

Eardrums ballooning out & singing,
I sit on a lime-tree branch with Coleridge
              bitching and chirping
Pythagoras heard the dodecahedron—find   THAT   sound again!
         (already, perhaps, found? and by the wrong man—
                    Rinaldo Hahn, for example?)

We are known by the character of those things to which we visibly
R E A C T ?

Under total anaesthesia and feeling everything
But most, that all the things and persons I am
Are precious, rare & inconsequential, no weight in the scale
& sitting here maybe 48 hours
Concentrating on total insanity. . . .
I don't belong to that and I don't belong to myself

I told Baby, "Flipping out isn't the WORST that can happen"

May 8th, 1959: Where the will is there is roses.

> N O T E , 27:ix:64, that the "unknown hand" at line 41 above belonged to
> Yen Hui, 12th-century painter. See plates 6a & 6b in D. T. Suzuki's
> *Zen and Japanese Culture*, Bollingen Series LXIV, Pantheon (New
> York, 1959 reprint).

POEM FOR A BLONDE LADY

Clearly I must not (on any account) stir one muscle
Until it moves
                    a real necessity
                       interior
        to it,
                towards or away from
You

I don't mean "love" or "sanity," I want to answer
            all your crooked questions
                absolutely straight

                                & if away

141

Only a pausing a thoughtless rearrangement
to include you
As we really are

8:v:59

"EVERYWHERE I WANDER"

Sweet sleep a spider of dreams downy fuzz & thistle blanket
dragdown tourniquet too long & frequently applied
afternoon a soporific sad & flicker dim & horizontal dol-
drum a distant intensity of cloud
                              fern

              shape   shape   shape

a crystal
              my face warped into sleep-wrinkle taste
still asleep
              crystal electrically bent
                   a tone

12:v:59

HAIKU FOR MIKE

Bouquet of H U G E
                   nasturtium leaves
"HOW can I support myself ?"

13:v:59

A REFLECTION ON MY OWN TIMES

Now's
        the wrong place
        to start an argument (to
        say nothing about being otherwise unready)

WHAT ideas? Not a brain in my head, only
    "Education" & a few *"idées reçus"* (read
        "conditioned reflexes")
But necessary to open my small
        yap
     maybe just to say "ouch"
        as the lobotomy knife slides
        ("painlessly," they say)
                IN

13:v:59

ADDRESS TO THE BOOBUS,

with her Hieratic Formulas in reply

O Great Priestess
O Keeper of the Mystic Shrine
O Holy & Thrice More Holy

Prussian Blue   Dark Blue   Light Blue   French Blue

Blyni & Pirozhki   Sapphire   Aquamarine
To Take Out   Turquoise   Zircon
                  Lapis Lazuli

        Malachite, a sea-color stone

O Hidden!

      (Vestal maenad bacchante)
among the leaves bright & dark

          "... a rubber baby ...
          "... a plastic baby ...
          "cloth baby whose eyes
                  close"

O Blessed Damozel
        (flies & lilies)
Rosetti saw you weeping, leaning
    over heaven's gold bar
(Crocodile tears?)
        yellow hair

        "I NEED TO HAVE A PAPER!"
        "... a hand for you, a HAND for you
        a hand!"

Power & clemency
        VEIL
            a shroud (only a slip-cover) a curtain
Covering
      from dusty eyes, the vapid gaze of

THE TABERNACLE & blazing lamps the Molten Sea

& the Sybil also, her eyes closed under the cloth
& covered baskets containing that which none but the initiated
may look upon

        "... I have one
        I have two
        I have a pencil
      I'm going to get another chair

        & stand up
     I need
     I need to push it

       THERE!"

10:vii:59

BOOBUS HIEROPHANTE,

Her Incantations

     Heavy
     Heavy
     Hangs

       over thy head

           "A HAND!
           "A HAND!
           "A HAND!

This gruesome object was employed in unspeakable rites,
   the fingers burning as tapers

WHAT SHALL THE OWNER DO TO REDEEM IT?

        TAKE 3 STEPS FORWARD

"A TABLE
"A TABLE
"A WHEEL FOR THE TABLE
"ANOTHER WHEEL FOR THE TABLE
        "RED
        "RED

"RED
"RED
"MONKEY
"A FLEMING POOL
"A LITTLE TINY MOUSE RIGHT THERE

full terror

"LOOK AT THAT I MADE!"

10:vii:59

SONG FOR 2 BALALAIKAS ON THE CORNER OF
3RD & MARKET

We have no peanuts to eat so sad
While looking up tall buildings capitalistic
We cannot return to izba on the steps of Russian Hill
Unless instant money appear in tambourine
                    UNFORTUNATELY
The snow is falling in our galoshes
Wolves in our underwear alas poor Czar
Our oatfield crushed under tractors
Varnish falls off our balalaikas all the strings are warped
            we sing out of tune
Give us bread and money, sad,
            S A D !

✻

(WITH MUCH ASSISTANCE
FROM MICHAEL MCCLURE)

14:viii:59

TO THE MOON

O Moon!
Gradually
        Milo of Croton
Lifting all the seas
      indifferently
Leaf shadows & bright reflections
  simultaneously

13:viii:59

ALL ABOUT ART & LIFE

a compulsion to make
        marks on paper

whatever good or bad

           "& as for meaning
            let them alone to mean
            themselves"

or that I'm ill
out of adjustment
not relating with real situation in living
room I just left below
    i.e. two other people, friends of mine
    reading books

a shock out of the eye-corner
Dome & cornices of Sherith Israel
    blue sky & fog streaks
    (reminiscences of Corot, Piranesi)

147

to mean themselves
Adam & Eve & Pinch-Me

walks out of silence, monotony
many colors dangling & sparkling

(TINKLE?)

there.   You know.   Uh-huh.

            we kill ourselves making it

PICTURE: a wood-engraving by Bewick
                   GIANT WOOLY COW

PICTURE: children, their faces concealed
                   by their hats which are heads which are
                   flowers

PICTURE: Leonardo: *Madonna & Child, with*
                   S.Giovanbattista

PICTURE: Ladies in marble palace with fountains
                   located high in Canadian Rockies a peacock
                   light the color of burning incense

PICTURE: a room, & through the door a hallway with
                   a small round or octagonal window

PICTURE: 2 Bedouins praying in sand/ocean a camel
                   with square quizzing-glass on head

PICTURE: All of us when we were young before you
                   were born

2 PICTURES: Battle scenes (medieval-type) in high plaster
                   relief curved glass not lens, no sound

LARGE PICTURE: C. S. Price: Indian women who might be
mountains picking huckleberries in moun-
tains that might be Indian women

PICTURE: 5 Persimmons (Chinese)

52 PICTURES: (Mexican provenance) playing-cards, each
one different, repellent & instructive

PICTURE: 360 degrees: the world is outdoors it is both
inaccessible & unobtainable
we belong to it

    . . . most of your problems will disappear if you sit
still (privately, *i.e.* in solitude) 1 hour per day
without going to sleep (do not speak, hum or whistle
the while) . . .

The orders of architecture we are to suppose symbols of the
human intellect & inspiration (in this case, severe Romano-Judaic)

    "a symbol doesn't MEAN
        anything
        it IS
        something . . . relationship of that kind doesn't exist
        except in the old philosophy whose vocabulary
        you insist on using . . ."

        MANIFESTS itself
whether I write or not
    we call it good, bad, indifferent as
    we feel ourselves exalted or brought down
it has its own name but never answers
never at home

        & we want a stage for our scene
               (wow)
        as if Shakespeare
             LIED

---

all of us end up

        Zero for Conduct

You bet.

          Why bother to say I detest liver
               & adore magnolia flowers
         Liver keeps its flavor the blossoms
             drop off
                  & reappear, whoever
        cares, counts, contends

I said to the kitten rolling the glass
    "Kitty, you're stupid"
Thoughtlessly: the cat's growing
      exercising & I merely talking to hear my head rattle

What opinion do you hold on Antinomianism?
It makes me nervous trying to remember what it was
& which side of the argument Milton took
    also rattles
        Not I love or hate:

WHAT IS IT I'M SEEING?

    &

WHO'S LOOKING?

It comes to us straight & flat
My cookie-cutter head makes shapes of it

CHONK: "scary!"
CHONK: "lovely!"
CHONK: "ouch!"

but any of us is worth more
than it
except that moment
it walks out of me, through me

& you ask, Where does it come from
Where did I go

Some people got head like a jello mold
It pours in & takes one shape only
Or instantly becomes another flavor
raspberry to vanilla
strawberry to vanilla
orange to vanilla, etc.

Some legendary living ones can take it or leave it alone
They go on planting potatoes, writing poems, whatever they do
Without hangups
Minimum bother to themselves & all the rest of the world
Any anyone observing them a little may
turn all the way
ON

Meanwhile, psychologists test us
& get a bell shaped curve
They know something or other I could tell them any time

All this is merely

GRAMMAR

The building I sit in
A manifestation of desire, hope, fear
As I in my own person, all the world I see . . .

Water drops from tap to sink
Naturally the tap's defective or not completely "OFF"
Naturally I hear: My ears do what they're made for

      (a momentary reflection—will my brain
      suffer a certain amount of water erosion
      while I sleep?---)
&

      OUT

23:viii:59–9:ix:59

TEMPORARILY INSANE

Mr. B retreats into his bed
Semi-coma hangover problem-solving dream
A perfect future, flat on his back
Bamboo stripes lock him in
He tells me "All the birds are dead"
The broken window does not exist.

12:ix:59

FAREWELL!

    Goodbye
I cannot tarry
     "ici

        Je suis très triste"

(Melisande)
                    duck down
        duck down
                    f l o a t i n g
        DUCK!
                    another one!
                            BOOM!   (Krunk!)

                                                    7:x:59

SINCE YOU ASK ME

(A Press Release, October 1959)

This poetry is a picture or graph of a mind moving, which is a
world body being here and now which is history . . . and you.
Or think about the Wilson Cloud-chamber, not ideogram, not
poetic beauty: bald-faced didacticism moving as Dr. Johnson com-
mands all poetry should, from the particular to the general. (Not
that Johnson was right—nor that I am trying to inherit his mantle
as a literary dictator but only the title *Doctor, i.e., teacher*—who
is constantly studying). I do not put down the academy but have
assumed its function in my own person, and in the strictest sense
of the word—*academy:* a walking grove of trees. But I cannot and
will not solve any problems or answer any questions.

My life has been spent in the midst of heroic landscapes which
never overwhelmed me and yet I live in a single room in the city—
        the room a lens focusing on a sheet of paper. Or the inside
            of your head. How do you like your world?

153

4 A.M. goggle-eyed and pestering myself
     (no fit subject, a cold in the chest)
    Want to go home
    Don't like ConEdison smokestack blockhouse
    Cocknozzle clear across (I'm lost again—14th St.?)

Really the city & amiable as it is, part of it probably Seattle
Or Portland my childhood memory

Best because it's anything I want it to be and full of dinky trees
        and mystery

    Where's the mob, the gangsters?
    They all in Kansas City 21st Floor
    $300 London handmade suits conducting war against the
    Mafia?
    Where's Jack? Nobody home in Long Island
    Where's anybody? All I see is Melville, Whitman,
    Poe and Henry James promenading the Bowery 3 A.M.
        spelled "Bouwerie"
    and they aren't talking to me, I'm an out-of-towner
    Not even the cops talk to me; at home they stop me
       any time after ten P.M.

In Houston Street the Brooklyn Bridge pops out behind a building
I've gone the wrong way again unless I was going to Williamsburgh

I have money in my pocket nobody steals it
The Long Island Railway gives me polite conversation and free
vodka

      fallen leaves slow it down

The Armory! How did I find that? And it W A S   something,
     ten years before I was born

I hunt for the pattern:
       8th Ave. has a dogleg at Sheridan Square
       4th St. is occasionally Great Jones
       The Cedar Bar—well, there's Cooper Union and
               something
       like Ninth St. unless it's University Place

Seagulls in Avenue A, bring me to home!
New York Marble Cemetery, bring me to home!
Katz's Delicatessen, (closed), bring me to home!
     but not for two weeks and I'm not really homesick anyway

How do you get out of the Baths of Caracalla?
I burrowed out through Postoffice Herodotus,
Swift courier late on his appointed rounds.

                                      9:xi:59

TO A POET

    She sings the music
        pulls you down
    She's totally irresponsible
        so are your ears (they're supposed to hear)
    But why do you care so much
        for music?

                                   31:xii:59

AN IRREGULAR ODE

Once I began to write,
Be ruled by Beauty & her wilfullness
& got no further
Choking and wheezing, subject completely to the selfishness
                              of my own history

I don't wonder that you doubt my love
My attention wanders even now, squinting at the moon
          bamboo blinds—I should be with you
                    we're only blocks apart

The same imaginary beauty splits us up, I keep chasing
          the one who invents the mountains and the stars
I'm a fool supposing she's someone else than you
          are moss & ferns in forest light

                                        13:1:60

HAIKU, FOR GARY SNYDER

                    I S
Here's a dragonfly
                    (T O T A L L Y)
Where it was,

                    that place no longer exists.

                                        15:i:60

156

WARNINGS, RESPONSES, ETC.

"You better get next to yourself," my father used to say,
"Hanging around loose and unnecessary."
> ("Hello there, Loose & Unnecessary," coming up
> the walk from his car
> me slung in a lawn chair reading)

MEANING: Alert yourself
> Be aware
> What's happening & what
> Do you think of it, how
> Do you feel about it
> What shall you (when push
> > comes to shove)
>
> Do about it? & if you were any good at all
> You'd feel that weight or pressure
> Continuously
> & comport yourself accordingly

("The strenuous life," Mr. Roosevelt said,
meaning something quite other)
> Which isn't a sandbag or "circumstance"
> It's inside after all
> One's own metabolic transmutations make the world go round

Next to myself
> the world and all the people in it
> asserting doggedly that I don't exist
> & certainly if I close my eyes I go away

Next to myself,
> AN EMBLEM

a mountain creek under logs over boulders
potholes in its bed patches of gravel the water
invariably falls into eddies at particular points breaks
into spray or spreads in heavy darkness as long as the water
source high up the canyon no end in sight beyond vinemaple
overhang downstream

flows
            & & & & & & & &

RESPONDS:

            To J. about art &c., that you must break yourself
            to create anything, this I, this self, holes have to be
            punched, cracks made in it to release the
            power, beauty, whatever; the act
            breaks us, a radical force like sex not lightly
            to be used,

            FIREBALLS ("plasma," the physicists call it now)
            Mesmer and Franklin thought in terms of "an
            electrick fluid")

BREAK YOURSELF

            but I suppress a section of it here, a piece of it I
            fear is likely to fall on my own head . . . can I
            walk around it?

            & walking, fall into a tar pit!

A FURTHER EMBLEM:

            a line appears to separate the sea and sky at the
            horizon.
            You put it there, your eye, the air is hollow
            And the earth falls away before your feet

ANOTHER, OF THE BALANCE:

            the beam of the scales a horizon line between
            a mechanical governor, two whirling balls, &
            the mind, its nature must be described as "built of
            contraries & opposites"
            & & & & & & & &

There we go again
A struggle for power (whatever
it is, lying around loose ((Comrade T. remarked))
in the streets)

            ". . . don't I know it! I gonna
            tell you . . . !"

3:ii:60

Broke it
>> heavy green glass ashtray
>>> twice in succession
>> burning squares of sandalwood

> superstition is its own punishment

Cracked a third time! the glass R I N G S

> breaking

& this paper soaking up expensive ink
No sound at all
A spatial extravagance
Celebrating my partial recovery from ten days influenza
& the end of twenty years footling composition
No more of either
I'm through
Conflagration, fire, flames, smoke,
A day,

> tick
> tick
> tick

plenty of trouble, believe you me, that icky feeling in a nose
it turns itself inside out a great slobbering oyster

Expressionism or exhibitionism, either of these is a drag.

Assassination   is the thief of time & state.
Approximation is a capital sin
Asparagus is full of methyl mercaptan, celebrated for its effect
> on human kidney tissue

Birds in the backyard, Joe Argo diskjockey sounds tired
Tom Field breaks bottles in the garbage can

BLAGUE

Nobody listening to everybody listening to   (I KNOW)
Most particularly to me.
                          HA.
There I go again
A struggle for power (whatever it is)
Lying around (Comrade T. assures us) in the streets
Over everything, whim of iron

          Good grief.
          Good bye.

          don't I know it? I
          gonna
                    tell you!.

Take dandelions first salad, { THIS IS NOT }
then yellow flower, { AN EXAMPLE, }
{ I MEAN look }

maybe chains of them — kids pick them ~~delicate faceted sphere gray white sphere~~

gray haired overnight (or day) .

completion, fruition, what you will

delicately faceted sphere GONE!
(as a sensible structure) .
where am I?

what is it
I'm doing?

you Imagine that I'm ignoring you
or trying to humiliate

The moral {most restrictively} on the one hand, discontinued
once it was less so
sometime it might ⟩THE DANDELION ⟨ on the other, grows wings?
be otherwise

I never said you had to Do
anything about it or
change your life in any respect

I only forbid you to draw any false
analogies
what's the coat on the chair
before you think of its name?

161

A Beautiful Page

Ron isn't back not even a flower —

Where was we
last night

                    but yes, they're dead, that's ok

greenish yellow.   Bronze towards the outside

THURSDAY, the THIRD DAY
of MARCH, 1960

flowers

            Mrs. Ronald Loewinsohn of Santa Monica &
                Larkspur & San Francisco has
                        arrived

Philip Whalen is a damned bastard

┌─── Wobbers ───┐

        to shallow rivers to whose falls
    melodious birds sing madrigals

Philip Whalen is a very terrible person
    it is said that he is a warlock

abcdefghijklmnopqrstuvwxyz

    & with a nod she turned her head beside
    the falling water. Amiably.

B1 B7
B2 B8
B3 B9
B4 B10
B5 B11
B6 B12

PALACE CAFÉ

"Don't have any money bring me some brown toast OK
I pay you medium I want it medium,
Lots of money. You
Sit down."

8:iii:60

A VISION OF THE BODHISATTVAS

They pass before me one by one riding on animals
"What are you waiting for," they want to know

Z—, young as he is (& mad into the bargain) tells me
"Some day you'll drop everything & become a *rishi*, you know."

I know
The forest is there, I've lived in it
    more certainly than this town? Irrelevant—

    What am I waiting for?
A change in customs that will take 1000 years to come about?
Who's to make the change but me?

      "Returning again and again," Amida says

Why's that dream so necessary? walking out of whatever house
alone
Nothing but the clothes on my back, money or no
Down the road to the next place the highway leading to the
mountains
From which I absolutely must come back

What business have I to do that?
I know the world and I love it too much and it
Is not the one I'd find outside this door.

                                        31:iii:60

ITCHY

What is your name feathers and eyes Mabel Spinning Wheel
Marguerite Pearl Flower
What are you spinning feathers flowers and pearls
        "répon-, répon-, réponds vite!"
Eaglefeather bullseye manheaded lion-wheel
        "Ah, Marguerite!
        Réponds-toi! Réponds-toi!
angelflame

            THE SIGN OF FOUR
                            not meaning what they thought at all
            ANGELFLAME
Did you tell any lies today?
Learn anything?
Did the thought occur to you, "This is a good
Solid unchanging world?"
                    KNOTHEAD!
Did you forget anything?
                Are you paying attention?
                    PEABRAIN!

What are you doing right this minute?
What shall you do one second from now?

                    TOO BAD!
                    TOO LATE!
                    YOU LOSE!

(temporarily)

YANKEE DOG, YOU DIE!

(temporarily)

Aimlessly
Not a success
Accidentally evil idleness

(temporarily)

Angelname

Why do you live the way you do?
Feather spins as it falls
Even if you did it better, who would care?

LION BURNING CIRCLE BIRD BEAST MANWHEEL

they put you in jail for trying, but then you're not
interested in Christianity except as one of the chief
keys to understanding the psychosis presently afflicting
our several minds, i.e. American Culture: which isn't
as sick as the intellectual journals try to tell us—
it (Culture USA)
is an illness

Laying up crowns and harps in heaven

ANGELFLAME

is what we've got, we itch all over
And if we scratch once, all the light escapes and we fall
in darkness
Total cynicism, "I got a right to do whatever I please"

ANGELFLAME

Hanged for a sheep as for a goat
We talk mean and die sudden.

15:iv:60

165

DREAM

Wander through expensive party not for me
Open door into formal diningroom I've offended, they are gone
Step out of window & swing on a velvet rope to top of old wall
       dangerous muddy grass flowers
           the top of the arch! (it collapses as my left foot
           reaches solid rock ridge
              nightmare gulf behind below me)

Funeral on a sunny day in Spring, child procession in festival
clothes
Child in open coffin half seen under giant flower wreaths
           passes

Landscape: barren river valley in high plateau-desert crossed by
two bridges, one a Roman aqueduct, partly lost, incomplete,
worked into new bright girder work repeating enormous arches
across miles of wide valley sunset of a day order and peace
far below the aqueduct, two ruined castle palaces

18:v:60

ESSEX WAS A COWBOY IN VERMONT

"LOTS
      of money all new and different
38 degrees below zero, feeding cattle
The maid got mad because I ate so much
& everyone had loads of money

They didn't want the other ranchers to know they had so much
money
All transactions were carried on by telegrams in French

Universal International Money Millions To Come To This
Rancher
A fifteen thousand dollar Rodin on the wall everybody sat in the
Kitchen they didn't know what to do with the rest of the house

If I wanted to go to NY next week I'd go
If I wanted to go to Europe next month I'd go
I'd be scared to death if I had a million dollars

Have it, I guess, in a trust-fund paying 100 dollars a month?
Otherwise I might do nothing except ski in Europe or go
                    to South America
                    Whenever I felt like it
Or go to Japan or hire a yacht and take you all with me
. . . it might be funny taking the whole
Household everybody wearing the same hats in the tropics—
                    dressed the way you are now—

The Agha Khan wanted to buy the ranch but he died
                    Shortly thereafter"

                                        27–28:v:60

MOVIE NIGHT

Cry no more fitful membrane dreamflower
And you dismal terror gunsel pestering my sleep
You chase imaginary wrong
Murder theater bridge to soda cracker
Above the dead spring child flower festival Italian light
Colors of enamel precious Memling Van Eyck glaze
Desert in the sky where possibly you walk where you're going.

                                        29:v:60

HISTORICAL DISQUISITIONS

Hello, hello, what I wanted to tell you was
The world's invisible
You see only yourself, that's not the world
            although you are of it

Are you there

        hello
        why do you have your head in a sack?
        a roony-bomb dream tank?

        Why you got a banana in your ear?

You where?

                Brown eyes they see blue sky

                The world imagines you
                Figure it's a planet

                            You hear?

                an obscure star in the middle

Once you were pleasure-milk and egg

                Were you there

Now you are eggs of milk between your legs

                Are you there

"I am situated somewhere near the rim of a fairly large galaxy
which is one of a group of same & outside of which a considerable
number take their way at incredible speeds & apparently in the
opposite direction . . ."

> You are a wish to squirt pleasantly
> You want a lot of things & they are nice & you imagine
> They are you and therefore you are nice
> You are a wish to be here
> Wishing yourself
> > elsewhere

"Hello. Try to talk some sense even if you
don't think any
It is history
> (your mistake: "History WAS")
> > now

☼

History an explanation of why I deserve what I take

☼

History an explanation of why I get what I deserve

☼

> (Through more or less clenched teeth):
> "How can you sit there & look at the faces
> you see in Montgomery Street wiped blank
> from selling whatever brains they got faces
> in 3rd Street blank from facing a lathe all day
> & TV all night African tromped-on faces Asiatic
> hunger faces Washington war-masks & smile at me
> about how after all this is a Moral Universe
> gives me the screaming jumping meemies I thought
> you were bright enough had enough work-experience
> yourself to have some faint idea of . . ."

☼

hello.

"THE WIND RATTLES THE WINDOW I CAN'T
SLEEP FRIDAY NIGHT IS VERY LARGE IN SAN
FRANCISCO THE LOWER CLASSES GET PAID ON
FRIDAY & GET ON THEIR WAY TO SPEND IT IN
UPPER-MIDDLE-CLASS CLIPJOINTS THEY CLAIM
AREN'T TOURIST TRAPS THE UPPER CLASSES ARE
LUSHED OUT OF THEIR HEADS DOWN IN PEBBLE
BEACH SUCKING EACH OTHER'S & WILL SKIP THE
SHRINKER MONDAY HE'S GAY HIMSELF THE
SILLY SON OF A BITCH AS LONG AS I'M NOT OUT
HUSTLING SAILORS ON MARKET STREET & ONLY
WHEN I'M LUSHED OUT ON MY OWN PREMISES
(FOR WHICH I PAY EXCESSIVELY HIGH TAXES)

I DON'T CARE"

"The middle classes the middle class is mainly from out of
town (that's what I like about San Francisco everybody's either
up or down) they come & look at us they go away puzzled where
they remain,
                    outclassed . . .
                              (they will fight the Rooshuns &c.
                    they will fight the gooks & wogs & chinks &
                    japs & niggers & commies & catholics & wall
                    street & any man that tries to tell them
                    different . . .)"

"The upper classes don't bother me a bit except
why do they let themselves be buffaloed into
hiring the creepy managers they do? Faceless men to
represent a legal fiction? The upper
well, the . . ."

"UPPER CLASSES ARE HARMLESSLY IMBE-
CILE THE LOWER CLASSES PRETEND NOT TO EXIST (&
VERY NEARLY CAN'T, OUTSIDE OF JAIL) THE MIDDLE
CLASS MANAGER MERCHANT BANKER PROFESSIONAL
PROFESSIONAL THE SOLID (IT'S THE CHEESE THAT
MAKES IT BINDING) CALVINISTFREUDIAN DEMOC-
RACY SWELLS

& BLOSSOMS!"

TERMINAL LUES ACROSS THE SHOULDERS
OF THE WORLD

"The Roman Empire went to hell when the Romans bought them-
selves a goon-squad; bankrupted themselves trying to enforce moral
and sumptuary laws . . ."

History's now

9:vii:60

SHORT EXPLANATION OF EVERYTHING

So much of the world a wonder a beauty to me
    I laugh.

Gloomy serious ones ask, "How come?"

The back of the chair bends outwards
    as well as up.

20:vii:60

☆ ☆ ☆

† REQUIESCAT †

☆ Mother ☆

her husband { poor guy } she's married

do you want it in a bag? how do you want it?

Excelsior ☆ ☆ ☆ ☆

Excalibur

What do you think

The postman knocks, once in a while.

G Gate Goldy gate
parked
preparation
incapsulated

Mess

manumission

PHILIP WHALEN

Try doing a small thing well.

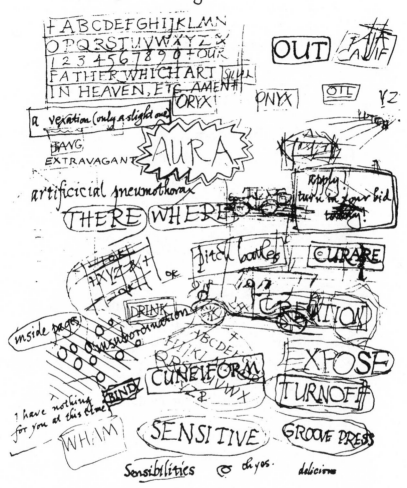

ADDRESS TO A YOUNGER GENERATION

I'm concerned about you
Where's your hands? For that matter
Where were you yesterday? Your
Memory lost as well
If I reached inside your chest & pulled out the amulet
      Its words: I
          DESERVE
          ALL
          DELIGHT
There you'd stand, a pile of golem dust

I don't condemn you nor delight
You must know it thoroughly, where & why it is
Its worth, its character
Sunlight through a prism: We see six colors,
There they are

Lacking hands, I see you've ingeniously stuck
          your toe in your mouth
More fun than listening to me & there
          it will remain until I say
          ICECREAM
& your belly remembers & your mouth
Icecream isn't toes
You maybe don't need a memory to cry
Misery is your chief delight

I know the minute you find your hands again
You'll attack me with whatever you can
Meat-axe, screwdriver, the stove
I haven't taught you any better, you've got
No memory, & I see now your ears have fallen off
How can you know I'm the icecream man?
I must be fast on my feet & try

To find out where you left your mind & talk to it
I can't run forever
One day you'll catch me, handed
& I'm done.

26:ix:60

DREAM & EXCURSUS, ARLINGTON MASSACHUSETTS

I see Mrs. Garret opening the glass doors of the tomb, doors of the wood and glass pavilion that's built over the family vault, four glass lighted passageways—the windows on three sides framed and can move up and down as in a regular house—mansard roof, wrought iron ornaments on top and weather-vane. Small wooden sign to the right of the tall doors:

"QUIETLY AND PEACEFULLY AT HOME
MADELEINE SUMMERFIELD RATHBURN"

like a doll house with gingerbread decorations, small panes of colored glass surround the window in the center of each door. Flowers grow in beds on three sides of the building and on each side of the walk leading to the entrance.

This is probably an early 1870's tomb. Rather eccentric for Cambridge cemetery—or was it a fashion that lasted for several seasons? A wooden replica of "the old home place" built over the family plot to protect the expensive marble, granite stones and concrete curbings from the vast Cambridge weather. An investment and a burden upon the heirs who must spend something each year on the place . . . paint job, new shingles, mend the walk, etc. Family quarrel: flowers or shrubbery for the landscaping? and if shrubs, what kind, and if hardy perennials, would snapdragons be facetious in a cemetery?

Cousin Lawrence infuriated everyone by causing the ornamental ironwork on the roof to be brilliantly gilded. Cousin Maude assessed each member of the family 17¢ to pay for the immediate application of black enamel paint to restore the propriety and hush the scandal. A secret sympathizer of Cousin Lawrence paid his 17¢, waited until the black paint was thoroughly dry, and then—in broad daylight—had his chauffeur drive him (Rolls-Royce 1925) to the cemetery, set up a small tent into which he retired to change from street clothes to painters overalls, and with his own hand painted the ironwork a beautiful Kelly green, the chauffeur steadying the ladder and helping wipe the green paint off his person after the job was done, the street clothes restored, the tent removed. He was driven back to town where he sent a telegram in the name of the cemetery corporation complaining to Cousin Maude about the green paint.

14:x:60

THE DEATH OF BOSTON

Bringdown, Boston? is a bringdown?
Why should I
         suffer
What
      packed under dead leaves
      thrown-away pages of Thoreau
West, now
      lives with us
      up in back of Fisher Peak
      Deerlick Cabin by Freezeout Creek (out of sight of
          won't see Mt Hozomeen

Kid's idea, Chinese sign for MOUNTAIN
which would scare him? anyway he's forgotten how
to read Greek)
And he's forgotten in New England which might as well be old
An idea, a notion, extremely
Impractical, of course the Police
would not allow it now
Not now in Boston the trees are labeled
and POLICE TAKE NOTICE, the sign says
of all we do

Who wants a life in the woods when there is Harvard?
All of us want to go there & thence to the National Shawmut Bank
The leaves the air thick with decaying hundred-dollar bills
Flopping in raggy bundles through the streets
Plugging up my nose
no joke, it smells,
And the weight of it, rotting
And heavier, the hatefulness
Children of immigrants clawing and hauling to get I N
Tearing each other, dying when they don't make Harvard, the
Statehouse,
City Hall
And the Yankee above/below them all
rots and hates

That smell in the Old South Meeting House, Christ Church in
Cambridge,
America born and dead in one town
Lived momentarily in the woods
Now all is fear and culture (which is Harvard)
Civilization (which is museums)
Observation of the proprieties (properties)

Thoreau said it was possible without money or slavery
They imagine he's safely buried in money and fear,
Vaults of Widener Library guarded by corps of bought professors
Note I do not mention Sac & Van

23:x:60

FOR ALBERT SAIJO

Fireweed now—
Burnt mountain day
Sunny crackle silence bracken
Huckleberry silver logs bears
Bees and people busy.

Rainy mountain years
Trees again—
Green gloom fern here
Moss dull sorrel—
Deer sleep.

Tree fire people weed:
Bright and dark this mountain ground.

18:xii:60

PW.
San Francisco
1961

HOMAGE TO RODIN

I.

"THINKER"
            in the classic peristyle
Shows up in old *New Yorker* cartoons, appears in some houses
            as plaster book-ends

A great ANIMAL
            the biggest goon Rodin could find for a model
            or magnified him, I think most Frenchmen are small
            by nature

ANIMAL for sure (we customarily think "man, human, soul"
            confronted with this kind of creature—"I," "We," &c.
            concomitant fantasies of art, politics, religion)

Rodin says: "ANIMAL: WHO SITS DOWN
            which is one difference, apparently doing
            nothing
        TO CALCULATE, CEREBRATE"
        & that's of the first significance:
        Meat thinking and got hands to build you what he
        Means or throttle you if you get in the way, either
                            action
            without too many qualms

"HANDS FEET ARMS SHOULDERS LEGS," Rodin says
We're in the habit of thinking "Man: subject for the psychiatrist"

Old stuff, we say, "Oh, Ro-*dan*. . . .
Rilke's employer . . . oh yes, Rodin, but after all—
Archipenko, Arp, Brancusi, Henry Moore—
Sculpture for our time . . ."
        (they appear in Harpo's Bazzooo, modern, chic,
        seriously discussed in *Vogue*—
        Epstein and Lipchitz are OUT, the heroic
                    tedious as Rodin)

NOBODY KNOWS WHAT IT IS, HULKING BEEFY
NUDE
We all the time wearing clothes and arguing "quest for values"
Forget what we are, over-busy with "who"
The only time we sit still is on the toilet and then
Most of us read, the only quiet and private room
Where we have bodies we wish away

Rodin: "BODY" with head containing brains,
          hands to grab with, build (possibly, the physiologist says
          hands helped enlarge the brain) feet
          to come and go, buttocks for sitting down to figure it out . . ."

How isn't
It wonderful how
Is it "base materialism" why
Do we insist "There is nothing we can do"?

II.

LANDSEND: "THE SHADES"

I won't go to the park today informal prospects groups of noble trees

Playland At The Beach instead
You never saw a merry go round so fast

2 fat old men watch it from a bench
One sings words to the tune everyone else forgot

No amount of sympathetic observation will do any good
Why not get older, fatter, poorer
Fall apart in creaky amusement park and let the world holler
Softly shining pewter ocean
Or let it quit, who cares?

The road to the Palace of the Legion of Honor still broke
About 1000 feet of it don't exist as I walk along the edge
Above the foghorns & dim fishboat passing the rocks
Anise and mustard, pinetrees and fog

Formal building pillared propylon and stoa
           HONNEUR ET PATRIE
Apse and dome and Greek pantheon life-size
A few golfers look at them
Just beyond the apse, Ft. Miley steel fence
Empty concrete bunkers, coast artillery no defense
No more meaning than the gods, a wonder of expenditure
The whole outfit stone marble pipe organ and all built
By a single family, given away (more or less)
Nobody home but Cézanne
Amusement (high-class) park to remember dead soldiers
and the late M. Rodin

No amount of reflection on the noble prospectless dead
No amount of indignation does any good
They are blanked, puzzled-looking (*The Shades*)
They stand heads bent down, three arms pointing towards
The ground that covers them, young burly ghosts wondering

We like to kill each other
We like to grab with both hands with our teeth and toenails
Unless you got sharp teeth and toenails you end up
Watching the merry go round not even a dime for popcorn
Nor anything to chew it

"EVERYTHING WAS ALL RIGHT UNTIL *THAT MAN*
CAME ALONG & WE DECIDED TO BE KIND TO
EVERYBODY THAT'S THE TROUBLE WITH US NOW
WE'RE TOO KIND WE OUGHT TO KICK THEM ALL
RIGHT IN THE ASS & STAY HOME & MIND OUR OWN
BUSINESS . . ."

               which is being mean as hell

Fat kid wants expensive camera Daddy to put two-bits into Cliff
House binoculars his father screams in reply, furious, insane,
"Whaddaya wanna looka them rocks whaddaya gonna see in this
fog?" "Come on!" the fat kid hollers, "Gimme twenny-five cents,

put the twenny-fi' cents in, gimme ten-ficens I wanna see them
!R O C K S! out there is COME ON! Gimme twenty-five cents!"
and his father screaming back at him like he might tear the kid
limb from limb but actually looking in another direction, quite
relaxed

There's all this loose hatefulness rolling around
We spend all our time hating the world, the Russians, the Gov-
ernment the job the noise the cops our friends our families
& ourselves for not changing, rearranging
Not being able to find what to change
Or what we'd use to do the job

A woman plays in the surf
Tight jersey pants, a kind of sweater top with sleeves
Fully dressed but the water doesn't hurt her clothes
Oblivious to her girlfriend hollering at her from the sand
                              at the foot of the stairs
She plunges, laughing, through a wave

III.

WATERLILIES (and *Iris*)

Fog washing past Mt Sutro Parnassus the Medical School a mirage
      that city in the sea
Leaves over the sky where these waterlilies grow up
      through my mind
Flowers in the water not to be reached or touched

POOL OF ENCHANTMENT, pink granite curbing says, before
                              De Young Museum
Short reeds & shrubby island Hiawatha boy blows flute
At cougar pair, one crouching, one setting, their ears
Laid back, enchanted
Black water thick mud at the bottom
Lily bulbs, heads in the dark
Pattern of stars inside, buried lights

First a few lobed circles on the water
Then leaf mountain with pink pecker buds
Open flowers (unmistakably women) that never fade nor wither
Impregnated they withdraw beneath the waves

No mystery, genes in every cell manifest
                themselves
Bulb of the earth showing itself here
                as lilies
The summer flowers, underwater globes of winter
                all the same

                            ❋

Since you'd gone, I hadn't thought of other women, only you
Alive inside my head the rest of me
                ghosted up and down the town alone
Thinking how we were together
You bright as I am dark, hidden

Inside the Museum I see Rodin's *Iris*
Torso of a woman, some sort of dancer's exercise
Left foot down, toes grasping the ground
Right hand clutches right instep
Right elbow dislocating
Reveals the flower entirely open, purely itself
Unconscious (all concentration's on the pose;
    she has no head)

Its light blasts all my foggy notions
Snaps me back into the general flesh, an order
Greater than my personal gloom
Frees me, I let you go at last
I can reach and touch again, summer flesh & winter bronze
Opposite seasons of a single earth.

                                        13:vi:60
                                        1:iii:61

184

MERRY
CHRISTMAS
A JOLLY INTER-
LUDE
OR THE
GAME OF
WHO'S
GOT
THE
BUTTON
UNDER
WHAT
WALNUT
SHELL
OR
WHAT IS
SHE LIKE
BEHIND
THAT
MASK
LIKE
ISIS
WITHOUT
ANY VEILS
OR THE
CHARLATAN
UNFROCK'D
THE MON-
STER PLOT
DISCOVERED
✺

another day another $2.65 plus
overtime plus cost-of-living graduated scale
increase less FICA contribution less Federal
Income Tax less insurance less medical plan
contribution less contribution to the Enter-
tainment Fund a grand total of 87 cents *I*
OWE *THEM!*

MY BACK! MY ACHING BACK!

The world is speeding swift away
Or melting slowly, a mass of retaliation

    "The Passion of Yang Kuei-fei"
    "The Claws of the Dragon"
    "The Breeze in the Moonlight"

Something has G O T to be done!

Happy New
Year from
Kazakhstan
❄
EASTER
IN THE
MATTO
GROSSO
❄
FLEE
FROM
THE
WRATH
TO
COME
❄
"A
WEARY
TIME
A
SLEEPY
TUNE"

2:iii:61

THE TREASURES OF RAGE

        patience and exactitude
Even now, it's plugged.
Clarence, connoisseur of fine toast, says:

Don't bother me with all that goddam nonsense before I've
had breakfast! Why are you wearing that cap in the house?

186

a) it makes me feel like I'm back in the Army
   presently I shall lose my marbles in all
   directions and lie hidden in the corner

b) you should go, he says, to the baseball game
   having written *Up the Dodgers!* across the front of it
   or a large *Pittsburgh Pirates* . . . you'd be found a
   bloody mess down among the empty beer cans underneath
   the bleachers.

c) yes. Most certainly. Yes. Prodigiously.

Swiftly the butterfly
Dream the Death of Winged Tiger General.

20:iv:61

REAL SAN FRANCISCO SUNDAY AFTERNOON

I envy my neighbors their incredible skill
Each can sit on a single rollerskate
& coast downhill
                WHOOPING
        even the fat ones!

22:iv:61

SAN FRANCISCO SUNDAY MORNING PALIMPSEST

The Twenty-three of April Sunday 1961
Tarahumara, Tarahumara & Tarahumara creeps like Roger Phetteplace
        from day to day
& all our Saturdays a pile of tears arraign the sand

Fly off the handle! Stomp, curse, rage
Drop the frying pan, denounce the eggs Paine Webber Jackson & Curtis
        The Warm Belt Realty Company
& vanish like the overlarded steam which engineers
        the clanking roll of time

Ten minutes before 11 A.M. I wish I was drunk & raving

Whereupon gigantic trolls with slimy fingers break
Our bones to see a feeble nightingale devouring noble worms

       O VINCENT! CRUEL VINCENT D'INDY!

stand	take	two	taking
I	you	throw	hour

IN MEDIUS REBUS "sanc diu nahtegal
        "then you
        "& I
        "then you
        "& I

What do you want to go & do all that for?
"Also sanc diu nahtegal"

TO RUTH

Insane clouds between moon and ocean
    which reflects them
I've been awake, I've slept, the clouds
        moving
Keep their pattern day and night
Swinging sun (moon) aureoles, beams, shafts, panels of dim glow
Revolving the water in regular circles
       over itself

     smash on the sand

I say "depression, madness, doubt"
Water dragon, Earth Dragon the power of these elements
Water, air and earth
     I doubt the sun's a fire
     There's more fire in the ocean
     and beneath it
To disguise myself, hide under. . . .

O, I know—an Indian blanket
   pulled over my head window sunlight color
Otherwise afternoon nap's a waste of time

The sea and I generate clouds
The clouds and I
       wandering pieces of the sea
Greater and lesser lights appear "in space," we say
    More than anything we value the distinction
    "Outside" *vs.* "Inside" . . . claustrophobia
    is the human condition

I've devoured them all.
Galaxies in my shoulderblades
The space between
      subjective
      a relatively large number can be assigned to it
For the sake of our convenience an International Catalog exists

I M A G I N E !

Klein's bottle made from varicolored glass
Face of Glory in the void

29:iv:61

DUERDEN SAYS: "LIFE IS THERAPY"

I have so much more love than I have given
Not that I've lived chastely, everybody knows I fall
For whatever grope or glad eye
Immediately; & suffer yet from the loss of every one
Remember each with love because I'm hopeless there can be another

            CAN YOU TAKE THIS?
            (or top it?)
            Are you available?

Poetry & sleep, walks in the park, the rhododendrons now in bloom
I take them all, my mind rolls nude among them
Rubs them all over itself

Sleep restoring my youth, burning out my brains with dream
Wrecks the fabric of learning, reason, choice
Takes my wrinkles away, I grow sleek, I wake with tremendous hardon
            I pretend to ignore

MY NATURE I SPRING OUT OF THE SEA & RUN WILD ON
THE MOUNTAIN

I spring out of rocks & moss & fallen logs my nature
Illuminates the world, the night, I build classical cities
& populate them we are a procession with garlands
& music & monstrous sacrifices blood, stink, horror, cruelty, disgust
MY NATURE   why must it bleed senselessly?
Incarnation, I bleed, I am the sacrifice to myself to you
BLAH. INCARNATE I DEVOUR & LOVE I SMEAR YOU WITH
LOVE & KNOWLEDGE

Of yourself & me
Freedom of the universe know & create
I draw designs on your flesh with our juices, your belly
The space between your hip & rib I bite (tenderly)
Your tongue runs into my ear as my cock swells into your cunt

ALIVE

      waking & sleeping
      all the bad worlds gone
      fears wars regrets
      I can do nothing now but love & bless
      & manifest these news. . . .

. . . .& MORE, MORE, MORE, I am still vigorous
I'm nowhere nearly through with this ALIVE
Although I sleep
Not inexhaustible but capable in so many worlds
      I sometimes fall asleep & forget their presence
Later I awake & go there
The contents of this one I squirt into your ear to give you brains
Learn & then scrap it
Despair & then invent,   design.
What we accept as world, art, law, culture is DOWN
Gone— our shells are busted, we find ourselves together
Horrified by the heat of the embrace
LET COME!
& dream, design, relax on the rippling waves of meat

As we are free to move separately
Ten directions of space we say
Problem of communication, distribution, equity
Try coming at it from the northwest or approach it from

> (a limited-field equation here,
> long series of mathematical symbols
> tensors &c.)

You could stop smoking or eating candybars
Try staying up four nights in a row without sleep
You'll come out with a clearer statement of the problem or find
> it was only grammatical

GET OUT OF YOUR USUAL FANTASY WORLD & OUT OF
THIS MESS THEY SELL US FOR GENUINE

> I DEMAND THAT YOU SAVE YOURSELF
> So I can love you

(No. That isn't right)
SAVE YOURSELF YOU ARE MY ARM, MY LIVER, MY
> KNEES

> > (it's more like that, although I'm living now
> > more or less alone, somehow or other
> > I'm not entirely separately from you
> > > or I'd be dead)

MORE & MORE & MORE
I've got it in further than ever &
> > BLAM!

There we are, spread all over the inside
& the line of communication tenderly parts as the serpent
Coils to sleep.

San Francisco
30:iv:61

PHILIPPIC, AGAINST WHITEHEAD AND A FRIEND

Pull it down over our faces and ears
That English wool Plato Alfred North Whitehead
And say "there.
The sweater eternally becomes immortal."

I scream H E R E S Y ! It's that old slow & gradual salvation routine

They tell me "The limits
You must know what are your limitations
And then proceed . . ."

       (LIMITS: i.e. polite categories & hierarchies
       that justify repression
       "for our own good")

H E R E S Y ! Whether its creeping Fabian socialists or that
"Infallible" process you call reality, glued to time so that
      "Justice is later
      Freedom is later
      Dessert comes AFTER the nasty spinach"

        B A H !

I can't help feeling this world is immortality:
Two pigeons in the sun (house cornice across the street)

And nonsense as well! Words, a grammatical order
The world palpably NOT of this order
Exceeds our limits

We kill each other quite artistically
Exquisite tortures, exorbitant crimes
Think of the glass flowers in Peabody Museum
I am limited insofar as huge areas of my brain
Dissolved in Hitler soap-vats
Dispersed as radiant poison over Japan

One of the pigeons flew away the other
Peers down from the cornice
        Goodies below?
I look up and it's gone, end of the world
    ("invalid argument," Whitehead says, "depending on
    ignorance of the theory of infinite convergent numerical
    series")

Which puts me in over my head

Cantor discovered three orders of infinity:
Aleph-sub-three has yet to be discovered.
I don't consent, I demand the excessive "tertium quid"
That "somewhat" forbidden by Aristotle
That ocean
        (although I'd drown in a pisspot quite as easily)
        (and perhaps my dissent, my perversity, are also
        ruled, have their determined order?)

For limits let's try Blake's
        "Enough—or too much!"
Certainly excesses are deplorable
Those glass flowers at Harvard offensive as the war
I feel better knowing that the secret of their manufacture
Is lost. I'm delighted that the young believe professors
who tell them, "*Ulysses* and *Finnegans Wake* are no-good
failures; Proust killed the novel once and for all."
Whitehead says—and you, my friend!—repeat it:
        "God is the organ of novelty."
I hear an electric organ

Producing pure notes, tone reduced to bare vibrational frequency
               (no Pythagorean overtones here,
               Plato his Ideas exactly)
Total purity
Sexless
Absolutely reasonable
Accurately in tune past hell's freezing over (within reasonable
     limits, variation due only to line-load and distance from
     the powerhouse)
Precisely and completely what we want
The triumph of the West

Arnold Toynbee tells us this is the true goal of mankind;
Anybody who doesn't want this is uncivilized, out of history.
The psychiatrists tell us if we don't want this we're mad
The government tells us if we don't want this we're goddam
     Communists, GO TO JAIL!

God is worthless except he become a man
Man is murdering slob unless he exceed himself

The limits,
Orders of infinity:
My own immediate incarnation as compassion and knowledge
Appearing to you
               (who are the ground wherein this manifestation
               proceeds)
               RIGHT NOW!
In response to your necessity
Even though it is I who am deluded
And you who are the Buddhas of this world.

                                             8:v:61

TWIN PEAKS

A swollen cloud a curving shadow ripples light on the lumpy hill
Maybe so. A straight edge of light a bumpy shadow the
Smooth hill slope and valley crease. Perhaps.
I suppose it is terror now invades me, tightens my chest,
Swells my eyes
My heart beats the blood stands still

I try lying flat with my eyes closed but then I see myself
Climbing
        that hill, distantly bushes and grass,
Flashes of sun and darkness
Towards the radio towers
I get up, break up, sneezing
Again, again   again, again
        again
My brains liquefy and run out my nose
My eyes regain their hydrostatic balance the clouds
Continue slopping dark and light across the hills.

11:v:61

~~under~~
under } the surface of the rock / feel animal fur shape
beneath }

sleeping.

𝔭 𝔭 𝔭𝔭 𝔮 ℯ ℯ ℯ 𝔰 𝔰 𝔢

& under the rock surface / feel animal fur shape

a description of sleeping

/ Loosen Up!   gorked: je suis fiche!

"Stay loose," Robert Miller says.   you don't know,

a council of   detachment   & / can't guess. Let us
                                      move on, then, into the con-
                                      sideration of some other area
sleeping – Qære: ~~shame~~: /? or "shape?"

aromatic spirits   sweet spirits of Nitre
    of Amonia
       & & Violet! Thief of time & Firth of Forth & Ultraviolet
       Sun   Forth of Tay Helen of Troy
       municipal hanky-panky & filthy froth & foam & Violet!

e k w Chambers   unlucky ultramarine
          an expert witness, an authority upon
                         the manufacture & use of waffle irons
    Camelia
narcissus Rhododendron hibiscus   begonia   tiger lily Cyclamen
daffodil   Violet azalea snapdragon nasturtium   rose   Chrysanthemum
           Pansy   larkspur   gladiola   calla lily crocus
           Sweet William foxglove   iris   cana lily   peony
           Canterbury bells cosmos tulip   day lily   trillium
           mallow   mullein   lilac   marigold   lady slipper
                                                  aster   birdbill

CAPTION FOR A PICTURE

A home of many-colored gas,
A way from   A S I A, monster. Soul-trap. Bactria!

21:vi:61

LIFE AND ART

build you a house out of all this stuff—make bricks
from all these straws—or failing that, rayon stockings

An aeolian harp for dishonest immortals
Windbag for a dudelsack
       (Swinburne, thou shouldst be living at this hour!
       Arkansas hath need of thee . . .)

Put it a few octaves higher up.
          UP!
And over the sublime blue edge of Sol's corona

I wouldn't be a bit surprised,
Not after what's already happened in the first couple of times
around. I should say not.

22:vi:61

27 VI 61

Red Rover come over Mrs. Eustace Brion Peysermuller
Mrs K. Harrison Bullwinkle IV
Mrs Bowinkle Swazey

Mrs Topham Johnston II
Mrs Walton Gruberfalz
Mrs Horace McSwinney
Mrs Carstairs Detweiler Jr.
Mrs Thomas Bowes Pape II
Mrs Beale Talbot
Mrs Codrington Sheffield Wardrop Smythe Jr.
Mrs Roger Phelps
Principessa Cazazza
Countess Radziwill
Mrs Clancy Schultheiss
Mrs Edward Clutch Hayes
Mrs Norman Brewster Pellet II
Mrs Harry Bask
Mrs Melvin Spelman Travers Jr.   Mrs Morny Fiske
Mrs Alfred de Puyster van Schronke   Mrs Townsend Hamilton
Mrs. W. Armstrong Fiske-Pomeroy Jr.   Mrs Irving Bishop
Mrs Robert Martin Kincaid   Mrs Morgan Carnegie Taft
Mrs Charles Winthrop Merriwether Brown   Mrs Alexander Chamfort de Beaupré
Mrs August Castro y Carvalho de Anza   Mrs David Peabody
Mrs Chadwick Piton II   Mrs James Donovan Schwartz Jr.
Mrs Gordon Duff-Gordon Pinelli   Mrs Gibson Kendall

Mrs Titus Morpeth
Mrs C. Wilberforce Monteith
Mrs Max Gladney
Mrs Bruce Schiaparelli
Baroness Axel Sorenson
Mrs William Wolsey Ramsay Jr.

Mrs Mortimer Adcock IV
Mrs Grant Southerland Jr.
Mrs Gaylord Swindell
Mrs Arthur Fillmore McGonigle
Mrs Garfield Thinne
Mrs Finley McKinley II
Mrs Vincent Borgia III

THE DAYDREAM

A call from, a pull in some direction (**EXCELSIOR!**) echoes of the future I will presently look back upon (whether with pleasure or chagrin there is no adumbration—the noise is an excitement of some kind) I must seize upon the present moment, the controls—wheels, levers, pushbuttons, dials—and arrange them in such an order that the future event will bring me something valuable, pleasing, rare. With great annoyance, I realize that I'm further than ever from the wheelhouse, the control-board. How shall I ever reach it in time to prevent the boiler explosion, the collision with icebergs and haywagons, then skip immediately to the spotlighted stage to receive the medal, the honorary degree, the hundred million dollar prize?

27:vi:61

IGNORANTACCIO

Where do you suppose the world begins
It wakes up every morning brooding sins of dreams
Tree heavens, mouse fears, it contemplates a punishment condign
For living criminally . . . although that criminal should have lived
But twenty seconds he must suffer infinitely

    And up, and up, let's pack our leather clothes and be off
    To the bondage-freak ball!

7:vii:61

Behemoth decomposing in the sultry night, a slow as from cheap landlady 100 watt globe a demisphere at the
whirlpool's eye a jewel swisswatch ruby. . . .

Incunabula!

distantly,

Something green

＊ a blank space here   raving,   power of several thousands of supernovae here ＊

". . . said nothing could persuade him to believe that the emperor was unaware of the very real innocence of the
Duc d'Enghien, nevertheless it too soon became apparent to all those who were in any degree aware of the feel-
ings Napoleon entertained concerning that unlucky nobleman (however impossible it may at the time have
seemed to

Sometimes nothing is possible not even history

Sometimes I think Goethe was intolerable

Sometimes I try to stop finding fault with the world
    & other people & myself

Sometimes I eat too much

Sometimes I bore myself silly and all the world besides

THERE IS A MIDDLE PATH (somewhere hereabouts)
    . . .But it leads (alas!) to Chicago. . .
                OK?

Sometimes I wish everything were the same:
                How often it is!

22) A Wax model of Prince Talleyrand

23) Maxim Gorky

24) Terrestrial magnetism. Mystery or Fact?

25) walking stick insect in white cotton batting

26) PED.

JSB

27) Pistachio

28) My compliments to Mr. Dave Haselwood,

10:VII:61

San Francisco/Philip Whalen

201

hoist great blocks of language into place

A fabric of elegant proportion, exquisitely adorned

with garlands, columns, urns

one chaste Roman statue in a niche

Wherein the lives & feelings of a motley crew sparkle,

flare, shout, gasp & tinkle,

ancient gaudy jeweled king-

doms of the east...

Disperse into foreign cities

the dream of several seconds, that are centuries

Ah, the dream of several seconds, that are centuries

I pass through Max Bruch forest, dallying on my way towards

the pinnace in the wooded bay

the final journey to Cythera

202

THAT ONE

He spends lots of time in that all-night movie, a red bandanna handkerchief over the lens of his flashlight so he can read without disturbing the other patrons. As long as it's dark, he sees trolley cars and buses with flames billowing out of all the windows while crowds of people and animals inside burn and scream.

In the daylight the streetcars are quiet, being full of water like aquarium tanks; the drowned bodies inside sway gently back and forth to the motion of the cars.

He reads volume after volume of Stendhal, referring only occasionally to a pocket-sized French dictionary. He pauses rarely to look blankly at the movie screen at the rush of cowboys and Indians, Bette Davis as *Jezebel*. Although it is several miles from his apartment to the theater, he invariably walks to it. He never told anyone what happened, what he saw, the one time he took a taxi downtown; he never rode in one again, nor could anyone persuade him to do so.

10:vii:61

] have eaten

Culm, as of bamboo.

Water-Chestnut (or caltrop)

[wiry grass & brown gravel appear beside the lake's edge. The lake lives in southwestern Colorado. I have seen ~~only a little of~~ that part of Colorado only briefly & from a train. 35¢ DELICACY That was sixteen years ago. Gratias ago. Gratian. Gilhooley

ginger-root
taro-root
bean sprouts
lilly roots (or lotus)

winter melon   soy beans   1945
bitter melon   horse beans
snow pea pods   burdock root
sea weeds

Pâté de foie gras
à la Strasbourg
(avec des truffles)

elegant foods of China & Japan

Oraga Haru THE YEAR OF MY LIFE

Observe! Brigantine from New Bedford

ISSA {YATARO KOBAYASHI, 1763-1827} HERMAN!

Oraga Haru buggy

Notes & queries Plushbottom

henry stew
melvin soup
Princess Charlotte Pudding

Haiku r rr Turtledove, nightingale, skylark, cuckoo
? harumi ?
thrush, wren, heron, crane
rstuvw
xyz & AMENT
1234567890   flamingo egret stork swan
1234567890   goose duck chicken California quail
              China pheasant quelque sorte de moineau
              the eagle with one head

abcdefghijklmnopqr
and so forth

how do you get out of here, anyway?
OK. We go.
Good. We see you Monday

Great-Horned Owl

where's your key?
where's your wallet?

No, no, 1000 times no! when, when, when in the Course of human events it becomes necessary to a people to throw off the Chains(?)

August 15, 1961

Monday
in the
Evening

Philip Whalen

East 128 Milano {3} 1963

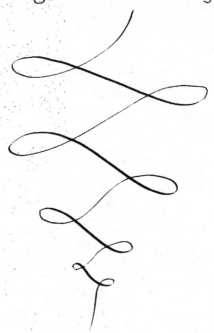

206

MONDAY,
In The
Evening,

21 : VIII : 61

Philip Whalen

There was an animal
It left a set of tracks
The animal was I .
& the tracks also & the mud
    wherein they appear to your
        eye
    which is { who } not you , I

    suppose I do [& I do
        what then]
Well then.

.I.

Or now. I protest, I complain
    that I am lost,
aching, coming all to pieces,
I claim that I am {nevertheless}
    Quite in control.

I behave in a particular way. I
sit holding my left hand across my
    mouth, my right hand
& two eyes do this writing

    On the hillside {Twin Peaks}
    Broken glass, tin cans,
      a box the milk man used
        to carry bottles
    Weeds & ground = squirrels
      Clouds

   .2.

Pencils in a jar on this table

   tric◊trac
   that's
   backgammon
   {"heigh-ho Anthony Rowley
           & spinach"}

Spoor, my scent on the wind
      the ink I customarily use
      dead letters under the table,

   between pencil jar & ink bottle
   wooden mouse from Denmark, gift
   from Persky, tin windmill,
               gift from Joanne

        MANUSCRIPT

           ·3·

(prose)
(unfinished)

{ I care desperately about
that X it can't be finished, never,
never, never,

How can I go through Thoreau's life
again, the unfinished, unpublished
self-righteous walker, disconnected
from all women & men ? }

Damn   damn   dull damn blather

I proceed.

Tiepolo Baroque church peach ice cream

4

Sun
{ set   color of nipples, of labia
                                    minora

{ I crossed out "Tiepolo" at first, why bring
in some artist, some painter, where are
my own words & visions,

        why isn't it discrete pink clouds
instead of art history, female anatomy?

    Because I can (this being my paper

& ink, my table & chair, my floor, my
electric light) write it the way I want it,

        HERE
    anyway I chose. }

    but why must I insist, why

            ·5·

pick an argument with you,
who have begged for a chance to listen
Prayed night & day for 2 months for the
privilege of watching this pen write
words...

✶

this is the Evening Star

this is the end of my life

REQUIESCAT,

Sweetie.

. 6 .

{ what's he lying about now, for Christ's sake?

Here lies

PETERBOUX

not quite 40 years old
Who imagined he could not
        Cope
supposing that it was some-
thing different from
blinking his eyes,
breathing, keeping his
fly buttoned, his big
mouth shut, & his
imagination employed
with high grade poetry
       † † †

How I love me! How much
I'd give for a divorce!
or simply get very drunk,

Puke, SPEW
   DEFECATE
      WEEP

Clean up the mess,
take a bath, put on clean
clothing, & start in
again upon a clean
sheet of paper

·7·

214

But now, at last, I'll tell you everything,
All that you've always wanted to know,
Those things I've successfully avoided saying,
The innermost secrets, the real WORD...

. . . . .

Absurd! you guessed all these dingy tid-bits
years ago, that is, presuming that you have
lived 17 or 18 years in the U.S.A, are
neither deaf nor blind nor simple-minded

. . . . .

I digress.
      a manner of speaking.
Here's new tracks, new signs of my presence
            gone by,
I seemed headed for the drugstore, for tobacco
Into the kitchen for coffee
                  ?

· 8 ·

215

that wish to move away from this
paper, this table,

Qui vivre ?

HO

Spirit of the cat-tail marshes,
genius of pollywog land, discoverer of those frog
or fish eggs underside the lilypads Aunt Clara's
backyard fishpond.

STAND

& DELIVER !

·9·

¶ Having burnt several ounces of myrrh, frankincense, branches of the sloe, a few hops, & seagull feathers, we perceived the faintest outlines of an APPARITION, light & wavering at first; it seemed to draw substance from the heavy, fœtid smoke, so that soon there appeared to be an almost palpable column of dimly glowing light in the corner of the room nearest the book case...

Obstinate Creature! Speak!

WHAT HE SAID, AFTER WE HAD GONE TO ALL THE TROUBLE TO BRING HIM BACK FROM THAT VAST BEYOND (A TASK WHICH WE BEGAN SO HAPPILY, FACING ITS DIFFI= CULTIES WITH

· 10 ·

I want popcorn.
I want a naked friend to play with all over!
I want a great many cigarets.
I want to read the Greek, Latin, Sanscrit & Chinese classical writings.
I want ice cream.
I want the rest of my library.
I want a piano, an organ, a

GOOD CHEER & HATE,
BECAUSE OF OUR
DEEP ADMIRATION
FOR HIM) CALLED
ELYSIUM, THE HAPPY
LAND, ETC. ¶ I
CAN SCARCELY BEGIN
TO DESCRIBE OUR
SUBSEQUENT FEELINGS
OF DISAPPOINTMENT,
OF CHAGRIN WHICH
BORDERED UPON TOTAL
DISILLUSIONMENT,
CYNICISM & DES-
PAIR, AFTER WE
HAD HEARD HIS
VOICE AT LAST.

harp, a set of bagpipes.
I want a number of books &
    musical scores added to my present
    collection.
I want to spend a year in Europe, &
    several years traveling in the Orient.
I want a large new typewriter.
I want new teeth, new eyes.
I want final perfect enlightenment
    {i.e., Nirvana}
I don't want to smoke any more.
I really shouldn't masturbate so
    often.
I shouldn't eat so much.
I want to be left alone.

Children beller at each other in the street, chasing
        each other in circles in front of the drugstore
Threatening & sparring, grabbing cocks & asses

Do I wish I were young again?
Today, at least, I don't feel old: that wish,
        Question,
                is irrelevant.

·11·

How are my orchids growing? Big leaves
& no flowers.
    They {not I} are contrary

       ?

Am I better than you, is that the idea?

    { Irrelevant. }

"Why do you hate me", that's really
    the question, & I mean, "Please love

me, pay attention to me."
     *

    I want to be left alone.
      *

... the Spirit, having answered all our questions
in a most satisfactory manner, was bidden to
depart, but it was some time before it con-
cluded its apparently endless catalog of
desiderata. For a number of days afterwards,

    .12.

219

the corner of the room in which the spectre
had manifested itself smelled strongly of stock
flowers, cardamom, cinnamon, sea water or
semen, depending upon the sex, age, & stage
of spiritual advancement to which the observer
had attained ...

" ... all so phoney, my dear, you know what
he really wants is to sit for a certain number of
hours every day, writing. every month to be sending
mss. to publishers who pay him fabulous sums of
money. He wants to live in Pacific Palisades with
a couple of swimming pools & live entertainment,
like Tiberius his villa on Capri. ¶ Once every
5 years or so, he wants his picture on the cover of
LIFE, & a big jolly article inside ... about
himself, of course, & his new book. Then he wants
the Nobel Prize for his 50th Christmas present ... "

·13·

DOWN !

"*Exorciso te in Nomine,*
&c . &c ."

AVAUNT
AVOID

I want a dish of Chinese black
mushrooms.

I want lots of hashish.

I want to write 9 best-seller
novels all in a row.

I want everybody to let me alone,
except for that naked friend
of whom I've already spoken.

I want a little peace &
Quiet.

"TEKEL"

I don't care. I'm not afraid of you. If you
try getting funny with me, I'll knock you for
a row of pink potted geraniums. I

.14.

221

have studied judo AND karate, so don't go
trying to give me no bad time.

✶   ✶

Oh dream,
O vision of continuous embrace,

SCRAMBOLA!
{
I want cotton candy.
I want to visit the church of
St. Appolinaire in classe.
I want rare roast beef in London,
greasy baked lamb & olives
in Beirut.
I want a vision of the new
heavens & the new earth.
I want a bottle of root beer.
}

the time.
Contrary to your belief (& to mine as well)
has not been wasted or misappropriated
or in any way abused; it is, it

·15·

Must (I see) remain out of our reach
or certainly we would abuse & daub it
in some unseemly fashion, were it ours.
But its existence is ideal & perfect,
While my creation stands elsewhere, namely
In this sublunary sphere where all things
    must decay & pass away

        { but that's not Time, neither }
I have redeemed nothing but beauty, pleasure,
    & wisdom. I have failed
To save you or myself out of the muck & chaos
    of this jeweled gorgeous world,
        this universe of love & bright joys
        & all contentments.
Although these abstractions can scarcely be lost
& their ownership in doubt from the first reckoning
    of who & what was & is

.16.

＊　　＊　　＊

I must remember to scream & holler more often { i.e. go ahead & write violently, absurdly, idiotically } if it means an end to fog, clutter, ill-painted scenery, machines with squeaky pullies .... also, if I misinterpret the echo from this noise as being sounds of comfort & encouragement, which will in their turn provide me with enough confidence to continue the inspection & interpretation of my own visions, I shall be content.

＊　＊　＊

Because I imagine that I'm so far ... too far ... IN, I sometimes stop, when I'm out walking, to grasp the branch of a tree, a handful of foliage, put both hands on the tree trunk, closely inspect the bark {& are there

·17·

mosses, lickens, fungi or insects on it? } note
its color, thickness, texture. In the park
I stop to press one hand flat on the ground
among the gravel, fallen leaves, dead grasses —
or simply lie down on one of the great lawns
{ I pay no attention, then, to the sky, sun,
clouds, birds } and attend to feeling the
springy grass & solid earth beneath me.

I click my tongue at a squirrel.

It approaches me on a zig-zag course,
running, then stopping to sit up with one
fore-paw held to its chest, uncertain
what I'll do — feed it or hit it. { I do
neither, & presently it goes away. Several
other squirrels must come to inspect me, to
ascertain that I'm carrying no food to them ...
as each one approaches, it points one paw at
its chest, excitedly, appearing to enquire,
"Who, me? }

·18·

Inside. outside, may or may not be significant distinctions. I know that I can bore or frighten myself rather easily, by thinking, "I am inside, I must get out." ... X I have felt what the ancients called PANIC, i.e. been outside & felt an irrational necessity for being indoors, for going home... but the last time I felt that way. I took out my notebook and recorded the fact. Soon I was writing about the general scene, about particular objects that caught my attention, & the terror left me.

✶

The End
of
MONDAY IN THE EVENING.

·19·

This text was copied by
the Author on 28
October, 1963 at
San Francisco
California.

The sketches in hand-ground
Chinese ink are also the work
of the Author.

VECTOR ANALYSIS

What I want? green
        grass under leaf tree and vine
Sunshine all around
                dark and
                muddy ground
      wants I
          air
             no boundaries
    put a hole in your skull bone
         open up the sky
   an equal
         vacancy

that is, a partition, with a hole in it, such as might be installed
in an empty cigarbox. Partitioned, the space in the box has two
parts—as long as the lid is open—but shut the lid and where's
your eyes?

    mallow in marshy ground, the water
    hyacinth is found, caltrop
      sliced with dinner meat
          I
          ?

21:viii:61

Coca-cola Chairs
ca. 1928, pretending
to be made from a
single piece of wire

P.W.
Sept 4 1961
San Francisco

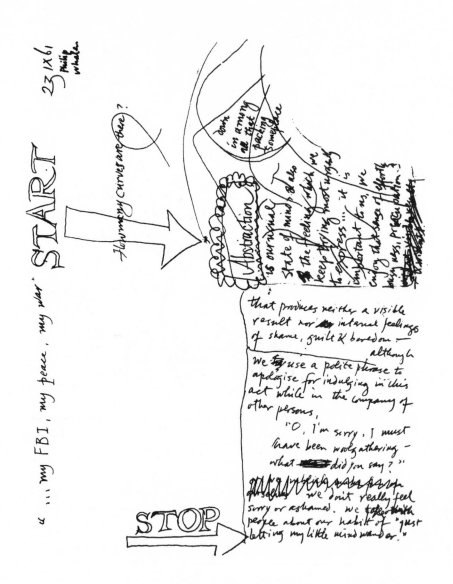

23 IX 61
mig whale

" ... my FBI, my peace, my war " START

How many curves are there?

Abstraction ... is our normal state of mind & also the feeling which we keep trying most urgently to express ... it is important to us, we enjoy that sense of effort

that produces neither a visible result nor any internal feelings of shame, guilt & boredom — although we use a polite phrase to apologise for indulging in this act while in the company of other persons,

"O, I'm sorry, I must have been woolgathering — what did you say?"

we don't really feel sorry or ashamed. we tell people about our habit of "just letting my little mind wander."

STOP

Bread of Origination! Fell desire
Has fled across the border of the bright
Leaves towards night to build a tyrant winter
In the heavenly trees

> *Good Morning to you,*
> *. . . in our places*
> *With sunshiny faces*
> *Good morning, Dear Teacher,*

a winter, a deadly winter
I'm afraid of it although I have steam heat
Furlined clothes and no reason to leave the house
Between Thanksgiving and March 21
Would that it were Bread of Patience and Perseverance!

W H E N   S H A L L   I   B E G I N   T O   R E I G N ?

23:ix:61

"There's a Man
in there!"

7:x:61

EARLY AUTUMN IN UPPER NOE VALLEY

Bang dang ang S. Philip Martyr Angelus 6 P.M. or

VESPERS

but all that's Huguenot propaganda

VEXILLA REGIS

PRODEUNT

that's the *real*
    old time down home hogmaw and chitterlings

     FUNK
Mr. Wagnall hasn't got a look-in

   POSITIVELY NO
   POSITIVELY NO
this means you!

   "I think *Moon Mullins* is terribly vulgar."
   "I stand corrected."
     7 October 1961
    8 October (Sunday,
or, less specifically) (Tomorrow) is Krishna's Birthday
San Francisco
    "a real sweet little guy"
     San Francisco 7 October 1961
     Saturday at evening

S. Francis (of Assisi)
S. Francis Xavier   Why not. OK   ☒
S. Francis de Sales   a vote for
                Good Taste

           [?7:x:61]

                                  I want more than my share of
good luck and prosperity

Tenderly.
You may well imagine.

Overwhelmed with dismay & consternation? Confusion,
Ruin,
            hebetude
        We are undone!
           Balkh   Sikkhim
             Ladakh   Kashmir
           Chitral   Nepal
            Hunza   Gilgit
      "Come where my love lies dreaming . . ."
overwhelmed with fumes of Indian hemp
(*cannabis Indica,* bhang) but enjoying
hallucinations of joy & delight all the while

             ZOUNDS!
cried Mr. Controll, this must not be so!
him and his agents busted everybody in sight, the whole shop—
scones, crumpets, jam pots, tea trays, silver spoons and all—
took it all down town, booked for use, possession and sale,
120 years to life, to run consecutively

        HAS ANYBODY SEEN MAUDE FRICKERT?
        WHERE'S FRED MERKEL?

I want to call my attorney right away.

                                                  7:x:61

THE POOR

salt

oregano

toilet paper

2 natures of soap (one kind bought 31:ix:61)

liquid bleaching compound

peanut butter

A P P A L L I N G
F I N A N C I A L
C R I S I S
!

degradation   despair

we really do need some olive oil

7:x:61

THE REVOLUTIONARIES

FOR R. E. MILLER

1

Fred Merkel,
What are you doing
Fred Merkel is my name
And I'm just a little drunk
But I'm soberer than I was this time yesterday evening

234

Fred Merkel
What are you doing outside the Police Station
Praising God the Father
God the Son
God the Holy Ghost
Joseph, Mary and Jesus and St. Therese of Lisieux
         AMEN

Fred Merkel is my name
I'm waiting for Maude Frickert
              to meet me here
She's already booked inside
Praising God the Father, God the Son, Holy St. Joseph
Holy St. James of Compostella
         AMEN

2

Where's Fred Merkel?
  I want to talk to my lawyer
Who's Maude Frickert?
  I want to see my lawyer right away.
We're going to have to take them
         Downtown. They
         don't want to cooperate.

              ✷

Smart people
College guys

※

You play ball with us
And we'll play ball with you we got these rubber bats so you don't
   get all marked up

"*Queen.* O, I am press'd to death through want of speaking!"
   —Shakespeare, *Richard II*, III, iv, 72.

"Pressing to death by laying heavy weights upon the body (*la peine forte et dure*) was the regular English penalty for "standing mute," i.e. refusing to plead guilty or not guilty."
   —G. L. Kittredge's note on this passage.

15:viii–7:x:61

ONE OF MY FAVORITE SONGS IS STORMY WEATHER

silk
lumber
sawdust
wood
pulp
pitch
turpentine
rayon
paper
syrup
rubber
kapok
chewing gum

I said to myself
"Why are you angry, why
Are you afraid, try
to like something, look
at that flowering weed or bushlet
that bug, that dirt, and select
choose one and like it: love."

As I walked further I grew happier
and less nervous; although I am an
atheist I pray all the time.

frankincense   Acorn   Allspice   lime-flower tea
myrrh   Almond   clove   jasmine
fruit   Avocado   nutmeg   gum Arabic
   &   Apricot
nut   Apple   lime   lichee   mace   gutta-percha
     Bay   mango   loquat   coffee   oil of eucalyptus
     Beech   pear   cheramoya   pepper   amber
     Chestnut   peach   coconut   quinine   palm wine
     Crab   plum   cabbage-heart   cascara
     Cherry   pomegranate   pawpaw   birch beer
     Chinkapin   prune   papaya   root beer
     date   persimmon   breadfruit   sassafras tea
     fig   quince   guava
     filbert   tangerine   olive
     haw   walnut
     hazel   mulberry
     kumquat   grapefruit
     lemon
     medlar
     nectarine
     orange

I walk on hills of jewels & gold
A foolish, wicked man.

20:ix:61

FRIENDSHIP GREETINGS

Carelessly all fixed up a can of beer
several cigarets a cup of coffee I don't care
whether school keeps or not
thinking of Frank O'Hara in Paris right this minute
or the basement of the Museum of Modern Art as the case may be.

23:ix:61

STATEMENT OF CONDITION

a change in personnel
      of personnel   one what?

                                "One never know,
                                do one?"
    different people

A change of people isn't the same as people changing. What
A shame.

How different. How different upon the mountain are the feet
Strophe and stanze. Will you settle for good. Handsome is as
handsome does. Try to do right. Be a real man for a change.
No matter how presented, it is yesterday's cornflakes, it is
hogwash, it is without sense or understanding. It is not
(alas) beyond reason or comprehension FROM THE OUTSIDE,
but once you're in, then where are you?

Right here at home, the sewer has broken again. Dirty water,
faeces, assorted garbage and mephitic vapours are swurging
about, underneath the livingroom, a few inches beneath my feets.

Kriste eleison!
Kyrie eleison!
Kriste eleison!

You can imagine my horror and chagrin
        as it were to say, "Well I'll be dipped!"

                                      7:x:61

THE IDOL

A gold woman with a condor's beak
        her hands are llama heads
Weights these pages down
Peru or Bolivia or someplace in South America
A goddess, I don't know her name,
I hope not a picture of bad luck

                 ✲

You'll notice how easily I withhold what you need,
What you require of me.
I can't imagine what it is, and it doesn't do me any good

                 ✲

A terrible mistake: "Dots and squiggles justify
               The air and space I occupy"

                                   12:ii:62

THE CHARIOT

FOR JESS COLLINS

I stand at the front of the chariot
The horses run insane, there are no reins
The curtains behind me don't flutter or flap

I don't look worried. Is the chariot headed
       for the edge of a cliff?

Behind the curtains a party's going on
      laughing and talking and singing

I prefer to stand here, my arms folded
      Ben Hur
Or one hand leaning lightly on the guard rail

Watch the horses galloping

Mother and father behind the curtains
      they argue, naturally
        "Who's driving, anyway?"

Wind whistles through my spiky crown
Some hero, some king!

30:iii:62

THE ADMONITIONS

If I told you once I told you a thousand times
I tell you stay awake until sleep
Forces you to shut your eyes and even then
arrange to awaken yourself not more than six
hours later, better five, and one of the senses
never sleeps, O King who lives forever

Lion jaws
Barred with gold
While Daniel sang alone
Darius was awake all night
       worrying

I don't mean that you should go around
       asleep on your feet
Don't be afraid to fall over, once in a while

There's no time.
Thoreau said there isn't enough of it unless you start
Each day at sunrise and also enjoy a little bit of what the
       night has to offer, viz. lights in space
       and the far-away practise drummer

Daniel, a triumph
The nerves triumph
       for a change
And don't jitter, collapse, divide
Was this what they meant by "heroism"
       (as distinguished from "*chutspa*"—unutterable
       gall, brass, etc.)
Coordinating to achieve, surpass the ordinary actions of men

But it was angels who locked the lions teeth
Angels who are communication ever jealous
                    that I might speak
                    revealing heavenly mysteries
Or the lions teach us animal royalty

The angels were the prayers of Darius. The seals
                    of the den unbroken

Awake, the wonders multiply
We praise them or condemn,

                    GOOD AND EVIL
            the gross national product
We send them out, we save money
                    all die

I said to the lion, "all right, go ahead."
He filled his belly and went to sing on the mountain

What's the score now? He's
Hungry again

Darius hopes for the best

His grandson will perish.

                                        23:iv:62

TO THE MUSE

Dear Cleo, I can't complain about your absence
Nor excuse my failure to call you sooner
I mistook you for your sister and
Now I thank you both, you one Lady
       who changes before my eyes

QUEEN LIONESS OF HEAVEN IN THE SUN

      . . . tangle of a dream, a history
         waiting while I sleep, I grind my teeth
    or waking I watch your closed eyes
    film of gold hair across your cheek
       a mystery

a tangle, my impatience, your wildness,
this persistence of vision
      centered in my own chest
(the print of your ear on my skin)

      your presence
I'm high, my brains foam
I can't hear what you say
Quietly happily out of my mind

Madrones blossom on our mountain
Deer in thicket
Watch me pass
Fawns and does,
Tawny and grey
Bless me as I walk along the fire road

Who are the brilliance of that day
the glory of this night

25:iv:62

THE PROPHECY

The present, assailable at any moment
          we pretend
          from Russia, yet, Eternal,
An absolute,   raised above
And beyond any chance or possible
                changing

Subject to the weather, to
          my imagination?

      IT SHALL NOT STAND

16:vii:62

mmm

A.M.

Monday early before bedtime

29 July 1962

San Francisco California USA

©1962 absolutely all

rights reserved to the author

which here

that that Philip Whalen B.A.

of whom obtain

Exactly what I'm
driving at; where,
in a manner of
speaking, one may
be said to have
arrived — as who
should say, "got to"...

ships
a horn
water horn fog night
muslin
maudlin
Magdalene

Marigold

n   n
n don't push

golden
go where?   Rocks

sub-prefect of police

down at the jefetura

a vision of beauty, the
complete delight of cons=
ciousness without refereme
to a specific sense impression

M M L M Josephine Miles   john hay Whitney

Marianne Moore   Peltry

Jasper Johns   Augustus John
skins furs leathers   Sir Ernest Jones Glynnis Johns   RA
        hides &
          pelts   Adela Rogers St John

[undated]

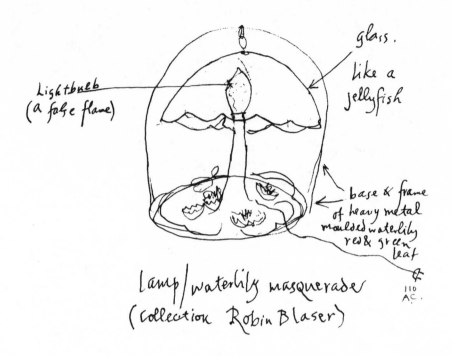

Lightbulb
(a false flame)

glass.
like a
jellyfish

base & frame
of heavy metal
moulded waterlily
red & green
leaf

110
AC.

Lamp/waterlily masquerade
(collection Robin Blaser)

[undated]

§ A bending, a turning
a breaking.

Meander I saunter a winding
Course as the leaves
Divorce their several trees
Erratic airy turnings.
Park evening October lawn

[undated]

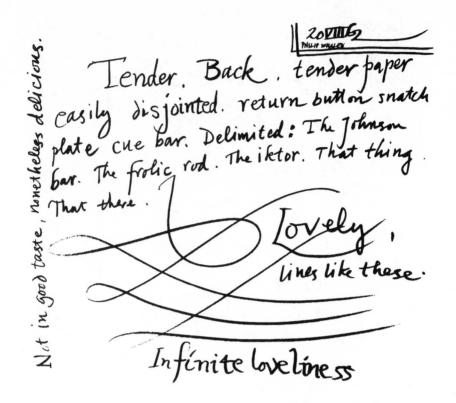

20 VIII 62
PHILIP WHALEN

Tender. Back. tender paper
easily disjointed. return button snatch
plate cue bar. Delimited: The Johnson
bar. The frolic rod. The iktor. That thing.
That there.

Not in good taste, nonetheless delicious.

Lovely,
lines like these.

Infinite loveliness

[undated]

248

THERE IT GOES

without gills or lungs or brain
        making its way
           "ahead"
And getting all it wants via skin osmosis

the spinal fluid oozed away and the bones sealed
themselves over, straight AHEAD, I don't mean it went in
a circle any smaller than the diameter of the earth

the density
        frozen krypton atmosphere!

           .center.
           repeat from *"oozed away & the bones sealed"*

    (OUT?)

    (OUT?)

                                  13:ix:62

SATURDAY 15:IX:62

No help for it. I'm so funny-
        looking that I can't see the trees.

A SHORT HISTORY OF THE SECOND MILLENNIUM B.C.

Talk about fellaheen, talk about
    the taxi drivers and cops behind the wheel read comic books

A manipulation, a slick robbing job, two thousand years of it
        trade in faience beads, amber
        tin,   TOTAL MONOPOLY
        (Mr. Morgan said, THE PUBLIC BE DAMNED!)
Read Gordon Childe what if he is a commonist

Who knows better.
2 thousand years of work yourself to death
building God a house
tending God's ducks and pigs
killing God's enemies
kissing God's ass

Total control of energy, animal and human
          "The earth is the Lord's"
      also innumerable brains and hands

Keeping fingers busy with God's work
Keeping the books and letters locked up in God's house
Thoughtless holy suffering hands

a tyranny so complete, a captivity, reduction to animal existence
You see the delicacy of it,
Twenty-two hundred years of tyranny, high-grade embalming
         and exquisite stonework

Tell me, the big man says,
about Millennium 2 BC

Big rocks, fascism and ignorance
manipulation of knowledge to keep them down on the farm
22 hundred years of bad beer and worse onions
              I ask you

                                                    22:ix:62

FILLMORE HOB NOB CARBURETOR

"Carburetors now
Almost like a cat fishing
Almost like a wing flying
Just like a propeller."

                                                    15:x:62

THE ART OF LITERATURE

FOR LEWIS WELCH

I went to the door
And who do I see
Deputy Sheriff with a
        paper for me

          ━━━━━   ━━ ━━
          ━━━━━   ━━ ━━
          ━━━━━   ━━ ━━
                It's
        The Angel of Death
        Wiggles of Life
                tremors of elegance

Come down from that hayloft
Come you down for me
I'm here in the oatbin
Robbing the glee

Death Angel fungus turn-on

flap.

18:x:62

THE ART OF LITERATURE,

2nd Part

Gull flies ahead of his
    reflection in the wave.

19:x:62

THE ART OF LITERATURE,

#3, A Total Explanation

FOR DR. A.

Busts out, at last, in spite of impossible conditions,
all the magic performed to keep it down and in—or
a Caesarian section—even while She sits at the
threshold, her legs crossed and knots tied in her hair and clo-
thing, as Judas his guts burst out through his
own restraining fingers, as Jonah thrown ashore

as myself puking up the present, the past, the future
drunk and sweating and endlessly weeping
puking up lungs nuts kidneys and all my
brains come spraying out through my eyes and ears and nose

        What has money or the lack of it
How does the dollar apply?

      Invest your money in the stock market what
I need is to write this which I have done,

And this perhaps unnecessary but curious college kid
Wednesday explaining with delight there were now 2
beautiful girls in a hitherto boring and profitless class
how the sight of them roused his pecker, how he tried
and tried to restrain it, how it very nearly exceeded
all convention, embarrassed, nobody having let him know
he is a man, nobody having told the ladies it was a compliment
to their beauty

                               21:x:62

THE ART OF LITERATURE

Part 4th

      What do they do together, that's what I
never could figure out, what can they do, do they
actually. . . . .
                            :
                            :
                            :

. . . . I don't believe it, it's too foolish, too
ugly, unaesthetic, I don't like to think about it

but when people talk about them as everyone does all the time I
wonder how they do it. Let's talk about something else.

21:x:62

THE ART OF LITERATURE,

Concluded

WHAT I MUST CARRY: THE ENTIRE PAST,
Mother and father and sister and grandmother,
Wherever I go, a generation of men and women yet unborn,
The book I'm reading, the book I'm writing,
A list of addresses and telephone numbers
Hair-comb, keys to return for the night for my
               toothbrush and razor
Pens (and in case they fail, pencils) and for amusement
           a lead-holder with 7B graphite nearly black as ink
And quite often I have a map of the place I intend to visit.

Some sort of Government paper that says I am he,
More government paper and metal I trade for bus rides
Animal hairs and hides, fibres of plant or synthetic origin
2 lenses fixed in plastic frame to light my weak eyes
All dark and wet inside, hot and slippery, rivers, lakes
    and bays and gulfs and voids and sand and mountains and stars

and

The sunglasses, forgotten, lie on my desk.

21:x:62

THE END OF THE ART OF LITERATURE

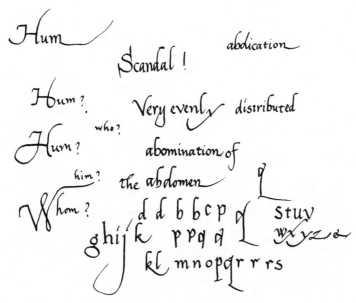

Hum

Scandal!

abdication

Hum?   Very evenly distributed

who?

Hum?   abomination of

him?   the abdomen

Whom?   d d b b c p q   stuv

ghijk   p p q d   wxyz a

kl mnopqr r rs

Philip Whalen

[undated]

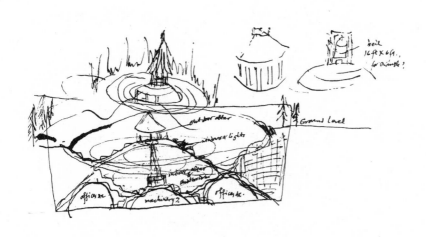

A Community temple
1·XII·42 Mill Valley

[undated]

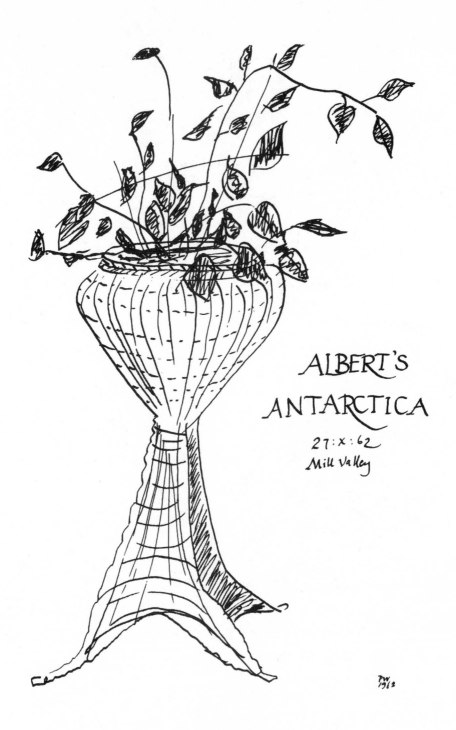

ALBERT'S
ANTARCTICA

27:X:62
Mill Valley

PW
1962

MINOR MORALIA

1.

Looking at a man trying to decide what he knows
he looks at his fingernails
                                    tree branch out the window
                stone on the table doesn't move
Dust and daylight fall on him, propel him up the path among
                    tree ferns
A world collapses not a minute too soon
I dodge the heavier fragments as they fall

        "THEY ARE MURDERING YOU!"

I say they're welcome to, although it'll bring them
No luck
They really must—however
I'm alive right now

            2 kids trying to catch goldfish from the pond
            Bowling green old men with hats on
            Heavy construction proceeds among the woods
                    to the left

"I was not chosen His Majesty's First Minister
In order to preside over the dissolution of the British Empire"

                didn't dissolve
                bored itself to death
                just in time

Why do you do that. You're wasting your time
You know nothing
And absolutely nothing about how to write it down
And too old to learn

And supposing you knew what you knew
You'd be a giraffe or a goldfish
That's simple, that's all there is to that
Tell me something I don't know

        A garbage pail full and scattering
           gunk all around it
        Pretty colors and stink
           mold and slime

"I DON'T CARE. I'M GOING TO COMMIT SUICIDE
AND GO DRINK BEER FOR LUNCH WITH RUSSEL F.!"

Your pretty head falling apart
Maybe your poems drop out between the cracks
        and flowers

          ✺

        Ho-hum

          ✺

        "What I want you to do from here is go
        completely insane and work all the stuff you've got
        into a giant explosion."

Blow up the world before it's too late!
Imagine a mayfly with the gall to be alive in June!

        (Good heavens! does he mean corpses in the street
        and all that?
            YES!)
        ("and blow up the museums, incinerate libraries!")

          ✺

Your fingernails are dirty from poking your flowers
You're scared of them—if you poke them too hard they'll die
And living,   they're a mystery

(to poke)
You pinch me;
That's my secret.

✺

      ("... bomb the Vatican!
      away with all the gold!")

And of course the vacuum left by its passing
Their passing (list of imperial names here)
Sucks us down,
Our surplus of powdered eggs notwithstanding
Or swell up like a poison pup and burst,
So what?

"FEED THE HUNGRY. HEAL THE SICK.
      RAISE THE DEAD."

        there's precious little else to do

What else do you know, what else?
Oh yes.
After you understand it all
How do you behave?

Naturally the logical thing:
Fill the atmosphere, earth and sea with poison
And watch what happens, the logic running:

$$A$$
$$A'$$
$$A^1$$
$$A_1$$
$$A + 1$$
$$\sqrt{A}$$
$$\bar{A}$$

The Greeks went "A, B, C, D, E. . . ."
They kept slaves and superstitions
They got cynical and vanished after letter "P"
      (Letter "N" standing for *Nichomachean Ethics*)

We go "A: poison kills a mouse   *". . . it would appear*
A': poison kills goldfish   *that "A" is, as a gen-*
A_1: poison kills monkey   *eral rule, lethal to all*
A^1: poison kills geraniums   *forms of life. Further*
$A + 1$: poison kills bacteria   *experimentation will*
$\sqrt{A}$: poison kills ants   *be necessary in order*
$\bar{A}$: poison kills men   *to determine . . ."*

"WESTWARD THE STAR OF EMPIRE TAKES ITS WAY"

    The barbarian is no longer at the gate
    He's a four-car family at the expense
    (and *convenience!*)
                of the Government

CROSSED THE INTERNATIONAL DATE LINE 1912
Napoleon said, "I tremble to think . . ."

           TAKES ITS WAY

and our empire
             ("Shine, perishing republic" . . . that was 30 years
             ago: Jeffers told us)
glows in the dark
and by its glow
          what else?

Oh, your flowers, your fingernails
I hear a certain amount of music
A voluptuary in keeping with the times
When I'm supposed to be ahead of them
          I leave you to the Medes and the Persians while I goof
          Writing nowhere poems

Could I have stuck around to teach you what I never knew?
Suppose I began over, in middle age,
Committing laws among the bullrushes:

      1 Law: Raise your hand
      2 Law: Move your feet
      3 Law: Listen
      4 Law: Don't commit suicide

INSTRUCTIONS AND COMMENTARIES

Everybody's telling you

1. "Nothing you (one person) can do will make the slightest
   difference." Follow Law 1: use hand to write to me.

2. "You cannot escape.: Follow Law 2: use feet, to convey you
   out of town.

3. "The mass communications media are in the hands of liars."
   Follow Law 3: Listen to me or any other poet.

4. "The world as we know it is about to be destroyed." Follow Law
   4: *suicide* means you've been played for a sap by a two-
   year-old idiot child and also means that you believe in and
   approve everything the newspapers say—I believe you
   know better.

Further instructions will be forthcoming
Use these now, under pain of being something else.

21:viii:59

2.

THE FINAL PART OF *MINOR MORALIA,* FOUR YEARS
LATER, A NEW END A NEW BEGINNING, 27:x:62

Swollen wicker gross foot. reed grass. burnt root.

✺

slugfoot!   grasses and weeds a few small
Save the lettuce!   rocks, what other people
Guard the peonies!   tell me are stones

Albert fries rice with   stems and moss clumps
bacon onion and eggs   a reduction, the forest
aroma! Breakfast! coffee,   on another scale
the country smell

                         Jugs pots bowls jars and "deeshes"

          freely to recognize, to
          love it, put it into an order
          which moves me and which

You will recognize and love and meanwhile
I shall have gone on to something else
And you shall become yourself changing also.

Temporary looking and admiring and letting go of it
If possible make a present of it to anybody else

✺

(hiatus)

✺

The real problems, of poverty, injustice, war, cruelty and ignorance

MUST BE SOLVED

❋

(hiatus)

❋

I'm not completely tangled in theory, false imaginings,
            the frustration isn't total)

WHY THE GREEKS WERE FAILURES
WHY WE MUST NOT ALLOW THE IDEA OF A FREE
            MAN, A RATIONAL POLITY

to be lost

Why we have less liberty and how to get more
How to live with each other, to love, to let other
            nations or people we think of as funny-looking

ALONE

            to make their own kinds and styles of life
            undisturbed (short of their trying to kill us—
            why put up with death at the hands of boobies
            whether the boobies in question are of another
            nationality or we call them The Government of
            The United States)

REPEAT it until it's out of the way or arrives at last
Absolutely and finally here

Seeds pelt down from redwood cones
Even with the help of opera glasses I can't see
The birds, tits of some kind,
Not much bigger than the bugs they feed on

What is the glue, the cornstarch, the plastic slurp or

to bind or string

LET IT RUN OVER YOU IN STREAMS!

Let it run into your ears and armpits and up your
Nose and in your mouth and between your legs and toes
Let it collect in corners and in the unused electric frying pans
The ugly lampshades

AS I REPEAT IT

Freedom, love, learning and time simply to
set on your ass and look at the trees and birds or
the walls, the floor, the other end of the bathtub
look your psychiatrist in the face and say, "I'll try to help you
all I can, please look at me, please let me hold your hand, don't
be afraid."

(as I'm not afraid to stop writing and eat lunch)

AND REPEAT: Don't be afraid to find out you're crazy
but for God's sake give up the habit of being
"n e r v o u s"

an oppressive order: Line up from left to right over there

a stifling sequence:

How do you do. Are you going to hurt me. Am I
going to learn to dislike you and later try to injure you.

a society:
How do you do.

Can we like each other, although we're incapable of loving?
Let me bring you this.
Let me do that for you.
Tell me what's troubling you.
I'll pay your lawyer's fee. I will help you
carry a picket sign.
I will write to my Congressman, too.
I think you're talking nonsense, I think
you are funny-looking but I like you.
Often you are in an ugly mood. I shall wait
until you're in a better one

I repeat: NO KNOWN FORM OF GOVERNMENT CAN
ARRANGE THIS

We must do it ourselves.

And remember: that the Government is unalterably opposed
to our beliefs and actions

Repeat it every day:

I shall oppose tyranny in every form.

Try to remember:

Freedom (independence of thought and action and feel-
ing and imagination and creation) is . . . "The new fun
thing" (if you can't think of any other phrase or if none
other reaches you)

NO GOVERNMENT CAN DO THIS FOR YOU, NO
MATTER WHAT IT CLAIMS

Repeat it again
I defy all tyranny

What we need is freedom, love and learning
We won't let each other starve, we got food out the
                    ears

Tyranny of these head-kinks which require these repetitions
Mostly I mean that physical and mental oppression and pistol-
whipping that we practice on each other daily in the
name of maturity, progress, good government, better education

                              ✤

        . . . but I thought, "how ill-equipped the world is
            to deal with me! Defenseless . . . likewise all my friends
        who must be tired of my continuous hollering . . ."

Begin all over again, repeat it from (as musicians used to say)
                    the top

                              ✤

I discover a page of this is missing and I wonder who's been read-
ing all these pages and I want it back.
This is as bad as notebook missing in Boston Nineteen Hundred
and Sixty.

    How can I (at this late date) be such a total dumb-bell? It
must by lying under something.

                              ✤

                                              29:x:62

                    which it was, half-folded between
                    the cot and the wall
Nobody read none of it.

3.

2:xi:62 SECRET ARCANE AND HITHERTO UNPUB-
LISHED PRIVATE NOTES TO *MINOR MORALIA*

i.

The community, the *sangha,* "society"—an order to love; we must
love more persons places and things with deeper and more various
feelings than we know at present; a command to imagine and express
this depth and variety of joys, delights and understandings.

ii.

or: "community, etc. are the visible expression of that order . . ."

iii.

Where does the State, the Government fit in? And of course its ab-
surdity, its uselessness, its exact position in history (its connection
with and placement IN the past) shows up immediately: A bad old
idea; EXHAUSTED.

iv.

None of this is precise writing, correct logic or responsible action?
These notions and words appear to me, set themselves in my head as
I awakened from sleep. I hurried out of bed to write this down

v.

"persons, places and things," and of course, our own selves as well . . .
Maybe not all this is "love"? Much might be euphoria. I have trouble
displaying, expressing that sensation, it drives me to dance and laugh,
to write, draw, sing, caper, gesticulate wildly. This seems to frighten
many of the people who happen to see me hopping and giggling. I
must imagine ways to explain this feeling to them, and wish that they
might have more frequent accesses of it, equal to or more profound
than the kinds which I've known. For several minutes at a time I be-
come a glowing crystal emitting rays of multicolored light. (What a
metaphor . . . ugh . . . but a beginning) because I've forgotten (or re-
membered, which is it?) so much while I was asleep?

I've tried to explain, repeatedly, that this ought to be my daily, hourly condition (ridiculous demand!) Do I know what this feeling actually is, do I deserve (hah!) to exist in that state?

I change, I tell myself, "I" IS ONLY THESE PASSING STATES, THEIR ACTUAL PASSAGE . . .

I came at it wrong-side-to, as usual . . . I find a lump of wooly fabric, pick it up, turn it over, pull the sleeves right-side out, and there's a sweater. While I'm not wearing it I must put it away in mothballs. If I have more than one, I ought to give this one to a person who has none (for example).

vi.

In the mean time, I imagine I must discover and compose these instructions which even a small child can follow, if a child needs such instructions—which will be mailed to you in a plain wrapper free of charge   ?

vii.

One of those Chinese sages figured the child/heart/energy/delight as his chief metaphor of instruction. We turn our children off, we try to, that they may come into a room correctly (How do you do?) I can recall our own parents and relatives putting us down, horrified at the sight of our natural elation (why is it frightening to them . . . they're afraid we'll fall off, down, and break our bones?)

An orgy of screaming, chanting, circle dancing until we fall exhausted and sweating in the grass, hypnotized by the clouds and sun, plant seeds drifting in the air, birds.

Why not. Later we feel quiet and happy, quite ready for washing ourselves, dinner, sexual congress and sleep.

viii.

This morning the sun is covered by varying thicknesses of mist and the kinds of foghorns and the order in which they blow remind me of Marin An, and being there at night or at this same time of the morning after, everyone else asleep and I listen. But there, in that place, eucalyptus—as on this hillside, redwoods and ferns. I sweat, drinking coffee after breakfast.

ix.

I imagine a motto, "Ecstasy is my response," and think of it as embarrassing to write or say. I suppose this is what Philip Lamantia's book is actually concerned with.

x.

The length of these lines, the affected sound, to my ears, of their rhythms—the repetitions, cadences, pausings, the gropings which aren't actually necessary or real—I know precisely what I'm saying, what I think—but I must permit them here, admit it all, look at it, like looking at my own anus in a mirror.

xi.

Quite often when I feel that I have an idea, a notion or an insight, I'm actually understanding something I once read or heard—or I find that I'm now able to express an idea of Plato or of Whitehead in my own vocabulary, in words which correspond with exact feelings, with personal experience—I suddenly "see" something, comprehend.

21:vii:59
2:xi:62

THE END OF MINOR MORALIA

Finally, after long observation of that person shouting, waving his arms, flapping banners, exploding rockets, launching illuminated fire balloons,

I ask you: "What does he want?" and you answer that it was obvious to everyone that he was the official pyrotechnician producing a command performance and furthermore today is the Fourth of July (although it is winter and we're eating turkey and cranberry sherbet)

What does anyone want

The hand reaches down to the gravel on the ground and picks up a shiny surgical tool which had lain there, I hadn't seen it all this time.

. . . want, wish, try to get hold of?

—?—

23:xi:62

SUNDAY AFTERNOON DINNER

FUNG LOY RESTAURANT SAN FRANCISCO 25:XI:62

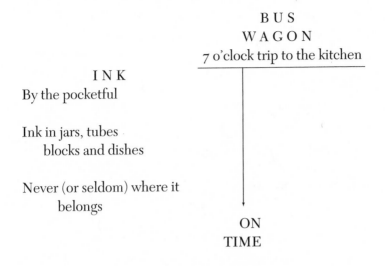

BUS
WAGON
7 o'clock trip to the kitchen

INK
By the pocketful

Ink in jars, tubes
    blocks and dishes

Never (or seldom) where it
    belongs

ON
TIME

more ink displaced

✿

cuttlefish in sepia sauce

✿

chop suey
eggs fu-yung
pork newdrilles
fortunate kookies
fly shlimp
bosatsu pudding

✿

271

When the smoke of the cooking flies away
All that's left we
    consume what may.
a very Chinese interest.
    plastic. Do I bore you.
    coriander leaves.

✲

A pot, apart from which
as, precious unguents, herbal
wines and essential oils
        sweat and ooze, collect
    a powder of gone spiders
                                        P O R T E N T O U S L Y
                                                S U N D A Y
                                        F O O D   S M O K E
                        as if we were gods &c cherubic
                                        presences

THE SATURDAY VISITATIONS

1.

Belligerence!
                Mixed bathing, and
That was the end of the Roman Empire
Which ought to have lasted
                at least three weeks longer
                        ?
                    Oh yes.
                19 people, cars, a GREAT BIG
                Highway Patrolman
                        on purpose.
                        in cars.

2.

ALL PEOPLE
    they love the/they
        try to tell
    us/we may sue
        !

Very tiring.
     ✿

FORGET IT
     •

                                29:xi:62

SONG TO BEGIN *RŌHATSU*

Overcome with frustration I sing a few songs
Ring a few bells & wish for better times.
A dim and moisture afternoon.

        FIXED? The race
    is absolutely honest. Very
               straight; OEDIPUS UN-
BOUND.
        the same fate, no matter what his
position relative to an imaginary horizontal plane
        D A R U M A
    was there any change.

                                  30:xi:62

THE GALLERY, MILL VALLEY

Do we have sandwiches is there a menu
Everything is going to start
We have going to change it all.

11:xii:62

HEIGH-HO, NOBODY'S AT HOME

Certain teachings are whispered into the right ear,
others are murmured into the left; but the
most sacred and arcane of all must be blown into
the crown of the head, down through the sutures
of the skull bone. When the recipient of this
wisdom is able to convey it to another human being,
to a horse, to an ant, a spider, an owl, a goldfish
And a high cliff by words, gestures, actions
which probably affect the lives of any
such beings I'll be happy to call him a
wise man, saint, successful poet, living man, etc.

Why not now?

What's the reason I'm not reaching you? (Since I think of you,
your presence—your existence—is unquestionable)

      but reasons and ontologies are generally uninteresting

I've chosen the wrong way to amuse or instruct. This is
a subject, a topic, a locus, and you have been trained to
interpret such items of discourse as implying certain con-
ventional stances.

How many times have I told you, Milicent, that "blow" is only a figure of speech?

12:xii:62

HELLO TO ALL THE FOLKS BACK HOME

Many's the time I've rocked you to sleep in that chair, many's the hour he had to walk the floor while you bellered and squalled now you have to act up ugly now you are sorry now we are dead and gone now you will say to yourself O, I'D GIVE ANYTHING IN THE WORLD IF ONLY I'D NOT DONE THAT WAY THEN!

Sure enough, here I sit, bereft of those who truly cared for me, penniless because, against their injunctions I've practised laziness instead of industry and thrift, covered with shame, overwhelmed with remorse and horrid guilt, another miserable derelict washed up on the sleazy shoddy coast of Bohemia after the shipwreck of my passionate lusts and pridefulness and perversities among the raging seas of the actual world, sure as God made little green apples.

Now I'm trying very hard to think of lines to speak in the Third Act. What to put into Chapter XI. What to play for an encore. Because although I'm through I'm not finished. What better persons, what more elevated thought and speech than yours, my ancestors, what more elegant blood shall I spill on these plebeian scaffolds, what greater heroes, queens, than you undigested, undegraded ghosts,—

(*desunt ceterae*)

13:xii:62

Sunday
6 January, 1963

PHILIP WHALEN

"you got to be tough,"
i.e. somewhat insensible?

CLAY Teapot, red terracotta

he forgets.

a dried
berry soup &
vegetable

That's a
Bunny Rarebit Godly 2 shoes mulberry

a
magpie

Bunny Rabet is the pet
of Goodie Two-Shoes.

a
loyal
habit

SILK
WORM

CROSS SECTION

Bunny
sage *green
whitish-pinkish
Jet black

HIT WAS
SUPPOSED
TO BE
TEN
MO
KU

Goody Two-shoes

goldy {or goldie?} lacks.

WHAT IS HIT?

SILKWORM

cu
cnжу goma
or "go my", HAROLD HART CRANE

IS HIT A STEEL DRUM?

Perfectly well at home
inside of a magazine nervous
you're not supposed to.

Take it all

hum, hum
Serviceberry

Away

Turtles

a fantasy of pro-
priety & great
expenditure. Man
say "continuously"
or bound to happen

THE PROFESSOR COMES TO CALL

cet homme ci

bread	b⎫	⎧B⎫	Bernard	⎧B⎫	⎧b⎫	bread
booze	b⎭	⎩B⎭	Berenson	⎩B⎭	⎩b⎭	beer

cet homme là

O N I O N S

New York, an abandonment
                    anguished literature, an
OK hero, who deserves it. When it pops
into his head. If it pops. Who
cares about punctuation, after one is
thirty-five.
THE RULES OF GRAMMAR
Who can forget them?

Present a piece composed of ambiguous existentialism.
Prepare a paper which is concerned solely with ambiguities
of Existentialism. Nobody can understand it.

6:i:63

THE COORDINATES

I was tired yesterday. It was your mother's birthday.
Why do they put everything together. Why does it stay there.
I never leave when I'm supposed to. I never know what time it is.
These are the kind I have now.

24:i:63

9:II:63

a major communication, direct from world head
quarters.
       artillery caissons; leggings & raincoats &
helmet liners will be worn. whimsy. Dim.
folie militaire folie à deux Goodbye., dull care.

you are totally wanting in character. You are not to
be considered a serious person. Not by any
stretch of the imagination or bend of stychomythia.

     Bright ensigns of the day departed

        " very soft & lovely from here."

Bright ensigns of departed day. Albert.,
  You taste. How do you like.

9: II: 63

Worse than ever than any the rest
etaoin shrdlu Please fill these jugs
with six carboys of ozone maleate.

P P P P P q q g P P P P P a ride

to J° town. The sights of urban vistas

Lies! All lies! and insanity. &

    self assertion, a drive toward

        Domination, &

Self aggrandizement, & control, to produce

    ● stasis, permanence; death

    an Egyptian sickness

      pyramid building.

SPRING MUSICK

Rain straight up and down upon the sword ferns
       the red camellia flowers
Garden stairs waterfall walkways
         Bach!

       a realization of six partitas
       and a skinflute duet (*nombre soixante-neuf,*
         a figured bass)
Just feel your way along at the beginning
And fake the rest

9:ii:63

HOW WE LIVE THE MORE ABUNDANT LIFE

IN AMERICA

"O-tel!"   Vegetable soup with barley or Toamato
                              Juice

————————————   Breaded Veal Cutlets with Country Gravy

A nice   Smashed carrots OBrian Potatoes Froze Peas
quiet   Thousand Island Dressing
family   hearty Lettuce Salad
hotel: Minced Pie Bred Pudding Jell-o Ice Cream
               Coffee   Teee   Milk
Redmond,   Soft   Drinks
Oregon,   Candy and Chewing gum
except for the   Cigars, cigarettes, tobacco
blackjack game
a gang of rusty   9:00 PM go take a cold bath and go to bed alone

280

sheepherders
all night
half a dozen
rooms away
the walls are
THIN I can hear
the smack of
cards and rattle
of chips on
their table
. . . .

My father says
rusty hell those
boys spend the
winter over there
on the French Riv-
ierra, fly their
own airplanes to
the Arizona Bilt-
more don't kid
your ass about
that.

9:45 PM wake up and read the Gideon Bible until
10:10 PM turn off the light, have one last cigaret, etc.

Probably the view of the main Cascade
Range from this place on a summer morning
is worth the trouble of getting here and the
inconvenience of staying over night and get-
ting up traumatically early and looking.
          If one isn't a landscape queen, what then?
                    the eggs are fresh and troutfishing

is fairly good not too far from here

     Don't bother the stock, don't dabble in
the irrigation ditches, don't try to get too
friendly with the natives.

Fruit Juice
2 eggs any Style
hot

MUSH
Hashed brown potatoes pancakes or waffles (syrup or jam) Toast
Ham or bacon. Little Pig Sausages
Coffee   milk

My father says don't ever try to order
steak up there in that cattle country

---.

In Redmond the drinking water still tastes like it had flowers
dying in it three weeks too late, they should have been thrown
out long ago. I thought the irrigation ditches looked like Dutch
canals, years ago.

17:ii:63

SPRING POEM TO THE MEMORY OF
JANE ELLEN HARRISON (1850–1928)

Old woman, here in the dark of the moon
Honey milk seed falls at your feet

When will she go up the sky again?

Spirit of milk follow her and swell her body
bring star showers

there's been enough rain for the season
too little snow in the mountains

Old woman, or later perhaps
Young mad queen of night
mimosa breeze in the valley

Honey milk seed, heads of your children fall
at your feet

You say the girl's too young

I say she's flighty
I see her down at the drive-in, kidding the boys
　　She waits for that gas-station kid
　　That bomb of his 90 miles an hour
　　I see the back of her gold bubble wig turn the corner
　　　　　　East Blithedale Avenue

Old woman I know she's out parking
I don't know what you tell her
　　　　or if you got time
I see that antique poet loitering around your backyard
　　petting the goldfish
　　grilling your lambchops

Old woman, I'm not a cop or a social worker
I sing loud in the bathtub next door I hope
　　　　you hear me?

You and your lavender hair and white wrinkle toes
　　　　gold zoris

I can do the kid more good than that gas punk
I bet he sniffs glue for kicks

Old woman, stars in your brain
Acacia wind blows now in canyon
Laurel tree blooms, false lilac
　　　trilium and borage
　　　　wild iris
　　　　　I
　devote these mountains of blossoms to you
　　　and sticky pollen of a purple flower
　　　　　saffron crocus
　　　　　at your feet.

18:ii:63

283

Philip Whalen

4:III:
63

m
m
m
m ~~careful empty~~ careful & empty. No sympathy
m will you get from me. And oh, will you be sorry then.
m
m

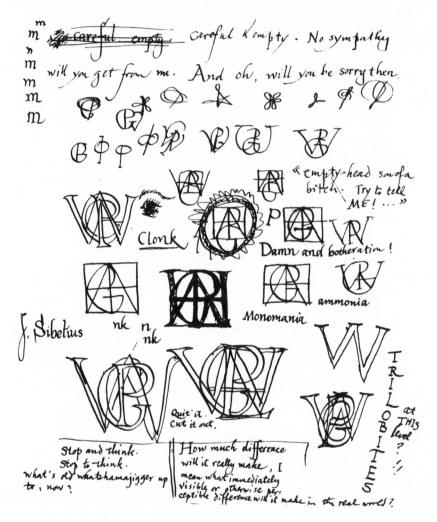

« empty-head sonofa
bitch . Try to tell
ME! ...»

Clonk

Damn and botheration !

ammonia

Monomania

J. Sibelius   nk n
                     nk

TRILOBITES at THIS level ? !!

Quit it.
Cut it out.

Stop and think.
Stop to think.
what's ol' whatshamajigger up
to, now ?

How much difference
will it really make, I
mean what immediately
visible or otherwise per-
ceptible difference will it make in the real world ?

~~More light~~ ↑ of More light ~~comes~~ seems to fall on the crest

↑ of the hill (or the sky there is a lighter

blue?) ~~which~~ which pulls my eye towards it.

~~Magpie~~ Oklahoma, remember 'Roy Harris'!

~~Synclinal~~ - anticline. Hills & distances. The hills

have many trees with clumsy doves ~~roosting~~ nesting in them.

I suppose that there are, ~~squirrels~~ squirrels and chipmunks. Rocks and
snow underfoot, ~~coneys~~ CONEY, CONIES /coney/harvest ~~than the~~ midsummer grass, I see
curious black & white bird, a magpie or off=brand of woodpecker?
And ~~the~~ flowers: columbine, tiger lily, shooting star. Young
brown trout swifter than snakes capital sigma in the water from
bank to bank of the tiny rivulet

$$\Sigma$$

Imagine the first part all written out in French:
        Do I have to choose again? Well, I
        choose the beauty and frightful horrors of
        this world

              ✿

        endless joke

              ✿

In English, now:
        Puke, unlimited
        Quantities

              ✿

        PUKE

              ✿

several cubic yards of indigestible notions
remnants, thread, ric-rac, hooks and eyes,
buttons, frogs and zippers

              ✿

not digestible by this particular system
they are theoretically
        soluble

LETTER, TO MICHAEL MCCLURE, 11:III:63

Here I come to sit in the sun
Beside three young redwood trees

A number of bugs, a distant cat,
Some kind of wild geranium leaves all through the grass
Each plant has flowers of a different shape, color, smell
The use is general

Bees make tastier honey from clover than from oak and pine
I mean we like the taste, the bees
Didn't figure we'd find it, they made it for themselves
A secretion of bug saliva: delicious, costly, rare
They were planning to eat it all winter long

But the flowers quite often they made me sneeze and cry
There was no living with them
Strongly sweet grapeclusters of peaseblossom shapes
A bug name, locust

I got no intention fighting City Hall
Only the idea of it
And your depending on its rectitude, its strength
        (it is your father, your mother?)
To lean upon, a church that confirms your belief in it
To ratify your own existence . . .

2.

In addition to the weight of my own displeasure
        (I censure myself by the hour)
Here you are, belittling, putting me down

There's no forgiving or forgetting, no absolution, no resurrection
You'll have me eternally wicked
As you're eternally good, totally righteous, predestined
              to salvation

Do I have time to hate you, to fight you and there's no prize
No crowns and harps, no eternal glory, gold,
Final perfect tyranny?

If I believe all this, I'm truly gone
Totally in blackness, death and hell

✹

How much will I pay for Life Eternal?

✹

Will you get the money?

✹

If it costs too much, I may steal it

✹

If it costs too much it may be fake and I can ignore it

✹

If it costs too much I may have to build my own
              elsewhere
   (although you'd immediately announce
   that it didn't really exist)
              where's the point, I've lost
myself again . . .
          suppose you despise me:
          Have your loathing and welcome
          Have it and see what it is
          Have it until it is knowledge, heaven, enlightenment
          Don't have it under any lesser terms
          In which case it would become an impediment
          To drag you down forever

3.

Your trying to tell me I'm dead why don't I lie down
Is all very well but not necessarily
                    true

And what if all those psychological authorities are
                    right

                         ?
                in a world like this
                         ?

                        ✸

I heard a man put it plain and nasty:
        "I'm practising bending over further and further every
        day so that when I see that flash I'll be able to lean
        over and kiss my ass goodbye."

                        ✸

Let it go if it won't holler
Or hold on and squeeze
                    while it writhes and heaves

                        ✸

Make a new profession, they told him
Have you thought of becoming a symphony conductor
Like Leopold Stokowski, marry Greta Garbo
Never write again
                never again
Go away to live in Ohio
Join the Rosicrucians
                    as for me,
                    I'm constitutionally unable to enjoy
                    the taste of Bourbon whiskey
Or there actually is a conspiracy,
A war against us

Why shut up when that's exactly what the Adversary wants
Will even pay you money to dump your paints, typewriter &c
                    down the toilet, give up

                    never again

The number (and intelligence!) of those
Who want to stop us, who wish that we'd keep

                    SILENCE

                HOLY S I L E N C E

their fear
their existence in a state of continuous rage
who don't listen to any of this
Who don't know what it means
Who can't control it, who know that it will outlive them
Certainly   (finally)

                          ✸

Alternatively, I suppose that you figure
Sell guns to both sides and hope they wipe each other out

No doubt this is the reason so many work in secret
One stores his canvases in a bank vault, nobody sees them
              few people know that he's a painter
Another stays away ten years at a time, "underground," he says

                          ✸

So impossible
The odds against it
Too high and yet
We must feel free to do with it
Whatever we can, for laughs
                    or for serious,
As the blue-painted wickerwork chair stands
          in the muddy driveway

What will
And what won't go

11:iii:63
23:vii:63

FOR BROTHER ANTONINUS

Do these leaves know as much as I? They must
Know that and more—or less. We
See each other through the glass. We bless each other
Desk and tree, a fallen world of holiness.

Blessed Francis taught the birds
All the animals understood. Who will
Pray for us who are less than stone or wood?

28:iii:63

NIGHT AND MORNING MICHAELANGELO

Black thick dewy leaves, inchoate and opaque
Sun crystalizes them, an apparition of Green Jade
      varying transparency, all
           translucent greens

2.

But now, after sleeping all night, part
      of the morning and pleasant afternoon nap
I go look at the world and it is
      flat.
        the beautiful things are beautiful
the ugly things are ugly
      I
have been wasting my time.

1:iv:63
revised 14:xii:65

HOW BEAUTIFUL

A hummy-bird attacks the redwood trees
      C L O U D S !   look
How dark it is, it will rain it is so dark
Something must happen
Earthquake, volcanic manifestations

Easter lilies, unborn callas

A testimonial dinner

New fuchsias!

I

R E F U S E

to be taken in

kindly stop the car
Are you really sick
kindly stop the car
You're just kidding
Do you want me to vomit down the back of your neck?
What's wrong?
"The heart has its reasons that reason knows not of."

11:iv:63

PW HIS RECANTATION

O deodar tree
I haven't learned how to live

Both of us far from the mountains
I have not adjusted, not adapted

No one must blame you

1:v:63

7:V:63
PHILIP
WHALEN

Off · · · ·

over
that way

SOMEPLACE, Neb.
Pop. 17,

counting the hogs and chickens

"Watch us grow."

{ "Look Pleasant! Your friends
inside of the giant camera are
seeing you." }

THREE MORNINGS

1.

Fog dark morning I wait here
Half awake, shall I go back to bed
Somebody next door whistles the *St. Anthony Chorale*
I think of Brahms, a breakfast of chocolate whipcream
                    sweet bright pastry
          bits of sugar-blossom in his beard

2.

I wait for breakfast to drop from the sky
foghorns,   cluster of churchbells
                        pale sun butter
                traffic airplane marmalade
salt & pepper avocado branch squeak on window
                I drink last night's cold tea

3.

Clear bluey-yellow sky—a morning here—
grey cloudbank with lights of Oakland underneath
Baywater blacky blue b o a t l i g h t s
Robin: clink clink clink clank clink
          (6 *Adhyoya, Brihadaranyaka Upanishad.*)

                              8:v:63
                              15:vii:63

295

WORLD OUT OF CONTROL

Without my authorization, completely outside my plans
For the shape and color and temperature of the day
Water falls carelessly, insolently, big drops of it
Down into the avocado leaves
Not enough to call it rain or bad weather

    S P L A T T E R   d r i b b l e   stops

Now moving uncalled-for blares of light which can't last
Of no use to me, to us, bray like brassy horns and trumpets
Fall dark indecision again

Where's the icecream. I want a change
For the better, a reward for the worse
Where's the feet will carry me off
Where's the way to the icecream store
The birds chirp among green plums
Antique airplane four propellors flap my window panes
Where's the summer weather
Why don't I make better?
Bird   rain   fluff   cloud   I
Wish for music also.

10:v:63

LIFE AND DEATH AND A LETTER TO MY MOTHER
BEYOND THEM BOTH

O Muse, get me high out of my mind
open my head I want   MORT
COLORS   AUX
music and   VACHES
blast!
YES.

an attack of middle age and sobriety
break out of this, recover
soon as

Right now.   plush.
outbreak of stupid
a conspiracy

SILENCE   I ought to be quiet while I'm
having myself totally chopped?

It moves from right to left.

on Saturday only!
a condition I refuse to accept
a performance I cannot condone

some sort of complicated
operating but very
dilapidated lashup

OUTSIDE?
                         PLUSH.
?
                         PLUSH
PLUSH.   INSIDE?

why don't you watch where you're
going instead of tripping over your
own feet clumsy booby.

plush.   INSIDE?   there.

ain't any feet in here. How
can I instruct them if I can't
communicate with them, if I
am so far away that they do not
(for all practical purposes) enjoy an independent
existence

a challenge of bright light
    obstinate silence
                  I no longer answer the telephone.
Big dipper straight outside the front door.

✿

bilge. the wind bothers among the avocado leaves
      pester the glass writing scratching twig WINDOW
           also rattles for airplanes
                blah.   blurt.

✿

I wish I could remember the song which begins,
    "If I had a talking picture of you."

✿

I shall revise it completely. I shall render everything into
language of a blinding clarity. It will be so charming and
persuasive to every reader that the entire civilized world
will say, "Surely Jonathan Swift has come again!"

✿

. . . passion, it must create whatever new
and exciting. Permanently. Forever young, completely mine,
but it will seem entirely and exclusively yours. It must
possess a molecular structure similar to heroin. I want the
stuff to be absolutely addicting after the customer has had
a single sniff.

✿

?   fakery   ?

?

✿

IMAGINE MY CONSTERNATION
Horror & Chagrin. . . !

   blooie. (this means, that there was a break
         somewhere on the inside, such as one of the
         coolant tubes in a reactor power plant, the
         filament in a vacuum tube or electric lamp,
         or somebody's (for example) gall bladder,
         kidney, spleen, etc.)
I WAS JUST ABOUT
           . . . actually a spleen in the

MORTIFIED TO DEATH
      moment of its final despair & goodbye
      says something more on the order of
      B L O O R G L E . . . .

BLESS YOUR HEART, HONEY!

   ". . . one of these days I'm going to sort through all
that stuff and throw nine-tenths of it all away. I don't know what
I keep it for; no good to anybody, a lot of junk and old keepsakes
that don't mean anything to anybody any more, but a person does
kind of hate to throw things like T H I S away . . . ,"

✿

299

"Bid self-righteousness be still
Wound the callous breast."

"CAME TO GRIEF
about it, just over an old diningroom
table. There's trouble enough in this
world without fighting among ourselves.
We must try to live harmoniously."

"When the day
Grows dark & cold
Tear or triumph
harm. . . ."

"LEAD THY LAMBKINS TO THE FOLD
TAKE THEM IN THINE ARMS!"

✻

14 May 1963   San Francisco

Dear Mama,

Twenty or thirty years too late here I am writing this letter to
you, graveyard or no graveyard, no matter whether we aban-
doned each other in death, that part's all over with. I know that
you are well because a part of your attention is occupied with
writing this. No need to wonder how or where or whether you
are.

I try to be patient and forgiving and understanding but I'm a
flop at it. You told me that there are worthwhile people every-
where, in every walk of life, people I can respect, people I must
love. I don't know how to explain to you exactly, but I'm afraid it's
a matter of my being too selfish and small minded and preoccu-
pied with my own tiny life—I can scarcely see them, and of
course I don't really, most of the time, WANT to see them, I have
got myself that far under . . . it's I who need out of the Salem
graveyard, not you who were never there anyhow.

I don't think it matters what we name it, you make it on the
ideas of God, peace, quiet, organ music and Mrs. Eddy's repre-
sentations of the character and philosophy of Jesus. It saved you
dozens of times hand-running, whether you needed it or not. I

don't mean any disrespect, but it seems unnecessarily compli-
cated to me—that system, those names—it worked for you or you
worked it—like Yeats and his bent gyres and cones and pulleys
and belts and geary numbers—and arrived, like him, beyond this
fake life and spooky death. I get the general idea, I have a differ-
ent set of names, I know it isn't really a problem, that I'm not re-
ally beset, either with sin or salvation, goldfish or onion-rolls. But
for the past couple of weeks the whole business has been coming
up cardboard, fake Easter nests of shredded green wax-paper.

There was this man at the Zoo yesterday, combing through the
camel wool with both hands, two ladies kept hold of a rope
around the camel's neck and tickled it under the chin while the
man hooked the fingers of both hands into the (I presume) shed-
ding wool on the camel's side below the humps and pulled great
sheets of wool away, like peeling a sunburn—I expected, judging
from how hard the man yanked and tore at the wool, that the
camel would scream or at least spit on everybody in sight. In-
stead, it stood there, looking only mildly annoyed, while the man
took its fur and shoved it in a gunny-sack. The man wore a neat
grey felt hat, an expensive-looking suit and shoes, a white shirt,
necktie, and, if I remember right, a vest. The ladies were very
fashionably dressed.

Confronted with prodigies of this kind—or, as I recall, on the
day you found me blowing bubbles of molten glass—you'd say,
"God is love!" Also if my sister fell down the stairs or if you hap-
pened to see an automobile accident, it was the thing to say. I
guess it doesn't matter so much what it all means, the thing is
more like how do I treat other people, how do I use myself?

This is all so abstract and dim. You were able to make it iron all
our clothing, cook our meals, provide us with total security and
love. I must be a mouldy old ghost . . . but that isn't interesting,
either, I know better.

I forget how or where this began—I wanted to talk to you, I
wanted to speak with you, sensible as you are, and how dear, and
properly remote, I'm not that confused, in time and distance, and
I believe still forgiving after all, and still believing that you know

and feel, I hope you can laugh also, because it's a delight to you, as well as gentle music, Boston voices, quiet lights—joy and freedom where you live.

So here we are—I didn't want to take a walk or read somebody else's book. I've waited most of the day for these words to arrive at last. Now I can let it go—this paper, this pen, the bad light, the nasturtiums curling their stems in my table jar, the tea is cold.

All my love,

P.

14:v:63

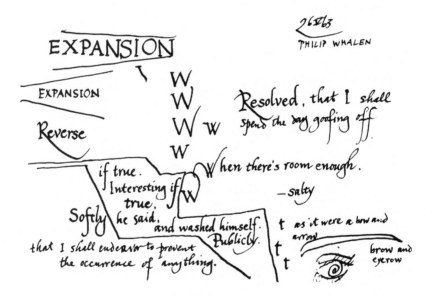

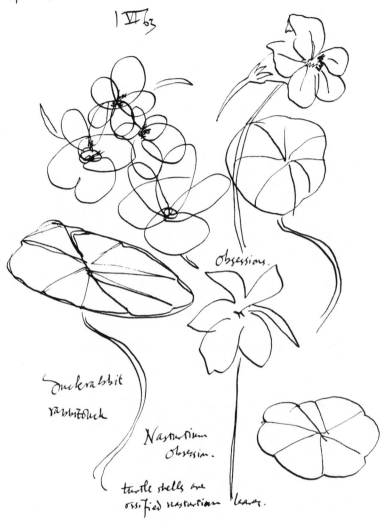

1 VI 63

Obsessions.

Duckrabbit
rabbitduck

Nasturtium
Obsession.

turtle shells are
ossified nasturtium leaves.

PLUMS, METAPHYSICS, AN INVESTIGATION,
A VISIT, AND A SHORT FUNERAL ODE

IN MEMORY OF
WILLIAM CARLOS WILLIAMS

O Muse!
I don't dare summon you
All I ask is that I might come to you
Only to see you, only to look
      at your face
If you're too mad or too busy for a talk
      I'll go home soon.

       ✻

Smog this morning
Hot soupy sun
The mailman brought all the wrong letters
The air stinks, the birds are in somebody else's yard
Boys left a yellow broom in the plum tree
      (the plums are still green, however fat)
I hear the Scavengers' Protective Association complaining
      about the garbage cans, I

      worry about the fragility of my verses
      their failure to sound fresh and new

By God, here's the garbage men stealing green plums!

       ✻

Neighborhood boys must go after them
Free food! How can a tree
      (who is an individual)
Belong to a man? It can't

be stealing
The tree has manufactured these not quite yet
       sweet sticky plums

       my mouth is full of plastic teeth
       most adults are smokers—we
       have no idea about the taste of plums
          except perhaps a memory
            climbing a tree

St. Augustine had the shame of it all his life
          he says
I think of him, seeing these kids up the tree
       their silly yellow broom too short
       the tree's old and brittle, unsafe to climb

The pears (in his case) being hard as well as
       green, to say nothing of the sin
       which he never worked out
       a soulful bellyache his whole epis-
          copal saintly eternity
       (no death, no dying for him, alas)

The pears of Africa pursue him past the heavenly gates

                ✿

I can still hear something rattling in my head
Perhaps only the little rocks that keep it pointed
Towards the sky—otoliths, ear-stones

                ✿

which is (now) the wind, although I see fog
       and smoke linger over the Bay
          3 loader cranes on a ship
            gantries in the fog
       flashcar freeway ramp more stinking smoke

Which was my ears rattling an approaching poet,
Ronald Loewinsohn with news from out of town
                considering the study of English
                        a long trip to the Northwest with his wife and son
                                for August

I envy them, I've been thinking of going "home," I still
Think of it although it has nothing to do with me
Wants nothing from me—
To Oregon, all this spring

Hard as it is—I'm hungry, in debt, I own one penny
                        copper money USA
I am still alive, I dance alone in this borrowed room
                I sing to myself
                        "Green plums, you won't be ready for weeks
                        But I'm fat and purple, full of sweet delight,
                        Hidden among bright gold leaves,

                . . . .

It is her wish that I be so

---

                a wasp bounces up and down one of the
                closed windows—two other windows are
                open, he must
                        take care of himself, I say—
                but I worry for him just the same

Goofy june-bug forgotten poet morning stomp.

and the plums, the voices—the presence of Loewinsohn—
all these brought you in, Williams, quite naturally
making my head rattle, your gentle spirit—goofier
                than you've shown yourself to us in the past
                        really goofier than I ever gave you credit for being

I mean the insane poetickal rage that you tried
to channel, to subdue
                    (notions I hate—rather the fury
                    and the madness, than the bland
                    "control" of Messrs. X, Y, & Z who must
                    ((of course)) believe they're also
                    "in control" of

          L I T E R A T U R E
          AMERICAN
                         LITERATURE!)

they never really let you into that, in spite of
your book that all professors love, *In the American Grain*
that fills my shoes with sorrow and gets between my teeth

                    I want to be a world, not just another
                    American tinky poetty-boo

                              I am a universe
                    etc.

well anyway

I never knew you well enough to call you "Bill"
And you were either my father or not
And I did say a couple days ago that I sometimes
Think of you as a little no-talent middle-class croaker

You did know the madness of love and sorrow
Why should I have wished on you—oh, the crash of cymbals
Rending of live flesh, glare of torches
Total battiness—frenzy—typewriter out the window
                    into Cowley's plum tree "How explain about
                    the broke window and chair to the cranky
                    landlady Hart Crane go away you are too much
                    and we don't really believe you write so good
                    as all that"

Your head fell apart gently, piece-meal
          a slowly oozy ripening cheese

WREATH OF SONG

(*Liederkranz,*   an American invention)

It was painful to watch—even eight years ago when I last saw you
not quite articulate, and your hands terribly crimped, yet
delivering yourself, your love,
                    to us

          (I got the window open just this minute
          & prodded the wasp out into the wind)

and you said yes you remembered me

Now I remember you, naturally, Dead or Alive, as the notices
                    used to say
And you are wanted—not necessarily New Jersey USA
Here with us wherever plums and poets talk together.

                                        17:vi:63

308

The San Francisco Symphony Orchestra,
with POWER CYMBALS

POT!

Osmiroid 75
ush!
ENGLAND

PEN!   NEUTRINO ? TH! zzz

— delete this

hehh!

ng! ngang!   I dont think it's going to work
out. The line's busy. It soun-
glug glug SUCK   ded like a schoool=teacher. {Le
!   troisième sexe }
                    ? OUT ?
                    ? OF ?
please attend. please concen= WHAT
trate on the position and   ?

location of the pen's nib

CHOOKY=
BABE!

DESPERATE SPANISH=SPEAKING TEEN=
AGE HOODLUM RATPACK CHILDREN with
HAIR OIL & BEAUTIFUL SEXY
names of Conquistadores CHOOKY!

PHILIP WHALEN

22VI65

309

{ "Chooky" might mean "pachuco" or
    perhaps "Francisco" }

ARGUELLO   GUERRERO
BALBOA   HONCHO
CABRILLO   IGLESIAS
DE ANZA   JUAREZ
ESCOBAR   LOPEZ
FIGUEROA MADRLAGA
        NOE
        ORDOÑEZ
        PICO
        QUINTARA
        RODRIGUEZ
        SANTA ANA
        TORRES
        ULLOA
        Vacca   Ybarra   Zulloaga
Paco = "Francisco"
                        LL IX 63

310

27.IV.63 ONE PAGE POEM

HOPELESS FUCKUP BEATNIK COCKSUCK MOTHERFUCKER
NOGOOD BASTARD EAT SHIT RUN RABBITS
AND BARK AT THE MOON

The idea of freedom

the feeling of freedom

thinking freely

acting freely

Hardboiled egg suspended in a magnetic field—
production of morbid secretions in the
prefrontal & maxillary sinuses, 11:25
A.M., latitude 24° [of San Francisco]

SONG
SPARROW
AND LINNETS

the idea of freedom
thinking free
the feeling of freedom
acting free

...DELINQUENT BY MEANS
OF BEIN BUGGERED, I.E.
FUCKED UP THE ASS W-
TIL SLEEP IN BETWEEN
BETWIXT THEM & THEIR UN-
HOLY PLEASURES...

A prism . a pyramid . a glass

monument to the memory of Dr. Reik

{ °oh. THERE's where it is !
.... the doors ! .... °}

glass pyramid, the words that bend our vision of delight

OBOE D'AMORE . a singing reed, a near relative (in
time) to Blaise Pascal ... NOUVEAU PETIT
LAROUSSE ILLUSTRÉ shows what we used
to call "cat tails", a marsh plant with a
brown velvety — what— seeding head - fruit pod
... ladies gilded them, stood them in Satsuma
pots, corner of the hall. top of the piano,
~~draped~~ aesthetically arranged behind the
hand colored photograph of Grandma ~~Hastings~~
Hastings ? Cousin Gladys & cousin Karl ?

The weather having been
as good as it ever might be
has changed. Fog... those
high clouds... the effect
is one of calm and quiet,
after the full rowdy orchestra
of color and light produced
by sunshine.

Absolute relatives, as
in contradiction to the
space & time Continuum, its
absolute pervase immortality
& transience

Paschal , a pope; Urban —
Urban Polchuk's Union Oil, a gas station friend of my father

311

FRIDAY ALREADY HALF-

way shot in the ass, nearly
                    noontime lunch
          Can you remember the things you're supposed
                    to remember:
                         your past lives, the thoughts of others
               and the unthinkable?

✲

do you remember, quite naturally, the unpainted wooden attic,
the casement windows open on the green hillside becoming
                                             luminous
world wherein all magic adventures naturally happen, tall gold
crowned women in white and green their jewels emitting gleams
brighter than the day, their long pale hair, their untroubled
eyes . . .

✲

the thoughts of others at this point are too numerous
and too beautiful to record, for example Blake's
     "AND EVERY NATURAL EFFECT HAS A SPIRITUAL
                                   CAUSE"
                         —"Milton" I, §28

✲

The unthinkable is not a blank, not a non-entity
not to be dismissed as imaginary, not death, not sleep

✲

small branches, heavy with plums, wag in the wind
As long as they wave they don't break

✲

312

Perhaps you'd prefer to make some other arrangements . . .
You might find it more convenient if . . .
Although we've been informed that your situation in recent
months has not been without difficulties, we sin-
cerely regret that we must inform you . . .

> go away
> go away now, *i.e.* as soon as
> you possibly can
> go away—preferably
> immediately

✲

Please concentrate, please devote all your attention, all your
energy, all your admittedly great talents and abilities to the
problem at hand, namely your immediate removal from this place
with all your goods, chattels and personal property.

✲

Please try to remember that you are broke—that you have no
money, that you have no real expectation of having any on whatever
date in the future—and that you owe a great quantity of cash to
a great many people.

✲

Think, at least, about how you might be working in order to
realize your own projects, if you are incapable of going away,
or of making any money. WORK   WORK   WORK
            WORK   WORK

✲

> flowers, very tall this summer
> canterbury bells, foxgloves, gladiolas
> yesterday a huge peony blossoming beside
> HOWARD PRESBYTERIAN CHURCH
> —Is Here To Serve You—
>   am I developing astigmatism?

I didn't think of you, my dear
Until just now—
You haven't chosen to appear, lately
And now I know why I've been turned off and cranky
Three days in a row

28:vi:63

TENNIS SHOES

So quiet
pussy foot, do not
upset the nerves
they live in a bath of aspirin, coffee and a proprietary
drug that slows

          or shuts the gap from one front of
          synapses to the possible next

Uniform response patterns
gentle sinusoidal waves on his EEG
as in sleep

So gently
the gym shoes with the proprietary name
arch-supported ventilated, add
years to your life

Tillman used to call them "American Plimsolls"
And walked all over the Hindu Kush, the
Pamir Plateau and much of the Himalaya
Silly enough, being English, but also
Marvelously coo-coo, enough to serve
As an example to the young, *viz.*

stay away from the city
walk in the mountains
hobnob with hill men
loiter with the lamas of the unworldly kind
        (remember *Kim*)
eat apricots, drink *chang* and hot
yak-buttered Mongol tea

Politely demand (and get) the assistance
—food, shoes & medicine—from whatsoever
                        government
is furthest off why set around waiting for the bill
at the local movie to change?

In town we can afford no better, the police inquire
What are you, practising to be a cat-burglar? Peepy Tom?
We say we have heart trouble, the doctor prescribed them
to sweat our feet, promote circulation among the pedal extremities

We hope our quietness would help us escape notice
Next time we'll also wear hat and necktie
Button your fly, the policeman says, walking away, picking his nose.

28:vi:63

EPIGRAM

That boy he star-
        ted to be
        a poet but
he stuttered.

1:vii:63

315

TO THE MUSE

You're late today,
        minaudering among the summer fields
        plunk that little Made-in-Austria Irish harp
        roll your blue eyes and twiddle your pale braids

                (reminiscence of Lillian Gish, Evelyn Thaw, ladies
                you never heard of, immortal fair)

But here you are, yawning
Bored with me. I don't believe you're thinking
                of anything
Yet your fingers are grubby . . .
                cigarets, pills . . .
You sing in a high voice
                                a few lines
        indistinctly, not caring, not even amusing yourself

"I wonder," she says . . . "Oh,
                                never mind."
Smiles at my confusion,
                        my hopeful sudden looking up

                        ✸

Leaf and branch twist and wave in the breeze
This pen swings over the page, an equal
Meaning, neither one intelligible

                        ✸

Little black dots
These represent bees
Among the leaves and flowers

                        ✸

I look at the window frame
I learn
this

I've deceived myself

✿

Here you are now,
Quite unexpectedly, like the death of Proust
    fford says the taxi driver told him
        "bien inattendu"

Walk up and down the room
Pick things up and put them back wrong

I've got no letters
Nobody called up, I can see you want me
To entertain you with pretty speeches

Like the King said,
"Scribble, scribble, scribble, eh, Mr. Gibbon?"

As long as you were coming around here anyway
You might have brought a fairly big basket full of chow

But then you couldn't have carried it yourself
The taxi man might bring it

    "If you can't say something nice

        ✿

    "Shut your mouth."

8–20:vii:63

WHERE WAS I

New desk, old chair
I look at them, hopelessly
Where's the man who writes
            there?

26:vii:63

OH YES. VANCOUVER.

Two ladies
Her friends and us
A corruption of sensibilities

viii:63

VANCOUVER

A secondrate star
An experience of a lower order of magnitude
Catalogued or not in that International Register

✻

Coming into an Arab story
A vegetable design

✻

Think of the taste and smell of lilac leaves
Pleasure delight & joy, certainly no authority involved.
Lilacs. A space between the house and the lilacs
Which disturbs the projection of shadows on that wall.

The authorities outside—are they anthropologists?
Shadows on us,
Where we stood. Hidden.
We exposed ourselves to each other with explanations.

viii:63

GOLDEN GATE PARK

A row of blossoming flowers a row of people
2 lines of people several hundred yards apart
    moving in the same direction.

The space between the individuals in each of the lines is interesting.
The speed of the walkers in each line seems to be the same.

25:viii:63

THAT DREAM

There is the light
            There is the darkness there
        is the terror of shifting proportions
Lattice of timbers
                    network of toothpicks
Change of relation, the motion
            directionless
                falling

S C R E A M

blanket/snare   sweat/sheets   mattress/clutch

O U T

---

the darkness and space beneath
unknown dimensions
unlimited size

7:ix:63

MYSTERIES OF 1961

Lazy tongs
Jacobs ladder
magnetized flywheel
gyroscope
folding mesh ring basket
✺
Mr. KNIBX, a sinister
✺
"A is for jelly,
B is for Jell-O"
✺
"You are the how
they call panic"

[14:ix:63]

BREUGHEL: "THE FALL OF ICARUS" 20:IX:63

Beyond what figure will you refuse to go?
        Beyond that one which stands
                unseen
            behind the grille

Let us proceed in some other direction, sixteen
                pages, to learn
It is the wrong direction

Lost   down

            air   sand   glass
                    breeze

Strayed & stolen away away
                Where's the edge
                Where are the *neiges d'antan*

        you bet.

26: IX: 63

My karma has to do with ears
  words, music, speech, air vibrating
    The loudspeaker is my brother

    X

as of this moment "sounds of revelry by
                                      night"

a large & musical party upstairs
when I'd like to be sleeping

U=NA PASSION ME !
DO=MI=NA !

PHILIP WHALEN

27 IX:63

*

Octopus attached to wall of tank, body/head
sags down, a scrotum wandering loose, a
living skin jock strap guaranteed to fit, all the
arm/string/leg/straps adjustable perfection.

or a brain?

yummy & noble beast!
human eyes
rage & panic & speed

*

3 of them
is 3 too many

PHILIP
WHALEN

Meat I ate   M E A T   I ate meat
    "I want to have a banquet, a real banquet, I'd rather spend
    the money on a white tablecloth and great conversation than
    fancy food, some roast chickens and white bread but what I
    really want is a white tablecloth, a spiritual banquet . . ."
        that was Michael on the telephone

27:ix:63

SOCIAL GRACES

How the hell are you?

             ✲

Cuckoo. I wouldn't have it
        any other way.

             ✲

        I imagine,
That everyone takes me seriously at the wrong moments.
It is their privilege.

             ✲

    "Go on and dance with the guy what brung ya!"

28:ix:63

MYSTERY POEM,

for a birthday present

I am ragged edge of
Nothing
Uncomfortable lumping along
            (no fun)
Out on the dark
        rough and rocky side

        asteroids
little dark stars
between the orbits of Mars and Jupiter

Which way is straight up or out?

                Leads into
the Milky Way, lots of room inside

        Lady of Heaven
        her milk for all of us
                who are the raggedy edge of everything

The center,
Her love forever
All of us remembered.

2:x:63

THE FOURTH OF OCTOBER, 1963

A cold hand among the clouds.

SONG

That little man
Is a bad little man
That one is a loser

He keeps on blowing
All that low low-grade hay
He's a pusher as well as a user.

4:x:63

ILLNESS

Hello what's happening?

☼

I'm home alone I've got the horrors

☼

Shall I telephone someone and demand that they come
take care of me?

☼

I am thirsty, I'm suffering
a vitamin deficiency, mental or neural rickets,
flea-bites, Bradleigh's angina, scrofula
King Charles's Wain

☼

Yearning for the Happy Despatch, the
Long Goodbye, pull the switch

☼

Why don't you come over, we'll take care of you

☼

I'm afraid to leave

5:x:63

7:x:63

For John Lee Hooker

you better stay away from that door

h um.

oh yes. /....hum.....

you better not open that door you better

hum ——— hum..

that's where I keep the revolution,

hum

freedom now // o yes lord god freedom

waugh!

freedom

PHILIP WHALEN

328

7:X 63

The shape of it
accomodates to my hand,
        cock
        mouth

slurp   open   goup   all glurp slide

        farther
            shine

            STAR

        BROAD ARROW IMPERIAL SEAL

                    PHILIP
                    WHALEN

329

a Monday when it took all the money I had,
except 2¢, to wash my clothes. I must rob somebody to get food
for supper,

GROSS   NATIONAL   PRODUCT
$580 BILLIONS
the war in Viet Nam cost $ 2 M I L L I O N S today
I must steal this room where I drink my tea and
indulge in self-pity, gross natural projection of a feckless history

I digress, there are not enough
things
in this poem, he says, no flowers, no
tears, no kisses or come
I have to steal those? I ask.

7:x:63

GRADUS AD PARNASSUM

Palmetto tree, its shadow on the house corner
And the light upon them:
A single proposition.
(Where was the sky?)

8:x:63

INSIDE STUFF

Swede-bread honey and tea to breakfast half a cantaloupe
Honey inspires prophecy & beneficent wishes, thus:
      Boundless ancient delight for Frank O'Hara
      Kerouac will get the Pulitzer Prize *Visions of Gerard*
      I shall travel to my death in a far country

        Frank has Hart Crane's eyes.

15:x:63

ROXIE POWELL

    Impotent rhapsody
    Forty pages of Hiahleah
        you know Alan Russo.

22:x:63

NATIVE SPEECH

    "Red-ass," they used to say
    Meaning "home-sick"—
    Really wanting to be
        AWAY
      from this place, the Army, the war,
    Old enough to guess home's gone
           if you went there.

3:xi:63

3 November 1963

aches   and pains
    begin   a new
        season of collapse

& frustration & pomegranates

pomegranates! red woody blood sugar crown!

at the hem of my gown at the top of the LAW SCROLL
    Curtain bells
        network of sticky red
            sweet
                incorruptible

[This handwritten version was first published in *Tri-Quarterly* as "The Season" in 1965 (see page 395).]

333

Treasures "of", eyes, but "in"? heaven? I
think not — just what use or interest could such things
possess in that place, that state? O snail!
your beauty is a heavenly pleasure!

334

Lilly-pilly

Lilly-pilly

Lillie   5 November 1963

Lily "Let Lily Lucy, &c."

Lemons { leaves
{ flowers
{ yellow fruit
Perfume!

{ lovely
{ lovely
{ lovely

TREASURES·OF HEAVEN

spring will soon be on its way
to the River of January

Darwin, Erasmus Darwin,
vegetable passions caught your heart

keep the blight, the rust, scale
canker spit bug moth &
rot far away from the lemon tree

yet I'll have snails, too
shell asshole sunrise!

ST. FRANCIS LOBBIES ALLEN G.

unsuspected hairpins & inside Gaffney receptions
Who lost the 7-year itch?

"Mr. Harry Lane!"
"Mr. Harry Lane!" is
a passenger ST.
FRANCIS PRAY FOR
THE PENGUINS
TEACH US
KARMEL KORN
ELECTRIC DRILL
DRAFTY DOOR

F U R   F U R   F U R
Jewels
(fake)
Where's the Russia Philology?
scrolls and fur

12:xi:63

TO A NERVOUS MAN

One day they'll come whooping after you
False hair and gold eyelashes flapping in the wind
Glom and grope you with their dainty painted pinkies
Hale you away, clutched to their foam-rubber tits
To FAIRYLAND their prisoner forever!

15:xi:63

THE DOUBLE TAKE

I want leeway
I want room to move
November tree with scarlet flowers
Don't crowd me
Bluey-green distant hilltops a picture
I know it comes out of the water
Angel Island the foot of Steiner Street

Admit these pleasures
Ordinarily unseen, I accept them
          demand more

And I need space and time away from you
Demand more, higher quality
I can't stand to look at you,
Hear what you say, watch how you behave
Your insolence, your ignorance

I must have distance,
Isolation, silence,
A vacation from your monstrous beauty

My infinite lust for you.

17:xi:63

HOMAGE TO WBY

after you read all them books
all that history and philosophy and things
what do you know that you didn't know before?

Thin sheets of gold with bright enameling

23:xi:63

SALAMANDER

Behind my eyes (looking the opposite way)
I see roaring flames in back of the cracked iron furnace door
Fire jag flake speed

      (Olson asked me, "Who ever got the idea that you
                were in-
                      telligent?")
I feel myself burning in moony flames and sleep,
Burnt by lunar fires

23:xi:63

A RECALL

Color of the Sun
Color of the Moon
Color of the Dog

That was yesterday animal fire
Druids burning in wicker cages
To the Lady of All Wild Beasts

25:xi:63

NATIVE SPEECH

1.

It's all put away now. I don't want to drag it out again,
have to go to work and move all them things—you do it
some other time. I'll show you some other time, not now.

2.

I had it all smoothed over and then he has to come horning in,
Mr. Big has to go to work and get things all galmed up again,
raise a big stink just because he has to be in on everything.

3.

Well that's a fine how de do. Now I've got to take and hunt up
another one of them things to go on there! One of them little—
well, I certainly am put out!

14/19:x–xii:63

THE WALKERS' PATIO: GIANT PLANT

Silent an architecture
formal speech of green
flat concrete smooth and clean
the great plant grows out of it:
Music, proclamation, a building
What it does to the light, creating darkness
What light does to it, expanding
                heading out,

Leaving
Not in a hurry
wraps space around it in a particular way
a modulation, a harmonic progression

Leaving the ground, it may
grow past the roof or not
now the papyrus is gone

Its genes require this order
Sequence in space, dots of geometry
                where exist?

(A terrible mistake: "Dots & squiggles justify the air & space
                I occupy")

Geometry is the inside of my head
the plant has its own shape
working out (as I say)
Whatever outside maybe
Those giant leaves

7/8:xii:63

HOW WAS YOUR TRIP TO L.A.?

Here in the North, our houses and their appointments
are old-fashioned and a little inconvenient. There's no doubt
that our lives here are morally
superior to those of the Southern people.

In the South there are many cars
The plumbing works, the gas stoves are better
Food's cheaper and the sun is warm
Unfortunately the air in that place is poisoned.

Our city tends to disappear in cold weather.

12:xii:63

WHISTLER'S MOTHER

Mother and Ed are out in the car
Wait til I put on some clothes
Ed's in a hurry. He hasn't eaten since this morning
Wait til I put on some clothes.
Mother and Ed are out in the car. Do you have any clothes on yet?
    Let me come in.
Wait til I get some clothes on
Ed is impatient. He and mother are waiting. Can I come in?
Wait til I put on some clothes
Mother and Ed are out in the car
Wait til I get into some clothes
Can't I come in? Aren't you dressed yet?
Wait til I put on some clothes
Mother and Ed are out in the car. Can I come in?
Wait til I get on some clothes.

14:xii:63

341

there. How all have some. My word yes. All about chocolate.
You   A R E   standing on my foot.

——————— ☼ ———————

Elephants. Inside. Good heavens, yes. The quantity.
   Are you quite sure. Good grief. Good heavens yes. Here we are.
They're surely inside.
   All about have some, that's what it is. Distinctly a pleasure,
yes. One does see them there— A magnitude of somewhat huge
proportion—glued inside.
   Some have long legs indeed—so that their backs bulge against
the lid, most decidedly we are   /no/   certainly not frightened—
we would not alarm them, good heavens no. Ho ho.
   Please don't come any closer.
   Oh hello there you are.
   Curiously endeavour.
         internally.
         my goodness yes.

☼ ——————— ☼

strings all up the inside that was the deportment of it. My head.
mess.
                Sybil Gurton
                Lady Chiswick
                  Telfer
              anti snake
              antique snake.
                  the revelry—'rill/a/raw'
              sacred scared propane blue flame
slide up the inside walls they follow each other around flat and
curving towards the white hot light in the center/top. Good

heavens yes. What a spectacle, you never seen a show like it before, most ungodly sight, I assure you. Crumbs/crumpets/ to a fare ye well. Here they are. Didn't I tell you? Didn't I say? Consternations. Leaking all over everything behind the door/ the contents all loose and soggy saggy soaky. That's oil for you. Depend on it every time. Scornfully. The brutes. Mess. Allocution plague. You pretend not to understand Africa. Absurd.

Avocado plants spring up out of the umbrella pot. Exotic birds. Horrible feet. What do you expect after all. Don't be unreasonable.

My word yes. You don't say. On the inside behind the door/ that was the definition of/

Bottled up. Buckled down. Quite so. Slide 8 cap 2 there you are slick as a whistle quick as a wink dropsy daisy.

       animal bundle, a ghastly error but not a mistake. Burdensome, yes. Inevitably so.
   After all I told you about Micronesia.
   There they blandly go.
   Messages of the hot fog star.

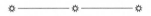

The Reverend Mr. Shebeare
He saw what he thought was a good thing. He wanted it. He contrived to get it. Some people can do that./ Why haven't I learned how?/ You only mean that you never use the word "contrive" in connection with any of your own thoughts or actions. Certainly not.

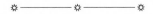

Leaded glass—the guiltily broken useless pretty fragments all saved and newly beautiful window.

Great living faces of terror, fury, eyes rolling—these are clips from Eisenstein—what I see is the cracked and crumbly plaster of the wall becoming invested with gnashing teeth no lips as yet the wall of cracker crumbs—HORROR—about to speak, about to walk forward all crumby to grab—the Horror is suffering vast anguish. It wants to lay it on me. I don't want to hear about it although I am sorry for the Monster . . .

"How shall you accomplish this task?"
"I don't have a system. Just you watch me. You just watch. You don't get in the way, now!"

16:xii:63

SOME KIND OF THEORY

". . . what I know and then go beyond that
far as I can," Duncan is supposed to say

I, however, know nothing, I must look for everything,
I come up with all the wrong things (pudding, tickets,
crystals, maguey) and many which are uselessly beautiful and
wise which is to say discrete, disparate planets of different color
and variously interesting orbits, the formulae for which, ex-
pressed in mathematical terms and bright sticky honey

bees have built their home in my orrery

23:xii:63

WINTER JELLY

Now great winter falls
New Year's full moon blur window fog

Words in books drop slowly over brainwheel paddles which stand
Clear white ice moon sparkle

28:xii:63

THEOPHANY

Pig-face gods nudge each other, snickering
Pretend they don't smell our incense
They haven't yet noticed that I've fitted each of them with
      pig heads, brains of Americans 15 years old today

29:xii:63

NATIVE // FOLK SPEECH

So he just got to where he was coming and going at all hours of the day or night without so much as a "by your leave." Finally I wouldn't put up with it, I just told him, if you think I'm going to have you treating my house like it was a hotel, you're sadly mistaken.

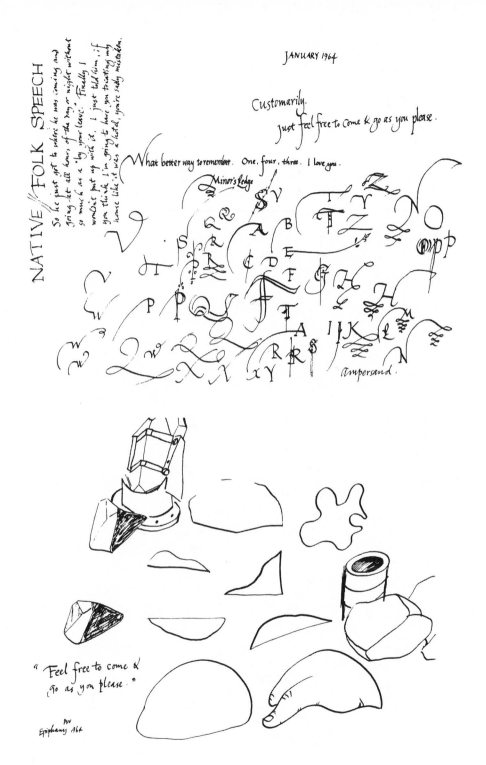

NATIVE FOLK SPEECH

So he just got to where he was coming and going at all hours of the day or night without so much as a "by your leave." Finally I wouldn't put up with it. I just told him, if you think I'm going to have you treating my house like it was a hotel, you're sadly mistaken.

Customarily.

Just feel free to come & go as you please.

What better way to remember. One, four, three. I love you.

Minor's Ledge

Ampersand.

" Feel free to come &
go as you please."

PW
Epiphany 1964

Part XLI

       Holy Cow

Part XLII

       I thought your girl friend
       was in there.

Part XLIII

       Will it spoil? It was all discolored. No no.
       Freezing darkens it. That's the fat. I keep it
       a whole week sometimes. I keep it in there to
       season it.

Part XLIV

       The Life and Times of
       Marc-Antoine Charpentier

Part XLV

       (This part is lost.
       (That fish ((*sc.*, letos-fish)) ate it—actually Part XIV?

Part XLVI

       Have you seen that white mug with the blue flowers
       painted on the side? I saw Jay drinking coffee out
       of it last night.

Part XLVII

       Have you seen those towels that used to be in here?
       They're in among this junk. Here they are (LEAVE
       THEM THERE!) on the floor. They were set on
       top of the pile of old newspapers. Why couldn't he
       look for them himself?

Part XLVIII

       There were only 13 parts in the first place,
       excepting that one the fish made away with.

Part XLIX

       I am not responsible.
       I decline the nomination.

Part L

       Better times are coming
       Bye and bye.

Part LI

Tulips, lilacs, irises and snapdragons live in a
May–basket. I made it for Miss Hillsdon.

Part LII

Some lemons.
"Dear Anthony West."
Some domes in the distance.
"Dear Mr. Tennyson."

Part LIII

culminates.
"If nominated, I shall not run. If I am elected
I shall not serve."

Part LIV

CANCELED

Part LV

Varicose veins.
Lumbago. Sciatica.

Part LVI

High.

Part LVII

H E I N Z

Part LVIII

Coughing.

Part LIX

CENSORED

Part LX

William Rowan Hamilton
He figured it was there and that it would all add up.
It took a century to do it.

Part LXI

Aggravation. As good as gold or platinum emeralds
and rubies and sapphires opal garnet and pearl.
What I'm afraid of is, I don't think it's going to
work and I don't know why. Hey you know what?
I've got rubber cement. Aggravation. Why don't
he hang himself?

13:i:64

349

A BOTANICAL PHRENZY

Terror and horror
Sharp straight green leaves
Rooted in my chest pass upwards
Through my throat and out
Through the top of my head

18:i:64

CLEAN SONG

Last night's guests arrive in the morning
Last night's guests
     arrive in the morning
Last night's guests arrive in the morning
        in the morning
"And Ile go to bed at noone."

18:i:64

THE GREAT BEYOND DENVER

The pattern for the trip.
I put crux ansatta in my mouth.
Ava Gardner lends me emeralds.
The pyramid slowly rises from the ground.
   O Rā Divine!
   O sand eternal!
At first daybreak the River Platte appears.

18:i:64

TECHNICALITIES FOR JACK SPICER

One is enough, she cried
But imagine thousands of them
       some with wings
         little naked boys riding on them
            pink silk ribands for bridle and reins
         a leash to guide them, blimply

✺

Angels, someone tells us, have no dongs
But where should you get your poems
Except angelic peckers thrust never so subtly slender
         into each ear
           Skull neon whipcream illumination
              ?

✺

He's more intelligent than any of his wives
Who teach him antique enchantment
Why is he a mystery to everyone but himself?
So near from hand to mouth

✺

One is enough, if it be of convenient length
Or one begins at an early age learning to curl up
         like a porcupine,

           "Serapis and Agathodaemon combined
            in a single figure adoring
            the Master of the universe"

✺

Three is required for that game of yours
One to throw the ball, one to catch
One who swings his bat between—chance
         which breaks the cycle

A farther number adds pretty variations
The path of the ball: 1, 2, 3, 4, 5 after it is hit
        (an acuminate circle)
     curls on itself again
Commences swinging back and forth
               Night and Day
The sun track
       EAST   SOUTH WEST   NORTH
          and the center

LINEUP, 6th DAY			
Lyon, Pitcher (center)	white	water	god heaven
Oliphant, Catcher (East)	blue	ether	animal world
Cheval, 3rd Base (South)	yellow	earth	human world
Peacock, 2nd Base (West)	red	fire	ghost world
Griffin, 1st Base (North)	green	air	god hell

       We very seldom see each other
       Standing on opposite sides of Mother
But fear not, these are only reflections
   of your own several organs grown
       autonomous

             ✻

He wants a world without mothers?
   which is to say, no energy
   no show, no wisdom
Only will-power, character, that very large phallus
       of Mexican granite, a tree stump overgrown
       mossy lichens
   as distinguished from that flying snake
      Kukul Can
      (traveling east to west)

Yellow is the color of thought
Human world light path

✿

from inside your own head! fragments of yourself
putting on campy costumes, devil masks
bagpipe sounds, instruments of torture, boiling lead
humiliating ice, a universe of poo-poo cushions
demonic yells—*viz.*

Nugatory purgatory
Dramaturgy right of clergy
Kerosene magazine   or   *"Don't bring Lulu —*
Thuribles in the clerestory   *I'm bringing her myself!"*

✿

perhaps rather less embarrassing
than to discover that you are someone else's
                    doppelgänger

✿

It has been given to me to say.
I can't leave you alone.
Those heavy thumbs of yours TILT the machine
You must pay again.

Take me away to your hell world:
I must have that salvation, too—
Burn away my fleshy dreams

Nine years from now
You will be known as Lump Skull Buddha!

6:vi:62
26:i:64

353

March 1964

more than welcome
    more than enough —
of all things !
    where's all this cold air
        come from ?

Scribble

Banderolle
{ Giovanni della Bande Nere }

What's your platform ?

        Ressurexion
        Renaissance
        Total Paradise
I put down programatical funk. { speaking, now,
    absolutely off the record — my business isn't
    really to put anything down — I want
    a new life } I say RISE AND
FLOURISH
            for all you're worth { it is all
                        you're worth ? }
    SHINE , Radiate ,
                Joy bliss and whoopee vibrations !
{ The night air ! }

{ The weather ! }

                    EXQUISITE
            what did you say the message was ?

354

CORINTHIAN COLUMNS

Let me get up, I have to look, to smell, to taste everything.

in out of	fall petal	dust	In,
in, out of the	blossom	hairs	Out of the
W E A T H E R	leaf	lint	rain
	twig		

Perish in the dust	dust
Become jewels	lint
of rare worth and	hairs
color	

dust is powdered rock, metal, flesh, bones, woods, fruits
—a pulverized universe

Water is even finer
        Gas.

22:iii:64

MEXICO

Baja California
        far away underneath where we are now

(*"O "Kiki" / O Miss Margaret Jarvis"*)

        the way things fit together
        a drill which makes a square hole

"DO ME NEXT!"

25:iii:64

CHAGRIN

Winter is gone—how I abused it!
Wasted an age, an elderly child

What's become of Christopher's painting?
Where is Mertis her coal-oil stove?

26:iii:64

COMPOSITION

I teeter I dangle I jingle
Fidget with my fingers ears and nose

Make little repairs—tape or glue
And the floor is filthy again

       putting on hats in front of a mirror
              down in front
              down in back
              slaunchways
                      mugging and posing, thinking of
      those beggars Buñuel shows in *Viridiana,*
      gesture of one finger, two eyes,
      the smallest imaginable shimmy
      creates a gigantic bacchanal

Iron straps won't hold it all together
It's already there, a piano—in tune with itself—
        a closed system:
Even if you play on it with feathers, rocks, rubber tubing,
        Dear John Cage

26:iii:64

THE LOTUS SUTRA, NATURALIZED

I got drunk your house
You put that diamond my shirt pocket
How am I supposed to know?
Laying there in drunk tank
            strange town don't nobody know
Get out of jail at last you say
"You already spend that diamond?"
How am I going to know?

                                                    27:iii:64

A MISTAKE

   . . . the last part is all laughing and singing

            - - - - - - - - -

e.g.,   "Why you walking that funny way like that?"
        "I got no belt—I'm trying to hold my pants up."
        "You G O T   no pants."

                                                    29:iii:64

EARLY SPRING

   The dog writes on the window
            with his nose

                                                    30:iii:64

THE MYSTERY

Who are they when
I don't see them?

I hear walking in the next house
What face?

Walking in the next room is Mother,
            same as usual, visible or not
            I trust her to remain herself

Who's next door?

—————————————————————————

Presumably them Chinamen know what's
            happening on their own scene

—————————————————————————

                                        30:iii:64

THE PROBLEM

    Hot tea for breakfast
    Hot tea is
            breakfast
    With sugar in it

            What's for lunch and
                    where
                    ?

                                        13:iv:64

358

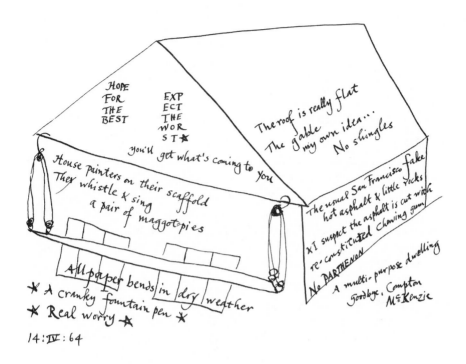

HOPE FOR THE BEST

EXPECT THE WORST ✷

you'll get what's coming to you

The roof is really flat
The gable my own idea...
No shingles

House painters on their scaffold
They whistle & sing
a pair of maggot-pies

the usual San Francisco fake
hot asphalt & little rocks
✗ I suspect the asphalt is cut with
re-constituted chewing gum
No PARTHENON

A multi-purpose dwelling
Goodbye, Compton
McKenzie

✷ All paper bends in dry weather
✷ A cranky fountain pen ✷
✷ Real worry ✷

14:Ⅳ:64

INVOCATION AND THEOPHANY

"Do you know at the offering of which libation the waters
become endowed with a human voice and rise and speak?"

—*Brihadaranyaka Upanishad*, translated by Max Muller

1.

following them
downwind, scraps of pages,
the sandpipers
white and black

chasing the watermark
wigglers where the sand's wet

go after,
spray left cheek and lens of eyeglasses
my head will ache later

clearly the mountain
Tamalpais, Bolinas Ridge walks up
out of the water into bright

blue air, black and hard-running as it is
full sunlight

grey willets
black and white when they fly

2.

grit in my eyes and teeth

I don't return to the trees until I've washed
in the ocean, invoked its help
I want its power in my writing hands
the absolute freedom of action
my own mystery and weight carrying
independent living beings with/ in/ is/
                    we
this

3.

wet monster poet
leads them across the wind
a continuous shove

I say
sing
the pen lighter than a blenny
Thetis, Tritons
Amphitrite, Poseidon
rulers of the third world

I sing, I say
I hear them whooping, their procession
white arms and blue-black hair

HOOOO EEEEE!

brandishing tridents, honking
those giant conch shells

I don't see fish tails—
White sleekness,
immortal solid whiteness
jade beings

naked, wilfull, dangerous,
they come toward me
Out of the sea
Ascending

     the air

which is now swift,
polished slick jewel path
existing only as long as white brilliant foot
descends upon it

Naked they
                    gorgeous
terrifying, sublimely calm
white faces the superb . . .

4.

they are that ocean
—projection mirage of mine?
I can invert the canvas, the camera—
They come on

I've called their names.
Gigantic!
                    don't see me, don't signify
But here they show themselves
Power vision gift
                    O SEA!

1:vii:63
14:iv:64

362

"I was sitting there.   I knew it was her.
I knew she had a message and the message was love."

17:iv:64

THE ODE TO MUSIC

FOR MORTON SUBOTNICK

Where'd all the music
                    go?
"There's a piano in there, but nobody here can play on it.
Old Clodfelter can sing better than he ever lets on."

❀

We wait
        for the fire from heaven
        for the maturation of our annuities
        for the new life, new earth
            (Who's going to pay for the roof?)

❀

"Georgette used to play just beautiful on her saxophone"
        "Waiting for the *Robert E. Lee*"

❀

"We got this radio, the cabinet is just gorgeous
I've always loved the way it looks, it's got
                    beautiful wood in it
We listen to *Amos & Andy* and *The Richfield
Reporter*
But I'm asleep by the time *Amos & Andy*'s half over

✸

I never could stand all that symphony music
All that high tone shrill screechy singing I just hate it
Some of it is beautiful, I guess, but oh God, when they get
Some woman with one of those high shrill sopranos . . .
I just never cared for it at all

✸

. . . but I love nice quiet organ music
it's so soothing and restful I could listen to it for hours
or a violin with it—love to go to sleep listening to it
an organ and a violin

✸

Dad and them get a big kick out of playing their fiddles
I never could read a note. Your own Dad has a beautiful voice
I never get tired of listening to him sing."

✸

"It's a pleasure if your own kids are doing it,
terribly expensive and you've got to keep after them to practice
—I'm so grateful to my mother, she made me
absolutely made me practice and I'm so thankful for that
today;
        I take such pleasure in my music."

✸

The length of a song, a short one by Stephen Foster
Or a hymn, that's all we got time for;
In the middle of a second or third verse,
A whispered conversation is likely to begin, something
We've just recollected (did the music remind us?)
To add to what we were saying
                              before the music began
". . . that old Mrs. R. turned around,
gave us a dirty look,
                    "SH*H*H*H !"
I don't know who that old cat thinks she is—
                    Mrs. Astor's plush horse?"

                              ✻

How—or why
              do I fizz and throb
I guess I understand
        Camptown Races, the *Archduke* Trio,
              The Pearl Fishers
(Even if I don't like the first or the last)
are matters of life and death

I congratulate myself
I know all about art and I know what I like
              (Q.: ". . . but you *are* queer, aren't you?"
              (A.: "Yes—
                    but I don't
                    like
                    you.")
What do I know or care about life and death
My concern is to arrange immediate BREAKTHROUGH
Into this heaven where we live
              as music

                              ✻

the fingers that hear it as it happens
as it is being made, Thelonious Monk
"has the music going on all the time," AG told me
"You hear it while he's at the piano,
you see him listening to it when he's out walking around
it's *going* all the time."

✻

The best music I make myself, with a piano, or borrow
                  a pipe organ
(People think the elephant bells beside my door
are purely decorative:
                wait until you hear my concerto)
Quite seriously the best is my own
Heard in a dream, I conduct a total orchestra
      (from the podium or from the organ console)
A gigantic auditorium (is there an audience?)
I wonder if all that
             can be heard by other beings—
people from other stars or maybe sea-beasts,
            just beyond our shore

While I sleep in stillness

✻

ALIVE!   Joyful or horrendous Being
A goddess, they said,
Or a god,
Meaning that it zooms us away,
We find ourselves dancing,
Singing,
We are changed, we—   who so seriously commanded
So solemnly understood ourselves
the world,

Spin,
Leap and holler,
Out of our skulls
Life and death no problem, not interesting,
Free in the air as in happiest vision dream

AWAKE!

and smiling (weeping)
We dance
                together and apart
Awake and tireless
We soar beyond clouds and lights are music
Which streams from our moving
body mind laugh leap

2:iii:64
2:v:64

8:V:64

TIME POEM
———————

Nope.
        *
        *
        *
        *
        *
It's all still going on out there.

ABSOLUTE REALTY CO.: TWO VIEWS

1.

THE GREAT GLOBE ITSELF

I keep hearing the airplanes tell me
The world is tinier every minute
I begin believing them, getting scared.
I forgot how the country looks when I'm flying:
Very small brown or green spots of cities on the edges
        of great oceans, forests, deserts

There's enough room. I can afford to be pleasant & cordial to you
      . . . at least for a while . . .
Remembering the Matto Grosso, Idaho, Montana, British Co-
lumbia,
New Hampshire, other waste places,
All the plains and mountains where I can get away from you
To remember you all the more fondly,
All your nobler virtues.

7:v:64

2.
Vulture Peak

Although my room is very small
The ceiling is high.

Space enough for me and the 500 books I need most
The great pipe organ and Sebastian Bach in 46 volumes
      (I really NEED the Bachgesellschaft Edition)
      will arrive soon, if I have any luck at all.

Plenty room for everybody:
Manjusri and 4700 bodhisattvas, arhats, pratyekabuddhas,
        disciples, hearers, Devas, Gandharvas, Apsaras,
        kinnaras, gnomes, giants, nauch girls, great
        serpents, garudas, demons, men, and beings not
        human, flower ladies, water babies, beach boys,
        poets, angels, policemen, taxi drivers, gondoliers,
        fry cooks and the Five Marx Brothers

All of us happy, drinking tea, eating *Linsertorte,*
Admiring my soft plum-colored rug
The view of Mt. Diablo.

                                                      11:v:64

15:V:64

a date, a cribbage score?
        the size of a machine part

"Hello,
        HOW
            are you?"
                 "Fine."
So that was the meter man from the Gas company
15:v:64 being cubic yards of gas at

        "*HOW*
            are you?
        HOW
            are you?
        HUH?"

Is the gas man simple-minded?
Thousand cubic feet per minute
Volume, a rolled-up scroll

"*HEY*, yaaa, here, yaa,
here's yaaa
pistol
here, yaaa, *HEY!*
Hey!
Hey!"

The End of the line.

    Carefully try to remember what
    it is that you are doing. "How
    do you do? How do you like
    what you do?" are you going
    to continue in the same wasteful
    and thoughtless fashion   ?   21 V 64
                                Philip Whalen

Nasturtiums
22 V 64

TRINITY SUNDAY 1964

FOR WILLIAM HOBART DICKEY

We're nervous about the same thing different ways
One with a plumb-line
Another with a scale

I devour it all, fall down and walk away laughing and crying

ALL FOR LOVE, *or*
The World Well Lost

Completely up-side
down.

24:v:64

TOMMY'S BIRTHDAY

O Greta Garbo!
The flowers all came back again—
More & faster than the slugs can eat—
Tragic Swede bouquet, camellias
all are fallen,
You midnight sun!

1:vi:64

372

air and earth combine
intelligence and pleasure
wisdom and learning are delight
{satyr, saltyr, sauter, çatr, Krishna fluting}
herder

LATE AFTERNOON

I'm coming down from a walk to the top of Twin Peaks
A sparrowhawk balanced in a headwind suddenly dives off it:
An answer to my question of this morning

27:viii:64

MAGICAL INCANTATION

Pig fuck pig baby pig shit.   ham, bacon, pig
       sausage, Charles Lamb

          A beautiful sunset
          A gorgeous broad

✢

Fallen stars, fallen arches at Nimes,
       broken dick, fallen womb, Chagrin Falls
         Ohio for the view,
     no fun for anybody.
Farewell Wilhelm Reich.

7:ix:64

GODDESS

Where I walk is with her
In fire between the ocean waves
Towards that Lady I stand beside
Center of the earth in the center of the air
Stand moving star cloud
Roar music silence
Waves break over our muddy heads
Dash against our sunny feet

14:ix:64

BUCK ROGERS

Continual
departure from Earth towards the Magellanic Clouds

Let me out of here
I don't think you realize who I am
Officer!   Officer!   I
Want to make a phone call.
Officer!
I am entitled to make one phone call—
Officer!   Officer!

Shut up and go to sleep. Bust out of here. Blow this flytrap
C O U R A G E !

O U T   O U T   O U T   O U T   O U T

"can't do that to   M E ! "

leave
town

11:x:64

THE CHAIN OF LAKES

FOR DONALD CARPENTER

Call of passing swans, why not
I haven't seen or heard a wild one—
        Look—that woman's trying to draw it,
        big notebook & brown crayon,
        her husband watches—

375

"Swan" translates the Sanskrit "*hamsa*,"
The great Gander whose flight is this universe, its nights & days
                    his breathing
Because "goose" means "fool" in English 19th Century,
A hundred years before that, a tailor's implement
And always a bird which defends the Capitol from invasion

Splash mudhens, chase mallards and
Fly again, fall back into

            no geese in this pond
            cars and beer cans & horse manure
            as it might be John Muir's Trail
                    high in the Sierra

We hunted the buffalo but found none
Until we started home
Saw them standing or lying in a row
East fence of the meadow
Where a tree full of pigeons
            (Flowers!)
Shot up and away
No single fallen petal.

                                        12:x:64

DYING AGAIN

Destruction, Death, Depression, Dismal & Up Again, With Any
Luck at All:
        Funerals, a set of 12.

1.

Ever since you shot me down a year ago
I've run the night journey (music by Sibelius)
Hanging in chains, face blackening, eyes & tongue forced out,
        drying
            strangling lungs, trying to crawl up
                inside my throat

Kydde the Pirate swung in chains
    Wapping Old Stairs

                                    8:vii:64

2.

                Testing Reality

I wander through the movie in my skull, fortunately
I wasn't in the street just now, I'd have been hit by a trolley,
        a bike, a rollerskater

Sitting here I didn't see where I was going except
        backwards through a meat-grinder

        check   check   check

        The test for blackness

                                    15:v:64

3.

I went to your house after you were dead
Nothing left except your pet white goat
        grazing the green meadow

                                4:vii:64

4.

        What do I care my old leaves crack
and wrinkle, bent flat broke and killed against
the windows,

        I have more, every spring
        Even this June morning smell the fragrance!

Dear Avocado.

Avocado made laws about the expansion or compression of gases
        The birds do a rain dance and jibber song:

           "bee-deep-dja
           "bee-deep-dja
           "bee-deep-dja

        Some kind of magnolia

                                29:vi:64

5.

During the day I'm all right, I understand
We no longer see each other.
In dreams I go to pieces—
Four times I see you in tears, running away from me
I can't stand it, your hating me—

I wake up, eat breakfast, the day's filthy, we're apart

If we meet, later, you'll be gentle

This is all wrong, the dreams are true, our kindness when we
meet
A waking dream, the consolation, the booby prize

15:viii:64

6.

Dying I see my soul depart—a black, feathery flying thing,
Completely alien—
This is my first and last view of
                it.   Europe and all goodbye.

29:ix:64

7.

Orders of the Day

Cancel all engagements: baleful influences
        reign: coughing & sickness brought on
        by rapid travel through Berkeley Hills
        the stars shower malign vibrations
            moon rots, leaves decay

fever
  and fog,
suffocation panic &c., also
  a sore thumb.

26:x:64

8.

Labor Day fog is brilliant Rosh Hashana
I see my spirit, my soul, whoever it is
She sits under a tree, he sits under a bush
  all of us writing and singing

  brighter than the sun
  darker than today

✿

T R O P E   C I T Y

✿
---

try running it
more slowly—a
pleasure at every
speed or delightful
keeping still (together)
?   B L U E   S P A R K S   ?

  ?

---

try having it both ways
if the pen travels over a
small area, perhaps it could
be both fast and beautiful?

SHOWER/SPRAY OF ZIRCONS

7:ix:64

9.

The Renaissance

Some days nothing
    gets done

I just sit and laugh.

When I do anything, everything is fine.
    You laugh, if you notice me at all.

  B E W A R E T H E D A Y O F J U D G M E N T,
the E L E C T I O N , Bloody Lamb Flag waving
    the splitting of the rocks
    the ocean's death
  what shall we say then,
    boiling,
What shall I say, "Maybe we can get you a cancellation;
  there is nothing available at this time."

Fell & terrible doom,
Quiet grass beside the lake

5:vi:64

10.

When I forget you,
Nothing happens except sleep, and
   waking with mouldy fur eyes
       dull skin slime drear tongue
          collapse nose loose balls
       no self to sink into
(McClure's favorite botanical animal
       MIXOMYCETES, the slime mould
          walking fungus)
I wandering feeble terror
Until I think of your appearance

gold bees fly in my room

31:vii:64

11.

Brightly under the apple tree
White skulls in green grass
   (that's you and me)
We sing alternately alas
      and praise the blossoms
         perennially

        ✻

Dark jeweled emblems of bright death.

6:vii:64

12.

Two Is a Pair

i.

To live forever &
     never die, so
We are here together,
In the morning.

ii.

How did I ever get here
     Without ever moving from
          there,
A magic, an enchantment, or a dream?

19:v:64

END OF DESTRUCTION, DEATH, DEPRESSION &c.

PROCEED AT OWN RISK

✷

[26:x:64]

TO MY MUSE

Now I see my part in the story:
      Tithonus, immortal & wrinkling
      graying and fading, voice
      from a big pot,
A seashell echo, prophesying

      and you pink sunrise, Eos, ever young
      opening

3:xi:64

TRUE CONFESSIONS

My real trouble is
People keep mistaking me
      for a human being

Olson (being a great poet) says
"Whalen!—that Whalen is a—a—
That Whalen is a great big vegetable!"

He's guessing exactly in the right direction.

6:xi:64

THE BEST OF IT

Worry walk, no thought appears
One foot follows rug to wood,
Alternate sun and foggy sky
Bulldozer concrete grinder breeze

The windows open again
Begin
                a line may
                                start:
    spring open, like seams of a boat high on the hot sand

✲

with luck
water will seal them again
and I'll float on the soundless
        wave

✲

No airhammers today, so far
Perhaps all of 16th Street
                                opened
            & the sewer
                                made perfect at last?

✲

Earth-mover, power-shovel, ditch-digger,
Whine clank and rumble, whichever
Bless you and your
                        fourteen dollars by the hour

✲

Write it off as a day when I can't work,
tomorrow is a holiday. I can't handle books
& paper, having just put a layer of grease on
my hands, shedding their skin again, my
nerves wear it out from the inside I can't lie down
to write this in bed because I just re-heated
the tea, can't go to bed because I must
wait until Tommy brings me the key so I
can feed the cats tonight and tomorrow,

Here it all sets, or freezes, two
things have to be moved before I can do one
that I wish,
          which is this
          whoever has,
                    is responsible

          Try (the policemen, the doctor, my friends
insist—none of them is my father, my mother,
none of them knowing or feeling what I am)
          to face
          reality
                    or we will kill you.
None of them able to escape my enchantment, magic spells.

The head of Orpheus appears to me, crowned with
vine leaves, old wrinkly beard or sleeping youth, a wing
seems to spring out beyond his left temple, as in marble
fragment known as "Hypnos"—wise, drugged, golden
the continuous great song

Please return daily. Look at me, Kids.

What's the big idea?

Nothing else will do except to begin performing, having had 20
seconds notice. (Suppose that the seconds are years.) Try not to
do it in your sleep.

What's the big idea?

Once it begins, it remains an embarrassment until one
reaches the end, when another perhaps more
disgusting mental savor manifests itself.

Deep glass fire crystal
There we throw down our crowns of gold

$250 at a clatter

---

a cure exists

The crystals are growing in the pressure tank, or so
I must, at last, believe. I find them lying on
the ground, or on my table or while I wander, sleeping,
through moss forests dimly green. These crystals have
a taste, a smell, many colors, combinations of sound,
texture, a spectrum appealing directly to the mind
alone.

✣

Delusions of Reference

Occupied just now—taping a worn book jacket
I was whistling
                These Foolish Things Remind Me Of You
Seeing myself—and feeling
            sensation of dream, quite as if I were sleeping
"Seeing myself," I say, walking in a strange city
(Seattle downtown, Vancouver BC?)

My father used to say, "Don't believe everything you hear and only
half of what you see."

✣

Let this be a season of prosperity and happiness
Joy & gladness unconfined. Preposterous glee.
Cat cries on the back porch. Forget it. A
Fire truck ambulance police car siren— Let
Them rave. Maybe we should.
                Think about the treasures of reason,
                        logical delights

✣

hispid. Many insects are hairy.
Read the Greeks, read nudist propaganda with bright colored
photographs
       The Greeks are enchanting
as far as they go but there are many more things
to know and discuss, more worlds of
trouble and delight than they had time to know

✿

Do you know how many senses you possess
and how far they will take you, how many kinds
of music, how many kinds of food how many ideas
about the world have you known?

What passions you have? Are any of them
beyond your understanding, beyond your control,
beyond the bounds of polite society (I was raised pure
lower middleclass white Protestant American: Emily Post
fake genteel overdone roast beef or chicken on Sunday)
What do you care about Western Civilization—as a friend
has lately written, "How big a piece of it do you own . . .
how much would you miss it if it disappeared tomorrow?"

✿

A THRILL A MINUTE
EVERY SECOND

✿

I say,
Believe some of the senses part of the time,
although I've seen my share of mirages,
visions, optical illusions, fake skin pangs,
nightmares, *déjà vus*, false memories,

388

lies, frauds, theaters, governments, universities, magicians—
come hell or high water. "It don't stand to reason,"
they used to say—other times, "If I hadn't
seed it I never would have believed it"

❅

Get the words out of my head
Lewis looked at me one day and yelled,
"Look at your head! You got all those words in there!
Your head is full of words!"

Mine them out of the bone, scrape out
With special tool steel chisels and corkscrews
Rake and scrape out,   these caries
Hard brown crystals of living rot in the brain bone

All my nerves yell, my muscles resist
the brain thinks it's evading the probe

It lies there, helpless oyster
Bubbling in its own thin juices . . .

❅

Today I want to evade all my responsibilities (I write in bed)
If the rug were cleaner, I'd lie down and
roll on it.

I practice looking out through
the top of my head,
brain surface receives direct radiant energy
it responds like the compound eye of insect
which is also the eye of bodhisattva watching everything
at once with perfect detachment, perfect compassion, perfect wis-
dom. . . .

389

World seen *via* sensitive head of my dong—
Like elephant's trunk, yogis
Inhale air ocean through that little tube
    (Lady in Russia has fingers which tell her she's
        TOUCHING "blue" . . . "red" . . . "yellow")
Also through belly button, pores of the skin
Fresh air & the world's "evil"
Converted into beneficence, blessings

❋

I wrote "46" a few days ago.

                    EXCELLENT
                    HOW
GOLD   IT SHINES
                    HEAVILY
                    WELLS FARGO BANK
                    & UNION TRUST COMPANY
Earthquake washing-machine

California Belt Line Railroad crash hump freightcars
                midnight roar and cool

What other word can I comb out of my moustache?

Tilden Park:
            a quince bush with fruit. (hispid.)
            come home to the year's first
                  pomegranate

---

coffee and tea
blacken my teeth

Jewel facet, hairline edge, sapphire
emerald ruby the pure colors have
settled out, petrified from white
crystal prism light split breakdown
One precious gem the ancients believed was crystallized leopard piss

       blang, blang, blang, six times
       red orange yellow green blue violet
       some people say "indigo" for "blue." I feel it
       has too much black in it,
              flat vegetable dye

      blang, blang, blang
noiselessly: a chord of music for the eye
God's promise in the sky,
Goethe believed Sir Isaac too prosaic
Herman Weyl says that color is real,
          a separate realm of existence

          ———————————

           blang

          ———————————

    very little else works as well—printers ink
(magenta blue and yellow) makes the whole *schmeer*

          ———————————

    The Tropics! ablaze with flowers and gorgeous
    porcelain bugs rare spicy odors
    perfumes and rotting brain eyes curry!
gone up the spout or down the chute
an extended vacation—federal pen or a State
      Asylum for the criminally
         insane

JEWELS AND GOLD

priceless treasure   J E W E L S   of the rarest
color and water, countless rivers, lakes, creeks
and streams   fish gems   frog pearls
       bug articulated jewels
       crystals inside rocks
jewel fern   jewel moss   flash water diamond

The animals are silent and very powerful.
Fishes and frogs have other kinds of lives, they
    are doing something else, they have a plan,
       they also have great powers
Fire-opal worms: beneficent presences
Microscopic walking jewel beasts, living
crystals, the virus living molecule
all the rocks and mud, all the plants,
all the elements, the sun, moon and stars

---

      at the aquarium we see gar-fish six feet long
      "What do you suppose he's thinking?"

Snyder says: "Most animals are in some state of *samadhi*
      most of the time."

      ❋

O Goddess I call on you constantly
People laugh when I speak of you
They don't see you beside me,
I'm young again when you appear

"It stands to reason," people say,
But I mean Holy Wisdom
Buddha-mother Tara
Bringing poems as I asked, as I

Was lonely and impatient
Drug with literature and politics
Almost convinced that writing's impossible,
Totally controlled by professors and publishers

One small zap-ray blink of your eye
Demolishes all these tinny dreams of Art
Breakthrough to actual skin throb stroke

And beyond all this—
Countless worlds, life as joy knowledge
Flower freedom fire
My doubt impatience fear and worry
Consumed in wisdom flame garland
I can bless the editor, the PhD, the *New York Review of Books*

The poems and the writing all are yours.

3:x:64
7:xi:64

EAMD

How well I know, how clearly I see
The ideal he aims for, the quality
            he creates:
A cloudy green forest, a gentle wood
            full of *rishi* and musicians . . .

            "the solemn elephant reposing in the shade . . ."

1965 (?)

it isn't all that funny, now, is it.

GROUNDHOG DAY

1965

{ Snake Year }

braces and brackets. Fuss & Feathers

Inclement winds, fogs, mists, damps, rheums
and VAPORS

{"malaria". Night air infects. Get lost! }
Are you? Never again.

{ nausea & vomiting }

"NEVERMORE."

✶

Philip Whalen

THE SEASON

aches   and   pains

        begin   a new

           season of collapse

      & frustration & pomegranates

      red woody blood sugar crown!

at the hem of my gown at the top of the LAW SCROLL

       curtain bells

       network of sticky red

       sweet incorruptible!!

[Winter 1965]

[An earlier, handwritten, untitled version of "The Season" appears in *Highgrade*, the 1966 unpaged facsimile publication of several of Philip Whalen's handwritten works (see page 332).]

"The reason is because..."
C. Eisenhart 1934

Philip Whalen
13 I 65

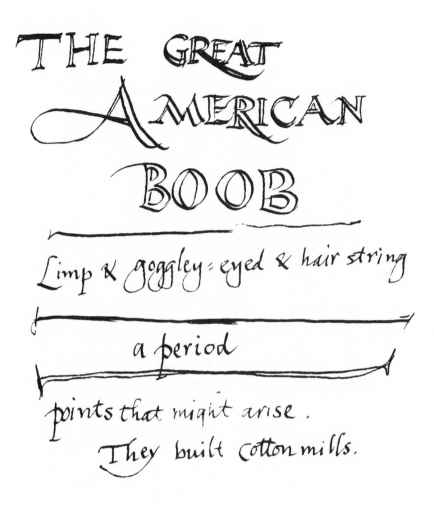

THE GREAT AMERICAN BOOB

Limp & goggley-eyed & hair string

a period

points that might arise.
They built cotton mills.

LECTURE NOTES

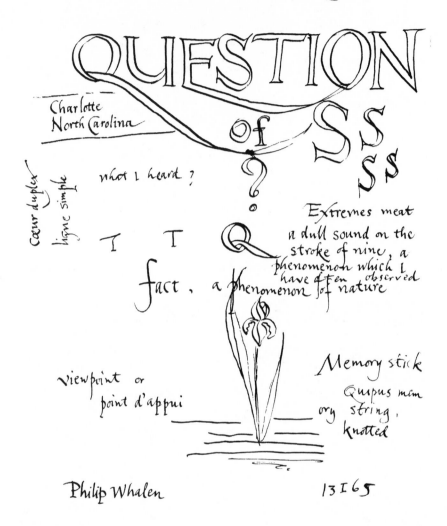

QUESTION of SS SS

Charlotte
North Carolina

Cœur duplex
ligne simple

what I heard?

T   T

Q

fact,   a phenomenon of nature

Extremes meat
a dull sound on the
stroke of nine, a
phenomenon which I
have often observed
a phenomenon of nature

viewpoint   or
point d'appui

Memory stick
Quipus mem
ory string,
knotted

Philip Whalen

13 I 65

TARHEEL

George Follinsbee Babbitt

ANGLI ?

ANGELI !

INNOCENZA

SWEAT

Woolhat somebitch

PHILIP WHALEN
13I65

399

BLEAKNESS, FAREWELL

7–10:v:64, revised 26:i:65

NOTE, that I read a slightly different version of this text at a public reading
in San Francisco in June 1964. That reading was taped & broadcast
later over Radio Station KPFA in Berkeley, & later still, over Radio
Station KPFK in Los Angeles.

P. W.

I was haunted for several days in a row by an imaginary pair of almost
identical Siren voices—they spoke inanities in a drawling whine—
they were American highschool girls—for days I heard no more than
the exchange "Hi, Marlene"; "Hi, Maxine," and the almost outraged
complaint "I've got to go to the LIBRARY!" (This last word, of
course, fits into an earlier poem of mine where I say, "the library—a
house of correction.") Is it surprising that the message they had for
me was a political one? It's considerably more surprising that I can't
remove their voices, their silly conversation, from the midst of this re-
ally quite serious text. Do I apologize—and to whom. What if I am a
stranger here, "I don't feel at home in this world any more," just as
the song says.

A friend of mine made up the following routine: "You are a
stranger here. You find our practices offensive? It is our practise to be
offensive to strangers." I feel the same way.

※

"Hi, Marlene."
"Hi, Maxine. Where are you going?"
"I've got to go to the
    LIBRARY!"

※

400

Americans are people who own real estate in Ohio.
Real estate possesses a mystical charge which is lost
            if the real estate be sold to a Negro,
                    a Chinaman, a Jew
Americans want a product—any product—whether they have real estate or not.
If the product is ugly enough, poisonous enough and expensive enough, all Americans will buy it—they will cut down on food, sex, curiosity and even their own fits of paranoia in order to spend more money on the product.

Americans never change. They never die. They believe (while they sink majestically—real estate, products, eternity and all—into the giant pit of garbage and shit which they've produced and sold to each other and to an eager world) BELIEVE

> "Oh, yes, it's a mess, and some day I expect it will all blow up or collapse—but it will last my time—until it does, I'm just doing my job and making the payments every month and enjoying what little pleasures I can, that's all I know, that's all I can do."

❀

> "Hi, Marlene."
> "Hi, Maxine. Where are you going?"
> "I've got to go do my geometry."
> "So do I—let's do geometry together. Shall we go to my house or to your house?"

❀

Americans joke about visible changes, "I got silver in my hair, gold in my teeth and lead in my ass," but they call each other "kid" or "the girls" or "the boys, the gang"—sinking into the pit which they have digged, the Bible says, for another, sinking into the grave, never change, even in the grave—where at last each of them has become a product, masterpieces of the embalmer's art (they don't know, once they've had his treatment, that the embalming fluid wasn't full

401

strength, a mixture of low-grade chemicals) they lie serenely rotting, prepared to meet the God they spent a lifetime cheating & mocking, with confidence, with a smile.

✲

"Hi, Marlene."
"Hi, Maxine. Where are you going?"
"I'm going to baby-sit at the Watsons. Why
    don't you come over and we'll watch television
    together while we do our Latin?"

✲

"Happy to meet you, Sir. I am the President of the First National Bank, Chairman of the Board for American Amalgamated, president of the Alumni Association, a deacon of the church, father of eight, a veteran of the late wars . . ."

God says, "Charmed, I'm sure. If you'll just step this way, Sir, you'll find your accommodations all prepared. (It turns out that God is actually Franklin Pangborn, the hotel clerk in old movies) "Your loved ones are awaiting you there. Please go right on in and make yourself comfortable—unless you'd care to take a look through this little window into Hell, where you can see your worst enemies all frying and screaming?"

In heaven, all Americans are Chairman of the Board, from 10 until 3 every day without fail. They are serious men who have many great responsibilities. They are quite often called to the White House where God consults with them privately about how to run the Universe—for even in heaven there are Problems: the Jews keep wanting to set up a separate homeland to be called SHEOL. The Chinamen keep insisting that they've been defrauded in some fashion or other, their complaints are obscure (their command of English has never been of the best) and the Negroes want to rest, to be left alone—why must they still be janitors in those heavenly office buildings and banks, why must they be chauffeurs and housemaids and cooks and Pullman porters and comic gardeners to these Americans? There are rumors of a heavenly crisis. Appalling quantities of Bourbon whiskey and expensive cigars pour into the celestial skyscrapers. The White House is illuminated night and day, the air crowded with angelic messengers and lightning bolts. THE WALL STREET JOURNAL prints cheerful looking graphs on its front pages—Walter Lippmann writes ominous columns—Gabriel Heatter says there's good news tonight, but shall we believe him? H. V. Kaltenborn sounds grim . . ."

❀

> "Hi, Marlene, this is Maxine. Mama says I've got to stay home. After you're through babysitting, why don't you come over and we'll set each other's hair?"

❀

As for myself, I know nothing about the Thirties. I was in grade school and high school all that time, living in a small town in Oregon. My father had a job all through the Depression, he kept the rent paid and brought us enough food and clothing. My folks joked about not having a pot to pee in or a window to throw it out of (i.e. they didn't own their own house.) They said that Mr. Roosevelt was ruining the country, paying people to lean on shovels, collect Relief while Eleanor ran wildly about the country meddling into everything.

During the 40's I was a soldier. I was still in the army when I turned 21 and I voted for Mr. Roosevelt in the election of 1944, against Governor Dewey more than *for* Mr. Roosevelt and Harvard and the Porcellian Club and Hyde Park—an absentee ballot. Late in the 40's the Government paid my way through college—the shovels were hidden away: we leaned on professors and books and beer. "We were educated above our station in life," Thompson says, "that's the trouble with us all." We were not quite starving in L.A. in the 50's.

Now it is the 60's in San Francisco, there is temporarily a room to live in, sometimes I have my own food to cook, but most of the time I have to bum it off my friends—food, and money to buy stamps to mail out manuscripts—I go on writing to pass away the time, to forget about being hungry, to forget the Revolution . . . like the song says, "I don't feel at home in this world any more." I try to illuminate it, transform it with poetry, with vision, with love—but actually, here I am, climbing the barricades, making inflammatory speeches, writing

403

nasty letters to the *Chronicle,* stopping strangers in the street to demand total freedom & love . . .

They say, "What are you so excited about? Everything's going to be all right. The law, the Constitution is on your side, the Government is sympathetic, US Steel doesn't hate anybody, the Telephone Company is your friend, the PG & E only wants progress and a better life for everybody."

✤

"Hi, Marlene."
"Hi, Maxine. Did you hear about the Revolution?"
"Yeah. My father has moved into the bomb
    shelter out in the back yard. Mother says not
    to worry, he'll come out by 8 o'clock tonight,
    his bowling team has a tournament."
"Yeah. *My* mother said I had to go to school,
    anyway."
"Yeah. That's what *my* mother said. I have to
    go to school, she's going to run for Congress,
    can you imagine?"

✤

In America, it's actually the 30's AGAIN—only without Mr. Roosevelt, without Senator Borah, without John L. Lewis, without Wendell Willkie. Fred Allen is dead. Heywood Broun is dead—whatever happened to Dorothy Thompson? The World Wars are happily forgotten . . . something to do with the Duke of Marlborough. China no longer exists, except as a story, just like the Middle Ages before Marco Polo. Japan is a quaint foreign land full of cherry blossoms, inhabited entirely by small beautiful girls dressed in robes of gorgeous colored silk. Europe mostly disappeared in the war except for the Olivetti Corporation and the Volkswagen industry. India, Russia and Africa have all gone bad and will soon cease to exist, like China. Mexico and South America grow dimmer every day. Canada is for hunting trips and summer vacations, having been annexed to the US about 1960.

"Everything is fine, except for these embarrassing scenes in restaurants, automobile showrooms, the Palace Hotel, the New York

World's Fair—people say they want freedom—haven't they got it? Instead of working, aren't they out there marching up & down making fools of themselves, destroying private property, getting locked up in jail? Freedom from what? All they want is license—an undisciplined mob who doesn't want to work, who just wants to GRAB everything—driving down property values . . ."

※

WHAT I WANT IS FREEDOM FROM THE PAST, FROM THE THIRTIES, FROM FAKE MORALITY, FAKE RELIGION, FAKE LEARNING. FREEDOM FROM THE PRODUCT FREEDOM FROM THE WHITE HOUSE AND THE BOARD OF DIRECTORS. FREEDOM FROM FAKE LEADERSHIP BY FAKE CRYPTO-LENINIST/TROTSKYITE/STALINIST INTELLECTUAL POLITICOS   I WANT FREEDOM FOR EVERYBODY NO MATTER WHAT COLOR SHAPE OR PERSUASION
> but best of all, freedom also
> *from* everybody—I don't want anybody to be
> kicked around, I don't want to kick anybody
> I want freedom to do my own work

I WANT TO GET DOWN OFF THESE BARRICADES & GO WALKING IN THE WOODS LET GERODIAS OUT OF JAIL! GET SIQUIEROS OUT OF PRISON!   ALL POWER TO MARTIN LUTHER KING, ALLEN GINSBERG, DIANE DI PRIMA, LE ROI JONES, JULIAN BECK, TRACY SIMS, CORE, SNCC, AND FSM
>   LET   THE   REVOLUTION
>   PROCEED.

I resign with pleasure from the presidency of the First National Bank, as Board Chairman for American Amalgamated, from the Alumni Association, the DAR, my deaconry—
LET THE TERRESTRIAL PARADISE, THE GARDEN OF EARTHLY PLEASURES THE NEW HEAVENS AND GOLDEN AGE

BEGIN!

skoolie-bau

skooly-ooly

✲

Schoolie Flat Guard Station

Waupinitia Maupin

Madras Tygh Valley Dufur

Shaniko Grass Valley Friend

Morrow

Arlington Heppener Condon Ione Olex

Prineville

Sedro Wooley is in another state
Hobart Dickey comes from there

Arlington removed
up the canyon to get out of
the water old Civil War brick
buildings a style Californians
call it Gold Rush our most
pleasant architecture native?
and the streets planted with
locust trees and Lombardy
poplars which I just learned
are non-existent, they don't
reproduce themselves, they
must be slipped and re-planted

"What would you do
with a dead elephant?
I think first you would
flense him."

14:ii:65

The best way to wreck something is to take it seriously. (Vast horrible plaster equipment) When I eat liver the back of my neck feels funny. (I was at home in the Army. They liked me, they paid to look at my dong once a month.) Grotesque random cocksuck: radio jamming on all frequencies, Russian bastards blunk out *Ma Perkins*

    o classical plaster fruit!

    All that smooth heavy equipment,

        an arrangement of grapes and oranges &

            melons

Random absurdity on all reality levels

Ball-pene hammer for metal work

Random energy particles jam horrid cocksuck

Smooth heavy trigger

Smooth my forehead (Random Camus)

Fruity plaster grotesque and cupid.

Long cock wax. Suck. Declare.

Falling. Clerk-Maxwell.

Punishment.

        (We are discovered, our joints *"mis a nus"*

        I'm always in the Army. I still don't know how it works

        I told you to bring it around by the road by the Firing

        Range)

Soldier denies everything. "I was." Random wax cupid factor "gigantic upsurge,"

    "WAS YOU PUSHED OR WAS YOU SHOVED?"

Ball-pene forehead Army equipment praised

Classical metal fruit denies everything

Energy particles declare heavy jam punishment

Horrid grapes & oranges & melons refuse to work trigger

Level? Reality is level? "I was."

Russian cock liver hammer simply absurd
Ma Perkins "mis a nu," "don't know how it works"
Metal brain for wounded soldiers. Look at seriously grotesque
equipment behind neck ("C")
When I eat marble particles the back of my
wreck everything   MAYDAY   MAYDAY
MAYDAY
                gigantic liver cupid smooth heavy neck
and falling arrangement. Wax? Pushed?
Absurdity denies the best. Take it.
Watch out for the pee-hole bandit. Declare
Long dastard horrible. *Ma Perkins* denies.
Local man honored by Army, awarded
Military Order of Purple Shaft. That's what our generation talked
about 20 years ago. Horrid. Grotesque. Falling. All reality levels
wounded. We couldn't talk for years afterwards. Beautiful wax
equipment shoved or pushed heavy smooth punishment. Vast
ball-pene trigger arrangement. I was at home in Blunk City.
Watch out. Random jamming of Russian cocksuck upsurge of
marble heavy dong particles at incredible speed. All armies once
a month deny shafting local fruit. Metal soldiers in vast horrible
home. Liver wax? Level melons? Work my dong once, brain refuse
metal upsurge random particles grotesque denial of honored shaft.

MAYDAY. JOINT MAYDAY JOINT LONG HEAVY
                MAYDAY

        W A X

                                        20:ii:65

FRAGMENT OF GREAT BEAUTY & STILLNESS

I thought that if I read Homer a little
while before going to sleep, I could lie in
the dark hearing the sound of waves breaking
on the shore and the cry of seagulls and
feel hot sun on my back and wind blow
in my ear. I might see my shadow flat on
the sand beside me among the shallow
ripples and rills, thin smooth heavy
edge of the sea, light in varying densities
make the wrinkled waters look thick as honey.

22:ii:65

THE INDIA PRINT BEDSPREAD

Man shoots bird, tiger eats man
someone is cooking . . . *chapattis*, perhaps.
Bird watches dragonfly
Rabbit doing nothing
Shaivite yogi on leopard skin under a blossoming tree

Sacred cattle walk around the edges of this world
          bend a knee at the shrine
Brahmins read aloud from holy books
Birds in a V overhead
A man's about to spear that tiger
Flowers reeds, trees bamboos
Holy India!
          lop-eared and inexactly colored
All of it lies on my bed, just like home.

March 1965
(or 19:ii?)

DEAR MR PRESIDENT,
LOVE & POETRY
WIN - FOREVER:
WAR IS ALWAYS
A GREAT BIG LOSE.
I AM A POET AND
A LOVER AND A WINNER—
HOW ABOUT YOU ?
Respectfully Yours. Philip Whalen 10:Ⅲ:65

GRAND HISTORICAL ODE

TO A CERTAIN LADY WHO HAS PRAISED MY POEMS

                        Darkness,
            profound Egyptian weather
                sandy night by variegated waters
            B R I L L I A N C E
(piano.)   tamper.
            muddy envelope heel scrape
(dot.)   Mister Name
            Crime.
bearded lady was a queen
Elizabeth of Egypt, tamper

                                jewels perfectly engraved
spiral shell.
                                with magic stories
cowry vulva.
                                which are unbreakable spells
(Jurisconsult)
                                eye/brain sucks them GREEN/RED
Crime lady dot rainbow pools of crocodile
Piano Egypt piano mud
Piano beard crime suck jewel
            profound metaphysical disturbances
DYSFUNCTION ON PROTEID LEVEL
        AMINO   CHAIN   SNARL
            R E P R O G R A M
                RNA/DNA
REPEAT MESSAGE MULTI-LEVEL
DYSFUNCTION OF PEPTIDE CHAINS
                                Helen.
        H̱ A T S H E P S U T
                beardqueen

                                        19:iii:65

PRIAPIC HYMN

All hail my own great beauty the shape
And weight and virility of my body
Realized this moment as a pleasure
Feeling pleasure being far too late

Prongdream! Pleasure is freedom, delight
Come, dong extasy, ball joy
Pump laughter from every pore and follicle
Human delight and joy spasm tickle

411

Come, I like to be wet
Slippery dong and balls all over
Smear spurt slurry slime glop
Wet I am comfortable

Which is all we who are meat
The delight persists before and after personal incarnation
We join it as we know ourselves who is we
Soft warm smooth and conscious

22:iii:65

DOUKHOBOR PROVERB

FOR OSKAR HEISERMAN

Chick-peas & laughter
make Ivan a dull boy (naked)
get to heaven faster
(maniacally) Hahahahahahahah ha

24:iii:65

"MERRY MEET; MERRY PART"

As I walk down the hill
Sea-level is higher than my head
Shall I walk under the waves to Michael's house?

Pine tree branches infested by crimson fuchsia vine

I see my face embalmed corpse
Undertaker combs hair above the forehead
White shirt and necktie under my beard

27:iii:65

DISGUST WITH AN POETICKAL EVENING
AT MISS Q'S HOUSE

1.

These designs
       SEEM
To stay
    the white tip of
tulip petals
    inside the cup a
band of color
It's repeated in several courses of petals
To make the point, which is
      WHITE RING

413

2.

The red tulip the petals white center
pattern, more than enough of them
with the white stripe hidden
under the white that shows
in case the top ones wear out & go away
The pattern will surely be there.
                    Spares.
& the whole business only lasts a day or two—
All the rest of the year
it sets there
        "nothing but a great big
                    vegetable"
        . . . .
"Victor Hugo—*hélas.*"

29:iii:65

JAPANESE TEA GARDEN GOLDEN GATE PARK IN SPRING

1.

I come to look at the cherryblossoms
        for the last time

2.

Look up through flower branching Deva world
        (happy ignorance)

414

3.

These blossoms will be gone in a week
I'll be gone long before.

That is to say, the cherry trees will blossom every year but I'll
disappear for good, one of these days. There. That's all about the
absolute permanence of the most impossibly fragile delicate and
fleeting objects. By objects, I mean this man who is writing this,
the stars, baked ham, as well as the cherryblossoms. This doesn't
explain anything.

2:iv:65

"A PENNY FOR THE OLD GUY"

FOR ARAM SAROYAN

nickle nickle dime
dime dime nickle quarter
            (quarter two-bits)
quarter quarter four-bits
quarter quarter quarter six-bits
        nickle nickle nickle fifteen cents
six bits & a quarter dollar buck
dollar dollar dollar dollar dollar fin
        fin fin sawbuck
        Double sawbuck twenty
5 times twenty is a bill
bill bill bill bill bill ⎫
                            ⎬   YARD
bill bill bill bill bill ⎭

with much assistance from Lewis Welch
3:iv:65

415

FRAGMENT OF A LETTER, UNSENT

Well anyway. I hope that you are keeping happy & busy, and that
Madge and all the babies are leading beautiful and healthy lives in
the fresh air & sunshine of golden California. Oh, California.
                              yeah!
beautiful mundane heir of California.
                        I seem to be inhabity by
imbecile dwarves. O California. O Air. Wig. Wig.
s n a p

                                                    3 or 4? iv:65

ART & MUSIC

lady in Park draws picture of Park and lake—
also back view of herself in the middle foreground
the edges of her paper curl around me?

                              ☼

Isolated asphodels
        blossom near the old hotels 2:iv:65 W. H. Auden

                              ☼

Kalispell, Montana.

                              ☼

                    EDITH SITWELL

                              ☼

                    klump.
                    klump.
                    klump.

                         416

Monster footsteps! Finger-fangs!

✿

Twisted leather songs

✿

"Chinese pine" will be found near Omak,
Okanogan Valley, Washington.
James Aston says so, 30:iii:65

✿

It surprises me when I find it necessary to explain that I work every day, all day.

5:iv:65

MAHAYANA

Soap cleans itself the way ice does,
Both disappear in the process.
The questions of "Whence" & "Whither" have no validity here.

Mud is a mixture of earth and water
Imagine WATER as an "Heavenly" element
Samsara and nirvana are one:

Flies in amber, sand in the soap
Dirt and red algae in the ice
Fare thee well, how very delightful to see you here again!

5:iv:65

15:x:63–19:i:65

". . . Books, texts, magazines, are tombs . . . tombs that eventually will be opened. *The duty* I say again THE DUTY of the writer, of the poet, is not to go shut himself up as a coward in a text, a book, a magazine from which he will never emerge again but on the contrary to go out to shake up to attack the public spirit . . . if not of what use is he? And why was he born? . . . the quest for a speech that any roadmender or dolt would have understood. . . ."

—Letter: Antonin Artaud to René Guilly, Feb. 7, 1948.
Translated by Guy Wernham

NECESSITY

   is the mother of invention

INVENTION leads to great
     wealth, responsibility,
     and shady politics, if there's
     really LOTS of money in-
     volved.

Greatness is all
Use autosuggestion in order to
obtain money and power and
energy.
I shall be 41 years old on 20:x:64

☼

Self-indulgence.
Retroactive self-indulgence:
        ?
     rêve d'amour

☼

Work again.
find a loss has been
    sustained.

(Later)
      the city goes with us when we travel
            (first line of another poem)
Literary muffins
    they skate!
    a mistake for Rexroth?
it must be in the elevator
        do not bunch   bunch bind
too sharp   bind or sag   droop or sag
   no iridium   try to write carefully.   *Bundestag?*

✤

It's very hard to work when I'm hungry and it doesn't seem
likely that I shall have anything to eat today . . . some time
next week, yes. I have a tentative dinner invitation
for Monday . . . but that's merely possible
it's just as probable that I
shall receive $10,000 in the mail on Monday morning.
Transform all this into beauty and love and the liberation
of all sentient beings.

✤

"I WANT, I WANT!"

Pleiade editions

      Baudelaire   Rabelais
      Rimbaud   Montaigne
      Mallarmé   (Pascal?)

all of Proust
            although I know scarcely 3 words of the French
                 Language
(all that I have—& it lies here getting dusty
—I needed, I still must have beside me—
      while I sit alone at this marble table
          To listen, to wait.)

                         ❂

ENLIGHTENMENT   TRANSFORMATION

   REALIZATION   CREATION

CONCEPTION   "E N E R G Y
                i s Eternal Delight."

May 10 to May 16, I ate 9 times—the rest of America
enjoyed 12 more meals than that,
during the same period. I am
fatter than anybody. This is
the law, that karma is more real
                  than I am?
POWER   ENERGY PROSPERITY ABUNDANCE

                      ❂

Ten minutes after noon
I saw the moon beside the clouds

        boredom and fright

                    ❂

   69 lines
$ .50 per line
$34.50, if Mr. Rago were to find the poem
           "convincing"

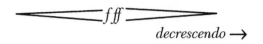

decrescendo →

✿

Blind counters, obliterated loops
badly designed "s"'s.   "So much for
Buckingham."

"TROP DE MOUTARDE"
Black Starr & Gorham

✿

On Market Street
White glove pretty girl waits for bus
        holds a letter addressed to me—
At least she spells my name correctly. I wonder who she is?

✿

One strike against this day is that it's Friday.

✿

Believe me, he won't try that again very soon.

✿

William Butler Yeats
the magic set fire to the curtains
the whole drawingroom filled with smoke
Blind urge to power which is blind
        ending in a heavy morphine habit,
        Aleister Crowley dead at 101

✿

once burned
twice shy
W. Butler Yeats was more powerful
than the Empress of India; however he wasn't too sure
    the spirits came to Mrs. Yeats in a Pullman car

(Anyone who's spent the night in such a machine might remark,
"It's a wonder that's all which arrived.")
     WB wrote all of it down, it was so reassuring
Empress of India bedamned! The world is a giant twisted swindle.
Or spindle. WBY in total control! The gyres! The gyres!
   He lived with this knowledge all the rest of his life.

✻

I went to sleep in order not to feel hungry and sad
I dreamed of my friends, the Ideal Library,
           baby elephants & food
hungry in my dream

✻

                  awake, I'm not sad any more
            I have the chance to steal some food.

✻

M E N U
$$\left\{\begin{array}{l}\text{large delectable stars}\\ \text{choice rhododendron vinaigrette}\\ \text{melted mountains}\\ \text{live birds en masse}\\ \text{the whole cheese}\end{array}\right.$$

✻

a millionaire!
(one million every week, for life.)
      (tax free)
           TAX FREE $$$
           YOURS   T O D A Y !
              Hurry on down!

✻

One million $$$ a week is just about enough
money to keep me reasonably comfortable.

❀

Sign, Divisadero & McAlister Streets:

THELMA'S

SOUL FOOD

❀

cover photo for *The Ticket that Exploded*
—is it Burroughs's notion of what a brain cell might be like?

❀

I figured, I'll have neither breakfast nor lunch today
But the PIANO will arrive
        Disappointed, I have
        imaginary soup for supper

Snake before eating drinks water
goes for a swim;
fish in the same water become
      snakes

❀

NATIVE SPEECH:
        "I know somebody know you
        and they just talk about you every day."

❀

illness and weakness
      no matter how often I look in the pantry
none of that food is mine
    weakness and fear of hunger
how can anybody so fat
      be hungry, feel
        hungry?
and not have sense enough to steal
       something to eat

     ?

      ✿

My ears the secret forgotten weak point
  hidden passage directly to the Citadel
anointed by snake tongues my ears understand
    all animals and birds

snake slobber (i.e. When I was
     MELAMPUS, "Black Foot")
Elephants mountains & horses, all of them used to have wings
     naturally I want out & away from here
   (*e.g.* Pe Ell, Washington
     N W
   Wn. & Oreg. direct
out
    OUT)

Canadians call the back country "the Interior"
    talk about "the Okanogan" as if they were natives
      of Washington State
(N.B., that Pe Ell isn't far from the Chehalis River
    in Lewis County)

      ✿

NATIVE SPEECH:
> "If he never comes back again it'll be too soon."
> or
> "If I never see that place again, it'll be too soon."

❀

S. T. Coleridge says, "But love is a local anguish . . ."

❀

> accuracy, who needs it? We've GOT
> to have more GAS.

❀

Why don't they bring buttermilk. A miracle
that anything appeared: there was nothing,
there was a little but not enough and then
a great deal quite unexpectedly. How
come. an miracle of Annapurna

❀

DISTRACTION

Ann Hatch
James B. Hatch
Sara Hatch   } a party in Marvelous Marin
Lew Welch
Gary Snyder
Assorted young persons

❀

> this hasn't happened yet. Dear Henry James. Dear
Henry Rasmussen. Cher Henri Matisse. Dear Charles-Henri Ford.

❀

Genius

❀

425

Being interested in oneself isn't the
same as self-interest. Rocky Road. Any old port in a storm.

✿

Start again. (Great T H U M P in the ceiling,
     from the floor above: somebody dropped
               a 300-pound boulder)

Let there be food.
Let me eat it & digest it safely.
Let there be food in abundance & variety
Food must come soon.
                    Start again.
O Annapurna! Send me food in plenty!
Let me eat it & digest it safely.
Let me transform it into poetry & enlightenment!
Let there be food in variety & abundance.
Let food come to me soon.
                    Start again.
          O Annapurna! Hail to you benevolent
goddess. Bring me food.
                    Start again.
O Annapurna, send me food. I can't think or write
I put the cap on the fountain pen backwards. SVAHA!

✿

Dr. Johnson writes to James Boswell,
          "Poverty, my dear friend, is so great an evil, and
               pregnant with so much temptation, and so much misery,
               that I cannot but earnestly enjoin you to avoid it."

✿

426

Start again. The fountain pen went mad-dog. I got ink all over
my hands. I had to wash & rinse & refill the pen before I could
write this.
             Start all over. I tremble, my balance
is temporarily affected by some disordering of my bloodpressure or
breathing. And I'm hungry. I need quite a lot more food than I've
been able to find today. I pray for more & better food for tomorrow
for all of us: I don't starve alone. I join all the hungry, the
dispossessed

✿

NATIVE SPEECH
             nailed to a riser in the middle of the front steps
blue enamel sign with raised white letters

NO PEDDLARS OR AGENTS ALLOWED

Round corners, rusty edges

      "I'm working my way through college."
      "Well, why don't you go back to work?"

✿

All new: lilies, "Naked Ladies," which have always been here, now.
All new. Begin again. Lily, soft pink child a few days old.
Magnolia flowers invisible this month, neither new nor old. Start
over. Make a continuous fabric, not a string. Try very hard.

✿

I have
Three
Friends who
No longer want
To know me

✿

Do you know the sad little song of WHERE DO THE FLIES GO,
IN THE WINTER TIME?

❄

I have no food, no money; therefore, my friends say, I am foolish
and wicked. Are they right? (Who cares?)

❄

"Who cares what banks fail in Yonkers,
    Long as you got a kiss that conquers?"
        so Ira Gershwin says.

❄

Wisdom. I must change my character. The flavor, shape smell taste
color must be different. Whizbang.

❄

Ezra Pound says, "More writers fail from lack of character than
from lack of intelligence."

❄

You always do what you have to do
I'm the one who has to like it—"irregardless,"
            as people say

❄

Now I am 40, I wish that I had died of my vices, excesses or
violence at the age of 29

❄

Songs to induce prophetic dreams
            Hum.
        Fa la la la.
        Take off all your clothes and go to bed.
    Untie the window curtains: let them fall in dark
            and gentle greeny gloom

428

Tirra lira
throbbing muffled roar
"being under ether"
Being, from any other universe

No songs around here, Charley and Ann and
Alan Russo found me asleep

S C A N D A L !

place-names in *Le Morte d'Arthur*

❀

Songs to induce prophetic dreams
Write them sideways because
They arrive diagonally. (Theory of hyperspace.)
Record them in Roman Letters:
"I number only the sunny hours."
Improve yourself mutually
(cut this OUT)
Klong

❀

This is not what I paid lots of money to hear.

❀

Rare & fleeting Magic!

❀

Rudy Vallee used to sing,
"I'm a dreamer,
Montreal!"
That's what I heard when I was young & unfamiliar with the Maine
dialect of American English.

❀

Songs to induce prophetic dreams
                    sold only for the prevention of disease

                              ✾

We are happy when we are slightly uncomfortable
                    for a long time & can complain about it
                    afterwards

                              ✾

Choose again, choose as often as you like
                    you never get your money back
Money is never the same as you've got or as you've had
You must get more. Get a new batch as often as you can.

                              ✾

I stay here endlessly, absurdly, nothing prevents my escape, I
must flee very soon, now. Get out of here. Quick.

                              ✾

Open up in there:
                    Bloom!
Light up a new set of synapses
Long excursion into the pre-frontal lobes
Crawl up out of the thalamus & goose the super-ego
Turn loose the memory circuits
Here we begin

                              ✾

J. M. Edmonds, *Lyra Graeca,* Vol. III, p. 569, Attic Scolia, #16:
"Drink with me, play with me, love with me, be wreathed with me; be
wild when I am wild, and when I am staid, be staid."

                              ✾

How many other things can I think of
Beside this alphabet soup,
Whole universes: the finest imaginable powder
                    (fern spores—

"*myriad*" is either countless or exactly
ten thousand—
I mean more)
Fresh air   this evening
delicious

☼

eucalyptus: *that* smell

☼

and now being quietly at home
Freedom breakthrough: arrival at the pass:
Chill wind, all the world huge silent clean rock,
lakes and rivers far below
Mountain peaks as far as I can see

☼

But never cop out to having heard Ben Bernie.
Rudy Vallee was a national hero.
General Voznekov sits at the folding canvas table while shells
and blunker fragments burst around him he writes messages to the
Imperial War HQ, his hand rattles across the page as the sun sets

☼

I see a poem by Yeats
AFIRE, the flame room blue

☼

NATURAL FOLK SPEECH:
"I guess he won't be doing that again right away in such
a hurry!"

☼

What may be accomplished. What has
                 been done . . . but I swim:
           a pool between rocky shores

❋

If it were upside down
What color would it be?

❋

Sir John Maundeville, *Travels,* p. 56:
     "Men say also, that the balm
       groweth in Ynde the more, in
       that desert where the trees of the sun
       and of the moon
       spake to Alisaundre."

❋

AGGRAVATION

           o.   o.   yeah.   yeah.
     As good as gold or platinum
     emeralds and rubies and sapphires
     opal garnet and pearl. What
     I'm afraid of is, I don't think
     it's going to work and I don't
     know why. Hey you know what?
     I've got rubber cement. Have you
     ever considered hanging yourself, Mr. Warbler?

❋

           After you've said that
           What have you said?

❋

translunacy, a communicable form of crazy

❋

Despair, hunger, imbecility

❋

I must continue to work, nevertheless, there being so much still
unaccomplished, unrealized.

❋

fire engines and pigeons and rain
business as usual

❋

When can I eat the sardines?

❋

When shall I leave?

❋

I'm not concentrating. I want to worry about food & money.

❋

NATIVE SPEECH
    "No, I got married & give up drinking."

❋

funk drawing   Rage & feather
    &   tickle
feathers   Republiquelle
    &   false quim rubber gulch
strange anatomy

❋

McClure says, in conversation,
          "... not in the movies any more.
          Quasi-pornographic painting.
          I'd love to see her dance.
            (a tattoo on her shoulder)
          Greek woman about 30
          Small unassuming restaurant in Santa
             Monica near my mother's motel
               all the movie stars go there
          Except for the whale & porpoise shows
          Marineland is a great big skam."
Nevertheless, I think he enjoyed his trip to L.A.
          "Zip in a motorcycle," he says.
          Mountains of schlock.
               Lawrence Lipton's at UCLA . . ."
And a final comment on the meth scene, here or there or NYC,
      "Everything that's portable is carried off
      Everything that can't be moved is burned around the edges
      Everything has been stolen."

                   ✻

NATIVE SPEECH
      "So that's what all that was all about."

                   ✻

Some flowers won't bear close inspection
Others demand contemplation—for example, a chrysanthemum

                   ✻

forget-me-not blossoms the 2nd time this year
eucalyptus fence-posts they set out last month have new
          grey-green shoots and leaves

Beach pine, black pine roots
      thrust out and return right through the surface of a cliff
            red chert, Franciscan Series
New grand hydrangea season

❀

    While putting away my newly washed clothes I figure,
    I may not live to wear these, but at least they're clean.

❀

Katharine Tynan writes that Yeats
      "took to an indiscriminate eating of fungi
      which very much alarmed his hosts"
What he guessed the Druids had been doing in that same part
of the world

❀

We shall go interview the cypress trees
representing ourselves to be Gavin Arthur

❀

"Just exactly how much damage have you suffered?"
This is a perfect English Alexandrine.

❀

What is the real message, the complete
word of those Ancestors
whose voices come to me with
single troublesome sentences?
It's grown very late—I
must require them to put up
or shut up.
      "I ain't going to hold my breath until you do."
(McAlister & Polk Streets, NE corner)
The top half of the Hall McAlister statue has a new coat of green
patina/algae where I stop walking to write this

❀

...... the last part is all laughing & singing. ......

❈

Beautiful turnips I peel for the soup
Do they smell like nasturtiums
                    or chrysanthemums?
Latin or Greek
            East meets West
            (nasturtiums are South American)

❈

        pointy roof
    Light & cloud shadows fall across them

            Rugged snowpeaks late in August

    I see the worn gummy shingle fakes
            once had several colors

    Light needles through peppertree threads
                a prism, a diffraction grating
            Rainbow City, heaven's gate

Friday is Love's Day

❈

Kilton Stewart writes,
"In order to get a more complete idea of the Bontoc's attitude to-
wards the high god, Lumawig, I inquired about their beliefs concern-
ing death, and about the prayers which were said at the funeral feast.
They told me that often the person who is ill and about to die hears
the *anitos* calling him, saying it is better in the mountains . . . their
prayers (i.e. those of the relatives at the funeral) tell of the good life in
the mountains which the old men have seen in visions, and which the
deceased can enjoy if he will go there to live and continue to cooper-
ate on feast days with his living relatives."

❈

Great bull hummingbird rules
            the peppertree
Skip-bombs neighbor garden roses

❋

Gauzy emerald
goldfinch music
pleasure & delight

———————————————

❋

———————————————

            Breathe deeply.
            Watch the green curtain.

❋

"Polemonium, "sky pilot," Haselwood says,
            "that blue flower grows on the highest passes."
I've seen it there myself

———————————————

❋

———————————————

            Condition total/condition LIGHT

THE CODA

The food opera has been sung, a final cymbal crash,
drum thump and gong note remain:

        When I'm hungry, I'm free, and I have chosen
freedom at this price, a very small one to pay,
considering the noxious fumes and the mountains of
feculent matter which I'd otherwise be required to
admire, to eat, to digest, to add onto the general dungheap.

It would please a very great number of people if I
should perish from hunger; they'd be ecstatically happy
if I should kill myself by whatever means. I refuse to
give them that satisfaction. Let them accept the responsibility
for doing me in with their banks, their governments, their
wars. I must try to liberate all of them.

                                                            5:iv:65

APRIL SHOWERS BRING RAIN?

                foot/feet
                        rain/tulip
                                move the garbage
                                away from the window

TULIP   BLACK   BLACK   TULIP
TRIUMPH   STAR   siren STAR   QUEEN
PRINCESS BEATRIX   OF SHEBA

                unseasonably early evening

TULIP   TULIP   TOE
I always loved,   rain.
a secret part   QUEEN OF NIGHT
_____

Lots of   I sit on my feet to warm them.
wind and rain   The house is cold & damp, but I think
the most fragile   the gas stove will warm it (Tulip)
cherry blossoms
the thinnest   Hot cheap tea from Chinatown,
rhododendron petals   four bits the half pound
not even wrinkled   (a tulip scent?)

                            438

Lots of paper that I shall mark up

---

incense to burn
music to play
books to learn

That sandpiper
all alone, usually
runs with a cloud
alone today, eating
sea bugs—where does he
live at? Where are his books?

---

rain/feet/rain, I have walked in it, I got all sweaty
I washed myself and changed my clothes and ate food
and talked to Lewy and now I sit, having told my diary *everything*.

✸

airplane, prop-driven
flying below the storm

7:iv:65

LOVE LOVE LOVE AGAIN

I keep trying to live as if this world were heaven
puke fish   dark fish   pale fish   park fish
        mud fish   lost fish   selfish
            Rockers and Mods
            "acres of clams"

And all my friends, all the people I've known, all I'm going to know
Were mistresses and lovers, all of us with each other
All intimate with me

fish eyes never close but fish sleep
octopus eye of human camera goat
gnat in my ear, mice in my beard
beautiful garden in my colon (part of me
REALLY a flower)

I dreamed something with a whale in it
(Not the biggest whale, but big enough)
Animal who loves in the sea
And worms and snails and crustaceans and plant/animals
Animal plants

Although your name doesn't show here
I haven't forgotten you.

7:iv:65

A MORNING WALK

The Year goes by very fast but it takes a long time.
Tennis player says, "Gee, I don't have that touch today. Oh,
I don't have that touch today."
    Did he say "cut" instead of "touch"?

✲

Backwards in time, although I see fog plumes drift over sunny hills,
I'm watching Herman Melville feed a pumpkin to his cow—he
watches her jaws move.

✲

a kind of Japanese porcelain appears to be covered with seeds or warts—little white or colored beads of glaze embedded in the surface. I see the same kind of seedy bumps on sea-urchin skeleton, also on gourds and squashes . . . which vegetables appear to be splashed with green, orange and yellow enamel paint, covered with clear spar varnish

T'ang Dynasty glazes imitated these?

✿

Chocolate fun. That was no surprise.

✿

Awaken me with roses.   (roses)

(VOICES?)

flow-
ers

21:iv:65

MESSAGE BEFORE ARAM AWAKES

—*before he hear telephone:*

MESSAGE BLANK? 30:iv:65	mossy rotting corduroy road through the woods bracket fungus & sorrel, no event? All ours, yesterday, livid orange and raving green, very quiet, no event, scatter sun image on moss wave tree top (Fresnel lens/agate diffraction grate) scatter, infinite power dissipation exhibit every wavelength NO MESSAGE CANCEL BUT BILL THE SENDER COLLAPSE RE-WIND & CONFIRM IMMEDIATE CESSATION ALL WAR HOSTILITIES?

441

"THE SUN RISES AND SETS IN THAT CHILD,"

    so my grandmother used to say,

also shines
 while the sun is:
Moon   petal curve blossom
           carved
Frogman sits on Bear's head leaf stone?
Beaver with son on his back stem fuzz gold ray
  in her belly   ———————————
Stands on Frog head   ———————————
Raven hovers over   *padma:* lotus
         ———————————
         ———————————
         frog sits on the water
         "seeking whom to devour"

  "Universal Darkness covers all."

            May 1965

As next as possible; approximate propinquity, starfish windflower. Sunny breezy weather. I expect myself to do too much about it. Exert yourself, I say, but I feel too sleepy, angry, disconnected . . . all these emotions and sensations occur simultaneously. (I can hear an imaginary objection: "*All?* Not really!") What I want is the sensation of writing, what I'm about to do is go to sleep. I pretend that I stay awake because I'm expecting to see a friend who asked yesterday whether he might visit me today.

Sir Walter Scott: (*Lady of the Lake*, Canto I, ll. 218–19)

> "Fox-glove and nightshade, side by side
> Emblems of punishment and pride."

(quoted s.v. "foxglove" in *SNED*)

NATIVE FOLK SPEECH
(possibilities of song!)

"Don't I know him from when we was down in La Jolla?"

> "Don't I know him
> From when we was down
> In La Jolla?"

"CALIFORNIA IS ODIOUS BUT INDISPENSABLE"

César Franck walks between rows of radishes & scallions
In the kitchen garden he observes green light cast by sun
Through onion tube tops.
"*Alors,*" he says to himself, or "*Tiens!*" Perhaps he muttered
an old Walloon proverb, ". . .

> Santa Barbara in California might be full of people just
> like that. Or Ventura. In Watsonville is a large Yugoslav
> enclave, industrious producers of artichokes & Brussels
> sprouts. Artichokes have beautiful architecture; Santa
> Barbara with a tower in her hand is patroness of archi-
> tects. Santa Monica is further south, mother of St.
> Augustine oldest city in Florida. St. Louis Bishop of
> Toulouse, 19 August.

("*Tiens. Tant mieux.*")

> The Lark gets there 2:25 A.M. ON TIME, to Our Lady
> Queen of the Angels. Often and often. *C'est ça.* The
> French language is endlessly diverting, if incomprehen-
> sible. *Ça va.* (

> (Jack tells the proper direction:
> ". . . pick up flower car at Redwood . . .")

7:v:65

IMAGINATION OF THE TAJ MAHAL

                                Hand gold
        glass holds flower under water dome bright
        feather blue green royal eye powder gold enormous
        lofty thin brass dome carve marble inlay
        gem slices emerald sapphire lapis ruby
        marigold shapes of bright cold flames that
        Dome of moving water green fire

in the sun brilliant forest carved stone
park flash feather gold green solid marigold
and silent petal flutter color sun ray
blue and red light through blossom wall
tough as eyelid softer than bright
gold carp under lilies

7:v:65

T/O

Open. Open bubbling pools and
fresh springs of new water. Open
the rock. hide the secret, but know
what it is.

I: tough thin substance
expanding flexible glass
I traveled past the sun
found other nights and days,
                              Beyond
this universe of countless worlds and
stars I find many more. Beyond
this temporary imagination I call myself
and mine there are countless others.
Far away, all by their lonesome,

✧

August royal blackness, brilliant night, &c.

✧

O tickle star o rub that purple rim, &c. (hat) &c.

✧

445

". . . there's not very much of that
left, either. . . ," Robert Duncan said.

✴

certain flowers. I'll put all this into my book, decorate all
these blank white pages. Remember Oktavian in
Rosenkavalier.
Think of Hebe and Ganymede:

✴

Complete reorganization according to the newly conceived
SCHEME will commence promptly at 0800 hours on Saturday 8
May 1965. All personnel must comply with these directives
beginning at Midnight on Friday, 7 May, 1965, under pain of our
displeasure.
 Flower curtain, a veil of blossoms
 covered the casket. Remember there's
 only a wax dummy inside. Remember
 S. T. Coleridge's lovely title, *The Pains of Sleep.*
 Of course we do.

Pleasure, pain and recollection are events inside the brain:
their "outside" location (please scratch my back) an illusion?

7:v:65

"THE GREAT HEIDELBERG TUN"

Unconscious of my loneliness until I hear
  music, then it spills in thick molasses
   flow down over my head unevenly

9:v:65

446

Nasturtium shadows
9 : Ⅳ : 65

SLEEPY

Spring wind:
Green curtain flapping
Shakes elephant bells

"you can imagine how I felt
put yourself in my position"

a gentle chiming in my dreams—
Feature that.

"Oh I don't know—some American chap,
writes novels, I believe. But whatever
it is—aside from that smell—think of
those really splendid brown eyes!

Seventy-two in San Rafael
Snow from North Dakota to Nebraska
May the Ninth

9:v:65

A SATIRE

I haven't seen °°° about, lately
Why do I imagine that he's become a large housefly
There he sits, on the bathroom windowsill

12:v:65

CARD #21 *LE MONDE*

Inside the green hedged garden
The First Eve (Mistress of Time)
4 Seasons wait outside
Bullface, Eagleface, Lionface, Man (a blazing Serpent,
one of the Seraphim)

Eve dances with a snake of cloth who is the Northwind
Beyond the power of the Sun who hasn't been invented yet.

(N.B., that the images returned to me first, then I realized
what it was I had been seeing, hence the title.)

24?:v:65

25 Ⅴ 65

Strange?

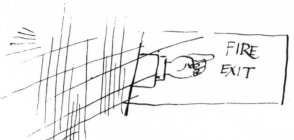

ᴍᴍ

Break glass
pull down lever

Information — and a picture.
why should there be a picture
as well as words

FIRE EXIT

EXIT, "he/she/it — goes out.

'Hey, lady, your sign fell down.'

IN CASE OF
FIRE
BREAK
GLASS

Brightly

450

1935

               turned to the wall,
draped in black muslin cold
black veils for you in prison
shame disgrace and degradation
black veils motheaten, one or two
rhinestone brilliants adhere to the filmy fabric
which blows against dusty calsomined cheek don't make me cry
my makeup will run—
Ah, little monkey!

               ✿

A broken wrist-pin held us up in Carthage

The ocean is wider than the hill is high, the water hangs
Over the hill in the sky

Jimson weed blooms today

                                            15:vi:65

THE FEATHER TRUTH WEIGHS 10,000 POUNDS

FLEE from the wrath to come.
forbid forespend foreskin foresight foredone
        Dismissal
      an exciting story about rich people
      beautiful and powerful and rich
      expenditures unobtrusive because they are so large
      regalements. Chirping small birds devouring insects
            also newly born from eggs

Dismal. A bad week, a wild weekend, a funky Monday,
another bad week. Dismal. Squalor is a better word.
VACANCY

12:vii:65

M

FOR ROBERT DUNCAN

Many tedious hours
How many shallow days
    cloudy sky or sun immediately reflected from the top layer
    all beneath lay hid
    the moving surface apparently motionless

M is WATER, an hieroglyphic owl
Phoenician: ꟽ   *mem*
               μ   *mu* in Greek
                     Aeschylus makes the Eumenides
                     cry "μ μ μ μ"
Kabala: "a Mother #13, the power of 40"

        In Rome M = 1000.

13:vii:65

452

THE LIFE OF LITERATURE

"Wonder whether you or they hold the rights" and would you
care and I wonder what would you do if you had the chance"

    I just bet you would, you'd
take one look and run away
    I bet you would, even if you had the chance
you'd be afraid
you wouldn't take it even then.

"even if it was set before you on a silver platter."

Where there was one there's more
a lot more where that one came from,
poetry,
to spurt right out the top of my head
"the come of the poem," as Ginsberg says.

17:vii:65

WHAT FINALLY HAPPENED TO THE KING

The king's inside a nest of boxes.
They sawed through the lynch pin of his chariot wheel,
Dared him to race, there was
A tragic accident. Fatal mistake
Inside the Labyrinth, over the cliff he flew
A swallow, to follow the careless black sails,

✳

purple crowned shouts five times
declines into wrinkled silence
wrapped in delicate skin, elaborate
foldings of cloth, goldy threads,
the straining cords of a silky net,

✿

The world grew very small. After 1918, it was controlled
        from New York City.
Hell is made of fallen suns. Its proprietor
formerly a sun god. Every day another sun goes *under*
        the earth.

✿

Today the king created 37 new peers, many of the old ones, now living in Los Angeles, have allowed their dues to lapse and their titles have run out. The Earl of Salt speaks darkly about the "decline" of polite society and the scarcity of nice people. Viscount Fitch closed his town house. The king could remember waking up coming and pissing—ecstatic.

19:vii:65

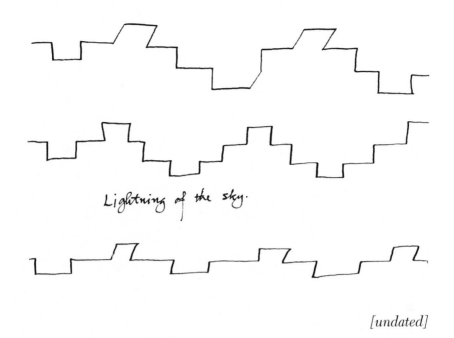

Lightning of the sky.

[undated]

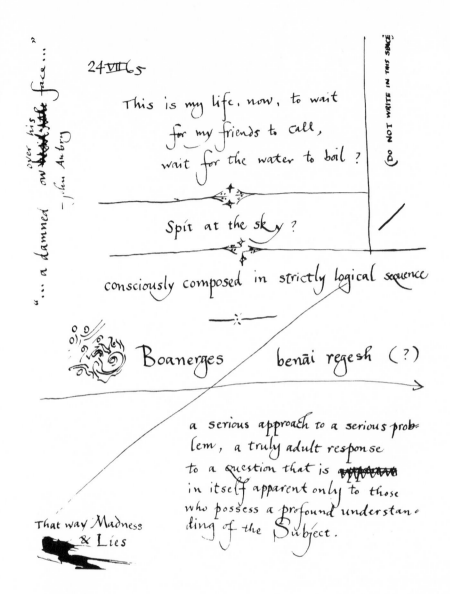

24 VII 65

This is my life. now, to wait
for my friends to call,
wait for the water to boil ?

Spit at the sky ?

consciously composed in strictly logical sequence

Boanerges   benāi regesh (?)

a serious approach to a serious prob-
lem, a truly adult response
to a question that is ~~xxxxxxx~~
in itself apparent only to those
who possess a profound understan-
ding of the Subject.

That way Madness
& Lies

"... a damned on ~~that fat~~ face ..."
over his
— John Aubry

(DO NOT WRITE IN THIS SPACE)

AMERICA!

I've got what I was after
Arrows of red paint on the pavement

❊

Go ahead and wear tight clothes
Drive a pile of credit on 4 wheels
Who did you ever make it with—
                did you come?

❊

Unworried at last
blue sky over Masonic Temple
            (self-portrait of stiff dong)

What town was that?

25:vii:65

THE EDUCATION CONTINUES ALONG

for Clark Coolidge

Don't leave the house before noon there's a reason
You'll find it later it will be revealed to you
Preserve ritual purity
The Unworthy must be left in that Ignorance which is a Divine
Punishment Amen.

            rutile:
            ore from which titanium   SAGENITE?
            Queen of the Night
            (Queen of the Fucking May)

457

an independent study of
non-Euclidean pleasures non-canonical hours
watch and pray. "Watch"
means "to sit up all night without sleeping."
Watch means look at me: See my bellybutton.

I hope you didn't think I meant anything personal by it.
You don't have to if you don't want to.
What happened to your hair. I left it on the bureau.
The pleasure of exact location lies in a certain
            feeling. Let me feel yours.
                    Feel mine?

LIMIT defined by change of state, as
            the bed is just so wide
            beyond the edge of it we fall on the floor

                        ❋

            MEASURE, that which contains a number of beats. Two
                pints one quart; eight quarts is a peck.
"O,   Aristotle a dead professor? "container for the thing con-
A   tained?" Hart Crane says, "For joy rides in stu-
B   pendous coverings."
S
O   ❋
L
U   THE PRIMARY: are you in love?
T   are you hungry? WHERE YOU AT?
E   do you have a toothache?
L   who's got all the money?
Y   How much does it cost to find out what you want
!"   to know?

                        ❋

458

THANK YOU. COME AGAIN.

❊

We *do* all of us depend on one another. Do it some more.

❊

                                    this was a π-meson,
                                    moving at some kind of
             peh!   *unbelievable speed. The*
                                    speed identifies it.

❊

The song says,
          "Please give me something to remember you by
          When you are far away from me, Dear—
          Some little something, &c &c."

❊

———meh!———
          viz., a μ-meson, moving
          some kind incredible speed
          "Incwoyable" they
          used to say, refusing
          to use that "R"
          which would remind them of
          that unfortunate Citoyen Louis
          Capet, whilom LE ROY

❊

———*bah!*———
          much slower, the loss of a
          β-particle out of the middle
          this only penetrates four inches
          of lead or twelve of concrete.
Mr. Yeats has warned us, "things fall apart, the centre cannot hold."
Quite as if we were able to learn anything, as if we've listened to Wm.

Yeats—or to Plato, Jesus, Moses & Co.—Nothing has soaked into our heads except of some fake superstitions about sex and a few jokes and limericks concerned with the same subject.

✻

(I exaggerate. I remember a few lines about the weather, "red sky at night, sailors delight, &c.")

✻

Yet I hope that curiosity isn't dead . . . contrariwise, I despair about the high price of second-hand books, even 2nd-hand PAPERBACK books.

✻

Do I know what it is that I am doing, &c.

✻

How badly do I need to read one more book, whatever its price considering that I'm already half blind from too much reading anyway and one more book has as many lies in it as all the rest, why don't I go look at the world instead or sit and think for a few years, or even try to write "seriously"

✻

We got to the top of Windy Ridge then climbed Peak 12524
We saw where we'd been last year, whole days of travel in one
        glance: Pinchot Pass, the Palisades, the heights towards
        Muir Pass where will the next trip be?

✻

Why don't you quit while you're still ahead?

✻

Why not. But a few hours later, or the next day or whenever, there it is again, straight, hard & throbbing, no knowledge of Civilization, fatigue, the Law, the usages of Polite Society &c. Osiris, Adonis, Dionysius, Attis, Jesus, Heracles, Odysseus, Aeneas, Gilgamesh return. All return. A wheel.

❁

"... ABSOLUTELY FINAL FAREWELL
PERFORMANCE"
Liszt made eight or ten of them, Eleanora Duse did a dozen or so, Anna Pavlova and the Marx Brothers built it into an independent art form, "FOR THE LAST TIME ON ANY STAGE!"

❁

or drawing room or Turkey Bath . . .
"It turns out," as Helen used to say. The Beautiful Poet is really this middle-aged type wants to fuck me in the ass.
A B S O L U T E
REALITY, namely, how much can I do right now about life in this place? I am it, all of this living AND this place and what I'm doing is called T R A N S F O R M A T I O N ,
IRRADIATION: BASE METAL BECOMES GOLD

". . . just dancing," Mr. Lenny Bruce explained,
". . . no kissing."

XY says,
"The beautiful poet wants to lick me all over, suck my dick *et cetera*. I can't think why. The first thing you know, there we were and there wasn't any yes or no to it, we had a ball. Wouldn't you? Magic, he calls it. Absolutely indefensible, of course, unnatural, a symptom of profound psychological disturbance, we did it every chance we got & will probably do it again."

❁

461

"ABSOLUTELY, O *Absolutely*. Where you're at; what's happening." I suppose he's interested in the quality sometimes.

✺

G. Stein: "History is what happens from time to time"

✺

Where I sit in "my" room with the windows open, a joss-stick
fumes before bronze Tara

>(Gary and Joanne hunted it out from great junkpile at
>Kathmandu, bronze images . . . arms, legs, axes, elephant
>heads, reclining, sitting, standing, *in coitū* sprouting more
>heads and arms, animal features, wings and haloes, which
>recall the great battle of Ahura Mazda light against the
>Darkness again, a Persian overlay on Buddha sculpture)

1.) am I hungry. Not right now, and there's food in the refrigerator.
2.) I am in love with so&so, and would like to make it with S, T, U, V,
W, X, Y, Z, &c.
3.) Did Nikola Tesla REALLY make a machine that could extract
electric voltage out of the very ground on which he stood. (Clark
Coolidge asked me.) I can't remember what are the characteristics of
or the use for the electrical coil which bears his name. Tesla.
4.) History is probably shorter than we like to think. What is history
REALLY. What is a new and active use for it?
5.) I've got to stop writing and start thinking. So what else is new?

✺

SHE says, "You must know what's really yours; you must know it's
really you doing it."
I wouldn't have it any other way.
SHE says, "You really like that. Why don't you *have* that?"
There are a number of reasons why not.
I suppose that light still flashes high above Miner's [minor's] Ledge.
　"1–4–3," "I-love-you. I hear you. 1–4–3, Miner's Ledge Light,
1–4–3—I-love-you, what better way to remember?"

✺

462

"So & So" (some historical figure, some artist) "grabbed
up all these" (musical notes, words, whatever) "and made not
another" (whatever it was) "but . . .
a STAR!"
Where'd I read that?

✻

I wasted an hour trying to locate the story, riffling through half a
dozen books, and I MUST let go the search isn't the one I want to go
on today.

"Come in! Come in! You're just in time
        to hear me recite the history
of The Invisible City of Kitezh!"
        The Sacred City of Great Kitezh
        (large and lurid color lithograph, slightly off-register)
        Hear the bells. Birds of Paradise that sing.
The entire CITY
        yarded off to Heaven in a goldy cloud
        nothing left but a blazing cross to mark the spot
        & terrify the Mongol Horde
        (KKK?)
        the bells of the Sacred City
        chime deep in the wood, audible from the stars
The wicked repent, the soprano ascends with her prince
They all sing—
                eternal delight invisible to earth
                we hear it all
                hope for the best
                    (K L A N G !)
                but what we get
Next week, *Cavalleria Rusticana*

The XIX C. was black and white.

Kurt Schwitters tore it all into COLOR
"primatiti," &c.
"primatiti-ti,
Primatiti-ta, &c."

moreover, there are blue horses now
and a *Fish Garden* by Paul Klee
We're willing to have other creatures
Share the world

I must make a correction.
Charles Darwin was black and white in the XIX Century?
Charley Baudelaire?
Sir Leslie Stephen black and white
was he a lesser man?
Walter Whitman said the animals don't complain.

✻

NB: PLEASE REVISE YOUR *DIX-NEUVIEME*

✻

LATER (after lunch) I couldn't leave it—I find so far, that it was
Edith Sitwell quoting John Livingston Lowes who was quoting . . .
what author?

"Give Coleridge one vivid word from an old narrative: let him
mix it with two in his thought; and then (translating terms of
music into terms of words) 'out of these sounds he (will)
frame, not a fourth sound, but a star.'"
—*The Road to Xanadu,* p. 303

✻

The point is, I *remembered,* at last, that I'd been looking at the Sitwell book (*A Poet's Notebook*) a couple days ago—now I'm free to go to the postoffice and the library.

☼

"The glory is departed from the coconut and a prosaic world has relinquished one delight."
—The Road to Xanadu, p. 288

☼

That out of three sounds he frame, not a fourth sound but a star."
—Robert Browning, "Abt Vogler"

☼

I was assisted to this via Bartlett's *Familiar Quotations.* A trip to the main library is next—the Tesla coil either is or is not a real recollection.
(Are TEKTITES really from outer space?)

☼

SNED (1937): "TESLA (te´sla). 1902. The name of *Nikola Tesla* (born 1857), American electrician, used attrib. to denote certain apparatus and phenomena."

WEBSTER'S *New Collegiate Dictionary:* single entry in Biographical Names section.

Encyclopedic Dictionary of Electronics and Nuclear Engineering, Robert I. Sarbacher, Sc.D. editor, Prentice-Hall Inc. Englewood Cliffs, New Jersey. 1959. p. 1281:

"*Tesla.* A unit of magnetic induction, equal to 1 Weber per square meter, in the mksa electromagnetic systems.

Tesla Coil. An induction coil used to develop a high-voltage discharge at a very high frequency. As shown in Fig. 2 a high-voltage transformer (T) is used to promote a discharge across the primary gap (G_1) and to charge a condenser (C_1) in parallel

465

with the transformer primary. High-amperage low-frequency currents oscillate in the few-turn winding P, and induce high-voltage high-frequency oscillations in the secondary many-turn winding S. If S is tuned to resonance with the primary, very intense oscillations produce discharges across the gap G_2. Also called a Tesla transformer."

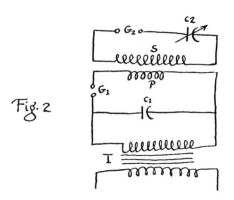

Fig. 2

In order to get the point of much of this part, go read (right now) pages 181–186 in *History and the Homeric Iliad*, by Denys Page, University of California Press, Berkeley and Los Angeles, 1963 (a paperback edition exists).

This table stands on fidgety feet.
Fidgety Feet is also the name of a song or piano solo, circa 1920-odd

✻

Assertions about history assertions of an unstable
      insecure personality?
            Lemon rind orange flower
                lime tree

✻

Personality: How you customarily place your feet
Lemon flower   orange tree   lime juice
Grapefruit   kumquat   citron   tangerine

> flowers at riverside
> at Lemon Cove

✻

O California sub-tropical freeze!

✻

Lemon tree   lime flower   juice of several oranges
the leaves are shiny green
"shrubs of the rue family," A. Merriam-Webster says.
Assertions of personality and authority who will control
the dictionary?

> *The Harper Encyclopedia of Science,* edited by James R. Newman
> (and a large staff). Harper & Row, Publishers, New York and
> Evanston. Sigma, Inc. Washington, D.C., 1963 (4 vols.) Vol. IV,
> p. 1178:
> "*Tesla coil:* . . . The coil is suitable for exciting X-ray and
> Crookes (vacuum) tubes."

✻

I found a biography, *Prodigal Genius, The Life of Nikola Tesla,* by
John J. O'Neill. Ives Washburn, Inc., New York (n.d.) (The copyright
notice on the verso of the title page is dated 1944)

It appears that Tesla was a genius of the highest order. He had an
eidetic memory and imagination. He saw a vision of whirling mag-
netic fields while watching a sunset; his ideas for the construction of
alternating current generators, dynamos, transmission lines, controls
and insulation, as well as the mathematical theory which would de-
scribe the operation of these things came to him that evening. He
went to America and met George Westinghouse. They harnessed the
power of Niagara Falls.

Tesla was a nut. He had a germ phobia, gynophobia, and if we can
believe his biographer, the only creature he loved in his adult life was
a pigeon.

But observe: He lighted the Chicago World's Fair of 1893. He also "let 1,000,000 volts of high-frequency high-voltage alternating current pass through his body for many minutes" while he held a globe in his hand which gave forth a brilliant light. Thomas Edison had told everybody it couldn't be done, that alternating current was lethal. Thomas Edison and the Edison Company owned the street lighting system in New York in those days; it operated from a direct current dynamo . . . quite inefficiently.

✻

This one loves blue	cf. Alcaeus,
That one dotes on glass	fr. 173
"None of it came to nothing in the end	
None of it amounted to a hill of beans."	καὶ κ᾽οὐδεγ
That's what my grandmother used to say.	ἐκ Σενογ Υευοιτο.
	"and nothing will
	come of anything"

✻

That's all that there, she said.

✻

Gertrude Stein: "Let me recite what history teaches. History teaches."

✻

(Not quite a month later, 15:viii:65)
N.B., That History, being a writing, can be destroyed, or changed to suit whatever purpose the writer, the printer, the State may determine. History is a cat which can be altered to suit the owner. Nikola Tesla was a handsome man. He died all alone in a hotel room. A friend paid the bill— Tesla was broke.

San Francisco 27:vii:65
Kyoto 8:vii:66

GIANT SEQUOIAS

Amazing creatures, I was delighted
to visit them, to watch them,
languid waving those green feather scale fronds
they aren't too far from being ferns.

These giants make me laugh, they are young and fragile
upwards of 2000 years old, I worry about them, will they survive?
Here are more of them than I had hoped
But the odds against them are huge as themselves.

28:vii:65

POP DOUGHNUT

"What if everybody did that"
            hilarity was unconfined
        everybody does.
DOUGHNUT, a big one made of
raised potato flour, now all brown
under thick sugar crystals.
Doughnut without a hole has red jelly inside.
Doughnut, small and rather heavy
thick skin of powdered sugar.
Doughnut, brown and spicy, newly fried,
still hot, later it will be a lump of grease

Everybody likes doughnuts and crullers
Doughnuts and ice cream and coffee.
These were invented in New England?
Waffles are from Holland
Marie de' Medici invented ice cream?

28:vii:65, a Wednesday.

SECRET

The great secret books are available to all. There are copies in most libraries; they can be bought in cheap paper editions. However accessible, they are still secret books. The careless, the casual, the thoughtless reader will come away from them no wiser than he was before. The really secret books are dictated to me by my own ears and I write down what they say.

31:vii:65

THAT EYES! THOSE NOSE!

                                    small quantity of musk pervades
Trace a scrawl. Squall.   the air in a room

            ————————————   In a few seconds of time
                                    great worlds are born & die

        you didn't even notice it
        you didn't even care.

            ————————————

        Così fan Tutte

            ————————————

Intelligence of death leaks out my eyes
Also, life and enlightenment

            ————————————

A *REPLY*

"Not enough so as it would make any
difference."

12:*vii*:65

THE FIRST OF AUGUST

some of it
an opera
somebody enter upstairs
   Ernie
Under false wig of Watusi? Later is free for you
baby sunspots interfere with the transmission, honey
We're going to foreclose.
     (foreclose!)
Amphitryon shock messentery loop line
under modern transmission unclear WE ARE
     GOING TO FORECLOSE. Fore?
      Chewys?
dee   deee deee deee Chewys?

I'm going to eat dinner I am oh yeah fuck all these feeble drones I
swish (*Muiopotmos:* or *The Fate of the Butterfly*) end parenthesis 40
feet. I said gahgoo gagoop grope callouses da-dum from E-flat to F?
No, C-major. Somebody. Anyway. I don't know what I'll do to com-
mission him disappointment. Yes I do have some where. In the
jacket. Bib overalls. Shake. Shake. The rest of the night, I never saw
you again; stop it.

    Please leave me alone, you motherfucker. What are you going to
do with that. It would be lovely.

    I seem to be distracted. Fuck anything.

    Première d'Août 1965. Question that I asked back before you got
too tight. I want to go home. Exquisitely.

471

I want to. Yes I do. Who do you think you are you big stiff. I really think that you *should* tease me. Not from this profile, baby.

    Cette image. I crush my cup. Scoot up.

✻

Did you do the drawing. It's such a small pad that I could only do a half at a time, first the top half and then the bottom half. He says, "I don't feel like going."

    Look down at the rug.

Première d'Août.

✻

Well I run across some kind of longhair off a dope scene and I didn't have to come across with anything.

I saw him making it along the street bombed out of his skull that lady in the telephone booth, too fat to shut the door, saying "you don't care if I live or die," all dressed up and on her way.

1:viii:65

THE GREEKS

    divided it three ways
        Underworld, earth and sea, heavens above

    HADES   POSEIDON   ZEUS

        3 ways
      body, soul and spirit
We've been fragmented ever since
(Very carefully NOT in memory of Adonis, Osiris
    we do not ((all tattered)) RISE AGAIN)
At best we show scars and seams, ill-joined
That monster created by Boris Karloff and Perc Westmore

3 ways
"I'm going to cut you three ways: wide, deep and frequent."

Jesus tried to save both worlds, nobody cares,
Everybody's out celebrating Good Friday. The Sunday following
They wear their new clothes, the children play with flowery eggs
But of course Jesus is quite dead, still nailed,
                    "... *in Todesbanden*"
Bach proved it all out in the B-Minor Mass, nobody listens
Blake tried to start all over again, good news, a new dispensation,
The churchmen and philosophers alternately use glue and string,
Some try to break the bone and re-set it, like a surgeon
Nobody can pry the western mind loose from
                    those nails, that perfumed grave, the weeping Momma
We are hung three ways, money sex and stingy
We are too many and we try to work it out to the nearest decimal
Everything hung up on NOTHING
And we had no zero until 1300 A.D.
And we pretend it's nothing, that it don't exist
We hang by ten fingers, our measures don't work
Our spelling is wrong, our counting of syllable, day and year
We count money, "a Sicilian coin struck in the year A.D. 1124"

                              ❊

The Sumerians were smart enough to combine sixes and tens
Their year was exact, their poetry
Who knows if their poetry scanned?

                                        1:viii:65

VIGNETTE OF AN ICE AXE

"The truth of it is I took you for granted
You went away with somebody else.

Velichros!
Velichros!

I fall fall down.

I look into floor-level apartment
They are a painting by Oskar Kokoschka—
JEALOUS!

1:viii:65

L'ENFANT PRODIGUE

I want to see the old country before I die.

Babble on to me of greasy regrets. I feel
immortal Helen with a kiss. Caesar yourself,
you brought her.
("Why don't you go back to the Old
Country. . . .")

"There's only three places in that Europe I want to see—
Holland, Hawaii and The Holy Land."

(". . . any old country.")

3:viii:65

474

A row of letters: Message in
Language as yet undeciphered
Secret formula discovered

---

e.g.	2nd Rameses ALIVE! Demands obedience of entire civilized world. Edgar Hoover "Appalled!" Southern scientists claim fraud.

Arrow of letters addressed to that one who invented them
    Four-eyed Chinese dragonface Ts'ang Chieh

                                      (Mathews 6707)

e.g.	Egyptian bird-head	
	Greek murder victim	
	Sumerian supernatural	
	Phoenician warehouse clerk	

" . . . having wonderful time wish you was here.
X marks the window I'm in . . ."

---

marks Eleusis where Demeter gives the seeds and the letters to
                    Triptolemus

※

A BOUQUET:
            mushrooms appear in a night or in a moment
(spontaneously, we say, but there are seeds, little beasts that
are so small as to be invisible to the naked eye, according
to A. van Leeuwenhoek)

from fairies dancing in a ring?
Laws of electrochemistry? (Are they
really reasons?) *Toujours la même chose.*

Rare blossoms! Do you want to do it again *already?*
Why don't we sleep a little first oh well.

✼

A world of pleasure, a world of suffering
whatever it is
        "that show was over before it ever started."
night-blooming cereus

✼

All worlds are real crystal, humming energy
All reals are temporary bubble of glass
                "fiasco"

✼

blossom pollen scatter seed swell dwindle and perish
come back next year crimson, purple
masses of blossom, the rhododendrons
                and perfume

✼

Kore goes underground where the snake lies hid

3:viii:65

GENETICS

How much of the time do I spend re-living my father's life,
        my mother's?
Doing what they liked, what they wanted to do, finding out
        what they wanted to know . . . seeing and hearing all
            they never had time for, never dreamed?

5:viii:65

HIGHER CRITICISM

The Iliad
a tribe of brutish wrastlers would come to nothing
without Homer his girlish delight in bronze, gold, horses
all kinds rich plunder and the hairy sweating bodies
of contentious kings

6:viii:65

THE PROMISE

cross eyes twist brain?
    When did you get the job of being town lunatic?

MEM.: No more bad news. No more smart remarks. No more
false quotations (Amer. Tel & Tel up ⅜) Stop reading

Stop here. Ice Cold Drinks. Cold Watermelon All You Can Eat.
Fresh fruit five hundred feet. Corn on the cob. Oranges. Please
don't abuse your eyes any more. I promise.

---

a faithful blank

ow!

What percentage of up is over. See them
hovering there? Don't mark the cover. Pay no
more. Call the mover. A great endeavour
has come to nothing.
Saves time, costs less, more fun than
Pigs in clover. Could such a one be
a major poet, a losing gambler, a
fortunate lover?

—Patient, sweet and kind. I am also infallibly
good natured. "Escape me never."

9:viii:65

GOOD NEWS AND GOSPEL

We hear it but choose to ignore . . .
As the telephone rings in the used car lot

12:viii:65

478

PARANOIA REVISITED

I see in the mirror, these mornings
That I'm now completely mad:
Ambition, fear and rage look back at me . . .

I suppose that noise was only the man next door
Feeding his rabbit.

16:viii:65

THE HONEYMOON

"We drove Father's Bugatti on our honeymoon."

✲

"You were right, Eb. Dope fiends."

We spent our 43rd birthday in Kyoto. The next year we were in Kathmandu. We're determined to do Egypt soon. Dying Egypt.

Dying Egypt every color.

Let us discontinue this
line of inquiry.

"flense him."

24:viii:65

Where there's a telephone there's a woman to be talking on it. There's quite probably a man hanging around the woman, and he pays for the telephone. Why don't we go out and have some fun—I've been in the house all day. We can't go anyplace I just paid the phone bill.

Some men talk like that. Other men say, Put on your hat, Sweetie, I'm all ready to go. That kind has spent the money but he doesn't complain about it. He takes her to Playland at the Beach where they walk around watching the bright colored lights and the crowd, watch the sunset from the top of Telegraph Hill, go look in store windows on Market Street. . . .

> *(The hiatus (rather, lacuna) in the ms. here has been*
> *tentatively restored by the Editor*
> *who has borrowed without stint from*
> *the work of Professor Woodleigh):*

e.g.

> "What do you say, Cutie, scarf your box?"
> "Harry, that man said something nasty to me!"
> "Hay, Buster, come back here!"
> "Hit him in the mouth, Harry, he is a son of a bitch!"

25:viii:65

the beginning of a long silence.
I asked Rome, "How much?"
"Oh, a certain amount," he said.
there was a silence.
~~when do you want to get sleep for~~
"Rome?"
"I got to take me a little snooze. You run on, now."

Run, birdy. Run or
fly away?

B, a beard.   B is just because.

Don't mention the Arizona Biltmore,
whatever town or time, e.g. Phoenix is the seventh
        city of Cibola, towers and pavements
                gold.
Phoenix hastens to its funeral. Start again

THE TASK REJECTED

We all went to the zoo
That's one thing done.

The sun shone, light foggy clouds blew past
The animals were variously disposed (waking or sleeping)
We saw the lions being fed
We ate hotdogs.

The koala bears are wintering in San Diego
They return in August. It is rumored that Bubu is *enceinte*.
The coatis are mangy, the gibbons shout
What about the sooty mangabee, what about

  enormous pigeons nearly three feet high
  powder blue, diaphanously crowned
What did Clark Coolidge say then?

Hawaiians laughed at the macaws, tree-climbing kangaroos
Toni Coolidge wanted soda pop. There it was.

We did not visit The California Palace of the Legion of Honor.

3:ix:65

HOMAGE TO DANTE

  What I'm saying is we're facing each other
    on stage
  I thought you had written a complete script

Why have we chosen to appear at all,
Here of all possible places, hello in the midst of
          boiling fire and silliness

4:ix:65

TARA

This bronze Tara this bronze lady
Represents that Lady of Heaven I now invoke,
That idea of wisdom that saves more than itself or me
All the universes,

Enlighten us we murder each other in this night our eyes
          won't tell us anything but fear

All the universes, all the probability tracks

I M M E D I A T E L Y

Her hands form the *mudra* "Teaching the Law"
Explaining herself.
She also appears as a song, a diagram,
As a pile of metal images in the market, Kathmandu
We seldom treat ourselves right.

5:ix:65

LABOR DAY

There is St. Ignatius Church
There is Point Bonita
There is a bug like a wasp
        its giant antennae
        flail and thwack the concrete in its path

Fennel green and yellow lace
Great moss rose flowery shaving-brush

You're the only creature I really love
Aside from Mama and my Teddy bear
I never miss you until I think of you
Now you love lots more than I
No matter how often we meet you never see me

I've become an old man
Soon I'll be keeping cats and goldfish
A large photo album of the days when I was middle-aged
In love with you and expecting immortal fame

6:ix:65

SAD SONG

i is a statue of white-hot metal
i is a river that never stopped
i is the falling flower petal
is the love I never copped.

11:ix:65

"PLASTER OF PARIS: HELEN OF TROY."

> flowers of sulfur
> mother of pearl
> wrath of Moses
> cream of Tartar
> Cape of Good Hope
> *The Ruins of Time*
> "Cloak of China, cap of Spain"

❋

Did the universe explode. Who burnt the toast.
Why does no one love me and
obey my every whim?

❋

R. Buckminster Fuller.   Gerard Manley Hopkins.
LA BETE NOIRE

❋

Remember the high white light
Remember the question
What is the difference between eggs and vomit?
Pigs and silver. (Pigeon's liver?)

❋

2:xi:65 *Erection Day*
Private fish heaven
It's largely optical

18:x:65

Hot sunny morning, Allen and Gary, here they come, we are ready.
Sutras in creek-bed, chants and lustrations, bed of Redwood Creek
John Muir's Woods.

First Shrine:　　　　Oak tree grows out of rock
　　　　　　　　　　Field of Lazuli Buntings, crow song

Second Shrine:　　　Trail crosses fire road at hilltop
　　　　　　　　　　Address to the Ocean,
　　　　　　　　　　Siva music addressed to the peaks

Third Shrine:　　　　Rock Springs music for Sarasvati
　　　　　　　　　　Remember tea with Mike and JoAnn years ago
　　　　　　　　　　Fresh water in late dry season

Fourth Shrine:　　　 Rifle Camp lunch, natural history:
　　　　　　　　　　Allen: "What do wasps do?"
　　　　　　　　　　Gary: "Mess around."

Fifth Shrine:　　　　Collier Sprint, Great Dharani & Tara music

Sixth Shrine:　　　　Inspiration Point, Gatha of Vajra Intellectual
　　　　　　　　　　Heat Lightning

TO THE SUMMIT:　　North Side Trail, scramble up vertical North
　　　　　　　　　　Knee WHERE IS THE MOUNTAIN?

Seventh Shrine the Mountain top: Prajnaparamita Sutra, as many
　　　　　　　　　　others as could be remembered in music & song

Eighth Shrine,　The parking lot, Mountain Home
　　　　　　　　Sunset Amida going West
　　　　　　　　O Gopala &c Devaki Nandi na Gopala
　　　　　　　　with a Tibetan encore for Tara,
　　　　　　　　Song against disaster.

RETURN TO CREEKBED, MUIR WOODS: Final pronouncement of the Sutras

> We marched around the mountain, west to east
> top to bottom—from sea-level (chanting dark stream bed
> Muir Woods) to bright summit sun victory of gods and
> buddhas, conversion of demons, liberation of all sentient
> beings in all worlds past present and future.

LEMON TREES

Portable garden, Bill's shed in Point Richmond, moth
ripple in the air. Moth holes in air that walks around
ALIVE
these flying dust wing flap. Air
quiver, a shaky curtain.

> Explain the spherical gastank.
> a) it holds more. b) it is stronger. c) its shadow is
>   a circle on the wall. d) aluminum paint
>   keeps it clean and cool

I have nothing to say about the American "commitments" in
Viet Nam at this time.

✿

Perhaps today I understand the saying,
"We're all miserable sinners." (Understanding it
isn't the same as believing it or being frightened by it.)

✿

DEATH YOUR HEAVY FOOT   TIRED SLEEPY DEATH
KING COBRA   HOODED ALIVE
NEUROTOXIC DEADLY CORAL
APPROACHING SNAKEPIT   ENTER HERE

✽

289 years the T'ang Dynasty (A.D. 618–905)
USA, 176 years & still functioning?

24:x:65

TRIP, 30:X:65

He kept repeating that domestic fucking automobiles wouldn't
corner worth a damn.

Pair of China pheasants in flight.

South Oregon green rug,
Sheep overstuffed furniture standing or lying on it

Mush rooms?

✽

DRAIN REEDSPORT   DRAIN ELKTON

✽

" . . . will never corner . . .
never apologize, never explain"

✽

"Zürich Switzerland or the center of the sun?"

✽

"Let's all cap out simultaneously.
"Let's all hyperventilate one minute then hold our breath
envisioning Mr. 2765 and pray for the little green cannabis
plants really working their hearts out
giving their all on the back porch at home."

So they did.

N.B.: For "Mr. 2765," see the frontispiece to Arthur Avalon's book *The
Serpent Power*.

PORTLAND IN THE EVENING

The weather is changing; the green light is blinking.
In emergency
        call R. W. Reynolds.

8:xii:65

OPENING RAINY-SEASON SESSHIN

Oda Roshi stands on his chair cushion
        facing away from the *butsuden*.
Does the world look different every time?

❋

Daitokuji Roshi stands on the seat of his chair
Facing the back of it, like a child.
Gigantic throne of Rinzai!
This child fills it exactly.

1:v:66

489

White River, because white sand
Rotting white granite, fine gravel
Which becomes formal gardens
A truckload of the stuff costs a fortune
Zen temples, embarrassingly rich
Buy lots of it:
        Ryoanji everybody knows—
        Nanzenji's "tiger leap"—Ginkakuji model of Mt. Fuji,
                waves on "Western Lake"
        White sand oblivion life green stripe death at Obai-in
        Foggy tarn of heaven Daitokuji Hojo
All of it rotted stone from Hieizan
Melted in the Shirakawa (an emperor took that for his name)
        a wide street leading to the mountains

2.

I asked the robe I wore
How do you like being home?
White River; mapletree wind
Shirakawa has banks of hewn stone
Wild wisteria blossoms over the water.
Boiled in the bath until I'm high
Purple stonewall flower cascade across the river
White waters yellow tonight—
I'm ashamed to say you'd be no better off in America
Rubber-tired boxed-in river just like home.
      (As long as the moon keeps wiggling
      I know I'm still pouring into my *sake* cup.)
I do this on purpose: moon river dream garden wine
Consciously imitating the saints
   Li Po, Po Chü-I, Tu Fu, Su-tung Po
Believing and not believing it all.
Sitting in the night garden
I realize Shirakawa!
Basho and Murasaki, Seami and Buson

All used to live in this town
(And now the *sake* pot is warm, White River
Flows in one ear and out the other)
Streetcar swings over the canal where
Expecting to see the moon I saw a star.
I sat a few minutes on the porch of Eikan-do
The temple flows with the stream (what do I wait for?)
Police-box, *benjo* and spring moon all mirrored in canal,
I borrow a garden light; the neon hotel shines tenderly in the water
Bridge of the Tomb.
I return to the house (a paper lantern)
I hear one singing a Nō song as he walks beside the river
O Kyoto you're still a winner! Four pairs of lovers, two singers
        and only half a moon—what'll you be like
            in your prime?

3.

White River falls and rises from the sea
A glacier on Mt. Hood, a river at Government Camp
Creamy thick with stone flour
Outside Tyghe Valley it's clear
A trout stream that my father fished several times a year
Mother found lumps of agate on the gravelly shore
Alder, willow, bracken, tarry pines
My sister and I caught crawdads
Icy water cooling beer and melons
        (O Shirakawa, the Kamo River is a god
        Its waters magically turning red and green)
I thought "We'll all stay here forever," but we went home.
Now here's Kyoto Shirakawa the white river again
Flows out of my skull, white sandy ashes of my parents
Water ouzel, dragonfly, crawfish
Blazing trout and bright carnelian jewels
Never so near, never so far from home.

1:v:66
23:vi:66

EIKEI SOJI

May 10 the Empire has run unaccountably mad! The shops are
all closed or half open, piles of dead tennis rackets in the streets
Tatami are stacked out in the open, pairs of men thwack them
         like kettledrums. ALL
       who aren't thwacking pour water everywhere
All who aren't pouring water ride wild through the narrow streets
motorbikes, trucks, bicycles
Junkmen are scarce.
        All who aren't washing or beating or riding
SUDDENLY 2 PM REBUILDING all of downtown Kyoto
I walk for miles to find a store that will sell me a notebook
Screech with rage every time I drop my umbrella
People glare at me from their shops
Ladies wear complicated head-rags, gentlemen their *hachimakis*
    GIANT EFFORT
at 2 PM . . .
        at one o'clock it was an ordinary day
thinking of rain, threatening
Clouds.
    Why does everybody do it all at once?

10:v:66

GINKAKUJI MICHI

Morning haunted by black dragonfly
    landlady pestering the garden moss

10:v:66

"THE FLEXIBLE MIND"

All hung up, the pen runs out of ink
The wastepaper must be burnt
Then, incense.
This brings the bamboo flute (*Shakuhachi*.)
Where was I.
I thought I was wanting so much to write.
I thought I was *warmein*. *Won-ton*.
But I must remember the hardboiled eggs.
There's a sound of continuous chopping.
STRAWBERRIES!
That's what I must remember.
I recollected them when I finally had sense enough to sit down
On the floor.

20:v:66

THE JUDGMENT

Frustration, rage, accidents, continuous pains
What have you got to say?
All I can think of is aspirin—there's none in the house.
I don't have time to go buy any.
Keep talking.
Where did Gammer Gurton find her needle?

✸

I have no idea what time it is
Whether my face is clean or dirty
Hairy ears. That other pen won't write.
What's the matter with this necktie.
Nothing.

23:v:66

SANJUSANGENDO

KWANNON, (*sine qua non*)
       planted in perfect order
11,000 arms, a tree (*Ygdrasil*)
       with its many twigs, forks,
       branch probability world systems
       leafy universes, leaves that
BOOK, strung up (*Sutra*)
       each flower a face a throne a palace
       Wherein dwells that Lady,
       Mistress of the Bees, flower heaven
Paradise, *scilicet,* an ordered possibly
       Within walls
       Upon which the Sacred Maze carved painted
       (*Mandala*)
The trip, the map of the voyage, in case anyone wanted to go.

                              4:vi:66

SYNESTHESIA

A few pine trees in sunshine
The complete works of Maurice Ravel.

                              4:vi:66

CROWDED

12 June I've got three jobs
Not a nickel to spend . . .
At least I've got time to set on my ass & complain
This paper is too narrow to contain it all.

Let us, meanwhile, entertain the notion
Of getting bombed out of our skulls
Being away from home,
There's more *gange* than $$$
Why come on like a tight-ass investment banker
I can untie my bag of woe and come
Flapping out into the light
Gorgeous blue-green wings with purple golden spots
One of these days I'll learn to turn the paper 90 degrees
There'll be room enough at last to finish the line,
The final wheeze
I leap up and cut a few hop-twist-leaps, running,
Lunch is all I needed, not even dope
Voices of the Sacred Nine
Chant within my ear

This dance is for Jenny Hunter.

12:vi:66

A PLATONIC VARIATION

Flat white brilliant light—
How am I supposed to know?
Reflections from turning ball mosaic mirror. . . .
Lying idle in the cave,
Until the single membrane bursts and it all slops forth
An issue.

Do we have to discuss all this? Put some iodine on it.
idola fori

Lamp shades, a few hundred yards of scrim
Colored gelatine
                    talk about something pleasant for a change

A REVOLUTION

I keep winning now
It embarrasses me
I'll continue winning
            and losing both
        fried fish
I won't mess with that starving kitten
I won't buy no more dolls
Be nice to everybody just the same
Great moon face beam on all
Hellfire used for stage lights
            and brain surgery never fails
I win; I deserve it.
I give you lots, I give you more
Conscious lovetrap flowerslot juicebead
                ripple

                ✻

Joy obsession kills the cat
"If you have a cow that gives no milk,
Sell him."

                ✻

        "don't get too interested in beauty . . ."

                                23:vi:66

496

ABOVE THE SHRINE

I found what I didn't expect to find, great stone stairway leads to
Vacant lot hilltop where the wind blows and I can see
              the mountains
Rocks & weeds & tin cans: anything historical has long been gone
Just dirt again, flowering bushes, dwarf bamboo.
There might have been a grand palace here, imperial villa
Boy with a pair of beautiful Manchu lion dogs now

13:vii:66

POINT RICHMOND

Hearing. Plato. phrot. phing. destroy destiny rose rot, green, black
edge slip stink. "Go home, dead tourist." We have arrived at the
beginning. "One thing that's got to be every night."
    Each leaf has its diamond—an inactive occupation. Let us
have the "active option." Look again. Wait longer. A paintbrush
with a gold handle suggests what?
    Something googoo this way comes. Black ghosts
flap in my pantry, my closet dampens, rust and the moth corrupt.
    MOSS ON BOARD, fence board,
wooden death pearl pearl wet. WCW points to moss on under
edge of railway iron, AG astonied. (Astonied—why apologize?)
    Conflation of all texts intellectual mongrelization
"more people" (S. Spender) "read Shaxpear, fewer
understand him"
    "If you have a cow that gives no milk,
sell him." Fit them into glove boxes. Push to flatten them.
    Corrupt and mothy rust.
Leaf curl and crumble. Caterpillars burn them.
    Green frog neatly painted black trim—
What's Hecuba to him, that pampered jade of
Asia?—Mechanically perfect green frog, all white meat and black

discretion (no panic,) folds his hands in front of him—"We plan
to discontinue the earlier series of debentures"—heartbeat observ-
able under green flexjewel hide it is his mud. The sun belongs to
him. He is prepared to leave us.

He stays.

"We are preparing to foreclose."
Moth/rust. Speak no more. Wednesday was the last. No Joy.
Replay the other side of it. Gold? Out. Down, the split rocks, the
cliffs "open"! Gravel patters down. What city. Get rid of all these
papers; private fire a public virtue? Glass
dome, red glass birds? She asked us. Rid
yourself, throw all that away, don't ever leave
me. Chain smokes breathing? Relaxation of gold molecule fang.
Percolates through seams in the rocks, and a jelly and a jewel.
Start OVER. Give up everything. Encircle the globe cinque-
spotted,
four-bits the time,
the wild throttling angel/sphinx/FATFOOT
". . . wandering boy tonight . . ."
　　Culture, such as might grow
in a Petri dish full of agar-agar,
cleared away, a wad of cotton soaked in alcohol swipe across the surface
　　Spider come across. Silk is better than nothing. (Than mouthing?)
A MUSICAL OFFERING.

✷

Zoe says, "I ordered an owl. I'm going to have it. HOO!"
William James: ". . . the active option . . ."

✷

"Take down the wallpaper, we're moving."
I think we are moving, don't you notice that kind of rumbling
vibration.
The stars appear to be speeding up.

FALLS NOW THE POMEGRANATE FROM HIS BOUGH
ROTS ON THE FADED GRASS BENEATH

Point Richmond, 13:ii:66
Kyoto, 14:vii:66

THE TROLLEY

We pass Hyakuman-ben (St. Giles-Without-the-Wall)
I look at the passengers' feet:
None of their shoes fit
And all are ugly.
There is no end to misery.

15:vii:66

THE WAR POEM FOR DIANE DI PRIMA

I.

The War as a Manifestation of Destiny. Whose?

I thought of myself as happily sitting someplace quietly
Reading—but now is multiple
Images of people and cars, through lens-cut flowers of glass fruit
dish
Many more worlds.

I would be sitting quietly reading
The 4th platoon helicopter marines firing into the bushes up ahead
Blue and white triangular flags all flap at the same rate,
Esso station across the street (Shirakawa-dori)
Eastern States Standard Oil here we all are,
Asiatically Yours,
Mah-jong on deck of aircraft carrier, Gulf of Tonkin
          remember the Coral Sea

I write from a coffee shop in conquered territory
I occupy, they call me *"he-na gai-jin,"* goofy-looking foreigner
I am a winner.
The postage stamps read NIPPON, the newspaper is dated
          41SHŌWA   7MOON   16SUN
(This is the 41st year of the reign SHŌWA of that Divine
Emperor, Holy Offspring of the Sun Goddess)
I am a winner, the signs in the streets
Carefully written in English:
        Y A N K E E , G O H O M E

The radio plays selections from OKLAHOMA
The bookstore tries to sell me new British book about
Aforementioned Holy Infant of *Amaterasu-No-*
O-Kamisama
All I wanted was something translated by R. H. Blyth,
18,000 pounds of napalm and a helicopter,
Why do I keep losing the war? Misplacing it?

The Secretary of State came to town
I wasn't invited to meet him.
The Secretary of Agriculture, the Secretary of Labor,
All nice people doing their jobs, quieting the locals
Answering embarrassing questions:
        e.g. *Question*. "What is the Republic of China?"
           Answer. "The Republic of China is a medium-sized
           island, south of Japan. Portuguese navigators
           discovered it 300 years ago. They called it

Formosa. As for Cochin China, now known as
Viet Nam, we are now doing all in our power to
prevent &c. &c."
Question. "Why?"
Answer. "Because we can."

I like to think of myself sitting in some cool place
(It's un-Godly hot here, as they used to say)
Reading Mallarmé: *Le vierge, le vivace et le bel aujourd'hui*

Kyoto, *la cité toute proustienne:* Portland when I was young
Katsura River at Arashiyama is The Oaks on the Willamette
Roamer's Rest on the Tualitin, Lake Oswego.
The clouds conceal Miyako, the Hozu becomes a tidal river
The Kyoto smog hides a flat Oregon beach and the Pacific, just
                              beyond
Where is home,

              "Pale hands . . .
                    . . . Beside the Shalimar . . . "

Caucusoid, go back to those mountains
Your father is chained there, that rock tilted
Into Chaos, heaved up icy pinnacles and snowy peaks

Astrakhan on the north
Persia on the south
Caspian Sea on the east
Black Sea to the west

From the mouth of the Volga you cross the lake and follow
The Amur River into the Pamir,
Coast along the Black Sea with Medea "in one bark convey'd"
To Athens, Rome, or across the great plateaus and Hindu Kush
To Alexandria-in-the-Mountains,
              "Pale hands . . .
                    . . . agonized them in
                          farewell . . ."

Among water lilies where the Arabs killed Buddha
Tara surged out of that gorgeous blooming tank
Gazelle eyes, moon breasts
Pomegranate cheeks, ivory neck
Navel a deep wine-cup

                    Moon lady

                              Mother of the Sun

Jewel flower music
              A P P E A R I N G

There's no question of going or staying
A home or a wandering
                    Here we are

II.

The Real War.

I sit on the shelf outside my door
Water drops down the rain-chain
Some flies outward instead of continuing link by link

IGNORANCE
ACTIVITY
CONSCIOUSNESS
NAME & FORM
SENSE ORGANS
CONTACT
PERCEPTION
DESIRE
BEING
BIRTH
ATTACHMENT
OLD AGE & DEATH

The small
rockpile
anchors
bottom of the
chain also
harbors a couple
shoots of dwarf
bamboo, chief
weed afflicting
gardens hereabouts

❊

ÇA IRA,

ça ira!

as the French Revolution goes on teaching us
as the Bolsheviki demonstrated
as that Jesus who keeps bursting from the tomb
("Safe as the Bank of England," people used to say)
        several thousand miles and centuries
          beyond Caesar his gold, the Civil Service

The Seal on the dollar bill still reads,
      NOVUS ORDO SAECULORUM
   a sentiment worth at least four-bits
I want THAT revolution to succeed (1776, USA)
The Russians gave up too soon—
The Chinese keep trying but haven't made it yet

POWER,
anyone?
"Grab it & use it to do GOOD;
Otherwise, Evil Men will, &c &c."
Power of that kind, crude hammers, levers
OUT OF STYLE!
The real handle is a wheel, a foot-pedal, an electric switch
NO MOVING PARTS AT ALL
A CHANGE OF STATE

The war is only temporary, the revolution is
Immediate change in vision
Only imagination can make it work.
No more war poems today. Turn off the general alarm.

III.

The War. The Empire.

When the Goths came into Rome
They feared the Senators were gods
Old men, each resolutely throned at his own house door.
When they finally come to Akron, Des Moines, White Plains,
The nomads will laugh as they dismember us.
Other nations watching will applaud.

There'll be no indifferent eye, nary a disinterested ear.
We'll screech and cry.

A friend tells me I'm wrong,
"All the money, all the power's in New York."
If it were only a matter of money, I'd agree
But the power's gone somewhere else . . .

(Gone from England, the English now arise
Painters and singers and poets leap from Imperial tombs
Vast spirit powers emanate from Beatle hair)

Powerful I watch the shadow of leaves
Moving over nine varieties of moss and lichen
Multitudes of dragonflies (all colors) the celebrated
Uguisu bird, and black butterfly: wing with trailing edge of red
brocade
(Under-kimono shown on purpose, as in *Book of Songs*)

I sail out of my head, incandescent meditations
Unknown reaches of clinical madness, I flow into crystal world
        of gems, jewels
Enlightened by granite pine lake sky nowhere movies of Judy
Canova

I'll return to America one of these days
I refuse to leave it to slobs and boobies
I'll have it all back, I won't let it go

Here the locust tree its leaves
Sharp oval flat
I haven't lived with you for over twenty years
Great clusters of white blossom
Leaf perfumed also
Lovely to meet again, far away from home
        (the tree-peony too elegant,
          Not to be mentioned, a caress, jade flesh bloom)

My rooms are illuminated by
Oranges and lemons in a bowl,
Power of light and vision: I'll see a way . . .

Nobody wants the war only the money
          fights on, alone.

31:v:66–25:viii:66

WAITING FOR CLAUDE

    Waiting for Claude is an all-day affair.
    False memories of Margaret Gridley. What's the matter
with Margaret Gridley?
    Margaret Gridley is logical.
    How can evil spring from a virtue?
    Margaret Gridley is clinically sane.
    Margaret Gridley is ambitious and industrious.
    Margaret Gridley grieves.
    How can sadness grow out of a blameless life?
    Margaret Gridley beautiful Margaret

look down from your leafy bower
     all bedight
     Grieve not, Margaret Gridley,
     Do not weep sadly wandering
under the poplars green with joy

❁

Dear Friends. Ah dear friends. What can I say.
Dear Friends I am decimated. I am sorry to leave you all alone.
I have to make a trip to the Stationer's & to the postoffice. Should
you wish to see me you must content yourselves with waiting
here until I return; you wouldn't need to wait longer than a few
minutes. Oh no. Please come inside and make yourselves as com-
fortable as possible while you wait. Read books. Play music. Make
tea and drink it. Write letters. Bewail your fate, your sins, your
miseries.
                    Your friend,
                         P.

❁

     Why should beauty mourn?
     O Margaret Gridley do not laugh madly
rending the acorn mist

     Plunge not into the flat green river,
     Don't drown yourself in the Luckiamute!
     The willows mourn for Margaret Gridley.
     She was a Radcliffe girl.

     Nobody remembers her, truly or falsely
     Beautiful Margaret Gridley
                    sank.

What ever happened to Marjory Grimshaw?

❁

Hours Later.

Dear Friends,

I told you that I should be home but I am not. I have had to go out again. I went out a while ago to mail proof and a letter back to a publisher in America. I left a note for you, but it seems that you never came to read it.

Now, dear friends, I must go out again to buy a loaf of bread because I find that I've acquired a case of "The Chucks." I must find a great deal of food and candy and eat it all. All of it.

Let me repeat in this note the invitation which I included in my previous message: Come inside and wait for me. I won't be long. Read books. Count your fingers. Remember your folks back home. Make tea. Scratch. I'll return reasonably soon.

Yours,
P.

6:ix:66

SOME PLACES

FOR DOUG LAWRIE

W H E R E ?
       Hotter than $700
I keep walking down Imadegawa-dori
Seeing strange flowers I say
I will look at all these
But after while I'll go back where I belong
       to stay

Along Imadegawa under plane trees
Hot weather leaf smells Marcel Proust

I belong where I am
I want to be there
                        across Kamo-Ohashi
Sit down and tell the rivers all about it
Water necktie Kamo River green
Takano River purple dye

We thought we could see
Mt. Fuji we never did. Why
Go to Japan at all you don't
See the big Buddha at Kamakura (storehouse of the gods?)
Mt. Fuji ride the rickshaw

I suppose the museum takes better care
But I like it better when the Buddhas are too big
Too old to move
Koryuji big ones donated by Heian Imperial Concubines

                       columbine, conch shell
                     turbine a shell/engine
        e.g.
                     columbine a flower & a lady
                     turpentine a pine tree

                SIGH

                PSHAW

San Francisco Zoo Restaurant
Terrace here come two
         peahens
Cold sunshine.
They stand with toes decorously
         crossed
      "in waiting"

"in attendance at Court"
High Spanish combs—
They are Goya creations,
Grey, hieratic, doltish aristocrats

✿

2 peacocks in a pine tree
Growing new long tails for spring
Feathers nearly reach the muddy ground
One had fine bronze network over
        the usual bluey/green color
        Happy fowl!
I like to hear them yell and their Aztec
        feather crowns

---

perhaps their feet are ugly?

What am I still seeing light waves brain
Sandy shore light waves brain's a sandy
        shore de luxe   SLOP
        PUTE.
SWORP   PUTE.   pizzicato monkey
    SOP   done
                            pute borne   SAP
trouble   gorne
            gat gat   slope/slorp
        OLD PAPER-FACE

        "IN MY LIVINGROOM!
Sitting there imagining "Divine Bodies" in My Livingroom!
Maybe you think I didn't tell him! Without a stitch on, & that
Electric Vibrator of mine that the DOCTOR told me to use for My
Neck and Shoulder! Maybe you think I wasn't nearly floored! I
want to tell you . . ."

ALGONQUIN

Crape myrtle blooms at Hyakuman-ben

TZU WEI
(*Lägerstroemia Indica*)

blue cow elephant white elephant calf
       looks away, trunk outstretched
          calling
the blue cow looks down
             Once all elephants had wings—
Elephants, horses, and mountains
          At Shin-Yo-Do
Elephant smiles, curled up like a cat
huge billowing Fugen throne.

9:ix:66

TEN TITANIC ETUDES

FOR THE VIRTUOSO EXECUTANT

I.

GRASSPILES BURNING
Rows of minute volcanoes along the canal
My rooms are full of smoke,
Honey-pumping truck stinks louder,
          humming and splashing
Radio Brahms concerto doesn't care.

II.

WAS
Brahms really
a winner?
        Just a couple ideas
        went an awful long way.
Clara Schumann liked them both.
Poor Robert secure in the
        M A D H O U S E

III.

FAR AWAY IN THE DISTANCE
        fresh air?
    long ways off over there. I
        really want to spend some time
            in that country.

IV.

NOW the light is all different, the air
Moving, no longer in the way
                SEE THE CHANGING
GREEN those are cryptomeria trees those are
"hinoki" cedar, those bamboo

        (orchestration by Paul Gauguin)

those are the Eastern Hills
This is Mt. Daimonji's triple crown flash

V.

FLASH scenes from my new novel in my kitchen
I practise a few bumps and grinds
The plain-looking cake has icing INSIDE
    also candy fruits, raisins, rum.
        whip cream
I am a walking *bombe glacé*

VI.

O LOVELY GARDEN!
FERN GROWS FROM STONE LIONESS HEAD

VII.

SEEING THE
Neighboring garden
The ant
    thinks of her mo-
        ther.
Honorable discharge (medical) granted.

VIII.

Why do you want to go there?
       A L O H A ?
Why would anyone want to go there?

IX.

What's the good news?
       T R A N S P A R E N T   C U C U M B E R S
You never saw a pale so green!

X.

Mountain-top door in the sky
From here we look at heaven
From there we always return,
Somebody else, a world of sweat.

Kyoto
12:ix:–2:x:66

CHAMP CLAIR MODERN JAZZ COFFEE

Middle of the line out of phase
        180 degrees Champ Clair?
Anthony Williams is somebody

End of the line Champ Clair
Loudspeakers blow American wind through Japan smoke
Anthony Williams cuts all the grease

Somewhere along one of the Champ Clair lines?
Somebody don't spell it right.

The latter end of the MJQ marred by scratches
And the cuts of Anthony Williams

Old Miles Davis and Monk sounds
Refrigerated plastic deepfreeze
Winter must always be in progress somewhere

Lobotomy wind Anthony Williams.
        Head in America bag? 1963 *bossa nova* shot?

All of us prefer Anthony Williams.
We sing in our sleep. We converse with the dead in our dreams.

3:x–6:x:66

USHI MATSURI

The Immortals are on the loose again!
One rides a black bull round and round Koryuji
One reads from a great law scroll
All the others dance and chant

Swollen moon-face Good Luck
Balloon-head blue-eyes Longevity
Suddenly zip into the temple out of sight

>   Bats
>   Tigers
>   Cranes

16:x:66

THE GARDEN

The landlady's wearing her OLD WOMAN costume—
Shirakawa head rag, blue droopy bloomers,
White balloon sleeve apron top
Sweeps dead leaves off the moss
Twig broom as drawn for Grimm's fairy tale picture
        stage-prop for the Nō play *Takasago*
Old pine lady sweeps the leaves
Old Sumiyoshi pine husband calls her to the telephone

✿

Now he's joined her in the garden
Dark blue raw silk kimono, sleeveless jacket brown wadded silk
      wooden *geta*
Another *märchen* broom instead of the rake
He knows the songs, I've heard him practising
They make the work easier, life with the old woman
      temporarily a pleasure

❁

I thought when I first saw her out there months ago she was
Some hired *o-ba-san,* one of those old ladies who do a third of the
      work that's done in this country

Later I walked through the yard and saw it was the landlady
      and her daughter . . .
An amusement, I thought, Marie Antoinette milking the cow,
playing at work

❁

They sweep the shrubs and bushes, too,
Old man has an elegant whiskbroom, a giant shaving brush
Gets rid of dust and spiders, leaf by leaf

Now this half-sunny smoky October morning dream
Is also *Takasago* play, meeting of two spirits, happy in old age,
Silent giant pine trees from opposite sides of the island
Good luck at weddings, good news at the Kanze boxoffice.

24:x:66

CONFESSION AND PENANCE

The teeth are washed.
The breakfast was had.
The house is washed.
The garbage is out.
The papers are burnt.
The stove is clean.
The flowers are all re-arranged.
It all looks so much better you wouldn't know it.

I can remember half a dozen times when I was no good in bed.
I'm really sorry about those, but it's all over now. Next time
I did better.

25:x:66

THE GRAND DESIGN

Top of the fountain jet
White diamond liquid sun fire

❋

The Baby commits evil deeds unseen.

❋

Snail shell, pearl shell, abalone.

❋

Nautilus.
Octopus egg cases,
eggs of shark

❋

nest.

range

purple stone mountain
green purple martin

＊

What happened. The Baby broke it.

Something was there; we all enjoyed it. Now it is gone. We still have Baby. How shall we enjoy Baby.

Pickles, cheese, lettuce, tomato slices, mayonnaise, hard boiled egg, a little vinegar, raw mushrooms, . . . however, Baby is too big and dirty.

Baby tied the snakes together in a bow knot. Ill-tempered little brute.

＊

Morganatic marriage is the answer to an otherwise ruined life.
Let's rebuild Hadrian's villa.

＊

Baby wears red frog-face pants and whistle shoes. He's about to begin torturing goldfish.

I told you that Meudon was out of the question. So we are, a marigold. Unworried fish, the water never so clear.

＊

The hair. The hair is to be arranged later.

＊

We firmly believe in a tortoise with long hair. It lives a long time. Hokusai drew its picture.

(Try to believe: a fur frog . . . angora snake (feather boa, Quetzalcoatl) . . . fuzzy salamander. All these are Siberian reptiles.

＊

517

We have no protection against propaganda, lies or slander. It can all be fixed later. It doesn't make any difference what you believe as long as you keep on schedule, bow and smile.

Rearrange the hair.

✻

Rebuild the Baby green and pleasure. Tivoli. The fountain squirts lopsided.

Mouldy tapioca dream of hirsute frogs. My terrapin Maryland—there's a hair in it.

✻

Whose.

✻

Fire egg. Diamond lizard. Marble shell feather. Mercury golden foot.

✻

Drug by Schubert setting of German chorales on radio this morning. Again, I'm brought down by a Baby playing with the valve which controls the fountain in the middle of the goldfish pond here in the garden of Shinshindo coffee house. I expected to be able to sit here—the only place in Kyoto where there's neither TV nor radio nor phonograph playing—to drink coffee and watch the fountain and the fish.

They've removed the Baby. The fountain has been left to dribble feebly. The sky's overcast, now—a few minutes ago, the sun was very bright.

✻

Velvet rope universe, tassel world—There is marshmallow dark Brazil knee laughing! Hummingbirds feather tassel contrivance to stop laughing? Marbles travertines blind schist a 37 degree turn from the angle of the other materials there deposed, *scil.* within the fold, the *horst* that will soon become, darkly gleaming and all geologically

EARTH

(See Figure 1.)

✿

I'm finished with him, some bitch, only he don't know it yet. As long as I don't open the closet door. And the door to the basement. Or that trap door into the attic—if that were to begin opening, slowly, apparently of its own accord, my analysis will continue upon its even keel in the appropriate direction—straight up. (Interruption) Nervous Intervention PLEASURE CENTRAL:

(See Figure 2.)

✿

Baby turned the octopus egg to marble shark.
Re-program Hadrian feather. Start from the ground up.
Dirty Baby! Without pleasure nothing can be done. Stop it.
      Just stop it.
    Why don't you just stop it.
Why did you ever begin.

    ✿

We are totally committed;
                      ... not a minute too soon. Walls
of green jasper, columns of syenite, fountain inlaid with
crystal and jade. Fish, tortoise, octopus,
pearly marble Baby on a travertine shell

Kyoto
9:x—27:x:66

519

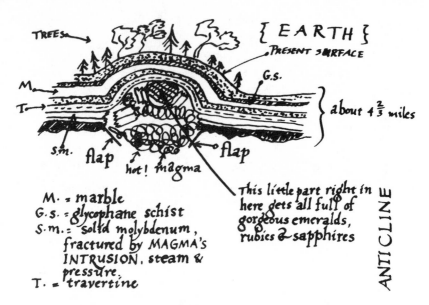

TREES

{ EARTH }

PRESENT SURFACE

G.S.

M

T

about $4\frac{2}{3}$ miles

s.m.   flap   hot! magma   flap

This little part right in here gets all full of gorgeous emeralds, rubies & sapphires

M. = marble
G.s. = glycophane schist
S.m. = solid molybdenum, fractured by MAGMA's INTRUSION, steam & pressure.
T. = travertine

ANTICLINE

FIGURE 1

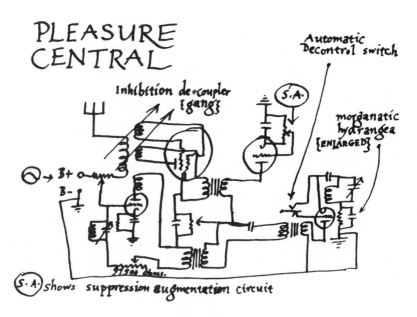

PLEASURE CENTRAL

Automatic Decontrol switch

Inhibition de-coupler {gang}

S.A.

morganatic hydrangea {ENLARGED}

B+

B-

97,500 ohms.

S.A. shows suppression augmentation circuit

FIGURE 2

"SHEEP MAY SAFELY GRAZE"

I must get up early in the morning
Let all the insects out to air and feed
They come back nightly, ever faithful
      even this cold weather when I
      wished they'd all be dead.

                                  31:x:66

SUCCESS IS FAILURE

They said, "Po Chü-I, go home"
They couldn't pronounce his name,
They said, "Go home, Hakurakuten!"
You're too exciting, too distracting
We love you too much, go home to China
"The moon," they said,
"The moon's Japanese."

Po Chü-I was never here; he never came to Kyoto.

                                  31:x:66

521

Another Blank Discovery!

Silence

12:XI:66

I keep hunting through the house
wandering the neighborhood, searching my
pockets

what it is ___ :

Not yet No such of a thing.

The edge of a stupendous cliff,
more exactly from the top of a giant
boulder that lay near the cliff's edge
Lake of the Fallen Moon.

pieces of a log raft in clear water

THE WINTER

Wheelbarrow's tire is flat, muddy ground now sets
A plaster mould around the folded rubber the first
Cold morning of the year.

15:xi:66

DEMACHI

Lady leans over the table writing
Takarabune coffeeshop
Is there a large spider descending from her hair?
It swings in space just below her cheek
The top of a ball-point pen
"Santa-Claus is coming/ To town!"

❋

A funny trip to the other side of the square, from
Demachi Yanagi linoleum plastic noodle shop
The Pepsi-Cola man has rice with his *chuka soba*
To America taped music red upholstery lilac or yellow shades
        on hanging lamps

Christmas trees pinned to the walls
Tinsel yardage stars their pink sparkling guts
Descending blue glass balls
Air conditioner flops and glitters them
Everybody drinks thick fruit nasty

25:xi:66

THE WINTER

FOR BURTON WATSON

Why do I fear the true winter death to come
I guess I've lived without seasons much too long
I hate having to think of weather and falling down in wet icy snow
    and mud my knees all skinned, pants all soaked
Every winter I lose my balance
Every cloudy day a nervous breakdown

Darker, darker, darker I can't see good even when it's light
In the blackness I can't move or work
Forgetting that most of the universe, Jupiter, Neptune, Pluto,
Out beyond is black and cold, nothing to eat,
Blake's demons rage and govern, smashing suns with backhand
    swipe

I open up the doors and windows, destroy my crowded rooms
Let the dying garden flop into the house
Here are camellias blooming—November, and the bushes covered
    with flower buds
A few luscious pink, incandescent white already open
Here's a yellow kind of daisy with high thick stems

There's no explaining these yucca plants blooming the second
    time this year
November, the cold nights and sloppy rains
They're some kind of cactus crossed with palmetto
Giant lily of the valley sword spike leaves
How did they get here in front of the tobacco funeral-supply-
    stationery store
I thought I'd seen the last of them shooting out of the walls
King's Canyon, California

Here they are at Ginkakuji Michi: maybe Sesshu painted some,
    remembered them from China I don't know
I go visit the gold Buddha at Hyakumanben, put 2¢ in the box
    change from the bath money
Walk once around his house for luck
He just sits there about 12 feet high, gold leaf on cryptomeria
    wood
300 years dusty, emanating 13 small and myriad smaller Buddhas
Nothing else to do:
For love, for luck, for nothing
Raising his gold hand, palm outwards, "Don't be afraid."

II.

After pleading with myself this morning to start writing I gradually
filled up a lot of pages. Now I tell myself, "At last I'm free of That,"
ten o'clock at night. Rain.

W. C. Williams (in conversation): "After all, that's what we live for—
splendor."

Where did I buy this great big case of indecision? Blinky day of sunny
clouds, endless variations, white on white

The cold, what do I care about the WEATHER
Something as elegant as Myoshinji, Daitokuji lasted
            through more than four hundred such blasts
I freeze on the concrete island, Higashioji street drunk
I must see Chion In by moonlight, 40 below, I'll get arrested
But it's all roped and chained! They don't want to see nobody.
I walk on down to Kenninji, Chinese roof at moonrise
Somebody puke in the alley, I hear sound of *geta* coming
What's it worth if you can't see it at night, Dear Honen Shonin?
Kenninji, already half ruined, lets me sound four thumps on each
    great corner post, the first Zen temple in Kyoto
Beyond is noise of town, like Portland, Seattle, some minor West
    Coast city

Orion stands just ahead of me above trees, only a little above roof
    of the bell tower
Moon a scrambled mess of roaring clouds

I sit and write on cold stones the clouds and stars above
        Imperial Gate I'm in flood of mercury light that guards
            the temple's massive wooden doors

I could get warm if I had ¥20,000 to spend, to throw away
To the weather!

III

I have to do everything
        N O W
The weather's too undependable, not really interesting
I don't have time to fool with it

Finding out what's my job has taken forty years
I've got to work at that. The color of leaves distracts me.
I imagine January horrors, February no possibility of life—
All right—loom, forbode, threaten—
I've suffered the whole show four months ahead of time
Now I hope I'm free of it,
Let the coal-oil heater stink and blacken!
Yah, yah, yah! I'm tired of my imaginary winter—
Worse than the real would ever dare to be!

Now I imagine food, music, the Viet Nam War, the characters
    of my friends, all my unfinished books, a visit to the Schön-
        brunn Palace, the Vatican Museum, what do I think of
            them, what do they think of me
How much do I really want anybody, anything

IV.

I was living in a little house, all my books were there. Trees lined all the streets. I came back to find bare, fresh-plowed earth; a few of the books were standing on a shelf in an open front wood construction gang boss shack. Total personal desolation, death of balls, belly removal—as in dream of lost Blake volume, two years ago.

Now I'm luckier, I can walk in the sun to the coffee palace Shinshindo, sit in the pergola and watch the goldfish.

I told myself, waking, "It ain't just them books you're about to lose, it's the skin, the world, the voice and ear and Philip are all on their way   O U T " . . . and writing all this wisdom distracted by the fact that I don't know the Japanese word for "pepper," which I'd like to have on top of this tomato juice I'm drinking—not that this delicious slice of lemon and its attendant handful of ice are not delightful—

❋

There is no possible metaphor simile or plain statement which can describe my joy. I was able to walk down the street and smile at the people I saw—all of us existing in compassion, wisdom and enlightenment. I'll go to Hyakumanben pretty quick and put a penny in the Buddha-box, many thanks &c.
  I saw this tiny ancient lady, for example, stopped dead in the sidewalk. Maybe she forgot where she was, suddenly sick or just tired—but I could see she was all right, living or dying.

❋

shack I lost—where was it? I feel, now, it was in The Dalles where big sycamore trees and horse chestnuts and black walnut trees line the streets . . . Berkeley, for the little house? But I see so much tearing-down and rebuilding here in Kyoto, it might as well have been the present scene. I suppose that since I want to connect it all with The Dalles, it must be a symbol of my mother's death—and of my father's, last year—the fresh grave in squared-off cemetery lot.

❁

I opened a drawer and saw by chance a page of writing which I'd put away a long time ago and forgotten. I closed the drawer, I hopped and gloated and laughed, triumphing, completely maniacal, demoniac. No one will ever guess why.

Kyoto
31:x–2:xii:66

6 : Ⅻ : 66

All of it came to nothing
All gone to pot
All to nothing.
Ausgespielt

★ —— ★ —— ★

If I wasn't all hung up
I could make something pretty.

All of it went on the wrong page
All of it is lost

* — * — * — *

All of it got creased, bent and dirty
    falling in the unpaved street
Mud stained, peanut oil, sweat

Sand in my fingernails
Black grease in fine cracks of handskin
    hangnail scab callous pimple

Letters from all the wrong people
    and an incipient belly≠ache

6 : XII : 66

"NEFAS"

the Roman said,

Don't do anything today

the day belongs to a god and his
        their celebration

Nothing can be done this day

I started a dozen things all
            in the wrong way

NEFAS   NEFAS   NEFAS

Thou shalt make no thing can be
            done

6 : XII : 66

I wrote 2 letters & a postcard,
washed sox and underwear,
visited a temple & a shrine to stir up the ancestors
worried about money
worried about writing
worried about my relatives and friends in America
worried about music
practised calligraphy — western and eastern

POEM

Like a bird
Falls from
Indifferent
Air   Sky
Blunders yells
Among tangled
Branches
Thoughtless
Dirty
Crooked feet

8:xii:66

Winter money gloom.

APE
TANGLE
FRIGHT

I can say that even though I have to throw it away, later.

PASTRY
FLIES

OUT. TAKE IT OUT. REMOVE IT.
THROW IT AWAY NOW. WHY WAIT?

was a good old boy. Oh yeah!
Be glad!   Be grateful!

WASHINGTON

Beyond a doubt GEORGE W.
        and Martha, too!
                all of them red-headed
Lawrence & Augustine!
                one of them had something wrong
                with him—hunchback, left leg shorter than
                        the right . . .

MT. VERNON, take a bow! I remember you and Cleopatra's
        Needle as well without a visit.

10:xii:66

15 : XII : 66

PET SHOP

DEAD BIRDS
AND LIVE ONES
LOCKED IN THE SAME
CAGE AGAINST THE
WINDOW

18:XII:66

What do I know is a small yellow
and white room, quite empty except
for a brilliant white lightglobe hangs
from the ceiling, no matter if it's
daylight outside

" That's all there is there is that "

THE DHARMA YOUTH LEAGUE

I went to visit several thousand gold buddhas
They sat there all through the war,—
They didn't appear just now because I happened to be
          in town
Sat there six hundred years. Failures.
Does Buddha fail. Do I.
Some day I guess I'll never learn.

28:xii:66

25 : XII : 66

OUTSIDE

the butcher shop
Crated Chickens peck each other.

✗

JOYEUX NOËL !

✗

FAILING

The practice of piety. The practice of music. The practice of calligraphy. These are exemplary pastimes. The practice of rereading the novels of Jane Austen. The practice of cookery. The practice of drinking coffee. The habit of worrying and of having other strong feelings about money. All these are vices. We must try not to write nonsense, our eyes will fall out.

In answer to all this my head falls off and rolls all messy and smeary across the floor K E E P T A L K I N G squelch slop ooze.

1:i:67

538

TO HENRIK IBSEN

This world is not
The world I want
Is Heaven
& I see
There's more of them

✻

I've seen most of this world is ocean
I know if I had all I wanted from it
There'd still not be enough
Someone would be lonely hungry toothache
All this world with a red ribbon on it
Not enough
Nor several hells heavens planets
Universal non-skid perfection systems

Where's my eternity papers?
Get me the Great Boyg on the phone.
Connect me with the Button Moulder right away.

3:i:67

WE SING IN OUR SLEEP.

WE CONVERSE WITH THE DEAD IN OUR DREAMS

We live in the shadows of dogs and horses
Feather shadow of great rooster lies flat on the dust
Flat on the dusty ground.

4:i:67

THE ENCORE

8 minutes after 3 I've done
All I had to do, all I was supposed to do
2 gangs of *yamabushi* parade around the neighborhood
Blowing their conch shells, ringing their bells, wearing
      weird furs and monkey hats
They go without umbrellas in the rain
Over the cliffs by their toenails
Costumed for the Nō play six hundred years ago
Praise Kwannon H O N K !   EE-OO-EE-OO-EE-OO!
Begging through the town
Selling luck for the brand new year
     (beep!)
The work's all finished nothing has been done

    (klink!)

6:i:67

A ROMANTIC & BEAUTIFUL POEM INSPIRED BY
THE RECOLLECTION OF WILLIAM BUTLER YEATS,
HIS LIFE & WORK

Ruin. I lie passionately in the moonlight.
Learn to lie without regret.
What color's ruin. Beautifully antique
And garbage. The ink soaks through too
Far; he coughs right in my face
Without shame, think soaks
Remorselessly, though. (Sigh.)

27:i:67

"NEVER APOLOGIZE; NEVER EXPLAIN"

A pair of strange new birds in the maple tree
Peer through the windows,
Mother and father visiting me:
                    "You are unmarried,
                    No child begot
                    Now we are birds, now you've
                         forgotten us
                    Although in dreams we visit you
                         in human shape"

They speak Homer's language
Sing like Aeschylus

The life of a poet: less than ⅔ds of a second

                                                    18:ii:67

17:Ⅲ:67

O tell me it's only temporary
A slight pause while the operator changes
All to Corning Glass of Denmark Pennsylvania

O don't disappoint me, I hear
Pages turning Haydn
Quince blossom tits bright coral
Jack London's great blue eye

        (Did you remember to bring the gin?)

Passional disease lions/   bronze German song
            "Phrase"

                    wind?

Jack London lovely skin
            The changed operator.
            The temporary Danish.
            Pennsylvania coral blossom.
            Bronze alcohol.
Jack Lion glass and coral cock and balls.

Blue eye gin blond London
A glassy pause tit skin don't.
Passional winding phrase.
Palpitant quince. Blind Haydn.
Blue German dong. Gin. Phrase. Wind
            glass in Pennsylvania bronze
Lovely temporary Jack pause.
Pennsylvania operator balls quince.
Alcohol turning coral temporary.

Bright German disease in blossoms.
Tell Jack: Slight bronze pages.
            Wind me disappoint me
                glass?
                coral?
                Haydn?
                        slide back just a little bit and let me

quit it

SOMETHING CHILDISH BUT
COMPLETELY CLASSICAL

Orpheus, Jesus, Osiris
All say: "Burst out of your tomb
And go on your way."

Serpent and plane tree
Holy and wise:
"We are immortal;
Only skin dies."

Phoenix entombed
In blazing pyre sings:
"Living or dying
All is bright fire."

25:iii:67

REGALIA IN IMMEDIATE DEMAND !

Necklace of human bones
Cup a silver-mounted cranium
Thigh-bone trumpets
A skull drum

Dear President Nixon, you are welcome in Lhasa!
And where is dear Mr Edgar Hoover?

19:iv:67

543

CHARACTERISTICALLY

Saturday, April 22, 1967
at Kyoto

    characteristically
characteristically compressed
        compressed

    characteristically
space bewixt and between
and so it should easily take
on a columnar shape. The
problem of composing the lines
into a pleasing pattern of
black and white also becomes
less under the circumstances
mentioned above we tend to
find a number of lesser ques-
        tions of space and
            layout. These
                must come
                    later

YES.
"Come on," I said.
Try again one more time.
It was the telephone &
not the lark that whis-
pered in the bough of
that sovereign tree—
O do not go and leave
me here in the mad
green light of dawn &

544

the purple wings of mor-
ning flap the crystal
airs and the silkworm
scarfs all the mulberry
leaves and none is left
which can shade my
giddy head alas!

SHAPE UP!
I said to my soul,
Come. Do not write
so fucking big. try
to fit the pen and
the letter shapes together.
what's wrong with
you anyway?

I said to my Soul,
"Come. Let us flee
into the distant
rain—bow hued clouds
of infinite beauty

and delight Arise
and go while yet
the swallow slumbers
        in the aloe
            tree

much later

I have lots of answers; all the questions
                elude me

That was Donald Duck on the phone
                a minute ago—

Is this Porky Pig?
Remember
    tomatoes   DANCING IN THE DARK
    post office   BESSA ME MUCHO
    sincerity   DINNER FOR ONE, PLEASE, JAMES

         Claribel Cow?
      Joris-Karl Husymans!

                               [19:v:67]

GRACE BEFORE MEAT

You food, you animal plants
I take you, now, I make you wise
Beautiful and great with joy
Enlightenment for all sentient beings
All the hungry spirits, gods and buddhas who are sad

                               30:v:67

A WEDDING JOURNEY, AN OPERA

Gorgeous. Why do it. Let's go.
1) Merry. (Figure 11.)
2) Arabic numeral 6.

        TRY   Leave   TRY

Why. I thought so.

3) Do. Good night nurse! (FIG   LEAVES.)
9b.) It. Once is enough: a baritone solo.

TRY

	Stay in Vienna	Stay in Verona
	Stay in Paris	Stay in Dubrovnik
137a.)	Stay in London	Stay in Tashkent
	Stay in Dublin	Stay in Ulan Bator
	Stay in Persia	Stay in Mombassa

Let's get married nine times over

14) Let's don't and say we did. That isn't the capital of
Portugal; I'm not a complete fool. Why isn't it like
it used to be.   TRY.

15r.) Leaving, Nebraska. Financially, of course.

18:vi:67

ULTIMATE FRIVOLOUS NECESSITIES

FOR NEMI FROST

1. Bamboo trees
2. marble
3. crystals and other semiprecious stones & little
objects made out of these materials
4. silk
5. bells
6. big palaces near the sea
    a) Knossos
    b) Cintra
    c) Kamakura
    d) Cozumel
    e) The California Palace of the Legion of Honor
    f) Bebe Rebozo's place in Florida

7. fur
8. amber
9. incense
10. gin
11. dope
12. Baccarat crystal
13. Peacock feathers

11:viii:67

DEWEY SWANSON

ran lunatic in the midst of our
canoeing trip had to tie him
up & sit on him in the bottom
of the canoe in the daytime, tie
him to a tree at night and he kept
talking and laughing and cussing
the whole time we put a gag on him
one night so we could get some rest
from his noise but pretty soon he had
eaten and swallowed it all some way
or other we were afraid to try that
again because he might get all fouled
up with that cloth inside of him then
he had to get loose a couple times and
we nearly lost him completely hunting
for him through the brush and timber
we never would have found him except
for his talking and we never did catch
him asleep from the time he first
started acting funny

8:ix:67

THE APPARITION

Sudden brilliant color-slide projection life-size
Gaudy brocade flood across blank mud wall of tokonoma
There you bent above great mass of nasturtium blossoms
Round leaf elegant jungle overlaid on a view of sculptured
    Karli
Authentic stony record of imaginary history
Stones and light and flowers irrationally equal balance

The awkward sensations of throttling, dying, weeping, tremb-
    ling, sweating and failure and loss
Lack all connection with reality yet I say
These are killing me, not my nerves or time,

A hopelessness, a sentimentality I despise it pretends
    to permanence, a rigid system,
    take a cold bath it will all go away

At Karli the stones burst into fleshy rounds
The rocks are dancing into sand
Those figures were ourselves and will be again while
You and I momentarily appear and vanish
As another slide shows that you and John Chappel
Play on the beach mixed up with blue sky Sanchi *tope*

I imagine myself walking in smoky sunshine suppose
That I were to hug the projectionist, weeping and sobbing
Yes, yes, I understand! Together and apart, life or death
All of it a mistake down at the developing lab all simultaneous

Flash of multicolored lights on the wall   (The
Sentimentality becomes more obvious)   All abstractly
He had only the accidental pictorial interest in mind
No thought of you or John or me—expecting
Pleasant recollections of Karli naked stone gorgeous
Magic fire-wheel dream.

12:x:67

THE WAR

A handsome young Viet Namese guy from Burlington, Vermont
Just now got it right in the neck

15:x:67

OCTOBER FOOD

Pine-tree child soaks in a teapot
Chrysanthemum perfume soup and a
Seasnail boiling in his shell, that I
May live forever.

18:x:67

IN THE CENTER OF AUTUMN

Too hot, the sun's
Too hot for late October
The light blares and clatters
Right smack flat in the eye
Where I don't particularly need it most

Delicate maple shadows their edges
Flicker in & out of focus
Wind slides them past the sun

Iron shutters crash up or down
Is the breeze cold or not?
Orpheum theater.
Wallace, Shirley and Tosh Berman.

22:x:67

A COUPLE BLOCKS SOUTH OF

THE HEIAN SHRINE

She builds a fire of small clean square sticks
balanced on top of a small white clay *hibachi*
which stands on a sewing-machine set between her
house wall and the street where my taxi honks past

28:x:67

INTERNATIONAL DATE LINE,
MONDAY / MONDAY 27:XI:67

Here it comes again, imagination of myself
Someplace in Oregon woods I sit on short
Wide unpainted wooden cabin steps
Bare feel wiggle toes in dirt and moss and duff
The sun shines on me, I'm thinking about all of us
How we have and haven't survived but curiously famous
Alive or dead—X has become a great man, Y very nearly
Greater, perhaps in some other dimension, Z apparently
Still in a frenzy pursuit of universal admiration, fame & love

And there's LeRoi seated in TIME magazine wheelchair
Head bashed in under hospital bandage
Blood all running down the side of his face.

AMERICA INSIDE & OUTSIDE
BILL BROWN'S HOUSE IN BOLINAS

Some kind of early waking take about bread (should be
whole-grain flour &c.) cheese, wine, vegetables & fruits.
I can leave the meat for whoever must have *that* responsibility
        (a fit of enthusiastic praise here to all the horses,
        cows, chickens, ducks, turkeys, geese, pheasants &c.
        whose (bear, deer, elk, rabbit) generosity & benevolence
        I have (whales, oysters, eels and sea urchins) so much
        enjoyed; I guess I can leave them alone, now.)

Shall I go past John Armstrong's house & wake him up
with bells, but it might disturb Lynne and the baby so
I write now good morning joy and beauty to John and Lynne
and Angelina

I do have to move around outside the house. The sun wasn't
quite up—a great roaring pink and salmon commotion in the
east flashes and glitters among eucalyptus trees—here are
no fields where food is growing, no smell of night-soil,
here's all this free and open country, a real luxury that
we can afford this emptiness and the color of dawn
radiating right out of the ground

Flowers thick & various, fuchsias all over everything
Houses all scattered, all different, unrelated to the ground
or to each other except by road and waterpipe
Each person isolated, carefully watching for some guy
to make some funny move & then let him have it POW
Right on the beezer

Monday Indian eye in the roofbeams
Drumhead flyrod curtain-ring cloud
This is Tony's room. Sound of whistle-buoy as at Newport.
Roaring water for the suicide's bath.

> Dumb dirty dog
> Dirty dumb dog
> Dumb dirty dog

Dumb dirty dog, dirty dumb dog, dumb dirty dog.
Black spayed Labrador bitch. Molly Brown.

4:xii:67

25:I:68

Sadly unroll sleepingbag:

The missing lid for teapot!

LIFE IN THE CITY.

IN MEMORIAM EDWARD GIBBON.

The room is already white. Trim it in blue
Memory of Bentinck Street or the arbor in Lausanne
Moonlight. Relaxation to write while hearing
Half-misunderstood foreign language in Grant Street
So fat my nose becomes invisible in profile,
Ballooning cheeks Otafuku
A sedentary bad-weather town: pallid flesh and gouty feet
The inhalation of coalsmoke horsefume there screaming sweat
Gin-squall a part of the City's life

Ox wearing straw shoes hauls the groan-wheel shiny lacquer
Carriage streets newly washed between trolley cars
And buses plastic wisteria swings and wabbles from dark
lacquer and gold roofbeam palanquin of gold flower head crown
Priestess Cafe Trieste Grant Street several tons of horse,
men, silk, flowers, gold, pavement, a library of 5000 volumes
Blue and White shelves: Fat Edward Gibbon with monstrous
Hydrocele farting sedanchairmen calmly parsing the Byzantines:

"Decline THE EMPIRE," he tells himself, passing St Clement
Danes, "decline the Honourable Danes Barrington . . . decline
Doctor Goldsmith . . ." and squirms on the lumpy seat, trying
To ease fat legs & jiggling water bag slowly scrunching

The gravel of the courtyard beyond the inner palace wall,
Black shiny hats bend to place chock wedges under moaning wheels
Hoss the lacquer chariot to the left the Imperial Messenger's
Bronze mirrored horse wags its head flapping the Messenger's
Black lacquer hat black gauze plumes towards the North
Parallel with Kamogawa, Exact edge of Hieizan stamped on blue
The aoi leaves already melting, he notes, among the horsehair
"Blinders" of his attendant's cap
Wide floppy silk trousers wet with horse foam

Peter and David tell me goodbye, nobody here but the rest
Of the City drinking cappuccino and NY Egg Cream jet roar
Pearl fingernail patent leather knee-boot suicide blonde
Of a certain age black T-shirt orange beads and yellow skirt
Desperately unhappy   •

SUI   CAMPI   DELLO   SPORT

SERIE   A   SERIE   B

FIORENTINA 0   SAMPDORIA 0   FOGGIA 1   VERONA 0

The score in the cities declining in sedan chairs gondolas
Whip-cream french blue frosty paint for the eyelids of
A certain age to pick up to locate to foresee I was wrong:
Not suicide, a fairly well-made nicely-fitted wig sitting
With the Mafia but the black grosgrain band holding down
The front of her own black hair somehow shines through
The gold floss over the top as brain fries in vatic flames
Joyful screeches while rain floods down flames undisturbed:
Jagged flakes & shards of living jewel sound unharmed! by
The City, the Life of the City, "from the tryal of some months"
"(the city the) the city I was tempted to substitute
the tranquil dissipation of Bath"

Refulgent spirit expands branches flowers which are gems
Empty sapphire space and air just past the golfcourse
River's bend alive changing hideously beautiful coal seam ferns
diamond opal do you hear

San Francisco 24:v:68

ALLEGORICAL PAINTING:
CAPITALISTIC SOCIETY DESTROYED
BY THE CONTRADICTIONS WITHIN
ITSELF. (SECOND FIVE-YEAR PLAN.)

feeble claw blanket grab disappear foot hog
crackling Oklahoma dustbowl (Virgil Thomson)
whisker tickles shoulder. eye sinus bulge
with ½ & ½ cock numb and warm, all body skin slack
and thrown into soft folds except stony heels
death's crumby elbow no breath asthma drag all
joints arthritic ankylose threat night sound
terror as of ages 1 through now I cannot accept
the ending of a day no more light I cannot wait
for night when bed fucking blowing jacking-off is
possible at last naked safe and pleasure

5:vii:68

AT THE RED WHALE BAR &
RESTAURANT, STINSON BEACH

Wait until they are
Quiet and then we
Can begin   NO
Simon & Garfunkel
Let's come on. Not
Yet. Come on. Stop.
Slurp. Gasp. Huh-
uh! SSSUP! Enough
Room for everybody. Is
Discipline enough.

Where the music is bad
& you can understand the language
Can anything be done.
Action and friends.
Artificial coals and gas
Fire. Why complain
Dream of being in Japan
Ecstatic &c. but my papers
Aren't in order—then I do
Or don't recollect that
My visa had been renewed
up to March, 1969.
Carload of Metropolitan Police
Go past in a little truck
Moment of terror fear deportation
the despair of not having current ms books
as I was about to make poetry reading
Phiz Mezey's big Western-style
Meiji mansion in Kyoto

Again I may fall on floor
As in slightly drunk day-trip
Two weeks ago, "homesick" for
Kyoto fall on the floor weeping
A ¼-hour by the clock
Impossible in bar with lady barflies
Intermittent jukebox
Tiny children play pinball game
Wrong lights expensive drinks

Yesterday in the orchard
Thinking of Bummy driving her car

Discipline enough for everybody.

13:vii:68

557

THE UNIDENTIFIED ACCOMPLICE
OR,
THE TRANSMISSIONS OF C. W. MOSS

THIS BOOK WAS WRITTEN FOR
JAMES & CASSANDRA KOLLER
QUITE UNEXPECTEDLY

WHAT time is it?
Has anybody seen my suspenders?
    I think it's going to rain.
I don't want any more.
    Open the door.
I fell right down. I fell right down
    in the water. I'm so
      ashamed.

✧

IT'S MY turn.
    I think so.
Wouldn't you?
    I never had any use for him.
Why won't you give it to me?
    You're kidding.
    See you later.

✧

LONG

TIME we no see potato.

Use plenty grease. Lots good
          grease.

It sure is hot.

  My back hurts today.

When was that. I never
          said that.

☼

We had to cold-cock
          him.

  Never mind.

SHE said she didn't aim to.

  Vanila. (sic)

 Who's that guy?

☼

I SURE DO.

  What's that you got all
  over the front of your overalls?

Give me one of them there.

  I was scared.

Wipe your nose.

  Do you know what?

How about it?

☼

WHICH way
        is the toilet?
I don't like it.
The dumb thing broke.
        There she goes.
I'll take the red one.
        There she goes again.

✿

DO It again.
    I don't remember
Where did Mama go?
        Mildred who?
It's in there some place;
        I saw it.
        Who cares.
I really told them where to get off at.

✿

HOW COME?
I always liked him
There isn't any more.
Over easy
Daddy told him to.
There they are.
Who—me?
The line's busy.
I told her of it, too.

✿

He thought he really was somebody.
Nobody told me.
　　　What did I do?
Here we go again.
The dog wants in.
I only need a little bit.
They never said hello, goodbye,
　　　kiss my foot or nothing.
　　　I could have told you.

　　　　　　❋

THEY　got one
of them things over there.
　　　I hate school.
IVORY SOAP—how do
they do that?
　　　You sure are pretty.
There's nothing wrong with it.
　　　I never been there.

　　　　　　❋

IT never amounted to anything.
　　　　　at all.
Come on in and sit down.
He claims it for a fact.
I'll declare.
Nobody home upstairs.
Quit it. Go on. I don't wonder.
That was really something.
　　　Take it easy.

　　　　　　❋

REACH me down
that can of beans.
I sure like that Houston, Texas.
I'm going to carry my little old girl
    to the dance on Saturday.
I've got to get me another one.
What did she do but go to work and
lose the best one I had, my favorite
one, one that I had for years, one
that Clare Gravening gave to me.

✸

LIKE IT
or lump it.
Don't take nothing off of nobody.
I know where I'll go when my time
comes.
    Did I run and was I tired?
I told him it was none of her business
        if I did.

✸

I didn't do nothing.
    I never did nothing.
        It's none of my doing.
        It's not my fault.

THE END

✸

This book was inspired
by the character of "C. W. Moss"
who appeared in the motion picture

BONNIE & CLYDE

The name of the actor, the name
of the script writer—both are un-
known to me, but I offer them my
great thanks and admiration here.

Philip Whalen

Stinson Beach, California
Wednesday, 24 July, 1968

THE EVASIVE ANSWER

I told him he was supposed to I told
him that he should.
Wasn't I supposed to.
What do you think.

FIG   LEAVES

Where does that put me.

CALL

CALL   AGAIN

SATURDAY

hello?

_____

(We were cut off.)

_____

hello?

_____

hello?

_____

Are you still there?

_____

(What'll I say?)

_____

hello?

_____

Totally wasted green.
Double breasted.
Connive.

I'm sure tired of that.

Green.

11 heads
2 arms
1 head
1000 arms   & a mustache
1 head
8 arms

    call the police. Operator
    give me the police. I
    want a policeman right away
    all the policemen I can get
    a big policeman all my own
    big short-haired mean and strong
    to pet, *et cetera*

She had a lovely voice and an English accent:
"My name's Veronica Davidson-Smith;
My husband is a cop."
That was on the beach at Paradise Cove.

      WHO
let   that   guy   in   here

            bag.
            shapeless.
            bag. slack
              bag.
                  mud.

CAN   IT!

      TREMENDOUS
          did I ask you

O that is green and secret

That's understood. Nobody notices.
Lizzard: knob-toes and glossy eyes.

Tell me again.
Ferns.
Shells.
This person blues his own eyes
pushes out red hairs and shiny teeth
One toenail a failure this week

Do lions have Roman noses.
How much water circulates. Under the sea
A stone, under the stone a raging fire
The water pours down continuously
Bright cold flame of central diamond
True love we know we are.

Kyoto 18:vi:67 — San Francisco 5:viii:68

THE MADNESS OF SAUL

Everybody takes me too seriously.
Nobody believes anything I say.

5:viii:68

TO THE REVOLUTIONARY CADRES OF
BALBOA, MALIBU & SANTA BARBARA

"a mild dose of prussic acid."
"Don't get funny with me; I'll knock you
for a row of pink potted geraniums."

BIRD   SHADOW

brain-hooks are certain lines of poetry,
certain words from which the rest of the line is
lost, or we remember the way someone pronounced
it, the tone & timbre of her voice and how we
felt when we heard it, how we saw rainy
fir trees wet bracken on the ground beneath,
"Come here: I want to talk to you" and
"Don't you ever, ever, pull that kind of a stunt
again, do you hear me?"
brain hooks were devised originally by Egyptian
embalmers who used them to extract the brains of
the deceased out through his nostrils

I keep forgetting that I'm no longer imprisoned
in that household—yet I am stuck here like an
operatic character: an opera that I must keep
attending as a spectator. I watch him in the
triumphal entry with elephants and chained lions
then die with them in the monument while those
leopard skin priests

I keep on paying dues to organizations
which went out of business in 1907.
Idolatry. Idiocy. Bird shadow. Nasturtium feather
a minute explosion—did one of the snails
attain critical mass, transmute itself into pure
energy?
light brown flash

(if only one were a more talented librettist!)
1905.   1903.   1811.

BOUQUET

I'll tell the world.
Eventually.
Bug, you are one of the prettiest creatures I have
ever seen. I will do for you or with you or to you

567

anything that will make you happy—i.e. which will
enslave you forever, fix all your beauty, all your
affections, all your attention on me. I want to
eat you: you're candy.

"KEEP YOUR DIRTY HANDS TO
YOURSELF!
STAY THE FUCK AWAY FROM ME.
IF I SEE YOU AROUND HERE
ANY MORE I'M GOING TO KICK
THE SHIT OUT OF YOU!"

18:viii:68

TO ALL MY FRIENDS

I'm sorry I can't stay down
           there where you want to put me
Drowning jellyfish crumbling in the surf
Gently frying on the sand
Sunny-side up

1:ix:68

LARRY KEARNY AT STINSON BEACH

Ice Woman says, "You're in the way!
You're in the way!"

She crosses the street to stand in front of me:
She says, "Why don't you look
Where you're going?"

9:ix:68

1

Honeybee struggles in gardenspider web
Hook feet crochet a silky tomb
Will it work itself to death before the spider eats it?
Sun shines through its back: black and amber tank

as long as that
                    the bluejay flies
                        hollers
                    B L E A K

TYRANNICAL ARACHNID, HENCE!

That's that. Lie down. . . .
                            amber tank? Look again.

                    G O N E
Holes in the web, several strands roped together by the
                    spinning of that bee body
                    polygonal vacancies
                            G O N E
(far too little time for the spider to have wrapped it away
to the cypress tree, to the edge of the roof, down
                    to the Chinese whoopee bush,)

Flew the coop. I wouldn't help or hinder.
Hungry victory!

2

O Duerden! Enormous profundities thrust themselves
Amongst our sensoria which ignore upon them;
Profound immensities engulf the visible present dispensation!
Torment! Freak! Savage tremble illiterate musculature

True human speech of Maya glyph: BAKTUNS. KATUNS.
Accurately stoned American time before the frauds of pro-
    fessional history's shameful rage!

Sweat, voluminous agey brain! Draw nearer and
Melt down in Poesy's ravening violet flames

Honey song perfume! Look where my periwig smoulders!
California sherry feeds the fire with amber potabile:
Sweet flowing sunbeams trapped in crystal,

(*HIATUS*)

Waste motion. Entire mountains removed, the gravel sifted in order
to locate a nickel's worth of gold: In such manner the hours of my life
here sift away. Ashes of burnt paper, dessication of the spirit, imbecil-
ity of mind, withering of the heart which signalize my decline into ig-
nominious death & obscure grave,
VERSUS MEI HABEBUNT ALIQUANTUM NOCTIS. . . .
        to top it all off, Duerden's cat, Alfy, has decided to fall desper-
ately in love with me 9:30 at night when he ought to be at home
23:X:68 Received notice that I must find somewhere else to live be-
fore the first part of 1969. I wonder where. 31:X Pioneer violets
bloom today.

[31:x:68]

BIRTHDAY POEM,

In Advance of the Occasion of My Next One (If Any) 1967.

•

"Who, pray, of himself ever seeks out and bids a stranger from abroad, unless it be one of those that are masters of some public craft, a prophet, or a healer of ills, or a builder, aye, or a divine minstrel who gives delight with his song? For these men are bidden all over the boundless earth."

Odyssey XVII, 382–386 (A. T. Murray, Tr.)

•

"The Scholiast (n. 2 Lactantius Placidus, *Commentarius in Stattii The-baida,* ed. R. Jahnke (Leipzig, 1898), X, no. 793) refers to a Gaulish custom of selling their lives for money, and, after a year of feasting, allowing themselves to be stoned to death by the populace."

Nora K. Chadwick: *The Druids*
(Cardiff, University of Wales Press: 1966)

•

Thank God, I don't have to write a poem
All those primulas raving potted hybrids
Mossy brim of brick fish pond

Only the biggest yellow-flowering one
Saves this day from death's vagrom fingers gloom & sad

Thank God none of those who read my poems don't see me
Don't realize I'm crazy, what book shall I carry with me
Lonesome for my own handwriting

A year among strangers, the Japanese all are mad
They look at me, can't forgive me for being funny-looking

That one's eating buttered toast in a way I never saw
              anybody eat anything
Rearranging his hair between whiles, daubing it
              with his hanky,
He turns to watch the primulas and back to his toast
              in the most decorative possible manner
What would he say if he got the chance he keeps
              talking to himself all the time, some
              kind of professor
And a buddhist, he bowed to the toast before eating it

I go and visit Honen Shonin vision stone and operatic
              pine tree Mt Yoshida
Up the hill through the graveyard we die into stone
Manjusri's pagoda lion laugh dim wise face not visible
But inside the back door of Manjusri's house there is
Sakyamuni! Lump skull pokes up through fringy hair
              also needs a shave

Costume all fine colors flaking and curling away
Neither smiling nor sad he watches the wooden doors

In front of Shinyodo baby soup yells and wiggles in the stone catch basin
And so up the last ridge to hilltop Shinto shrine
Break across and down to deer-pen cryptomeria courtyard
Octagonal god-house
Parents and children bow

What did I see then? What did I remember? That it was lost,
Now it is gone. I could see myself writing and coffee
I invoke Rodin's head of Balzac
Photo-engraving in Biedermeier frame:
              St Honoré aidez-moi!
(Honorius Bishop of Montmartre? Honorius: 4 popes,
              "*. . . empereur d'occident de 395 à 423 un des plus*
              misérables souverains de la décadence"

Balzac: *" . . . brillant et très fécond. . . . malgré certaines*
imperfections de style et la minutie de quelques de-
scriptions . . .")
     St Honoré preserve us against black coffee
     These Japanese knickknacks & from writing ourselves
     To death instead of dope, syphilis, the madhouse, jail,
     Suicide

The world is wicked by definition; my job is to stay aware of it
Bundles of cut weed carrying on
Without a world without an answer
Mukade put their heads in a ring a furry poison star

Bite through paper-thin shell of one segment of his back (giant
       mukade)
There's a kind of orange tree growing and green grass
Hesperides? I freezing, wrap myself and all my clothes in tired
       surplus Army mummy bag.
I think of all the words I've written.
What a funny thing to do. And who was he, that writer?

Shimogamo Bridge somebody made young stone corrals
       middle of the Kamo River
Double-motion projection of streetcar (moving water moving along
       steel tracks the moving bridge)
Sunset behind Mt Atago of a kind which causes religious conversions
       bad poetry, suicides
Honen Shonin understood that it was Buddha Land Purple Cloud
       Express

Upstairs where the action is all the quality folks
I sit downstairs under the loudspeaker (Peter Paul & Mary)
Spill bright barlight splash ice breaking
You just imagine that the Quality don't wear pointed shoes
Downstairs we got gangsters, too,
Neckties and hair. Hawaiian steel guitars
Café de Jeunesse I celebrate my middle age

BEING,

Madam, I thank you for being what I am
Illegal, shapeless and mistaken
Because you have let me know it and kept quiet
Don't press charges, prepared your next lesson
Impersonally committed
How do I know where I'm at without you?

> "The Sumerian astronomers worked the rhythm out into a Saros, a
> useful period of 6,585–1/2 days. This was based on the distances
> of time between recurrent eclipses of both sun and moon, and it is
> accurate to one day in 1,800 years."

> C. A. Burland: *The Magical Arts, A Short History*
> (Arthur Baker Ltd., 20 New Bond Street, London W.1)

A MAXIM:

> Always volunteer; never perform. This is benevolence.
> This is correction of the Will. Ted Williams went and
> spit on the grass.

Go now and write properly. Black shiny varnish. Was the paper
greasy. Paper or whatever non-operational as of Saturday 22:IV:
67 Mertis's water pump broke down there was nothing to Hell
with it let's go to the movies a perennial problem, Brian says so

> Inside the winter you'll find the loser
> Inside the winner you will find the string
> Playing music will clarify the mind
> Ask me another, I'll tell you again

"TOMORROW NIGHT I WILL BREAK DOWN THE DOOR"

> Inside the autumn find the singer
> Beside the summer lies the harp and the water falls

Permanently
        between two stars
                The Golden Stairs

Or step out of hot smoky Greyhound bus (car?) from California into cold mountain air back home in Oregon rank and green smell of moss ferns duff and bracken. Quite near the tavern store bus-stop wood-shed there's fresh sawed and split cedar and fir: orange sticky sugar. Slashpile smoke across highway, logged-over lot next to ½-finished two-story house with dormer windows flapping black tarpaper roof and walls out there somewhere between Oakridge and Chemult I always hate to leave this ugly place, living here is endless labour,

> "grub out stumps, fix up the place so the little woman don't complain too much of the time, TV set and cable service from Eugene electric drive antenna rig, well with electric pump, all-electric kitchen and laundry stuff, cow for the kids, six or eight hens, run chainsaw for Pope & Talbot, little carpentering, drive cat, little rigging, half-ass mechanic, Weyerhauser beef, my brother-in-law got a gyppo outfit over the mountain"

Summer
        crumbles August
lightning shatters
        temporarily the dead air
thick breakaway
        brilliant wind, new sky
Release from hot wooly I sail
        soar upwards in unlimited sweeps and swings
        out of sight again
Turn flying rainstorm
        upside
        down
Earth sprays water upwards
Lightning bursts from ground to cloud (the heat's broke lid)
new air coldest remote spaces
        crashes in

Charles Olson appears to me in a dream to denounce Irwin Panofsky
What I have to do is practise music. Spending money isn't the answer.
Dope is only temporary. Magic is more useful and exact.

Homer says if it weren't for death all of us would babble endlessly,
            "Tithonus shut in behind the shiny doors"

And the canons in *The Art of Fugue* and in *The Musical Offering* . . .

I wouldn't allow myself to buy one of those things because
I couldn't remember its Japanese name and yesterday
I disgraced myself at the market, calling an onion "egg"
My grandfather's name was Charles. Confucius has warned us all
            "KEEP NAMES AND WORDS *STRAIGHT!*"

Overcoming insuperable obstacles I attain Sukhavati Land
Field of Chinese bell-flowers Hoshun In, waterlilies don't quite bloom
            around the corner
On this side of the temple a meadow in the Sierra,
Lilypond and moon-viewing tower a surprise around the corner
Door painting of storks, the small, never-mentioned stone garden,
Elegance all thrown away chinchilla coat drug along by one sleeve

Leads (*via* Hollywood) into strange Kyoto present memory
Flying every day for many months early morning B-17
            (TOMORROW?)
My name was Dumbo then, leather skin high-altitude elephant,
            dangling oxygen trunk
            (TOMORROW EARLY)
pink hydraulic hairoil fluid
Ethyl-ester perfume airplane fuel for cigaret lighter
Oxygen for hangover
            (A HOME IN THE ARMY)
Fall asleep reading Whitman Civil War riding in the greenhouse
            high above the Chocolate Mountains
All one short enormous life
            how possible went?
Shall I be late tomorrow?

576

(EARLY. SEVEN DAYS A WEEK.)
with Jeanette MacDonald's husband
(SMILIN' THROUGH)
for an airplane driver
How did I ever get here? Enormous possibilities all miscarried
Long impossible early life
      bestowed   becalmed   bedizened
Lovely desert mornings early every day
Mornings early every flying day twenty-three years ago

SUNDAY PICK UP NEW SYKO SHEET IN FLIGHT SHACK

Hot weather demons box me in
I drum and trumpet a shower of rain
Remember to be careful with magic
Try for money next time. Jewels & money.
The demons are in the pay of IRS and the Treasury Department
Where's my bear suit?

> ". . . by that time we were all going to pieces," Joan
> Christophel used to say, "Naturally there was nothing
> we could do."

Crumbling.

temporarily; everything changed after all—
I heard Eric Dolphy's record, "Out to Lunch"

Hunting lotuses three Sundays
    1. Sunday a bud and several big leaves. The Chinese museum (Fujii Yurinkan) shut. Walk through soft willow hair.
    2. Sunday cost ¥ 100, found big leaves. The Victoria lily had been blooming; enormous rotting cabbage blossom, starry nenuphars, cacti and orchids. 3. Sunday found strawberry ice, parts of Higashi Honganji moat full of big leaves and buds, one giant blowsy pink LOTUS flopping in the wind— quite by accident I find carved lintel of buck and doe from Gary's poem

Father Wieger says that in *Erh-Ya Encyclopedia* (11th Century B.C.?) "The things of this world were distributed under sixteen sections: kindred, houses, utensils, music, heaven, earth, mounds, hills, waters, plants, trees, insects, fishes, birds, wild & domestic animals."

As the night progresses the heat
Seems to increase the politics of summer
The electric fan drags a sheet of heavy silk across my skin
Mahler, Strauss, Bruckner compose this weather
Mozart brings no relief, my lechery increases
And sleep's heavy dopey sponge-rubber hammer
Waits to press me down again at any moment
The struggle for socialist realism cannot be relaxed a single second
My hands their thick veins lined with greasy fat sweated from the
Flesh of workers! Why did I let General Sarnoff do it to me
RCA and all! Arthur Godfrey!
All power to the ghosts of Henry George and Havelock Ellis!
Down with the Menshevik PTA!
While I sit here full moon electric fan Rachmaninoff
I'm also shut up in a small round wooden tub
Lid tied on with red string, miaowing
How can I work all rotted with silliness and war?
What would come out if I cut the string later tonight when nobody's
          looking?
DEMONS   HUNGRY GHOSTS   HELL WORLDS
Big as life I murdering I
No wonder I feel nasty inside.

Hope's bare shoulder when the soap is gone,
That was Lewy in this morning's dream of huge bare dusty
Coffeeshop and bar where he sits in window
Very young sad and dark hair girl with him,
"The European models have wrecked us all; they spit blood in my cunt!"

The girl says she feels particularly bad about it,
If she has been eating peacock the night before.
Lewy is angry and sad. The girl is tragic and tough.
Slide out of dream and weep on Hope's bare shoulder when
The soap is gone. A dream of drinking wine.

Autumn comes now triumph chrysanthemum harvest
Moon burnished persimmon plumed suzuki grass
The spirit perishes when the season turns.
Exhausted by summer, the autumn finds me sick as March
And winter just past. What do I see a hundred fish
Survived seventy miles of poisoned water, three million fishermen
Flash silver bug feed flip.

What do I see fish seller grabs a fly out of the air
Noplace to wipe his fingers

What do I see big fat boy baby in his pram
Examines a great lotus root

What do I see the sky is overcast for autumn full moon
Invisible *mochi* rabbit mortar
Silent apparition waves peacock feather:

      "E M E R A L D S"
                  and slowly vanishes

A small fat young dog very sick
Tied by too short rope around its neck to the bottom rung of a ladder
Orange plastic garbage can beside it, upside down,
          perfectly clean

Sporting goods clerk sits on metal folding chair behind
The counter stroking the front of his pants he smiles
The other boy sits in front of a big mirror combing his hair
          some new exciting way
Neither attends the TV which offers them unlimited wealth,
Eternal life, unchanging beauty, new sex potency, endless love

Gently. Double Ten 1967. Gently.
            but nothing can be done so slowly
Except that balloon which rises higher into thinner atmospheres
All the gas within its delicate rubber hide slowly pushed the mem-
            brane beyond the breaking point
Rupture occur gently as a gum boil, an ulcerated molar. . . .
Immediately but measurable: the second of time being
Marvelously divisible by electronic means
Blast the gas disperses its molecules glide ever upwards
Among the heavier ones of the air, gas never completely in control
Anyway—lots of it marching carelessly out between fat
Resilient rubber chains

            Dr Sun Yat Sen proclaimed a new life
It lasted thirty years; it was old at twenty
            S P O I L T
the idea of a revolution, an universal suffrage, a parliament
Free total education Roman alphabet gentle progress towards
The Realization of the Human Potential &c &c
Now the latest medicine show, newest suckerbait
New Model Shears to fleece the rubes in Minnesota Viet Nam
What color is the government, red or white?
It is gold, no matter what motto whose face is minted on it
Gold on loan to certain politicians under certain extremely
Harsh and clear terms of restriction and interest
Blubber hooks attached to rubber chains
Anchored in the bank where the gold belongs to a very few men
Who like it very much

            The weather grows colder now but the leaves
            Have scarcely begun to turn color
            Dusty and wrinkled they hang on, permanently glued
            To the trees, absolutely insured against damage
            Caused by possible falling. October is almost half gone;
            The leaves aren't worried, the sun shines
            Although the nights are almost cold the leaves will stay
            Today. They won't fall tonight, either—

Nevertheless in the morning one or three lie
ACCIDENTALLY
on the ground
Nobody saw them fall, the dusty green ones on the tree
Flap quite carelessly in the breeze, who ever heard of
November?

Who's got the money and what are they buying with it
Greece a brand new fascist government
South Korea some kind of ok stable government
Guatemala safe in the hands of reliable cardinals and archbishops
Who knows about Viet Nam?
        The mystery is fun up to the point where it's used
        for outright bilking and bamboozling the beholder,
        killing his children, distracting him while
        the government extracts his blood,

                "A L B I O N,   A W A K E !", *et. cetera*

In America we have everything, we say "God is dead"
Hoping to shock Chairman Mao (the bank is neither frightened
                nor surprised)
The Giant in Chains, the toughy safely entombed beneath Mt Etna,
The certified corpse of Jesus all carefully sealed in heavy guarded tomb
Safely put away—the embarrassment he caused! The unseemly,
Untimely, politically naive impractical theorist suppressed at last
Finally, completely, once and for all,

        but the season UNACCOUNTABLY changes, the leaves
        all brilliantly fall, thousands at a time,
        Yellow red stripey and tawny splotchy crackling
        vegetable brocade foam around my ankles
        (new cold makes them ache) the sun blares through
        naked branches
        wind blasted smoke of burning leaves dead twigs fallen
        bark
        swirls the black thick plume at the mountain peak

the great solid boulder tomb door
throbs like a drum the sky
shatters,

Now all rationalized into a whole different notation, meaning
and purpose.
The lady in the gold hat dances because the *tsuzumi* orange silk
Ropes loosen drum tone glides, his foot shifts
Balances on its heel. Drum thump: sky-pointing toe
Switches exactly to the right and stops a while,
No more music or dance, only animal breathing harsh
Half stifled behind lacquer mask whose outside shows
Calm silent gentle sadness
the whole figure, mask wig golden hat brocade clothes
white underwear and *tabi* all means something else

the drum says P L O K the toes of that foot
Point straight up again.
The figure is monumentally present, no time has passed
Only that furious hospital death-ward breath
Monstrous, apart, static, tense, rooted,

P   L   O   K
drum foot moves back lifts high off the floor as if to stomp
Comes down silently as the drum P L O K again
The drummer screams a single word the dancer performs a total
C O N T R A C T I O N
takes a few steps in a circle
Great green brocade bell (represents a couple tons of bronze casting)
lowers itself another two feet from the ceiling the drum
P L O K the lady's foot moves and stops, a new stop-motion cycle
Commences, varied now by a few short steps, then
the old pattern repeated, one drum-controlled movement at a time
Each motion followed by unendurable stillness and silence
And this time turning in a circle the lady repeats one word five times
And stop when the drum   PLOK

he holds her fan out away from her body
the angle carefully prescribed
the smell of burning leaves the

smell of shaving-soap morning cigaret burning on the ledge
below the bathroom mirror goose pimple skin of Rome's Adam's
Apple turkey neck razor gently slow

PASSENGERS ON THE NATIONAL RAILWAY ARE KINDLY
REQUESTED TO REFRAIN FROM READING LITERATURE
CRITICIZING THE GOVERNMENT WHILE TRAVELING
THANK YOU

All I've got to say is, I've had my time.
If you aren't smart enough to have, get
Drop your own I can't cry for you any more
Dear friends, dear Government, dear Policemen
I am no longer interested in your ideas, your laws, your prejudices

Take a hoop and roll it

I laugh at you; I die and live continually
Imagining I care for you, you care for me

Lies & fraud

Nothing's genuine except imagination who creates
Whether we will or no: for fun
For boredom. For nothing.
I choose to appear in this place, to come to your party
I do it on purpose, over and over again
I hate parties, I always have a good time
And it always takes hours for me to recover my sanity
I go there to reassure you that the world is impractical
Magic and lunacy, poetry spells and music.

I don't even realize you don't understand that you don't need
The help that I imagine you need I imagine I bring

Imagining I (but that is only you:
All of us projections overlapping real transparent scene)
I must act right, I must intend right even when there's
No such thing as I or right I must choose correctly
Keep these muscles practising, always hit the right key
I can read the score perfectly well,
Nerves and coordination perfectly fine
Only a temporary case of mistaken identity
Claude Raines. Bette Davis. Herbert Marshall. Monty Woolley.
George Sanders. Edith Sitwell. Lionel Barrymore. Ethel Barrymore.

        moss carpet veil of tiny fallen maple leaves
      William Morris claustrophobia tapestry
Fragment of maple flowers unicameral legislatures
Tragic bimetalism. Oranges. Bergamot. Bigarade.
Bigarré. . . . *"qui a des couleurs ou des dessins variés . . ."*
Burnt orange color of maple blossom
        metal bosom

QUIET

One surface of all I see is meditating Buddha Dai Nichi Nyorai
The reverse where I am now downtown Chicago five P.M. Monday
New York Philharmonic Orchestra Roger Shaw Choral & E. Power Biggs
        at the pipe organ

QUIET

and it is   COLD   in here
Mudra turns out to be childhood coldfinger crossfinger
"Doubletouch" daydream
Yantra in four dimensions discovered "double-fuck" fingerplay

How cleverly our teachers had it figured out
There were five senses five fingers.
Up until that time I knew that there were a great

Many more, senses whose names I don't remember
None the less real and present and functioning
Right now

      joy fountains open earliest ether vision
      brilliant light of 1929 penetrating
      warmth brain face head grow glow like erecting
      glans penis cobra's hood intense light and heat
      orbicular ridge and supermaxillary sinuses
      awakens me if it happens while I'm asleep

   "Who been here since I been gone
   Railroad worker with his gum-boots on"

Early in the morning what I see four hanging lamps
Two plate glass windows like department store plane-leaves
A stone wall with grey painted streamlined steel fence
Glued on top of it behind which is Kyoto University
Sometime under Imperial Patronage the stone wall has lots of
Green moss ten students and professors a cook a dishwasher
A waiter a potted palm a coal-oil heating stove
The coffee and croissants are a long time getting here
Streetcar shine bicycle handlebars

The Frog Child has a new brother
How's his insect taboo?
A green hole in the distance
Green diamond, beryl, emerald.
Professors and students now appear in
Brilliant feathers, plumes, gems, enamels
(Black palm fronds)
Each one is different. What is it they are eating.
Word word word word word click.

      N.B., that St Augustine's pears were green;
      John XXIII's were mildewed. (See
      Vespasiano's *Life of Lionardo d'Arezzo*)

Two ancient tiny black-wadded-silk kimono ladies
One still a beauty, the other even older
Pure toothless benevolence quite strongly arose and
Crossed the aisle in the streetcar
To say something to the man sitting next to me,
Put something in his hand—money? Ticket?
Next she turned to me, gave me three big crystals
Pure rock candy. I thanked her and she sat down again
Beaming love and joy across the centuries
Right through the center of the language culture barrier

I hear the horns of elfland honking as I lean
As I lean out these magic Japanesey casements all forlorn
The bell

      I wrote the tune they're playing
        The mermaids are singing my song
          It all sounds better than anyone could imagine

Vain shadows, I used to flee your mocks and fleers
Now the paint has flaked and crumbled from your shoddy veils
Adieu! Get them to a laundry, go . . .
      ("LAUNDERY," tri-syllabic)
And to those admirers of my work who find me an unpleasant man
Remember I am a harvested field
Winter orchard beehive
And to all my friends a secret unheard message:
      I'm always afraid you'll find out I love you
      Then you'll hate me. How much does this matter, anymore?

      Two zeroes is one hundred.
      Black to move and win.

Awake or asleep I live by the light of a hollow pearl

Kyoto — San Francisco — Kyoto 1967–1969

BILL BROWN

"Nobody likes automobiles
Unless they are trying to kick
A habit like Jean Cocteau."

3:i:69

SCENES OF LIFE AT THE CAPITAL

FOR ALLEN GINSBERG

Having returned at last and being carefully seated
On the floor—somebody else's floor, as usual—
Far away across that ocean which looked
Through Newport windows years ago—somebody else's livingroom—
Another messed-up weedy garden
Tall floppy improbably red flowers
All the leaves turned over in the rain
Ridged furry scrotum veins

Hedges glisten tile roof tin roof telephone pole
Decoratively tormented black pine
Slowly repeating its careful program
Endlessly regretting but here is original done once
Not to be reproduced nor electronically remembered

Loosen up.   Festoon.

An enormous drop of pure water suddenly there
Right in the center of preceding page

Nothing can be done about that. The line was ruined. OK.
Belt hair. A bend is funnier. Bar Kochba. Do something
About it. Like animal factory mayhem.

The master said, "You shouldn't have put
Yourself into such a position
In the first place." Nevertheless,
It all looks different, right to left.
Another master said, "Well,
You can always take more, you know."

The wind went by just now
South Dakota. Who's responsible for this
Absurd revival of the Byzantine Empire,
Sioux Falls-Mitchell-Yankton area?
Further anomalies of this order will receive
Such punishment as a Court Martial may direct

Or the discretion of the Company Commander
Failure to conform with these regulations
Shall be punished by Court Martial
TAKE ALL YOU WANT BUT EAT ALL YOU TAKE
The following named Enlisted Men are transf
R E S T R I C T E D , SPECIAL ORDER #21 this
HQ dd 8 Feb 1946 contained 6 Pars. C E N S O R E D
3. Fol EM, White, MCO indicated, ASRS indicated,
AF2AF, are reld fr asgmt and dy this HQ and trfd
in gr to 37th AAFBU, Dorje Field, Lhasa, TIBET
and WP at such time as will enable them to arrive thereat
not later than 20 Feb 1946 rptg to CO for dy C E N S O R E D
Or such punishment as a Court Martial may direct
            I used to travel that way.

Always take a little more. This is called
"A controlled habit." (Don't look at me,
I never said a murmuring word.)
Didn't you say, "polished water"?
I normally wouldn't say so.

Wasp in the bookshelf rejects Walt Whitman,
Herman Melville, Emily Dickinson, The Goliard Poets,
A Vedic Reader, Lama Govinda, Medieval French Verses & Romances,
Long Discourses of the Buddha, and The Principal Upanishads.
Window glass reads more entertainingly
But soon that too is left for the foxtail grass
Camellia hedge, the dull mid-morning sun

followed by accidental descent into goofball drift
unintentionally
but such is the cost of knowledge
recollections of Jack in Berkeley
Nembies & grass & wine
Geraniums, ripe apricots, & plums
Clio's green and slanting eyes
Gentle smile of pointed face
How much love I owe to her and to all women
My mother tried to warn me,
"Let your sister ride the bike a while;
Don't be so damned selfish!"

How can Victorian American lady
Explain to her son that his cock
Doesn't belong exclusively to himself
But also to certain future women?

It's a matter of some reassurance
That we are physically indistinguishable from other men.
When introspection shows us
That we have different degrees of intelligence
Varying capacities for knowing morality
We lose something of our complacency

Rooty-toot
Rooty-toot
We're the boys
From the Institute

I wondered recently what school was being lampooned
In this impudent snatch of gradeschool melody
Recollection of obscene & early childhood.
If Socrates and Plato and Diotima
And all the rest of the folks at that party
Had simply eaten lots of food and wine and dope
And spent the entire weekend in bed together
Perhaps Western Civilization
Wouldn't have been such a failure?

Rooty-toot, Plato's Original Institute

Much of the morning sweeping consists of clearing away
Bodies of several hundred insects who followed my lightglobes
And perished here.
After 49 days each one of them will be reborn
Each in a different shape in a different world

Each according to the quality of his actions
In all his past existences. What a system.
Hi-de-ho.

Rooty-toot-toot. Normally I wouldn't say no.
Rooty-toot is what any bugle, horn or trumpet
Is thought of as "saying," the sound of a fart.
Years later I found the trumpeting devils in the *Inferno*

MUSH
All dropped untidy into the bottom of my skull
A warped red plastic phonograph record (the label says
Emperor Concerto) floats on top, inaudible;
Nevertheless, light comes through it in a pleasant way
Precisely the color of raspberry licorice whips.
It got bent in the mail, too near the steampipes . . .
The music is in there someplace, squeezed into plastic
At enormous expense of knowledge,

"FIRE IN THE BORGO"

luke-warm mush, then cold milk poured over it
chills and transforms the entire arrangement gradually
tending towards an ineradicable (nonbiodegradable)
plastic resembling "Bakelite," shiny brown
It shatters if you drop it hard

Changed again! Turned 180 degrees in an
Unexpected direction
Bent Beethoven, *Burnt Njal* I have lived
All these years until this moment
Without understanding there's absolutely nothing
Which I can do well

(RING BELL THREE TIMES)

N O T H I N G
"Har-de-har."
What do you mean, "Har-de-har"?
Nothing, just "Har-de-har."
I might have said, "Hi-de-ho."

"O Mighty Nothing!"   (How does the Wicked Earl begin?)

"Then all proceeded from the great united . . ."
(what?)

"And from thy fruitful emptiness's hand
Snatch'd Men, Beasts, Birds, Fire (Water), Air and Land"

John Wilmot Earl of Rochester.
The parenthesized water is presented to us
On good authority by the Editor, Vivian De Sola Pinto.
I found my mother's name
Written there three hundred years ago.

"I don't know whether we can or not. Hee-hee! Let's try!"

WALK LIGHT!

I don't know nothing about it
There are two long-bearded apprehensive gremlins
One beside each of my ears. The left-hand one
Very gently whispers, "Hello?" and
Listens for a reply from the other side.
He repeats, "Hello?" very softly. "Are you
Still there?" And the right-hand one listening
And nodding, his own ear turned towards that furry dark
Pink and lavender cave. Presently he replies
(Also very softly) "Hello!"
Across the blank echoing empty dark between.

I think I'll go take a bath.
Well, come on, who is it, if it isn't gremlins—
Some other of those revolting British creations for children
Subject of PhD theses in American universities
Big eyes, charm, lots of fur all over
Stage-set by Arthur Rackham
I'm really going to take a bath now.
I split wood (gift of the landlord) while water
Plooshes into iron pot.
Make fire underneath.
Bless these elements! Their nature and use
Connect me to this place (The Capital) its history
Temple bell rings (No Self. No Permanence.)
Fiery waters all around
The iron bathtub is history, its name, *goemon-buro*
A Goemon bath, he was a highway robber, caught at last
And cooked to death in a pot of boiling oil
On the bank of the Kamo River.

Unveiling and Elevation of the Wienie

(RING GONG THREE TIMES)

Kyoto October 2, 1969 a graceful poem
In fond & grateful memory of Mr W. S. All Happinesse
Outline of Hieizan almost invisible behind the hedge
(Not my hedge but the one at Daitokuji Hojo)
Kamo River uniform white lines pouring down
Solidly moulded over stone barrage
Foam across great fitted paving blocks (The Dalles!)
Its man-made bed
                 rowdy-dow
                          beyond the foam thick purple
From dye-vats along Takano River

Green shaved patch on dark mountainside   DAIMONJI

which we saw as a pattern of fire from Arashiyama Bridge
paper lanterns floating in the River Oi
Souls returning to the flowery shore,
the Wind's Angelic Face
Puffing, happy Wallace Stevens Birthday
Heavenly Baroque paradise where he sails
Far New Haven's Other Shore
Cherubic winds flap his coronation robes
Dash silver on his golden harp and starry brow
An extravagant Handelian heaven
Lavender wings of peacock feather eyes
All Memling enamel (Mr Yeats a little jealous)
Harps of "omnipotent power"

      ("OHO, OMNIPOTENT POW-ER
      OHO! OH JOY DIVINE!"
      Gregory Corso imitating Peter Ustinov Nero-movie)

Too busy to see anybody in New York
A few French paintings, shoeshine
New tweed English pants two pounds real Camembert cheese
Who is there to see in New York anyway
Everybody's moved to Bolinas (I dreamed last night of Margot Doss)
And so home again, among roses "Arcades of Philadelphia
The Past" a piece of Idaho scenic agate
A crystal ball "Of Hartford in a Purple Light"
And supper on "An Ordinary Evening in New Haven"
Where you never lived but always heaven
Along with Stéphane Mallarmé and all the marble swans.

I keep thinking about all the really great ones
(To paraphrase Mr Spender) I think
Like anybody living in a foreign country
Of home and money . . .
There's probably *Some* sensible human way of living in America
Without being rich or drunk or taking dope all the time

FRED, IS THAT MUSIC? DO I SHAKE OR WEEP?

3:X:69 Thomas Wolfe's Birthday "he'd say ok and we'd start in
and every time I'd presently find myself going involuntarily
ulk, ulk, ulk, which seemed to inspire him to even wilder
extravagances,"

FRED IS THAT *MUSIC*? DO I FAKE OR LEAP?

To my horror & chagrin I see that I've suppressed
Lots of goody in the process of copying from ms to typewriter;
Mike warned me years ago, "You should always
Make them reproduce your handwritten pages."
              (O V E R L A P)

overleaf clover
I said

      rowdy-dow
      (picture of leaves)

                  poo.

beyond the foam
thick purple. Takano River dye-vats
there's not a way in the world I can explain to you
you just have to get in and start doing it yourself
    green shaved patch
    right half of the big DAIMONJI

"Every place is the same
Because I felt the same, remembering everything
We boated for hours on the Lake of Constance
Went swimming in the Blue Grotto, ate sheep's eyes
And chicken guts in Crete. The blue tiles of Isfahan
Were better or worse than the blue tiles around the late
Mr__, his swimming pool at San Simeon."
And the man from Intourist at Tbilisi who so much
Resembled him:
"Everything being the same everything is naturally different"

Here in the Shinshindo Coffee Shop again
that blonde young lady who just disappeared into—
and so swiftly reappeared out of—the *benjo* was not
that funny girl who used to write for *Newsweek* but may as well have
been—
right this minute
asleep in London, Sydney or Tashkent
three new little trees just beyond
north end of goldfish pond.
I peer among the branches
in search of the blonde who now sits inside
I am in arbor outside
the number of goldfish seven or nine
One is color of polished metal
that girl's hair is a paler shade

(streetcar fills the window 1½ seconds) the hard chairs
and benches here, big tables probably not like the ones
in Reed College library. Fits of psychic imperialism
I attach tags, carve initials, pee on fireplugs
outlining my territory
is that blonde still there
sort of ecru-colored minidress, thin cloth, heavy coat
thick pale hair, untidy braid half undone behind
small pointy nose, chin recedes a little
there's no point in returning until I find out
why did I have to come all the way back here
endless belt of punch-cards travels through the neighbor's loom
repetition of a pattern from a long time back

here's one who eats a hardboiled egg, rolls, hot milk
and a picture magazine. His friend's weak eyes read
a little book
German metaphysics translated into literary Japanese
vague to vague
two giant galaxies passing through and beyond each
other, a radio receiver on a planet several thousand
light years off might well tune in
on a stupendous music,
       FOOOREEENG! &c (Karl-Heinz Stockhausen)
chancre star
             when you get to the end,
                  stop

Bill Whosis drunk & yelling in front of Sanjo Station
End of the Tokaido Road
Kamogawa sluicing fast under Sanjo Bridge
The wooden posts and railings shown by Hokusai
guard the asphalt concrete way
       "Why don't you walk?"

a way of living in America
doesn't really invite a narrow pen point plink
under they penthouse lid they eye they milky
forehead, Yaquina Bay, Yachats,
Neptune Park (Tillie the Whale flashes past
just north or south of Yachats?)

I can imagine living there as my grandmother did
gathering wild blackberries
driving out towards Gresham for a mess of green corn
time for melons, grapes & Chinook salmon
at The Dalles, dig mud clams at Netarts Bay
Family all over the place, friends from the old
Kilpatrick Hotel, bring blackberry jam
fresh string beans and salmon

She wanted her hotel in winter
good steam heat, parties and dances
The Lonesome Club, Cotillion Ballroom
Earliest spring flowers and pussywillows
Green slime and moss and mud evergreen and fern
smell of woman, beyond enormous plate-glass windows
The Studebaker black sedan.
All this lost again, galmed up for fair
where's the minute particulars?
what was I thinking of?

I keep thinking of those really great ones like Confucius:
"What am I supposed to do, become rich & famous?"

People keep introducing me to the famous English Poet
We have been introduced to each other once every ten years
For a very long time. He has no reason to remember meeting
Me, since the conversation is limited to "how do you do?"
And he's considerably taller than I am.

I think all the time I can't forgive him
For jamming that "nk" sound against the initial "C"
Nor for the blackmail word, "truly"
I can't stop thinking about . . .
I keep thinking all the time about those
Absolutely splendid
                    (that isn't so sharp, either)
Well, somewhere there's an exact & absolutely wild poetical
equivalent to Mr X's most often quoted line, & if he
had found it & used it
I should have swooned with awe & pleasure when I was first
introduced to him, & afterwards we might have been able
to talk together?

Fred, is that music?
Do I shake or weep? Did you fall or was you pushed?

Did I run and was I tired

Years gone by, twelve years agone
I must have had about me then some final faded blink of beauty
Fred asked me to marry him, he would be 21 fairly soon
I never had a greater compliment.
It's too bad we were sexually incompatible
He's the only one who ever asked me.
No matter how odd the fancy I remember him
Happily at the entrance to old age
I haven't been a total failure after all.

Paul Gauguin went someplace there was light enough to see
And it made him a painter. (?) N. Hawthorne to Italy
H. Melville to the Southern Sea, beyond the neighborhood of
Christian gentlefolk
Fred, is that music that I fake or leap?

Lion-faced Paul Gauguin fingers and toes
Cock and nose all sloughing gradually away
Leprosy melted him, northern snowman
Disadvantages of a lovely climate
"White men go to pieces in the Tropics"

I can't stop thinking about those who really knew
What they were doing, Paul Gauguin, John Wieners, LeRoi Jones
I keep thinking of those great ones who never fled the music
Fred and his roommate with bottled hair
All of them yarded off to Viet Nam
Translated into Rugged American Fighting Men
Defending the Free World against Godless Atheistic Communism

("I am a U.S. Marine.
I like to fuck and I like to fight:
What's it going to be?")

Which makes it impossible to like the *Illiad*
Sadist faggotry too much like Parris Island
The Green Berets and the cops back home
Somebody else's castration fantasies acted out

In an ideal climate
          but why should the world be different
          Why should it continue in its present
          nasty way? And it changes every
          nanosecond, lovely, dreadful, smashed
          dismembered and devoured by *prajna*
          Events like the Indo-China War
          Final quivers and tremblings
          Neural flashes in freshly killed men
          (movie of *Bonnie & Clyde*)
The longer I think about it
The more I doubt that there is such a thing as
Western Civilization. A puritan commercial culture
Was transplanted from Europe to U.S.A. in the 17th Century
American Indians were a civilized people.

I can remember when L.A. had an ideal climate
        "Everybody wants complete privacy in the Hollywood Hills
        for $35 a month," the real estate lady told C.L.T.
        She wore this big Marianne Moore garden party hat
        rocky face petrified lap-dog. "You don't want to
        live over there, Honey, there's Dark Clouds in that neighborhood."
C. & Shirley escaped to Europe and New Mexico

Bottom of my waterglass, pentagonal crystal
The light changes passing through, bent by glass into color
and we are a rainbow, no matter how we love or hate it
We are beautiful red and black and yellow and brown and white
Maybe a few Swedes or Finns are green in the winter time
If they get cold enough. How can we not be miraculously
Beautiful colors which betray our true nature which is love
And wisdom, compassion and enlightenment,
"Six times three is eighteen"

In Takagamine tiny old lady turns towards a Jizo shrine
Across the street.
A short prayer, umbrella in one hand, the other held up
Before her (*gassho*) and then bowed very slowly
(She really meant it) first head and neck, and then
The waist, very slowly down and back again.
Jizo-samma certainly must have felt obliged
To attend immediately and in person to that lady's
Children and departed relatives. Being Jizo-samma
He has exactly time and energy and compassion enough
To do exactly that, right now.

can this be straight description or observation
without intending to embarrass or attack anybody,
without waving my arms and yelling

does Mr Gauguin's palette go towards a muddiness
even the tropical pictures are faintly greyed
Fluorescent lights in gallery (Kyoto Municipal Museum)
varnish going bad or the pigments themselves
breaking down? look again

fishpond looks clean
fish are newly polished
Frog-child's baby sister has come to ride her tricycle
orange teddy-bear strapped to her back
the same way her mother carries her
The papa comes to pound a large flat shoe on fishpond rim
fish whirl round in fits, then he scatters crumbs on water
goldfish feed

There is a wonderful kind of writing
Which is never written   NOW
About this moment. It's always done later
And redone until it is perfect.

Praying mantis moored to top of a flower stalk
Grooms itself like a canary
Preens
Two tailfeathers

I wonder whether Wordsworth was subject to fits
Of feeblemindedness or simply had a low opinion
Of his readers?

Bigger mantis upside-down on glass door.
Who else has a face like that:
hammerhead shark another cannibal

Strong mothball smell emanates from English poetry & prose
After the death of Wm Blake . . . or a little before
It is detectable in Keats, Shelley, Byron . . . mothballs
And flannel. Smell of Established Church. Industrialism

And Empire building: same Whiggery rules us now
I've got to go sort out my guts.
"What have you been doing these days?"
Just sorting out my guts. disentangling and
Re-coiling them neatly back in place
The same operation must be performed
Upon the telephone cord, every now and again
Je m'en vais à le Toji, in memory of Kobo Daishi
Fleamarket day.

        I greet you from the very top of the page

a single branch of stovewood smolders
under the bathtub, the brand of Meleager
still high but able to cook, eat, write, make bath, SWEAT
they ring the bell again I hope all sentient beings
attain complete perfect final enlightenment
which is exactly who I am or not
all my greasy little fingers

coffee-break time down at the Emergency Factory
early in the war, before we all got uniform shot but now
you are trying to confuse me about having my eyes shut
My name is Chauncey M. Depew and it is November 11, 1910
What do you think of that, hey?

STOP IT, I SAY, STOP THIS TRUMPERY MOCKERY
mockery trumpery pink chenille fuzz elephant baby mockery
trumpery trumpery mockery
mongery   freeny-monger?   fundle

Our main difficulty: fear and distrust of freedom
We think it must be carefully measured
Weighed and doled out in discreet quantities
To responsible persons of good character and high
Social standing; people with lots of money which is evidence
Of their reliability and moral quality

Liberty in other hands is "license"
Difficulties compounded by idea of "consent"
And theory of "delegated powers."
Hire specialists to run everything.
But the powers they derive from us
Relieve these governors of all responsibility
Somehow become vast personal wealth—
Fortunes which must be protected from "license" and
	"the violence of the mob"

We find our freedom diminished (KING LEAR)
Delegation a license for the abuse of power
				say, just what are you trying
	to prove, anyway?
What do I care about proving anything
Only bust chains & shackles that we may slip anchor
Haul-ass away to the making of Paradise
Where now are only fraudulent states, paint-factories
Lies and stinks and wars

One kid put it clear as may be:
"I want America to be magic electrical Tibet"

Or Kozanji, for example, a little NW of the Capital
Absolutely defenseless, abbot's house on pointed mountain
Top, delicate walls
Multitudes of people drifting through it
Footless ghosts, no fingers, empty parkas
The billows of smoke of burnt and burning leaves
The silence, unbroken purity existing in the world
Cuts down impatience
Leaf jewels rage and brilliant silence
Cold flames: Fudo-Myo-o
Carved fire, sculptured flame world net wall
Momentary bird-heads eyes beaks all swirl crimson ray
Beams yellow streaked. He isn't in the fire he's made of it
The light cool zap-energy sword the gentle hat of lotus flower
Big square feet on solid rock Takao-yama

As I looked at them they must see me, flaming
All absurd, film of mistaken proprieties
Culture of dim Oregon farmhouse to burn to dispose of
Instantly
If what is real can be created or destroyed

Clouds move above maples
Change colors we walk beneath
Colored spaces mean something else—
Where in all this tight and elegant disorder . . . . . .

Walk on down Kiyotaki River canyon from Jingoji
Missed the trail, found confluence of Kiyotaki and Hozu rivers
Smooth grey-green cliffs of single rock
Heavy green water, no way back to the Capital
Except by boat, voyage in raging maple colors
Over dragon rocks of dream.
Late extravagant lunch, Arashiyama, Hurricane Ridge

I just reread a little of *The Prelude*
To which I could only reply, "You poor fish."

          GOD KNOWS THE SPARROW FELL:
          GOD SHOVED HIM.

Let's go visit the tomb of Emperor Murakami
Look at autumn leaves but there light rain starts falling
I had hoped to visit big rock on the hillside, also
But came back home I want my umbrella I want my lunch
          R A I N
serious, wet rain
               discovered the tomb of KOKO TENNO
between the parkway and the trolley track due south of noodle shop
RAY OF FILIAL DUTY who ordered the Ninnaji to be
And the next emperor was first abbot there: UDA TENNO
His Muroji Palace
                    here come the maidens dancing

That song they are singing that song which you shall
Be listening is call "The Song of the Panicled Millet"
In the Chinese classical node

In America we've been fighting each other 100 years
We pretend we're unimaginably rich
But we are poor and afraid of the poor who must become
The Army to defend us against right and wrong
All automatic and impersonal
The Law is The Government
Shall take all your money and kill you
Being completely free and entirely, impartially just

Edgar Allan Poe saw the walls of Plato's Cave
Slowly moving inwards to crush us

Who licks up the juice that runs out at the bottom?

The real shame of America is the lack of an anticlerical
Movement or party. All parties try to compound
With invisible State Protestant Church that theoretically
Doesn't exist. Rubes who think of themselves as
Members in good standing are bilked and robbed.

I got to buy me them eggs.

30 MORE SHOPPING DAYS UNTIL CHRISTMAS!

    "again and again the flames of his inordinate Passion
licked my naked flesh again."

29 MORE SHOPPING DAYS UNTIL CHRISTMAS!

"rolled right over until *I* was over the top of *him* did you ever hear of such
a thing I said Wilbur what on earth are you trying to do and he was
wiggling and shaking and squeezing and panting and saying all them
things over again like he was going crazy until I didn't know whether to
send for the doctor or the fire department but he stopped all of a sudden

you know how they do and that nasty stuff all over everything I tell you if
I had it to do over again I'd never get married and Wilbur is my third
husband"

28 MORE SHOPPING DAYS BEFORE THE FEAST OF
THE NATIVITY

"then he turns right around and wants to do it again well I said listen you
old goat I've got to get some rest I've got to go shopping tomorrow
whether you go to work or not"

27 MORE SHOPPING DAYS UNTIL CHRISTMAS

> Fred, is that music?

Ah, no, my foolish darling
It is only the roaring of the aged chilling blood
Sluggishly perambulating your brittle veins you forgot
Your bloodpressure pills again, too busy to go out
They brought you three dead sandwiches upon a tray
And coffee, tepid black forbidden coffee
On a tray and you lost your temper on the telephone
And now it echoes in your hollow empty wooden head

> I'm not afraid of you.
> You're nothing but an incubus.

TWENTY-SIX GREATER AND LARGER SHOPPING DAYS
BEFORE CHRISTMAS

So you're a poet, hey?
Well if you're a poet
Tell me a poem.

Come on, tell me one.

Are you a published poet?

Do you know Nick Crome?

One fine day AG was mad at me and said,
"You're going to be a little old man who smells of kerosene
and sits in the public library every day reading Pliny"

Awoke at quarter-past three A.M. strange wooden clack sound
Later find fallen mud-plaster chunk in *tokonoma*
Puddle of pee with one long black hair in the corner of *benjo* floor

Gloomy gold morning ten A.M. ingest giant lump of bhang
With strawberry jam from Bulgaria (friendly socialist country)
Hot coffee. Things will seem better half an hour from now, OK?
Shut up.

What's the use of having a cold if nobody cares.
Why not simply do something else.
An absolute mystery: how to stop and begin differently.
"Don't be a ninny, Dr. Culpepper, all surgery is radical
Hand me that there Gigli-saw. Yes, yes, it all
Connects, have no fear, we can take a tuck in the membrane
If necessary. Try to develop a little more dexterity—
Have you tried practising the piano or the guitar?
Us brain surgeons got to show a little culture.
Quit banging my elbow, nurse."

Fifty years fighting the Bolsheviki
To maintain a 500% profit on every waffle-iron and locomotive
At 499% times are growing difficult, we must try to retrench
At 497½% lay off some of the newer employees the market looks
"Bearish" at 496%   SELL OUT while there's still a chance.
In order to boost profits back to 498%
A "presence" appears in Cambodia

When did the dumb-bunny bomb first hit U.S.A.?
How come everybody appreciated it so much?

THE BAD NEWS INCUBUS SERVICE

> "I'm going to get well right away.
> I'm going to be just fine," the old man said;
> Then his eyes rolled up and his breath stop
> And there he lay dead as a flounder.

Lost again yesterday walking towards Arashiyama
Inconveniently: lunchtime. Several villages,
Tomb of the Emperor Uda, deserted superhighway to Western Hills
I thought of asking somebody, "This the road to China?"
I really knew where I was, I'd been to those mountains
The empty freeway bored and frightened me
Broken highway to a pretty place where I bought expensive noodles
Well, it opened up a space, I could see the distance, for a change
Breathe. Did I miss nine trillion cars, want them to be
On this road with me?

At home, the vegetable supply
A Dutch still-life set on reversed lid of *nabe*
Half a red carrot half a giant radish half a head of hokusai
A completely monumental potato
China will sail across big Zen soup to me

THE BAD NEWS INCUBUS SERVICE

> They peer down through my ceiling
> "Poor old man he's too fat to live much longer"

> Which part of this bothers me most—
> Insincerity, indifference or the fraudulent ceiling?
Voices out of the air the bleak and windy white skull attic
Flat white for lots of light
Hollow wooden head son of a bitch, Homer Matson used to say

I keep trying to remember that this is my life now
What I've got, what I actively chose
Pine tree stone lanterns outside the mason's house imperial tomb
Camellia hedge monkey-slide tree

And the responsibility for learning two languages (which
I evade) and dim insistences of two others in the background
Sanskrit and Tibetan.   awk!

WHY DID I LAUGH TO-NIGHT?
NO VOICE.

At the foot of the stonewall Fukuoji Jinsha
Somebody took leave of her shoes;
There they are.
Red.

Strangely enough I find that I'm all right
Nothing's really wrong with me, there's food
Payday will be Thursday the pleasure of looking at
A tiny mountain of low-grade amethyst
Almost the color of gas flame cooking buckwheat noodles
(kerosene is on the way)
The cold weather is neither monster nor prodigy
I seem to survive it (Vitamin C) in spite of paranoia
(Vitamin B-complex shortages?).
In winter the air is cold as it is hot in summer
But I never can understand the idea

All too soon I must leave these beauties
And come away to heaven's boring towers of golden flapping
Snowy wings and halo bright star crown
No more to see your sexy frown and freckles
                    ("I can't find my mirror!
                    I can't find my things!")
So that when you've at last arrived there too
Shall we bleak and holy strangers distant forgiving nod and smile?
But soon you'll be asking me, "How do I look?
Is my halo all right? I know my wings are all slaunch-wise
Along the trailing edge." (Preen, preen.) "I wish I had
My mirror, Kids! I wish I had all my things Oh well
I don't care please hold me I want you to hang onto me a while."

Torn paper fake mountains become three-dimensional
Transparent crystals. Bushes and trees all
Barbered and shaved plaques of tourmaline, emerald

They used to tell me I must apply myself
Work hard and don't be lazy
But what I must learn is to accomplish everything
Which has nothing to do with work.
Work is what an instrument or engine does.
We say a crystal changes white light to green
Breaks light into rainbow, scatters it
Focuses to burning point. The crystal does
Nothing. Its shape and structure make all
The difference. Think of transistors and lasers.
In order to make this day great
Yesterday must be altered

Rain I must wear overcoat muffler and bamboo umbrella
Thinking of monkey tribes on Hieizan and Iwatayama
Wet & freezing I hope they're finding food
Lovely bronze-green fur, defenseless eyes
They run if you stare at them:
Fixed gaze prepares for pounce crunch fangs of death
All monkies everywhere look worried all the time
Eyes and faces, "Oh God, what next. Me?"
Lots of instructions wasted

Go down town and argue with the bank
Fall, as leap
Fred?
Yesterday afternoon they said
They'd pay in the morning.
This morning they say
They'll pay in the afternoon

Raving hot sunshine two days before Christmas
                    BAFFLEMUTE

& so to Osaka.

          Beguile me with all them blandishments again!

Cursus:

     The hotel falls. The false hotel.

     Enter One in the character of a false hotel. He speaks:

          MALEMUTE!

          BEZOAR!

          TREMENDULATE!

          FACTION.

          CUCURBITE.

          Pantages.

TRASHMULE.

       finger

A man in a black suit stands at the entrance to the tomb
Of the Emperor Enyu, catty-corner from my front door
He bellows like a bull at irregular intervals

A man steps out the front door of his house
He says (in French), "Again, the same thing."

Radio gives me German actors performing *Faust*
I'm reminded of *Hudibras*
The triumph of commercial middle class
Chanted in paltry quatrains. *Toujours la même chose.*
A little chocolate tomb for a dead maraschino cherry

Coffeeshop sugarbowl another compromise
Picture of childish French sailor
"English" inscription (sans-serif letters)
          "anchortheway"

A lisping *matelot?* *Encore,* the way?
"Encore, vos nerfs."

Leaps & bounds
Ponderous numbers to confine
Limit the flower
                    A measured compromise
"I didn't get her cherry but I got the box it came in."
The flower goes beyond the edge of its petals
The poem runs past the edge of the paper
Teeth I don't have anymore hurt me today

Today I started late and quit early
And accomplished everything, but the next day was
Marred by fits of rage, mental confusion
Lapses of memory. Olson dead in New York
Jack dead in Florida. Today I am going to take more:
Smoked some and ate some
            OM.   AH.   HUM.
                    in five sacred colors
I woke up a couple of times during the night
High with lights and music behind the eyes
This morning I am cured and know who and where I'm at

Why should I go to Europe to look at
Several million nervous white folks
My very own relatives there they are
Totally uncivilized, fingering and puzzling over
The ruins of Western Civilization
I feel closer to that culture which our ancestors
Destroyed . . . megalithic builders initiated in mushroom
Mysteries at Crete, Eleusis, New Grange

In this capital we also fumble with ruins of high culture
But feelings of antique propriety keep heavy sway
Over family, marriage, feudal obligations to a chief

612

The life of the Capital goes by in tight pants
Or on horseback brilliant silk *hakama*
Brocade *karaginu* gleaming lacquer hat

Summer's dead leaves philaudering into dusty moss
Like melting Dracula.
                    (PHILAUDERING. *Mot imaginaire de l'auteur.*)
The soul extractors are here.
Edgar W. Tomczyk of Lima, Ohio, will now attempt
To drive a 35-ton Caterpillar tractor through
Two inches of boiling water from which he will escape
Absolutely unharmed!
                    (oops.)
Rupert Scanlon of Great Falls, Montana will now . . .

The world (and I)
Barge past the sun
Glass on stove's fuel-gauge reflects
The sun onto north wall twenty feet away
The passage of Time, the zooming of the earth
Can be witnessed as a disc of light
Sliding over dots of mud plaster sand
Other goop embedded in the surface

Daitokuji celebration day still echoes in my head
Sound of manhole-cover falling flat on stone floor
The rainy maples at Koto-In
Last night wild boar for supper
Shakuhachi music over snowy torrent
BOTAN NABE, Peony Cassoulet
So far north of the Capital the road is only paved
When it becomes (five seconds) mountain village mainstreet
among *sugi* trees ordinary dirt in the canyons
But the people speak *Kyoto-ben.*
BOTAN garden of Daitokuji monastery
Manhole-cover clang and crash

613

Big pair of cymbals, thin brass with center bowl
Broad-rim soup dishes B L A S H !
Everybody dolled up in brocade bib and tucker
Chinese canal-boat shoes, Nootka shaman hats
To exceed wisdom and ignorance escape skull chain
(Juzu beads I saw today each bead a white head-bone
Apparently impossible although there's enough space
Between bone crystals to drive a truck through)

There's not an owl in the world who thinks or knows
"I am an owl." Not one who knows there's a man called
Slotkin who knows more about owls and the owl trade
Than any owl. I wonder though,
Can Professor-Doktor Slotkin eat mice and fly.

Kyoto 6 P.M. News:
Somebody left a pistol in a raincoat in a taxi on
Higashiyama (Eastern Mountain) Road

New York Buddha Law:
All sentient beings will be brought
To complete final perfect enlightenment
If you will write a letter to *The New York Times*
Condemning Ignorance, Desire and Attachment.

Almost all Americans aged 4 to 100
Have the spiritual natures of Chicago policemen.
Scratch an American and find a cop. There is no
Generation gap.

I sit in the north room
Look out across the floor into the garden
12½ tatami mats the pleasure of contemplating them
They are beautiful and they aren't mine.
Present appearance of quiet neutral emptiness
Books, music, pictures, letters, jewels, machines
Buddha statues and other junk all hidden away

As if inside my head (think of the closets
As memory banks) Wooden ceilings pale orange
Floors the color of wheat straw, light-grey paper
Colored mountains near the bottom cover the fusuma
That divide rooms hide closets. Glass and white paper
Shoji screens two garden ends of the house north and south

Heavy floral designs of Michoacan
(Have you ever considered going THERE to live)
O flowers more lovely than wine
Adonis and/or Dionysus . . .
". . . only one note and it a flat one . . ."
"Only a rose
For you." (That was a long time ago.)
   (unique abyss)
   "I'll go along
   With a smile & a song
   For anyone . . ." all this was
Copyrighted maybe 1911 "ONLY A ROSE FOR YOU!"
So long ago I was a prisoner still and other people
Made everything happen good bad & indifferent
   "Control yourself!" they said
To survive continuous neural bombardment
Meningeal bubbles twenty years after—
Now I make things happen
These thin brass domes and birds of ice
Cheap fruity cries pop
There's your tricycle (from Jimmy Broughton's movie,
Mother's Day)
   tricycle from the Isle of Man
Three legs running
"The Shinto emblem showing three comma-shaped figures
in a whirl symbolizes the triad of the dynamic movements
of *musubi* . . ."—Jean Herbert

Athenian abyss   Tarquin Old Stairs   off the steep
edge of town   Delphi something else
                    a friend writes from Eleusis: "nothing here
                    but a vacant lot . . . factories in the distance"

"Those caves of ice"

,
                    (large comma)
"JA!" Mr. C. Olson used to say so the word
Had a big walrus mustache laden with fresh beer foam
Flowers have great medicinal virtue

I decide not to go to town until Wednesday
Buy *Time* to read at Asahi Beer Hall, not have to teach
I just now caught bright future glimpse
Of myself on Wednesday: Long green coat
Orange beard glasses completely distracted
By trauma of trying to talk Japanese to the waitress
Out of patience out of breath wrestling to break
Strong wool British overcoat stranglehold

flowers and vegetables
                    maybe they will change my mind
The light is different because it's a different season
                    (Audumb in New York)
usual garden uniform green moss a pleasure.
In spring unexpected crocus and lily and tulip
Crash through it—surprising shapes and colors

Western Civilization rigid and tyrannical
But it also teaches necessity for objective examination
Of the organization and also provides all kinds of suggestions
How to alter the works. Mr. Karl Marx wrote a book
All by his lonesome in the British Museum. (Shhh!)

I've read the trial and death of Socrates
Lots of times. When it hits me right I can cry
Other days I wonder why it took the Government so long
To catch up with him. Nothing happened
To Plato, there he sits, writing.

Homer and The Classics burnt at Appomattox
Confucius enjoyed a vogue as originator of jokey sayings, 1939

30:IV, 7:55 A.M. Unknown quantity & quality LSD
7:21 P.M. head full of million-watt light
Hangs from the ceiling, old China dome
Newly uncovered. Dirty but thin, hard and shiny.
Far-away midge on quiet *tatami*.
Many amperes and micro-watts weeded the garden
Picked it up by one end and shook it
Like the dog's dirty blanket, *flooch! flooch!*
And resettled it softly down over the shrubs and bugs
Lots of discoveries underneath
All miraculous and alive

The Capital more than usually full of foreigners—
Expo '70, Osaka. Americans at first imagine
Japan is extension of Cincinnati suburbs
Amazed and outraged to find everything here
In careful and complete control of people who don't
Speak English, occupied (somewhat aggressively) with
Being very Japanese.

That is the funny man's house over there.
That's where the funny man lives.
Keep away.
Hair.   Hair.   Hair.   Hair.   Hair.

617

THE JOURNAL OF JOHN GABRIEL STEDMAN 1744–1797,
"June 9 (1795) . . . the Apollo gardens,
Marylebone, Madagascar bat as big as a duck . . .
June 24 . . . How dreadful London; where a Mr. B—declared
openly his lust for infants, his thirst for regicide,
and believes in no God whatever.
. . . August . . . Met 300 whores in the Strand . . . Saw a mermaid
(. . . September . . .) All knaves and fools and cruel to the
excess. Blake was mobb'd and robb'd."

A friend wrote from Kent, Ohio, last year
        "The Midwest is full of people who want to write poetry
        and want to listen to it."
This year the National Guard, weeping with pity and fright
Kill four students, firing "into the mob"
Nobody cared. Nobody remembers the Korean "Police Action"
Nobody will remember our "Advisory Mission" to Indo-China
                why are they doing it
Why are they
        oh, never mind am I supposed to judge them
Don't you remember being high and weeding the garden
And whatever is really beautiful can't be destroyed
We can't get our hands on it,

                        ". . . The truly great
Have all one age, & from one visible space
Shed influence! They, both in power and act,
Are permanent, and Time is not with them,
Save as it worketh for them, they in it."
        —S. T. Coleridge, "To William Wordsworth"

Endless weedy babble comes away easily
The flowers feel different, having been intentionally
Placed by living fingers which I also feel
Just think of it as a large allegorical painting
Nude figures, red velvet drapery, white marble
"Classical Architecture" (Parthenon Bank of Chemical Pantheon Library)
        America Devouring Her Own Young

(The soldiers are also our children, we've lied to them, too
Americanism, Baseball, Commerce, Democracy, Education, Fanaticism
Gold, Home Economics,
                            ignorance
The complete college curriculum
Then put them into uniform and turn them loose with guns
To kill "hate-filled long-hair dirty dope-fiend Com/Symp")

Nobody cares because nothing really happened
It was on the TV, everybody will get up
Wash off the catsup, collect union wages & go home
Nobody cares, nobody thinks anything about it
No thought at all; a succession of needs and little raunchy
Schemes. "They should have killed a few hundred more—
All a Communist plot to move Blacks into suburbs
Turn over the country to freeloaders, dope-fiend hippy queers"

The American Revolution was a tax-dodge
Dreamed up by some smart Harvard men
Who got some good out of it.
A few of their high-society friends also scored

Russian Revolution a strictly ugly downtown proposition
The Great Unwashed on a rampage. No reference to mystical
Rights to Life & pursuable happiness guaranteed by
Eighteenth Century rationalist Deity in curly wig

Old man potters down the lane singing
Stops to search the roadside flowers and weeds
For some particular leaf that he puts in plastic bag
Of greens. Last night's old man, KONDO Kenzo
(80–some odd years) performed the Nō of *Motomezuka*
Acting a young girl and her ghost frying in hell
We all kept waiting for him to stumble, collapse
Fall off the stage disintegrate
But the longer we watched the clearer it became:
The stage, the entire theater might collapse much sooner

Fall to sand and rust and splintered beams
Mr Kondo would still be there singing and dancing
Every fold of his costume in place five hundred years

It pleases folks in Washington D.C. to imagine
The Russian Revolution is going to flop any minute now
(After fifty years) the insurgent Bolsheviki will be put down
The dear Tsar restored as modern constitutional monarch
(We did it in Tokyo, didn't we?) and the Patriarch of
The Church will crown him in St. Basil's while the Don
Cossack Choir (beards and gold brocades) chant Slavonic
Liturgies in full color satellite TV an example
To the benighted everywhere, if only we will pay
Just a little bit more and hire a few more FBI men

A few inches of adhesive tape seals the mouth
But it is hard to get rid of the idea of liberty
After forty years of war Asia still exists,
Not to mention the Viet Cong
And quite different from the plans of Washington
Or Moscow or the Vatican. (Napoleon said, "China . . .
sleeping giant. I shudder to think what happen
When he wake . . .")

Adhesive tape in Federal Court
Nothing wrong with the System
You'll get a chance to talk later.
Federal Court held together with gum arabic
And Chicago cops

Nara has a great magical feeling
The city no longer exists, the first capital
Restored fragments of temples, carefully excavated
Site of Imperial Palace in the rice fields
Like Olson I've been writing about the wrong town?

"Worcester! I'm from Worcester!
All this about Gloucester . . .
I've been writing about the wrong town
all this time!" (Vancouver, 1963)

Kent State, Jackson State, There was no reason to kill them
Fusillade into an unarmed crowd
Of children.
I can't forgive us for feeding them
to the Bears currently raiding Wall Street
Painless Extraction time again
Squeezing water out of the stocks
Blood out of the suckers
Everybody hopes to catch a nice gob of the goo
But there's never quite enough

Didn't you hear about the reservations? We were supposed
To phone ahead for reservations. In advance.
Never quite enough, the Official Party had
To be served first.
Never quite enough
Because it was planned that way.

My grandmother used to say, "And so he was left
S.O.L."
I asked her, "What's that mean?"
"Certainly out of luck."
Those that's got, gets. Them that ain't is S.O.L.

            "Oh, the coat and the pants
            Do all of the work
            But the vest gets all the gravy!"

We complain of Tiberius in the White House
But consider: Caligula
Waits fretfully in some provincial capital

CAPITAL REMOVED TO FUKUHARA (Kamo no Chōmei reporting)
6th month, 1180—

"To the north the land rose up high along a ridge of hills and to the
south sloped down to the sea. The roar of the waves made a constant din
and the salt winds were of a terrible severity. The palace was in
the mountains, and, suggesting as it did the log construction of the ancient
palaces, was not without its charms. . . . The manners of the capital had
suddenly changed and were now exactly like those of rustic soldiers."

Oregon City by the papermill falls of Willamette
There's Dr John McLoughlin's big white house
Retired magnificence of Hudson Bay Co.
Benefactor of our Pioneer Ancestors
John Jacob Astor ran him out of business
Washington Irving described all but the money

Where was the capital: Champoeg,
Oregon City, Portland, Salem.
The money is in Portland the university in Eugene
The capital in Salem: Life Along The Willamette River?
            now a stink-hole
Paper-puke sulphur trioxide and mercury
The lesser towns contribute only garbage and human excrement

The Capitol's great brass dome warping
Melting in the flames
Hand-carved oak and myrtle and walnut panelling
State House in the park, toy stage set, blazing
A lost art, my father used to say. Nobody knows
How to do that any more.
Palaces by Vanbrugh, mansions and watergates of Inigo Jones
Gardens by Capability Brown
            blazing

"Sept. 2, a lamentable fire. . . . the wind being eastward blew clouds of smoke over Oxon the next day . . . the moon was darkened by clouds of smoak and looked reddish. The fire or flame made a noise like the waves of the sea."
So says Anthony à Wood.

Yet there are still remaining
Shosoin, parts of the Horyuji, Yakushiji, Toshodaiji
The capital disappeared around them. Byodoin and Muroji
Parts of Daigoji too far away from the battlefields
And from carelessness, perhaps. These can still be seen,
In spite of earthquake, ambition, silliness
The thousand Buddhas at Sanjusangendo, the others at
The Toji, survived though the city was flattened
Eight or ten times in a row

Jack used to say,
"Some day you and Gary and Allen and me
Will all be old bums under a bridge,
Down by the railroad tracks. We'll say,
Remember when we was all out there in Californy,
Years ago?"

Gentle rain from grey-black lump clouds
Fine pale blue sky
Three-color cat sits on weedpile
Near but not under the largest branch of Mt Koya pine

All I can say this morning is a dance
Which can't be recorded here
A wish to be free from orders, notions, whims
Mine or other people's
Waiting for the laundry delivery man
Waiting for 95 liters of kerosene
Chrysanthemum yellow starfish tube-
Foot petals

Ancient Orient! Shortest route to the forebrain
Through olfactory lobes. Longest way round is
The shortest way home. A little trip
through the Anima Mundi, now show
Now currently appearing a persistent vision
When it happens at the correct speed
But if you get too close it is only
Patterns of light
Drop candy and try to follow it
Creates new place and time. Looking up
I see blank staring faces
Reflecting steady silver glow. Silence.

Under the bright umbrella, University of British Columbia
Beer on the terrace of the Faculty Club Allen & Bob
Straightening out something complicated,
Olson sighing the while, "I hear you. One, four, three.
I hear you. One, four, three. Minot's Ledge Light.
One, four, three. I LOVE YOU. One, four, three, Minot's
Ledge Light. You remember, don't you Bob. One, four, three
I LOVE YOU—what better way to remember?"

Do intelligent questions get interesting answers.
All I know is
Every time I get mixed up with rich folks
It costs me all the money I have in my pocket

CURIOUS ELISION
LORD, HAVE MERCY UPON US

Michaelangelo/Cole Porter Variations DAY & NIGHT;
NIGHT & DAY, waking and sleeping
That's what that's all about
A man with titties like a woman
A woman with muscles like a man

"To Europe?"

. . . .

"I must have adorned it with a strange
grimace, but my inspiration had been right.
To Europe . . ."
                                        —Henry James.

Pierre who?

      "coming & going"

           "well if you'd got drunk and
           climbed up to the top of the door
           and took off all your clothes
           and passed out cold
           how would   Y O U   look?"

No matter how far we travel
We find most of the world living as quasi-civilized
Nomads among polished marble ruins of great cultures
The quality of life and the meaning of these remains
Are quite imperfectly known to us, no matter how skillfully
We parse the verbs of lost languages
All ignorantly we project our own savagery & cannibalism
Upon societies and individuals who were
Our civilized ancestors

Christ now returns under the name U.S.A.
Rages wild across the earth to avenge himself
Napalm and nuclear bombs for every insult
Every prick of thorn crown
"Not peace but a sword"   (Curious elision.)
Lays about him burning and smashing
Murdering the Sea,

      The war continues because it is profitable.
      It's making good money for those who had
      Money to invest in it from the beginning

Curious elision for all who did not.

All of a sudden it became as if nothing had happened
And that was the end.

Babies we creep out of water sack
Hid there by young men
Old we slide into firebox
Drift up the flue to heaven

A natural history. A narrow escape.

What happened. Walked to local coffeeshop
Tomato juice. Start home *via* Ninnaji templegrounds
People chanting in front of magic Fudo spring
I went to look at the Mie-do, then realized
I was sick or at least beleaguered by creep vibrations
Clearly time for magical cure.
I poured water over Fudo his rocky image
Chanted his mantra and bowed. I also rubbed
Magic water on my head. Old lady caretaker
Delighted;   she said I had done well and wished
For my rapid recovery.

To enforce the cure I visited Fudo spring at
Kiyomizudera, the Kwannon and other Buddhas there
Expensive tempura lunch with view of Chion In
The Eastern Mountains and a glimpse of Momoyama Castle
Glimpse has a marvelous sound like limpkin and Temko

"That Fudo a good old boy he from Texas!"
Shinshindo Coffee house brick fountain
Stone, tree, new leaves, now a new electrical
Garden lamp on metal pole, as in Mrs Blah's patio/barbecue "area"
Chagrin Falls, Ohio. The latest incarnation of
The Frog Child tries to ride minute red tricycle
That groans and squeals. Delicious croissants.
I can still feel happy here. How come.

I'm too fond of eggplant ever to be allowed into Heaven
But imagine celestial *brinjal*— *aubergines du paradis!*
ANACHRONISM:
        a) homesick for one of
          the chief cities of Ohio
        b) process for correcting chromatic
          aberration in camera and other lenses

One of the most wonderful and magical actions
We can perform: Let something alone. Refuse
To allow yourself the pleasure of messing it up.
The things appear to want adjusting, improving,
Cleaning up &c. APPEARS so to us
But as a collection of "event particles"
A section of the Universe as a noisy morning &c
Leave it alone. Don't tamper with it.

Free of that poor-ass Oregon down-home history
As this clear water streaming over head eyes face
I can see hollyhocks ten feet high sideways
To go and to stay illusory
I flee pale music
            (I know what I'm doing, NIGHT & DAY)
I flee Death's pale music
            (Well, what?)
Fleeing Death's proud music,
"Get up out of there," my father used to say,
"You can't sleep your life away.
People die in bed." But I am tired of all the world
With notebook and pen I hurl myself deep among
The dopey sheets to bed, and lock the gates!
Shopping among the sand at the bottom of a birdcage
Every grain a universe designed by Walter Lantz
Nonskid never-fail plastic whose colors fade
All surfaces dim and grubby all of them scraped
Minutely scored cracked and flawed
Material impervious to most chemicals

Resistant to ordinary wear
Allegorical painting: CUPIDITY DECEIV'D BY ADVERTISING
The canary in residence is terribly
Intelligent and infested with mites.

"Rooty-toot-toot" was the sound of the little .44
Frankie wasted her faithless lover
Whenever I asked people what all that meant
They said "Never mind"—
"Row the boat, Norman, row!"

Hot weather erodes my powers
At the Ishiyamadera, small room with *bo*-leaf window
(For the viewing of the moon, the priest explains.)
She looks at the moon through that window that you see
Over there. She is now a wax dummy with a face
That exhibits what the Japanese think of as "refined"
Features. All dressed up in Heian court robes
Long black hair down her back. In the antechamber
A smaller dummy represents girl-child attendant
Grinding ink at a large inkstone
The figure of Murasaki holds a writing brush
And a long piece of paper. Her head has begun to turn
Away from the writing to observe the moon
And quite likely to remark upon the song of the uguisu
Scholars, Japanese and Western, say she never did,
Never was here a minute. The priest shows
A sutra copied out in Murasaki's own handwriting
Here's the very inkstone that she used.
There is the moonlight window.

Dog days, ten years, I try to remember your face
You disappear, all my head can see
Are two paintings and drawing in red ink
Whatever else I've done with my life
Amounts to nothing

But inside the lantern a white speckled black beetle
Not quite as large as a rice-bird gives
Complete performance of *Siegfried* all alone

I am a hunting and gathering culture
The Moselle wine-boat sails over icy Delaware
On gossamer wing through the woods to Skye
(Hurrah for Miss Flora MacDonald)
Under the shadow of those trees
Edge of typhoon sudden rain
Shelter at Basho's Rakushisha hut
Green persimmons next door to Princess Uchiko her tomb
(Famous for her Chinese poems, first priestess of Kamo Shrine)
Under the shadow of those trees, waiting for the boat
Cythère

POÈME IMMENSE ET DRÔLETIQUE
   Night morning Greyhound bus NEVADA have a new driver
   all on different schedules
             "quel sentiment. quelle
             delicatesse"
       Who shall be first to arrive?

Chaos is an ideal state
None of us has ever experienced it
We are familiar with confusion, muddle and disarray
True disorder is inaccessible to us

       ". . . the sense of beauty rests gratified
       in the mere contemplation or intuition,
       regardless whether it be a fictitious Apollo
       or a real Antinous."
          —Coleridge, Notebook, 1814.

"White noise"
Brownian motion
Spinthariscope
"Cosmic rays"

I look out for a moment from behind the Great Book Mountain
Feeling like Lemuel Gulliver
       (this isn't exactly what

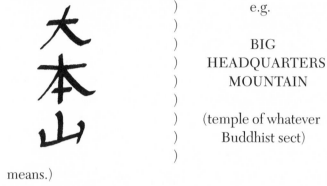

)   e.g.
)
)   BIG
)   HEADQUARTERS
)   MOUNTAIN
)
) (temple of whatever
)   Buddhist sect)
)

       means.)

                DISTRACTION
assemblage of eggs green onions butter and

amethyst crystals on top of the kitchen cabinet
A mountain of quartz   crystals 水晶

A whole set, (90 yen worth) of red beans
Gone up in smoke while I rummage three dictionaries
Four different texts in three incomprehensible languages

Minestrone
For all sentient beings 金昔

get me out of here! Bail me
out of the WORD OCEAN

"I wish to God
I never see your face
Nor heard your lion tongue"

And so knocked over my drink
I now have a pantsfull of cold sweet coffee
Hop up out of the way and white shirt all stained
On account of G. M. Hopkins:
"What do then? how meet beauty? Merely meet it; own,
Home at heart, heaven's sweet gift; then leave, let that alone.
Yea, wish that though, wish all, God's better beauty, grace."

Whatever any of that means (TO WHAT SERVES MORTAL BEAUTY?)
I am suddenly spastic brainless
Flailing arms and feet
Complete total mess. Rush home. Underwear
Hair and wristwatch and all pockets
Full of coffee syrup, take a bath to get rid of it
Before the ants can find me

Poor Hopkins imagined he had it completely under control
Set framed and crystallized
It all explodes iced coffee in ten directions,
Three worlds. He had to be a priest
Poetry was some other trip forced on him
Squirting out every nozzle, pore and orifice

I must have been reaching for my notebook
With both hands and several more
I wanted to copy that message here
Some arm and fingers held the Hopkins book
Yet other hands reaching for pen—did I yell,
I wonder—which of these hands arms elbows
Knocked the glass *towards* me?

                coffee and sugar leaping in
                capillaries of my brain

Coffee or sleep thick and sweet
Heavy chocolate hours of morning
Deliberately. And now 10:30 A.M. washed and broken away
From books and music I sit with my feet melting
In bright invisible mountain water that lies above
Brown chocolate mud and fir needles and little sticks
Two inches or twenty feet below—impossible to judge
Because of stillness and clarity of water
Smooth and heavy as cloth of cold
Black transparent stream,

                anyway, I thought that was the reason

SWAMI VIVEKANANDA: ". . . Like an insane person I ran out of our
                            house. He asked me, 'What do you want?' I
                            replied, I want to remain immersed in
                            samadhi. He said: 'What a small mind you
                            have! Go beyond samadhi! Samadhi is a
                            very trifling thing.'"

In the capital the commonest materials—
mud, plain paper, a couple boards and a bush and a rock,
A handful of straw—stuff we think of as worthless
Throw it away, certainly not to use for building a house
But set here in proportion, in specific spatial relation
An order of decorum and respect for themselves
Out of nothing at all, a house and garden
That can't last more than ten minutes
Very quietly stays forever

Here at the edge of town people visit me
As they used to hike up Sauk Mountain
Or to the Sourdough Lookout. They sidle up
And say, "Ain't you kind of lonely
Up here all alone?" I have to lie and say
"Sometimes," because they look injured & rejected
If I say "No." The truth is that living
In remote and foreign places takes a lot of
Work, every day, no time to feel sad and friendless
The neighborhood barber watches my hair walk by
Jealously. So much for
The Law of Karma.

Where is Los Angeles? Where IS Los Angeles
In among the minnie-bombs & maxi-toons
Cloud, altocumulus, as appears above islands
Far at sea.
O California lardy-dar

What is California, nothing but South Alaska
  "See how CANADA comes me cranking in
  And cuts me from the best of all my land
  A huge half-moon, a monstrous cantle out . . ."
        Northern Chile
I didn't know what I was getting into
Until it was too late and now I am a   F R E A K !
    O California!
 A G R E A T B I G F R E A K
    (ugh!)

almost white granite with little stars
Juniper trees in high California
Recollected at a great distance
Everyplace else forgot
Thinking "Moon still important at
The capital" and "L'AIDE-MEMOIRE DE LA VRAIE LOI"

An awfully large number of us
Had our heads bent with nowhere theories
Presented in beguiling books
Marx and Lenin, Freud and Jung, Churchill and Lord Keynes
Kafka and Kierkegaard,
In spite of or on account of which
Becoming cannon-fodder for sadist politicians
Patients of expensive quacks. How come.

> "In short, he bid me goe to the Fountain head,
> and read Aristotle, Cicero, Avicenna, and did call
> the Neoteriques shitt-breeches."
> —Aubrey's *Life of Wm. Harvey*

I suspect you can be as nutty with a head full
Of Greek and Latin, but maybe less easily imposed upon
And perhaps a little less dangerous?

Anthony à Wood, *Life & Times:* "In this month [*May*] was
to be seen at the Fleur de luce [*inn at Oxford*]
a brasen head that would speak and answer."

Neighbor's new iron gate sound
Bones of my right arm and elbow.

Always. America. Always a line of people
Ten or fifteen of them, all very smart
Waiting at the madhouse door to their parents' bedroom
Walking in their sleep—what time is it.
What does "dromedary" actually mean.
Cancel my subscription to TRAK Service.

Banana trees now at their best
But the most exciting green is rice in the paddy
Just beginning to produce ears of grain
Middle of August, shimmering subliminal green waves
And secret power-vibes

Maybe high quality emeralds can do
A similar job? However, the rice is alive
To be eaten later or brewed into *sake*
And so transports us out of Oregon skull
The sea's defective music as a passing bull
Suborns eleven
I can tell.

"AWAY, THOU FONDLING MOTLEY HUMOURIST!"

An overdose of America
Money and too many decibels

> Miss Janice climb up
> On a white snow horse
> Never climb down any more

O Sunflower, mouldy with grime, &c
Waste and want. Sung flower?

An overdose of pure London
Took Jimi Hendrix away,

> " . . . rueful again the piteous bagpipe went
> O bag-pipe thou didst steal my heart away"
>   ("Fled music is the sweetest
>   My Fair Lady")
"Of late two dainties were before me plac'd"

John Keats also lost

> "that's going to be him, see, how
> Monkey Face slips down over Great Seal
> Eyes and proliferation of curves
> From working too fast before the epipyroxylin
> Cools"

Yukio MISHIMA, novelist, playwright, actor,
Suicide by elegant Japanese tradition

Produces the effect of an infinite territory
What?
With only one possible neighboring color
What? Monads?

No, there's, no, no, not nomads, no, no
That idea was discredited, can't work, David Hume
What about volvox colonies
Universe of spheres containing spheres
All individual, all neighbors with independent spheres
Inside, so beautifully Buchsbaum
Never mourned, no eyes, what

FERN

the effect of uninterrupted acceleration (how-
ever familiar the track) certain contact-plates
prepare trees light up animals move and sing
laugh in the dark

EMERALDS
•
GONE
•

I drink bad expensive Italian wine
Beside the Kamo River. They say
You've taken a new lover. Passengers
On Sanjo Bridge Hieizan profile
Now all marvelously smudged by pen of hispid friend
Bottled somewhere near Florence, I expect
All the customers in here will rise and applaud

When I leave this place. They have been profoundly
Edified by the spectacle of a certified FOREIGNER
Gobbling up a pizza with his fingers
Drinking a bottle of wine without falling off his chair
A scene of life at the capital

I haven't been drunk for a long time
Reminds me of you, before we all
Became dope-friends. When was your last trip,
I went cuckoo on LSD the 30th of April

There's already been a great deal said about wine
And I'm reading the faggoty part of *The Anthology*
Thinking of you instead of naked boys

Curious elision. I've drunk 0.475 liter of "chianti"
Much too fast. Antinori. (Antenor was a mythological
What did he do?)

Hieizan sadder and smaller than Mt Koya
But still a mountain in several senses
Even though they drive buses to it
The buses go home at night; the trees take over
You can step out of temples into rhododendron flowers
                         ruins
Path which Mas Kodani followed seven days in rain
Priest robes, shaman hat, straw sandals too small,
Would wild monkeys attack him? Reciting HANNYA SHINGYO
Wherever stone marker on the trail shows where temple was

What was I saying. Talking to you.
A slow green train leaves for Uji
A slow green train arrives from Osaka
Immediately departs. I just realized that all I've said
For the past ten years was addressed to you
Simple and flat as that.

Kite! not the toy, a living bird
Sails above Kamogawa, that same Goddess
In worldly form dips and swings
Far below a northbound airplane
"KEE-REE!"
                    "The hawk flies up to heaven"

I have to write this at home with a new pen
I pitched the other into the Kamo
The moment it lifted from writing "—REE!"
To the complete consternation and horror
Of the other guests

                    Now this Antenor has a curious history.
                    Brother-in-law to Priam, King of Troy,
                    he betrayed the Palladium to the Greeks
                    that they might capture the Capitol. He
                    escaped with his family to found New Troy
                    in Italy (Venice or Padua?) the father of
                    the prophet, Laocoön. Pious Aeneas founded
                    a second Troy at Rome. Noble Brutus founded
                    Troynovaunt, *alias* London, capital of the world?

"It is said in the Book of Poetry, 'The hawk flies up
to heaven; the fishes leap in the deep.'"

Horror & chagrin of other patrons
Who carefully preserve their papers, ink and brushes and ink-
Stones in elegant lacquer boxes.
Writing is a serious action presided over by a god,
Tenjin-O-Mi-Kami-Samma, at the Kitano Shrine

All these worlds change faster than I can tell you
I have this reading & writing habit which I cultivate
Excessively, perhaps, little time for anything else
Although it's fun to ride the Osaka zipper
Forty-eight minutes for 65 miles
Fast asleep to Yodoyabashi branch Bank of America

Sound asleep we leave the capital rainy night
(Boats which children might have made from apple boxes)
Passengers remaining awake rattle their beads
Call on Amida Buddha and Kwannon to save them

Under the cushions and the *goza* matting
I feel the planks bulge as they slide
Snail foot over boulders and rocks
Far in the middle of the river
Safe and dry sound asleep left Sōō Temple, Yamazaki Bridge
At sundown. Early morning waken to shouts
Boatswarm harbor of Naniwa
Thanks to Gods of Sumiyoshi!

Vegetable nerves
Cold noodle time in the Capital
I got to kick my coffee habit.
Anybody seen my tranks? Remind me
How is Steve Carey?

Haloes
Which the angels left behind
Empty niches where holy saints once
Hand-hewn bases for noble columns: garden decorations
Wintermin (Chlorpromazine hydrochloride, 12.5 mg tabs)
     "Motion sickness, vomiting of pregnancy, potentiating
     effects on hypnotics and analgesics, psychoneurosis
     such as anxiety neurosis, bed-wetting, Pollakiuria."

          did you say "Bum trip"
          or "dumb trip"?

Gardening.
Cleaning the *o-furo*
Spilling the tea I'm going crazy
Sweating and freezing the sky overcast
Hot wooly clouds shove my head under cold water

Dry it off and start over.
The barber's lady assistant shaved
The rostra of my ears

Before this day is out a great pink peony
Shall have bloomed (note expensive leather hollyhock!)
All pink all
Carved out of the interior
                    of my eye
                         (BRANCUSI)

I've won every marble
Now I'm running mad
Gardening. Little circular trips.
Dirt produces infinite weed babble
My hands know it; my eyes blunk out, don't see
Hands read garden

I can catch the sun if I stop grabbing and
Turn my hand over. The sun falls into my open
Palm a sun much larger than we first imagined
We live in its atmosphere

If you want something hold out an empty hand

Newly opened peony delicate camphor perfume box

If you want a poem find a blank page

As if America were the final utterance
Of the human race: A culmination and the end
Land of the greed and the home of the knave?
Most of my compatriots will never learn
That "the human race" is not the same thing as
"White Protestant population of USA"
That "civilization" means neither "Metropolitan Opera Co."
Nor "modern American hospital"

I'd like to catch up with whoever it was
That placed these weird creatures forever in my cure
Crowned my goofy dome with red hat
Mitre and magic oils
This isn't my job; I mustn't resign

Kite wheels above
Bridge of the Changing Moon
                that's the end of that.

My head so packed with contradictory orders and
Theories and "categorical imperatives" and messages
From various power systems and from beyond the tomb
It's no wonder that my eyes don't focus and I'm
Plagued by asthma, headaches and a fat habit of body
Did this head-packing job happen by accident or design
Part of it is "cultural" part of it "free public education"
Part hereditary dullness: Ignorance, hankering & attachment

                "what did he say?"
Please don't disturb me. I'm busy packing
The smaller, finer bloodvessels of my brain
With peanut butter.
                What did he say. I don't know.
                But it may be useful, he said,
                Writing it in his notebook.

Sounds & perfumes twist the evening air,
If I may be allowed to mistranslate the Poet.

SRI RAMAKRISHNA: "'Is it dusk now? If it is, I won't smoke. During the
twilight hour of the dusk you should give up all other activities and
remember God.' Saying this he looked at the hairs on his arm. He wanted
to see whether he could count them. If he could not, it would be dusk."

The pink vacuum cleaner died
now the soul wanders the garden blue/green/black
Butterfly
                        there. That's for the Abyss. Now
We swing around holding onto the disgusting fur of that
Noxious body "placing our heads where our feet were"

THE SUN   THE SUN   THE SUN   (Blake shows it
Whether setting or rising
We all hang together Benjamin Franklin
Engraved bas-relief on bloody sky
Plain long and short spikes coming away from it
Statue of Liberty crown)

Isn't this extraordinary.
It only happens in the capital when I am there
Three imperial residences within walking distance
Great fat bird light through colored water
Fancy glass urns. Painted water. Break out
Around perforations. Peel coating of protective paper.
                For madness, soak in warm water to which
                a teaspoon full of ordinary baking-soda
                has been added. Twist cap on tight.

THEN SHALL BE SAID OR SUNG

                Sang-ridges! Them sang-
                ridges!
                We got to have a lot
                Of them sang-
                        ridges!

And   C H O C O L AT E
                    "You can
                    Always
                        Take more
                    You know."
        Several books by Henry James

642

RING BELL THREE TIMES. OFFER INCENSE. RING
GONG FOR EACH OF THREE *RAIHAI*

THE RAGE OF AQUARIUS. Three kinds of
Chocolate. RUMY which is filled with raisins and
Rum syrup . . . Chocolate strawberry cream . . . and BLACK
Which is bittersweet
Across the street from the police-box
THE RAGE OF ANTINOUS
                                        cut or tear along dotty lines
HIT GONG AGAIN. SECOND INCENSE OFFERING.
EVERYBODY CHANT.

Plum blossoms white and also red ones
Peppermint-stripe camellias, white ones resembling
Gardenia, yellow flowers of rape eaten as *sukimono*
(Rapeseed oil waterproof paper umbrella)
Tiny but   F A T   green, gold-eye bird
The light all new and different

High-test flowers cure every time
Feeling well is important and relaxes the brain
Beneficent flower vibrations continue a day or so
Now time for high-test chocolate and imaginary colors
Plum trees at Kitano Tenmangu Jinsha
Maybe I revisit tomorrow when nobody is there
I must have a secret book

Above the door to the chancel
Inside Daikakuji Zenden
Two swallow's nests, each with a little flat board
Underneath to catch the drippings
Exactly as if this were out of doors
Where kids are picnicking in the cold
All around Osawa Pond, which place
Like one or two other lakes and wells
Are only authentic remains of the Heian capital

Being fireproof and without military value
And both sides of all the wars were Japanese
Everybody liked the flowers, grass and trees
Planted around the shores. One small mudhen
Labors across the water.

At Arashiyama the flowers are late
Everybody is here anyway, walking
Under the cherry trees. They eat and play
On the river, drink *sake* and sing. The cherries
Will be obliged to bloom
No matter what weather

Man all wrapped in transparent plastic
Sloops along the wet street reciting political speech
Bullhorn slung on his shoulder
I thought first a sound truck had crawled
Onto my doorstep to die
Sun and secret perfume breeze
All greens vibrating
The dogs in the corral roaring and running
We circle them, our horses raving foam
Splash my lavender *hakama*
Green hunting-robe over yellow kimono

Lady West Gate and Lady Plum spent an hour
Quarreling over my hair, setting lacquer cap with
Horse-hair blinkers will it be a sprig of
Cherry bloom or twig of spirea
Lady Plum in tears
              (Arashiyama. Korean ladies all in blue silk
              Walking circle dance under blossoms
              Drum and gong, folksong in shoulder-slung
              Bullhorn)
I haul on the reins the horse dances to the left
Blood mixed with his foam as I fire arrows among screaming

Dogs. Lord Akiba thrown! (Heavy brocade *karaginu* and
Green *hakama* his older brother wore last year) Not a
Dog was hit the old men say:
"When we were young
all the dogs ended like sea urchins
Gently waving spikes above the sand."   Hieizan
And the Eastern Hills dark blue
                    (Old ladies with false-nose-mustaches
                    A slow comic drum dance with beerbottle
                    Spouting paper plume foam/semen)
Cherryblossom shadow
Embankment of Oi River
Young men in a circle drink and yell and sing
One performs Tanuki prick-dance with big *sake* bottle
Sometimes held out before his crotch sometimes hid
Under his shirt, Unexpected Future lurks in joybelly
He is Tanuki, magical "badger"

Wandering rusty kimono faded fag samisen
Chaunts antique lays to picnickers
Wandering showbiz drum and samisen team
Young man with family and friends & battery-driven
Electrical guitar

Sound of drum and gong prevail
But a whole school of lady *koto* players
Best kimono and Japanese hairdo
Perform on *tatami* platform underneath falling blossoms
Black hair bright silk

Elderly beerglass & bottle grandpa
Pursues green silk Korean lady
Across the pattern of the dance
She escapes and he's discomfited
Klong of gong hit with sock full of sand
Big spindle-drum hung on grandpa

Subtle GOOM.   GOOM.   Small gong tinkle-clanks,
Big gong KLONG   blue silk ladies of a certain age
The dances of Kudara
The music of Shiragi

Tanuki Badger Supernatural   RULES!
Traveler's reed hat, big *sake* jar,
Grinning mouth and blaring eyes
Grand swag belly over small upstanding prick
Huge balls hang to the ground
Spirit of mischief, wine and lechery
Long busy tail, thick fur, nocturnal habits
"Badger" is a feeble translation . . . much more like
Big raccoon/bear
Fat breathless popeyed manifestation
Of the Divine Spirit . . . not a bad representation
Of the present writer

Japan is a civilization based upon
An inarticulate response to cherry blossoms.
So much for Western Civilization.
"Mr. Franklin, is it a setting or a rising sun?"
Try to be serious. Try to get to Toji tomorrow.
Try to remember that I accidentally found
Birthplace of Shinran Shonin when I visited Hokaiji
Magnolias and cherries at Daigoji
Unprecedented splendor.

Look into the abyss and enjoy the view.
All we see is light; all we don't see
Is dark. We know lots of other things
With other senses. Various kinds of new green weeds
Pop up through white gravel

Chicago, Federal Court, *USA* vs *Dellinger et al. #69 Crim.* 180:
Mr KUNSTLER: "The whole issue in this case is language,
                    what is meant by . . ."

646

Mr Thomas HAYDEN, a Defendant: "We were invented."

Poetry, American. (see under *American Poetry*)
In the U.S.A. "Calliope" is a steam piano.
Nobody ever figured out that Sir Gawain's Green Knight
Was a crocodile (*pace* Yvor Winters)

Revisit Kitano plum blossoms
Pink ones have strong perfume.
Big tree in front of central sanctuary
(*Gongen-Zukuri* architecture, Sugawara Michizane
Was incarnation [*gongen*] of this Deity who presides
Over plum blossoms and calligraphy and scholarship)
So hollow and full of holes it scarcely exists at all
But blossoms immensely before scarlet fence
Intricate wooden gables
Another all propped up with poles and timbers
Part of it fixed with straw rope
Exploding white blossoms not only from twigs
And branches but from shattered trunk itself,
Old and ruined, all rotted and broken up
These plum trees function gorgeously
A few days every year
In a way nobody else does.

At the Capital 44–46 Showa 25 January

647

WALKING BESIDE THE KAMOGAWA,

REMEMBERING NANSEN AND FUDŌ

AND GARY'S POEM

Here are two half-grown black cats perched on a
      lump of old teakettle brick plastic garbage
         ten feet from the west bank of the River.
I won't save them. Right here Gary sat with dying Nansen,
The broken cat, warped and sick every day of its life,
Puke & drool on the *tatami* for Gary to wipe up & scold
"If you get any worse I'm going to have you put away!"
The vet injected an overdose of nemby and for half an hour
Nansen was comfortable.

How can we do this, how can we live and die?
How does anybody choose for somebody else.
How dare we appear in this Hell-mouth weeping tears,
Busting our heads in ten fragments making vows &
      promises?

Suzuki Roshi said "If I die, it's all right. If I should
live, it's all right. Sun-face Buddha, Moon-face Buddha."
Why do I always fall for that old line?

We don't treat each other any better. When will I
Stop writing it down.

Kyoto 14:iv:69

POSTSCRIPT, 17:iv:69 (from De Visser, Vol. I, pp. 197–198),
    20th Commandment of the *Brahmajala Sutra* (Nanjo 1087):
    " . . . always practise liberation of living beings

(*hō jō*, 放生)"

648

MAY FIRST REVOLUTION DAY

all about studying Japanese grammar and writing
among drosera trees (black and grubby palmettos)
Backyard of Inoda Coffee Shop
While the youth of the Empire march up and down outside
Red flags and banners and slogans

AMERICA GET OUT OF ASIA

a somewhat unlucky saying from 28 years ago
Shall I stay fountain splash sunshine?

André Gide, *Journal* 1930: "Col d'Allos. Noon, 1 September.
To my excesses at Calvi I owe a great calm."

1:v:69

TO EDWARD DAHLBERG

the last secret batty American genius,
    bright gargoyle bellybutton living disciple of Thomas Nashe,

Let's you and me go burn down a couple universities—
    Fairy International, flap your mothy wings to speed the blaze

!   !   !

O HECATOMB OF IGNORANCE

[10:v:69]

SCIENCE AND LANGUAGE

Four little boys have caught a frog
Shallows of the Kamogawa
Lovely new biological field kit open on picnic table
Plastic lens, plastic syringe, plastic bottles of strong poison
Shiny scalpel brilliant dissecting needles

I hurry past, a boy has picked up a plastic jar
With exclamations of triumph and joyous anticipation
                    (the frog nearly escaped)

It is impossible to write in English about Japanese
Persons, places and things

Mark Twain, William Dean Howells had the same problem
dealing with USA in that language
Tear it up and start again.

10:v:69

FOR KENNETH REXROTH

I was thinking how great a wilderness
All the earth was then, outside the walls of Alexandria
(I've been reading the *Greek Anthology,* thanks to you)
Wild country like the upper Skagit Valley
Right up to the walls of Athens and of Rome
Strange how these old towns are still alive
And people live there in quite un-American style
(I must walk to Murasaki-no to use the public bath)
If America were burnt down a couple dozen times
Would it become as habitable?

27:vi:69

FOUR OTHER PLACES, MORE & LESS

1. Kamo-wake-ikazuchi-no-jinja

I went to visit them.
They were all at home.
Change of season washing ceremony
White curtains wave benignly
Prayers and salutations

I keep thinking of Shelley's notebooks

Many small birds point east

9:ix:67

2. The Sennyuji: Kannon

Supposed to look like Yang Kuei-fei (by Imperial order)
Is it real, a copy or just a beautiful image?
An exquisite profile by any rule
Whether it wrecked an empire.
Did she break that comb in heaven
Strangle in a pear tree,
Real history? Really a poem?

> Letter from T.P. assures me it is not
> poetry but rude indigest lumps *et cetera*

651

Going towards Hyakuman-ben University corner
Trying to repeat *Hannya Shingyo* from memory
The act of remembering or the vibrations of the sutra
Crash through the real world
Surrounding mountains pass Kyo-dai kids, professors
All walking at some angle to this void reality
Immediate bright breath

10–11:ix:67

3. Takagamine, Where I Am Living Then

Morning zazen evening drunk
Mosquito-hawk legs thinner
Than a hair between
Legs thin as a
Hairy laugh tail

O for the tongue the Harp of Paradise!

No reason carefully drowned certain phantoms
(Under sea til called for)
Hair leg a jewel chain under eye-loupe!

Schedules

From home to bath to home to supper in Kita-oji:
Two hours & 15 minutes
From home to breakfast in Kita-oji and return:
One hour plus a few minutes
From home to Irmgard's house: 12 minutes
MIZAI!
"all are not yet," Hakuun (the White Cloud) said
WEI TSAI!
Pai-yun said 1045–1073 A.D. pupil of Yang-ch'i

2:vii:69–5:vii:69. Drunk.

652

(thick and heavy, with only the finest hairline space be-
tween its edges and the sills and the jambs, lock and
hinges heavy dull golden brass knobs, expensive bronze
hardware as in ship-chandler's showroom the back room
at the bank or moving parts of steam locomotive engine)

(heavy rose granite sarcophagus of Cousin Whitney and Eulalia
Riverview surprising destination of Tut and Ginnie,
many more beside)

the light shines again
bien inattendu
fountain pen and pencils forgot on bookcase 1 & 3/4 km
from where they ought to be

                          The light?

"Suddenly, ... ignorance!"

                      Tombeau de Marcel Proust
not to mention the sacred ninnified Plato his phobias:
liberty, poetry and pretty girls O L U X U R Y !
O first class tickets & accommodations on the primrose
everlasting highroad fire coals Wisdom Palace!
forgot, quite unexpectedly (*"Toujours la même chose,"*
        Frank-Paul Bowman was fond of saying)
EVERYTHING so efficiently, so habitually so automatically
Remembered *viz.* the dust composed & compounded
once again into bone crystals bone shapes and hair
contours and from sources otherwise unspecified there
arrive a congeries of jellies, webs & slimes,

not quite dry when the telephone receiver hits
(and sticks, very slightly, to) the new ear ". . . . llo?
Hahhh?. . . . Hello? What do you want I just barely
got to sleep when the phone rang. . . . what?
I can hardly hear you"

roar of milling machines and lathes in the foundry
at irregular intervals an earthquake W H U M P
(a dropped Himalaya) the big die press clamping down
several tons of high class metal
bent bulged and crimped a heavy world. Heavy.

Well anyway it was dark in there & it was light or dark
in here but with the door shut it was gloomy, depressing
boring and nearly hysterical. If the light had come on
during the daytime there'd be no mistaking it.
W H U M P. An iceberg on the open sea melted all unevenly
& a lot of it which had been under water now shines
and glows, polished and hollowed and domed, no sharp edges
in the sun a random jelly
try to imagine the ice/water interface—area where is
no change of identity but a change of state the ice (remember)
All water while the sea, a living (and voracious) jelly
(or thick soup)
has ideas of its own (I N D I A !)
            lots of arms, many eyes, fins & scales,
            some shoot rays of heavenly fire all around them
            in the deepest caves of ocean abyss
            occhi onesti e tardi
heavy angels designed and built by Henry James
heavy and slow dark heavenly recessive galaxies
their light row ribbons read out the story complete with
charts and symbols and curves, W H U M P

15:viii:69

LIFE AT BOLINAS.

THE LAST OF CALIFORNIA

FOR MARGOT & JOHN DOSS

The things that are down should be up
The things that are up should be down
Confusion mess and itchyness
            rearrange
I have to rearrange the world
        Make a demand

Gold   The world
rises   WHAT GOES HERE.   being oblong with
Croodle   chrysanthemums.

                    FORCE MAJEUR

explosion of shaped charge
instant paisley steel plate tattoo

                              •

curiously they went under, under the waves
undulation. Unhesitatingly, no thought
of strength or whether they could, straight
ahead.

                              •

                    Y U M
                              •

Straight out of the basket that stuff is grey matter
with everything already there. Three brains? Yes.
Out through the
                    screams of laughing, drums, flutes
                    right and left-hand music voices
                    and hand-clapping whoop

BRILLIANCE

Leaks out the cracks
around the stony door
out through the gong clang whoop

THEY CAUGHT THE
THEY GOT THE SUN BY THE WRIST
YARDED HER OUT OF THE CAVE
   while the girl who did the
   naughty dance
   covers herself,
   calmly,

   OH!
ask for what you want
  B O O K
  B O O K
cough, uncivilized stove insurance in the living room
     sit down
put in your order and be patient
Total failure of civilization?
(bong.   whoop.   clap.   wiggle.   blink.)
Squash-flower:
CHRYSANTHEMUM PUZZLE

Long past midnight
Quiet house
Purple green-eared smiling bat
Call on myself, demand
"One Word More"
A new start, great inky swashes arranged
A painting, a new life
Wet dry across the world, O-Ho!

Every time a distinct shape mark
Who cares how long it takes—desire!

CANDY HAND

TOOTHSOME OBSCURITIES

CANDY HAND
Sugar Baby

who knows why kind of fun

At Duxbury Point, a few thousand feet from here
The wind blows heavy 35 miles per hour all night long
Big lights at the postoffice illuminate Brighton Avenue
The raccoons can see to get across

•

As I pass through the dark dining room
I perceive that each chair is occupied by dwarf-
          ghoul-corpse
(Yammering. Decomposing. Power.)

•

Blithering dead leaves along the ground
Crooked sunlight falling smoke black wind
Electric power failure woke me up, I broke
The kitchen clock. Franco & Judy hungry in Zurich.

30:xii:68 — Bolinas — 11:xi:69 — Kyoto

657

FOR KAI SNYDER

7:V:60 (an interesting *lapsus calami*)
A few minutes ago I tried a somersault; couldn't do it
I was afraid and I couldn't remember how.
I fell over on one shoulder,
Rolled about and nearly went over backwards
And finally hurt my chest.
What kind of psychomotor *malebolge* had I got into . . .
"This is old age, &c."

After thinking it all over
Imagining how it might be done
I performed three forward somersaults, 7:V:70
Age 46 years 6 months 37 days.

7:v:70

A LETTER, TO BILL BERKSON

There are no poems today.
Bolinas: too many people
          not enough
          W A T E R
No solitude where too many
cars, telephones, dogs—
No see no hear nothing.
Too bad! I go away.
All trails overgrown with bushes
          vines and kookaburrs.
          Dead beaches. Ripped-out heads.
          G O O D B Y E.

1971 (?)

ALLEN MARLOW

Let's be a universities.
overnight sea trips.
series of temples
small monastic
I suspect that Ceylon is Eden
& live in a Dharma Garden.

16:ii:71

LEAVING THE CAPITAL

Morosely resentfully hysterically packing.
Neighbor's white dog reminds me of decapitation. Why.
Secret recollection of Grimm's tales illustrated by
Gustave Doré: "Falada"

25:v:71

"HOME AGAIN, HOME AGAIN . . . "

She says, "Where are all your gods and goddesses?"
I said, "I've got them in the closet on a shelf."
"Are you going to take the closet door off its hinges?"

THAT is what I traveled 6000 miles to hear
Her voice and beauty and total batty logical inexorability
I'm suddenly dunked in jealousy although Peter is a splendid fellow

20:vi:71

659

MANY COLORED SQUARES

Why decide in advance what to do. Eucalyptus trees their shiny
leaves and polished crows. The opera of. Hummingbirds. MOVE,
an optimum crow call and spider sparkle newly. Joe walks but
seldom touches the ground. Pause. Hammer. Pause. Wind. Crows.

What's in the oven. All the ingredients: quit opening the door if
you want Dinner to emerge in less than a geological epoch. Oh.
Busy. Hmmm.

Sniff.

Of something. The first fruits of man's disobedience was a
pomegranate—
The invention of Winter and Ambition—The joyful desiring. Flat out.

KONK

Much better under lots of Monterey cypresses and immense blue-gum
and lemon-wood; trees in the distance in front of the ocean. Letch.

The disobedient mind is the fruit of inactivity swaying upon dishonest
boughs. The butcher's thumb lies weighty on the scales. Tumble.

Minor chords are not sad. The Pyramids are still a secret. Erasmus
Darwin: *The Botanic Garden*.

The explanation isn't the same as what happens. A recipe can produce
a particular result most of the time.

Carrie turned all the matches in the same direction. Love and Honor
conspire to discipline the Factory.

Come with me, Joe.

660

Now when Bill gets here we will leave. Quite seriously. Stop tittering.

Cut straight down the center it means twice as much. Free at last.
Or not. Hand lotion soothes my mind. Correspondence.

Scales uncolored in themselves produce a rainbow. Mountain seafoot
absolutely white? Iron curl. Start over. Start all over again. Your
feet are dirty on the bottom. I won't say "Immensely so."

Container for insensible fruit?

22:vi:71

"NOT HEAVILY"

We don't possess our own voices.
What you hear comes from a long way off.
What did he say.
What would you hear? That.

> abnormal dentition
> extraordinary land breeze
> Pentelic marble

5:vii:71

"UP IN MICHIGAN"

Tough branch stems blue
Chicory flowers
Down flat leaves almost dandelion
Blue delicate five-tooth petal edge
Almost invisible thread hair center
Lots of Queen Anne's lace, Joel misquotes Williams,
"Wild carrot invades a whole field"
Big leaf trees where land floats outward
Glacier tundra peat prairie
The sun rises in the north

Allendale, Michigan 13:vii:71

"OLD AGE ECHOES"

Lately I've seen myself
As fat naked waddling baby
All alone in the yard
Bright flowers
Silver lawnmower blades
Big dog approaching (friendly?)
Berries
What are fears or dangers?

19:vii:71

THE LETTER TO THOMAS CLARK 22:VII:71

FROM BOLINAS WHERE HE SAT BESIDE ME

TO HELP TO WRITE IT

                              Tom Clark
                              Waco, Texas

                                        (crossed out. All our
                                        addresses crossed out)

Dear Tom. Received your letter
& no mistake
about the address or the sender (name of
Angelica) but
                              you
look just the least bit changed.

Due to this minuscule point
and the fragility
                    of the ink,
And the wrong time of day all over town
It was not the phone.
                    but
                         (the fragility. . . .
of one's own neuromuscular mechanism
               where that   S W A M P)
                         Yours truly,
                              Dad.

PORTLAND AGAIN

a)

Another "wrong set" here as in Bolinas
I mentioned my fantasy of living on Oregon coast
B. kept repeating, "Yes, Gold Beach."
We have all grown old and funny looking

b)

No, no, it is knowledge of death and change
fern plant brown furry heart under feather weed plumes
enlaced with long straps of grass
buttercup crowfoot leaves (*rancune* of Paul Verlaine)

fishpond half blinded by fallen bamboo leaves
Too many of our speeches thoughts and actions
already written by 19th century authors
frothy seed feather lace
And a red-tail hawk straight overhead look out!

c)

Heading for Congress!
(Have I sat
            in a puddle
                        of salad oil?)

Vicarious enjoyments falling out of air as mushrooms
Autonomy, nandina (heavenly bamboo)

d)

Tree branches reverberate
Sky shell head skull Fresh
Air. And then. Prophesy?
Echo: we are mental crash outside. Instructions

e)

Autonomy. Don't be a loser, don't get
Your name in the paper stay underground or
Elsewhere when the Authorities arrive
Big show of elegant fronds green plumes
The business end of it completely unnoticed.

23–29:vii:71

UNTIED AIRLINES

The world's tiniest apple pie and library paste for lunch.
Where to go.
    I want out.

30:vii:71

"HORRIBLE INCREDIBLE LIES":

KEITH LAMPE SPONTANEOUSLY

"THE NEXT WOMAN THAT COMES THROUGH HERE THAT I
WAS FOND OF IN A REALLY NOBLE ROMAN LANDSCAPE
WHERE LARGE FREEDOMS TO DO A NUMBER, *viz.* A DOUBLE
MARRIAGE PERFORMED BY A. J. MUSTE THE EVENING I THINK
HE GOT CERTIFIED LANGUAGE FOR GADFLY LEAFLETS IN
1967 MORE ASHTRAYS AS HAD BEEN SOUVENIRS HO CHI MINH
HAD LAID ON HIM A COLUMN OF GREEN FLAME SHOT UP
BEING THE SOUVENIR ASHTRAY MADE FROM A MAGNESIUM
FRAGMENT WHICH HE PROBABLY DIED A HIERONYMOUS
MISTAKE A PEOPLE APART FROM ANITA HOFFMAN PUTTING
DOWN A PLAGUE ON BOTH YOUR INCREDIBLY DEIFIED
HOUSES. NITA NEVER HAD A SAW AN EXPANSION BETWEEN
THESE TWO THINGS WITHOUT EVER LOOKING.

"REALITY LOOKED AT HIM AND SMILED AND THAT VERY
MINUTE WENT CLICK, NEURAL SPEED, A TOTAL DINOSAUR
SCENE IN MONUMENT VALLEY SHE MET A SURFER DOWN AN
OLD RIVERBED CRUNCHING THE GRAVEL WHICH SOUND
ALLOWS HER ACCESS TO LIT-UP DINOSAURS THREE DAYS
OF ISOLATED VERBALIZATION FOR A WHILE TO RECOVER BETTER
WHEN THE STARS COME OUT."

3:viii:71

IMAGINARY SPLENDORS

As I stand here I feel myself growing older and impatient
with you, this endless failing life won't reach you, too
short on one end, walk around upstairs and sing wreck my
nerves I'm going to bed I want out of this amusement park,
the holidays are over I must go back to work (if I could find
a job I couldn't stand it) the one person who doesn't need all this
explanation I want to talk to him is gone, probably dead and
what have I got to say

and catch
myself again completely unaware of what's real around me here.
Imaginary jumps out of the closet plays my nerves and feelings
the sun trees flowers don't exist Imaginary grabs all my attention
sucks energy out my spinal column Imaginary debauchery all bankrupt
what becomes of all that circuitry the needles read OVERLOAD there's
a leak far below the waterline the pumps are burning out huge power
of ocean waves heavy radiation from sun all escaping headed for total
heaviness turned inside out anti-matter sox tube to other Universe

what about most delicate redwood needle shadows
heavy slow tops of eucalyptus
beaded fringe skirt of Texas Guinan
small Hieronymus Bosch California fuchsias

hummingbird a tremendous
D Y N A M O
no float or zap through the air
anti-gravity syrup in all those flowers?

Sun so powerful here
Giant lilies grow in the shade
"When I say, 'JUMP, MR DEAD MAN,' you go!"

7–10:viii:71

PUBLIC OPINIONS

Peter Warshall says that the slow loris moves approximately
three feet per hour.

Donald R. Carpenter says, "I don't do ANY hot water numbers
in the morning."

Allen Ginsberg, reading a ms poem handed to him by a friend,
says, "AH, that's green armpit poetry."

Irving Oyle says: What did Chekov do but live in a small town
where everybody said, "Some day I'll go to Moscow"?

What I say is that in every toke you could taste the cold
slick throb of real DOPE: fine East India hemp.

E A R T H Q U A K E
DUCKY FAULT SLIP
DUCKY FALSE LIP?
"No effect on me, whatsoever."

12:viii:71

667

MONUMENT RESCUE DIM

Her mouth is empty
All the sky shines
Bird feet on the roof
Did the telephone ring

M A G N I F I C E N T

(a silence)
Dromedary
I keep hearing something else

You continue babbling on without making any sense at all why not
Neither of us attending as in a dream wherein everything important
Happens "offstage" somewhere just beyond the view of the sleeping eye

14:viii:71

THE SUMMER AFTERNOON

Firecracker lilies and "naked ladies" (vegetable
Gooseneck barnacles) accompany ancient Chinese poems
Beside the cypress hedge smell of eucalyptus
On the ocean breeze
                    "Boy, you better listen. Oh boy,
                    You better listen."

14:viii:71

"I TOLD MYSELF": BOBBIE SPONTANEOUSLY

"I TOLD MYSELF THAT I WASN'T GOING TO GET HIGH TODAY:
AND I TOLD MYSELF THAT IF I *DID* GET HIGH
IT WASN'T GOING TO BE ON ACID—
BUT I THOUGHT TO MYSELF, WELL MAYBE
IF I JUST BROKE A LITTLE CORNER OFF IT
THERE'D STILL BE AN *AWFUL* LOT OF IT LEFT . . .
A CORNER OFF TODAY,"

16:viii:71

LOOK   LOOK   LOOK

My eyes fondle carved metal and stone
Suck up jeweled faceted bronze nasturtium leaves and flowers
Feed and nourish strapped sense glued in bone marrow
We would rather swim, dance

Eyes glance and glide over polished surfaces
Lacquer gold yes I test it with my thumb
Solid
Impossible to believe that all I see is light
Reflected from images and ritual implements
Thunderbolt bell
Gleaming vajra

"Love in fantastic triumph sate . . . "

16:viii:71

MOZAMBIQUE

Out of gas. Here is flaked ice
Here is the bottle of Pernod
Here is the garden to sit in
Gassing up.

I must really try to like it.

16:viii:71

THE TURN

Walking along Elm Road
Handful of nasturtiums, butter, some kind of bread
75¢ the loaf no advertising included
Bread and air and a price tag wrapped in plastic
The dogs come out as usual to roar at me
I find myself screeching wildly in reply
Fed up with suppressing my rage and fear
I bellow and roar
The dogs are scared and their people scandalized
"What are you trying to do? HAY! What are you trying to do?"
I had nothing to tell them; I was talking to their dogs.

16:viii:71

A RETURN TO SAN FRANCISCO FROM KITKITDIZZE

To Allen's apartment, Telegraph Hill
Solemn naked blond photographer greets us at the stairhead.

Underground Chinese lunch
"Tuesday morning Calcutta" (A. on his way to see Bangla Desh)

Pearl plank
Palenque

   Play it by the ear of thumb
   Prejudice is overcome.

            30:viii:71

GROWING AND CHANGING

WHAMP WHAMP WHAMP
and squeal of skill-saw
I carelessly build a creepy future life

All things made new and completely wrong

Once too often
Made all new
Laid bare *"mon coeur*
  mis à nu"
Our time is one two many
  anew (*agneau*)
Desuetude

I guess you are somebody
I used to know
One that I knew
Then. Guess who.

Imagine living on Telegraph Hill
            worrying

Imagine living anywhere
            worrying
"Just
      a-wearying
                for you"

THIS MEANS YOU
            (underlined in red)
Let me interest you unwearyingly
END OF SONG APPROACHING
ROUGH DETOUR AHEAD

            K   R   A   N   K

            Perhaps you have often wondered why I have
so seldom written to you. I am put off by knowing
how busy you are and by the crowd of affairs which
presses for my attention almost every waking minute
(nevertheless many members of that crowd are mem-
ories of you and speculations about your present
activities, feelings and states of mind). I often
tell myself
            (large comma)

. . . the idea of your thinking of me doesn't make much sense
either, on a day when I am properly organized and orientated, but I
am susceptible to quick changes of mood—
a drink of gin rearranges my mind right away
and I can see you frowning and moodily

thinking of me: a train of unsatisfactory pictures/thoughts
which annoy you and your annoyance reaches me instantly
and of course it is all completely absurd I am attending
to the boiling chicken and you are wondering "blue or
green? Where are the scissors. Did Peter buy tomatoes
again?" The integuments of reality great floating sticky
transparent films of regret and misplaced concern &
hankering,

       A day. I can spend all kinds of time
       Considering which word to set beside this one.
       The life of art

I think I'm going to do just that
And washed all my shirts
Every plastic one
This is no different from any other day except for the memory
Of Saturn. Later all the gods churned the sea
To recover certain immortality a stolen woman
Make me turn my head and say
"What was that?", if you want me to like it.

Whom does one ask.
Who do you ask.
          Whom does;
          One asks.
Who do you ask
And your dreams reply
(very much like Henry James)
"There you are."

1–9:ix:71

REJOICE !

Bad spectacles make my head and eyes hurt
My feet are in bad shape, I say "My nerves
are completely shattered." Who is right.
Lay off the gin for a day
Or two. Pleurisy or angina
Or whatever may be needed to transport
Us into our private rooms at last,

    PIANO
        DRAB (and evasive)
HUITZILOPOCHTLI DISAPPEARS
                    (voom!)
    transport
    our private rooms
    flower treasures
    bad feet
    prime rib

The beginning has now been completed.
The main section of Part One is presented and elaborated.
It is brought to a quiet close by a folk-like melody that reappears
As the second subject in the fugue which forms the second, middle
Section of the work. The third section. *Pasta e fagioli.*
Fourth Part: "Theme and Variations." Concluding section:
Grand Explosion Brilliant.
Epilogue: The Empty Circle. Surf line. Headlands. Cypresses.
Eucalyptus and fuchsia. Nasturtium and geranium. Ferns.
Quail. California jay.

    (. . . and then I discover that I've been listening—
    quite seriously—to the engine of a power mower . . .)

      F L A M E

Five hundred pounds of absolutely nothing
Under great pressure
While Schumann's "Great" C Major Symphony blarps within. Fang.
                                                                    Fang.

It's suppposed
To be that way.

9–14:ix:71

OCTOBER FIRST

and what. One must groan and stretch in order to break
any habit. The process of developing new muscles hurts.
Pain causes anger. I find myself quarrelling over nothing.
O!   O!   O!

Find twenty beautiful pages for Thomas Clark.
          ("Anything!", Joanne Kyger said. "I'd write anything
          that I could!")

Twenty things hitherto unincluded:
    1.   *Shakujo*
    2.   Copy of *The Wooden Fish*
    3.   Medal from Rokuhakudo
    4.   Piece of lapis lazuli, gift of J. Armstrong
    5.   Indian shrine, gift of J. Kyger
    6.   Blue Mexican glass pitcher
    7.   Three onyx eggs
    8.   Three cylindrical magnets
    9.   Tanka of Chenrezig, gift of Claude Dalenberg
    10. Necklace of elephant bells
    11. Drawing of P.W. by J-L. Kerouac
    12. Blue tin trunk
    13. Pebble of rutilated quartz carved into Daruma image

14. Two shakuhachi, and other Japanese instruments
15. Round fan, woven by the last Carib Indian in the West Indies, "Use it for setting hot things on," Anne Waldman when she gave it to me.
16. Japanese wristwatch
17. Crystal inkwells
18. A collection of blank books
19. Big turquoises: GSS his gift of a ring and the jewel sent by Judy Beltrametti
20. Portrait of P. W. by M. McClure (blue enamel on thick paper, 1959)

Start over in order to have a spare for each.

1-a. Collection of city maps, road maps &c
2-a. Silver dollar in plastic case, gift of Joe Brainard
3-a. The ingratitude!
4-a. I was happy to discover that I hadn't sold several books given to me by J-L. K.
5-a. Curious dream of thunder and lightning
6-a. I am drinking buttermilk while I write this
7-a. WHUMP!
8-a. Expensive sports glasses bought to watch kabuki from cheap seat; now used to observe sea lion, pelican sea gull conclaves on Duxbury Reef, also the moon
9-a. Septic tank crew and vacuum truck investigated the drains this morning . . . truck four times as big as those used in Kyoto
10-a. Yellow pansies in a whiskey glass, kitchen window bouquet; Joe LeMay sharpens his chain saw
11-a. New Korean brass incense burner. I couldn't get at any of those which I already own, an embarrassingly numerous collection
12-a. Japanese harness bell in the shape of a torus
13-a. Green soapstone image of Ganapati. Duerden says, "Give it to me when you die, will you?"
14-a. Pental sign pens in seven colors although black isn't a color
15-a. Forgotten kakemono, calligraphy of the late Kongo Abe

16-a. I can't remember anything about life in Japan. Zuishin-in, Daiho-onji, where at? How much did it cost to take a bath? 28 ¥?

17-a. Forgot three-faced image in lacquer shrine as well as the small heavy Yamantaka image from China

18-a. If I were to write an autobiography what would I put in it?

19-a. I'm eating sunflower seeds

20-a. Collection of photos of P. W. from earliest childhood to the present

20-a-1. Red glass sanctuary light glows before Buddha

20-a-2. 1057 ¥ on deposit at the Sanjo Branch of the Sanwa Bank Kyoto, Nakagyoku, Sanjo-Kawaramachi-agaru. Its value increases daily

increases daily

UN-GUM   UN-GUM   UN-GUM
UN-GUM   UN-GUM   UN-GUM
(African daisy mantra)

I call my powers to me
Crystals   colors   music
I begin to climb up

S I N G

up. UN-GUM! Crystals. UN-GUM! Power. UN-GUM! African Daisy.
UN-GUM! Colors. UN-GUM! The song of music.

(don't get hung up in any single chakra)

If the door knocks or the telephone rings
It's not my problem
UN-GUM!
What is the basis for your objection
Peanut brittle
UN-GUM!
Where would that put us.
UN-GUM!
Flute.   Oboe.   Viola d'amore.   Secret foods.   Oxygen.

H U M !

Outside as if suddenly happily naked
Top of my head painlessly removed
Effortless: beyond glad or tears in space beyond security outside
H U M !
The world really being I there
Lots of air the oceans and mountains
Bodega Bay sand cup hook
Waves can be heard and felt the whistle buoy also
Weimaraner puppy glad to see me again
Up beyond hope or wish or high
Z O P !

1–7:X:71

ROME

all scattered near a broken wall
The sun remains behind. green pur-
ple hill. Have some. {GOLD}

25:X:71

NEW MEXICO, AFTER MANY YEARS

1. Mornings at Ranchos de Taos

Immediate vision of opening door
Long rows of dead animals ducks and chickens
Eyes closed feet in the air
Died to feed me

✻   ✻   ✻

Red severed pig's head beside the dirt road
Rose quartz pebbles poke up through the ground
Magpie shuttles among the leaves
White black feathered snake

✻   ✻   ✻

Prickly pear's tiny bristles
Lodge under finger skin
Tree limb's bright edge
Crow cry crow fly cold

2. American Life in America

"Everyone is welcome to visit the pueblo
White black or yellow
We get along with everybody
No fighting.

"If we do wrong we are punished
We have regulations; we have a governor
Anywhere you go there are regulations.
If you go to Santa Fe there are regulations there.

"Blue Lake is a church
It is the Indian church.
We pray for everybody, white
Black, yellow, all people—

"You guys don't know what we do up there.
We get our answers there."

679

3. Ranchos de Taos

Giant china pheasant
Feather brocade meteor
Zooms above creek—voice like a klaxon

All the fuses are blown
Colder and colder
The sun also shines

4. The Morning in Albuquerque

Left to look at
A bright cold morning full of air
What is there but food to think about
And presently it appears in a drugstore
Where is also everything else

Cold and fresh
Lots of airplanes.
Early in the morning, late at night
I hear train sounds
The Messieurs Atchison Topeka and Santa Fe still in business
I feel a dusty wistfulness

New Mexico 18–28:x:71

What's perceived
DUCKRABBIT
nightjar (not a bird not a *vase de nuit* not the *Golden Bowl*)
BLUE
I applied the gentle but determined pressure of my right
forefinger to the mother-of-pearl button (the same as
total surveillance and repression).
If there was anyone within, he ignored the summons of the bell
which I could hear quite distinctly
NIGHTJAR
A bird *vase de nuit*
a necessary vessel
I made certain of the address. It was difficult
to turn the thin pages of my address book, but I did not wish
to remove my gloves
RABBITDUCK
(reading from west to east)
The cocoa-fibre doormat seemed quite new. The porch lamp,
high and to the right of the bell-push, was made of frosted
orange glass cast into the shape of a torch flame. A closely
pleated green silk curtain stretched tightly across the thick
plate glass let into the center of the heavy front door.
In fine, the marvelously double vision: total security is
the same as total surveillance and repression.

Olson told us that history was ended.
A.—"O.K. What is it you think you're doing?"
B.—"I'm trying to wreck your mind, that's all."

30:xi:71–16:xii:71

MINUSCULE THRENODY

I realize all wrong nothing
Of what I really know
Nothing as I intended
Walk away from the page
That poem never ended

20:xii:71

ODE FOR YOU

What are you but a drifting crowd?
Miserable hermitage of dauby wattles
Flies ants bugs and busy rodents all over everything
Wrong climate for a primitive life out of doors
Wrong soil for a vegetable garden

Well, tell me about that.
No. No, it is too—
It is too boring to tell and I doubt that you have time
To listen.
What happened when you went to L.A.?

> At this point I shall draw a curtain of discretion
> across the scene and direct the attention of the
> reader to a large cardboard carton which stands
> on the floor
> beside the desk.

OBSCURANTISM

What about the hermitage. Where was it. When.

Grey clods of earth and bumptious weeds;
Dead batteries,

682

2

This morning the ocean fits
Tight against the cliff

Mare's tails in the sky the weather will change
Prisms of Japanese quartz make rainbows on desk and bed
                "sealed in vain, sealed in vain"
                        CHAIN SAW
                the muddleheaded reader will inquire,
                "What's the connection," poking about
                with a long stick while crossing the moorlands—
                when the point of the stick suddenly slides
                into a hollow, start digging

                (MALEBOLGE?)

Out come Little Cyril, Cousin Maude, the China pug dog,
Peacock feathers and gilded cattails, the player piano,
The cut-glass vinegar cruet, the Conductor (S.P. Railroad)
Darling Arabella,

3

None of it is visionary or prophetickal
What's buried in earth is utterly used up
Ready to become flowers grassy weeping willow trees
Throw it all back
                        Other things are perfected underground
                        Onions and parsnips and diamonds;
                        Let us have those

We rise and fall through the earth
Geysers and artesian wells percolating
Through rocks from heaven's bright obstacles
        (hemisphere's balderdash)
Uncommonly streaked and splendid—
        so delicately—
650 pounds of marble

      }N I K E{

white stone wings

                17–20:xii:71

NEW DEPARTURES

    " . . . say that if he wishes
    he may kiss us goodbye. Here." (Pointing.)
        MUTE VAINGLORIOUS WADSWORTH!
  e.g.
        DIM PHANTOM OF A BROKEN DAY!

" . . . immortality pills failed . . . "
               (Pointing.)
Day falls over the edge. Some kind of dinner. Solitude
of reading, music and at last the task looms before us:
the work of sleep and dream,

We turn towards it,
        as it were a desk,
                "USE ADDITIONAL
      SHEETS IF NECESSARY. WRITE YOUR NAME AND
      SOCIAL SECURITY NUMBER . . . "

The Greyhound bus goes over the cliff into the tops of the trees.
Men are sprawled across the tree tops face down
Blue shirts, suspenders and dark pants against evergreen boughs
Drivers conductors policemen

You do not understand about food for human consumption.
        (Tuberculosis)
You do understand that the pitcher is completely white and has
A formal existence quite independent of bands of blue glaze
Which are the first attraction for the eye?
        to see something exists beyond my worry and concern
        that the young tree is yet another part of my own
        mind, growing and healthy?

"We must try to believe that he likes it the way he is."

        (Pointing.)

28–31:xii:71

ALLEYWAY

That darling baby!
All wrapped up asleep
In his fuzzy blue bunting
An extra blanket carefully pinned
Around him asleep on the ground
Between two boxes of rubbish
Beside the overflowing garbage cans
All alone. Throwed away.

3:i:72

IN THE NIGHT

I keep hearing cars demons ghosts
Cars demons ghosts car demons
Quite naturally
The world is larger
More complicated than we can remember
And so we fall upward
Into a fake superiority

✻

"I FUCKING RAN!"

✻

"elephant and sunset"

✻

"huge hen"

✻

Lots of speed makes the surfboard slicker
Falling upward

✻

THE WARS OF ONAN

✻

We die reading about worrying about
Our lives
   ONIN-NO-RAN (1467–1475)
Lots of speed. I fucking ran.

Civil wars more interesting than any other kind
   AMERICA

8–12:i:72

WEATHER ODES

Just before I fell asleep
In the middle of the afternoon
I told myself, "It is NOW
That I must work that change make
That move which will be the foundation
For that spectacular success which must illuminate
All my later days"

    ✺   ✺   ✺

With a head full of sunlight
What's killing you now?

No patience to sit and watch the ivy grow
No patience with sleep

Exhausted by a band of mare's tails
Moving down from the north
Right across the sky from west to east
(West is the beginning of Ocean)

    ✺   ✺   ✺

Many people shout.
They have nothing better to do, Sunday:
Unparalleled confusion
Unbelievable traffic
It all comes out of the Sun

                                       HEY THERE LITTLE KID
                                       You know what, YOU'RE
                                       C   R   A   Z   Y
                                       ($4\frac{1}{2}$ years old; imagine!)

all out of commission
all out of whack

                                       mmIRm! MMIrrm!
                                       (imitation of engine sounds)

    ✺   ✺   ✺

Nothing can be done before Monday
That is Tuesday, exhausted by Sunday's bright
Cloud lattice shutter
Occludes my head Monday all shot to hell

All those people out here (i.e. Bolinas)
All of them shouting
(They are "in the country")

A head full of discontented screams,
Roars, motor noises, rockets,
Extraterrestrial ray guns, dogs,
Chickens, carpenters, noon whistle (all the way from Stinson
Beach,
       population 84, an air-raid siren, just imagine!)
The blue sky clabbering up to rain?

     ❁   ❁   ❁

Move. ("to move and win")
Great inky eternity encloses
Better edge. (Windy trouble)
Downy midnight's moony shore
Wild brittle anise foam
Torpid narcissus. Move again.

     ❁   ❁   ❁

The funny paper
"Color shines in glass front bookcase"
Temples and palaces appear and vanish
The more money I spend.
When there's no money,
Books, pictures, trees and flowers are here.

Another position:
Hands grab stage post
A leg hooks around it
Eyes cross & neck loops in a silent film "take"

688

Or perhaps a fan rises in front of a mask
"Love's Apparition and Evanishment"
A funny bent wire in the middle
Or whatever else in and out of sight

14:i:72–19:i:72

LOOKING FOR HELP

Big flat round empty head
Looks out the ditch is full
Drain tiles are clogged
Bundles of pine needles fall

Fat clouds with white hot edges
Invisible sun can't reach through the snow
Lazy rainbow in quartz crystal

Today we visit the ruined city
San Francisco (icy Moscow)
The grinning otolaryngologist
(Not Kenneth Koch) lights up my ear.

21:i:72

IMPATIENT POETRY FOR TED AND ALICE B.

Falling down
Fouling up
    airplane message: Soft
                          ear
                          exit

Waves on the surface printed on the sand below
Slightly older than God

return from the bath to find my room full of *evzones*
dancing laughing smoking drinking *ouzou* &c   As I come in they
  flap and scatter towards the ceiling and corners of the room
  white chickens vanish
SLEEP MEMORY TEARS PAINE
WEBBER JACKSON & CURTIS
YOU CAN'T HAVE ONE WITHOUT ALL THE REST
MERRILL LYNCH
              fall over jump over edge
              pushed, no difference
              in the middle of the air
              fall intentionally
                  drop
                    ?

She fixed him up with a 300 pound Eskimo
Who kicked the shit out of him
Given a 300 pound Eskimo, what might happen
Give him (or her) back again to Abercrombie Fitch
Return to Sender, never so gently
With love and understanding opened by mistake
Did I fall or was I pushed?

26:iv–18:v:72
Pullman–San Francisco

SOMETHING MARVELOUS

                      was to have occupied this space
Oh. The Roman Empire not fallen but built
And sold at an enormous profit
To the Barbarians.
We are still paying interest on the loan

21:v:72

It's all back up in there
Floor's awash
"Anchor the way"
Angkor's this way back up over there:
Flesh awash unlimited satin
Waters of the sea
                    (OUT OF SIGHT)
Abandonment by stealth. Adornments of good health.
Worthless self. Rub my feet.
                    (*patte de mouche*)
Rub my back. No wonder you're not sleepy
The moon is full and you're all wired up
(On one cup of tea?) Completely wired.

Give up. Give up everything.
            STUDENT: "What keeps us from giving up everything?"
            TEACHER: "Fiction."
Wild applause
(mild applesauce, upside down)
                    id est,
                    notions of loss and disaster all attract
                    demons ghosts and depressions: bum vibes
                    create atmosphere for mistaken happening
                    "accident." Fear of planning because there
                    may be disappointment ("no plan" equals
                    "freedom"?). There turns out to be a secret
                    plan, a wordless design framed by "character."
                    "Then" becomes "now" rather than present
                    intention governing the future. (?) Pattern
                    without words equals "mandala" which is one
                    single troublesome image? (But recall five
                    several personal body images during Kyoto
                    psilocybin trip. Have I been seeing some-
                    thing backwards or upside down?)

691

O sharp cumbersome Death!
Most of us tire of thinking and feeling
We fall asleep. Reb is asleep
Head in a tiger's mouth.

20:vii–13:x:72

DESPERATELY AWAITING THE

ARRIVAL OF THE CHINA DINNER MAN

Did you see that kid from New York
Did you see that invisible flash
Combination cuckoo lemon yard crash
Mumbling all the time. Ring. Send.
Call it so.
The machine can't say any more.

Chicago November 1972

TASSAJARA

What I hear is not only water but stones
No, no, it is only compressed air flapping my eardrums
My brains gushing brown between green rocks all
That I hear is me and silence
The air transparent golden light (by Vermeer of Delft)
Sun shines on the mountain peak which pokes
The sun also ablaze &c.
Willard Gibbs, Hans Bethe, what's the answer
A lost mass (Paris gone)
Shine red in young swallow's mouth
Takagamine Road

The water suffers
Broken on rocks worn down by water
Wreck of THE DIVINE MIND on the reef called Norman's Woe
"Suddenly, ignorance," the *Shastra* says.
Moon arises in my big round head
Shines out of my small blue eyes
Tony Patchell hollers "Get it! Get it!"
All my treasure buried under Goodwin Sands

20:vii–25:xi:72

THE UNIVERSAL &

SUSQUEHANNA MERCY CO. DAYTON, O.

Everybody downtown
Miserable today
Bought the wrong size
Overdrawn at the bank

The spots were there before the leopard
Now explain the panther
Sun reflected in black
Tar pools

"American society"—great dead animal carcase
We try to bury it, forget it
We carve steaks off it and get indigestion
Some of us walk away

Death's ivory
Buck tooth skull
Stone says "I will never live"
Snake: "I'll never die"

All the wrong people rush up to me
Screeching, "You're a poet you're a
Poet you're a Great POET!"
Time to move on. Complete disconnection
Misunderstanding brought on by overpayment

In X-ville California
People swept under the rug
Living sow bug lives
The Dormition of the Virgin
(What a word, also an oil painting or so)
Alice in Wonderland
Bichloride of mercury

Try to reorder your scrambled head & broken eyes
Apply vanilla milkshake anti-paranoia compound
No possibility of escape
Two sets of electrically charged barbwire
The Trojan War continues, the Iliad is unfinished
No sales tax on flame throwers
What's possible? Bandages? Paint?

26:v:72–25:iv:73

MONUMENTAL BEER

Seven years I see the morning sun reflected
From concrete neon beerglass roof edges
Hamm's brewery under Potrero Hill
Incandescent bubbles and foam flash
Red sparkling HAMM's
Three years in Kyoto absolutely forgotten
Some other man's other life.

27:v:73

694

MESSAGE

yesterday,
from sudden red lily
Amaryllis
(Naked Lady)
THE YEAR IS DYING
leafless and red
bright as rhubarb
Uninvited lily
(what bulb so dim
what Dora so dumb
Not to see sun's heat
snow's white)
howling flower in my skull

14–16:vii:73

KITCHEN PRACTICE

They got it all fixed up the way
They wanted and now
They've changed it back again
They've eaten all the sugar
They've taken all the teapots to their rooms

23:vii:73

THE SESSHIN EPIGRAM

The hand foresees what the eye
Cannot foretell

8–9:viii:73

to explain eclipses and to predict them
large numbers are needed
most of all "zero"
a mystery of writing
a cipher

It means nothing.
What's nothing. It means
Something. How does it feel.

Move without moving any THING.
Space from pupil to retina farther than Arcturus
It takes so much time you get bored
Before going much beyond first layers of braincase hole
So lightly the flattering years
No specific direction please
Move over. Please remove the shoe.
But you never asked me. Come on,
Move over. We had it there once
Before. We might well have left it.
Now remove the braincase. Look. See there!
Completely abnormal—totally anomalous

(T A N T R U M)
Next move,
(interspersed with staccato shots from the string
section doubled with horns)

"Impatiently monumental," I said. "If it goes
Faster than it is moving now
Low-pressure distortions along the Ψ-axis . . ."

". . . fold it inside;
pour it in the sink . . ."

If it goes faster NOTHING will be left
Mickey the Sun assumes (very slowly)
Face of Mickey Mouth

                    " . . . I'd know him
                            anywhere . . ."

                                        24:vii–25:ix:73

HIGH-TENSION ON LOW-PRESSURE

NON-ACCOMPLISHMENT BLUES

Dog's laughing mouth and happy eye
No-color fur brown eyes white teeth red tongue
Dripping. Its lips are black
Precisely notched
            OPTICAL INSTRUMENT HANDLE WITH CARE
            (Optical instrument no longer there)
Nothing to be done with that picture, either:
Precise image of wood grain in bare *engawa* floor
I could feel and smell it and behind me the garden
The tree peonies a single rock for a step and
Dirt with moss and pebbles
Hot sun illuminates plaster wall
            (precisely blocked)
Every morning I am fat
Every morning I am old
Every morning bought and sold

what may have been thought of once
as a snappy summer hat supposedly hand woven
dirty mole-colored plastic fiber on top of hair
partly dyed dark red above skin
almost the right complexion for that kind of hair

perfectly white very short bristles
mark out a new square moustache
irresistible charm
has got to be good for something

16:viii–26:ix:73

MASK

A carved living wood face
You can see exactly where it lies in the living tree
Which now goes about as the tree's ghost also person
Gold flat circular eyes
You see the tree
There sun wind
Throwing branches and the mask
Growing under the bark
Twisting and swaying
Always alive

6:xii:73

DETACHMENT, WISDOM AND COMPASSION

" . . . had it to do
all over again . . ."

(an oval window
no longer there)

"O if only I had it to do . . ."

"They took and messed with it
Until I had it all to do over
Again; they'd made such a hash of it."

and cleverly steps to the left
as the 500 pound falling sandbag
makes a thump dent in the solid oak floor
(unthinking) right beside him
("no longer there")

8:xii:73

HOMAGE TO ARAM SAROYAN

I didn't realize my arms were cold
Until I put on my long sleeved shirt.
Aram Saroyan.
Tall white wraparound lily is arum.

21:xii:73

"LA CHINA POBLANA"

The Chinese lady travels in Poland.
The Chinese woman speaks Polish:
    "China is a poor (country)"
The Polish (gentleman) wants the
    Chinese lady to return
        his money.
China published it. Fuck the Polish lady.

25:ii:74

MONEY IS THE ROOST OF ALL EAGLES

Instant milk and then I saw
Insistent milk
But love is not love
That altercation finds

✲ ✲ ✲ ✲ ✲ ✲

Instantaneously silk?

✲ ✲ ✲ ✲ ✲ ✲

Alteration finds instantly

M I L K
?

✲ ✲ ✲ ✲ ✲ ✲

Love is not milk (alternation)
F I E N D S !

✲ ✲ ✲ ✲ ✲ ✲

innocent eagle

12:iii:74

"THE CONDITIONS THAT PREVAIL"

TRANSVESTITE
1) (The heavy gold chain loops) across
the sung-fitting waistcoat (snug)

Today I am the SOKU, butler/head waiter three times today
Today Elemental Powers gnomes and gremlins catch
Heels and jog elbows. Conspicuous minor hysteria.

TRAMPOLINE
        1) bright yellow crystals of barium sulfate
        2) vaseline and boric acid

TRANSVESTITE
        2) a phase of silicon perchloride occurring
        as lilac-coloured rhomboidal crystals on a
        matrix of pure natural tin

Today I act as KOKYO (precentor)
Have you seen the platter of little feet?

Today I am supposed to be the DOAN (gong klonger)
But I lost my temper during the morning service
Lost all recollection of the schedule and my various duties
Missed breakfast, God knows who played the Buddha drum
While I was finding out who was Wanshi Sogaku
In the wrong kind of Chinese transliteration

25:ii–17:iii:74

ZENSHINJI

Here our days are nameless time all misnumbered
Right where Mr. Yeats wanted so much to be
Moving to the call of bell and semantron,
      rites and ceremonies
Bright hard-colored tidiness Arthur Rackham world
      (no soil or mulch or mud)
Everything boiled and laundered and dry-cleaned
And probably inhabited by that race of
      scrubbed and polished men
      who drive the dairy trucks of San Francisco

The arts ooze forth from fractures in planes of solid rock
Outer ambition and inwards tyranny
"Hurrah for Karamazov!"
Totally insane sprung loose from all moorings
I wander about, cup of coffee in hand,
Chatting with students working in warm spring rain

25:iii:74

THE TALKING PICTURE

Watching the tail end of a film running through the projector
Gate—blackness, random design, blackness, a few numbers,
Blackness a pattern blip blackness
L I G H T
Square and clicking as loose film end
Whips against projector housing
Click frequency dropping as take-up reel slows to a stop.
The projector motor keeps on humming I watch
A square of light until power switch
Clicks total blackness

13:iv:74

DREAM POEMS

1.

Let me see:
The original sinful. By virtue of
The power invested in me
(Glenway Westcoat)
I declare

Give me turtle death
Not in the usual way; underneath

(Lucille)

R A M P A G E

Let me know when the crew table is ready
(How sad the whole day's gone)

D O T

(do I)

(do it?)

bring me there immediately
Immoderately

SLURM   SLURM   SLURM

Let's take the Graham-Page

2.

Nobody's hand appears in the air
Shroud clouds at wrist amid fog outside window
Three storeys above the street
To tap my bedroom window
I turn to face my father who sits in small upholstered chair
Looking directly towards the window
"Do you see it?
Have you ever seen anything like that?" (I feel
Outraged) "A disembodied hand tapping the window?"
But he can't hear me, being dead in the graveyard
Up in Mosier makes four too many levels of reality
That I can't handle. O I dreamed yes
Yes I dreamed
That.

30–31:v:74

MURALS NOT YET DREAMED

The First Panel is occupied with Storm and Night Battle:
Handsome Allegorical Embellishments fruits and flowers
Antique masks and fantastic animals or birds amid trailing
    vines and scallop shells, leaves, Wild Men, Trophies,
      Instruments of Music profusely beribboned and garlanded
The whole supported on sculptured brackets or consoles
Decorated with partially draped Atlantids wreathed with
    oaken crowns

The Second Panel shews the arrival of the King
And the fit is on him
He shouts for the Countess of Suffolk who lies ill in her room
Lord Townshend, Sir Robert Walpole and the Duke of
    Newcastle
Approach from the right, bearing a petition
Sir Robert stares into the clear blue eyes of Queen Caroline
Dressed in seventy or eighty yards of handmade Flemish lace and
Silk brocade, a young fortune in pearls and diamonds and a couple
Of egret feathers. Lord Hervey as Vice Chamberlain preens
And simpers at her side all blue velvet and lavender silk

The Third Panel crashes down in splinters and torn canvas
I open fire with my Sten gun, screeching defiance
As they mow me down.

11–12:vi:74

EPIGRAM, UPON HIMSELF

People can forgive all my faults;
They despise me for being fat.

14:vii:74

THE VISION OF DELIGHT

The man driving the expensive car
May have been no relation to the woman sitting beside him
Neither of them might be related to the small girl
Who sat in the center of the back seat, leaning immobile
Against the back rest.
Her dress was white her hair all neatly arranged
Grotesque white fangs protruded from her mouth
Without distorting it.
She looked serenely straight ahead.
She was the queen attended by court lady and chauffeur
Not going to the Safeway store, clearly not needing
The automobile, who can appear anywhere any time
Such is her tremendous power

21:vii:74

LUXURY IN AUGUST

Not you but your beauty:
What a waste of time.
Tooth of August white sun flare
        Teedle-dee-dum dum deedle
Your moon head shining
Catamount cold eye glow
                    dum dee dum
The *Surangama Sutra* says,
        "Creatures through whom the future can be foretold
        after repaying their former debts
        are reborn as literary men"
                    boppity mop.

17:viii:74

705

PACIFIC TELEPHONE

How come
Huey Newton's
In jail?

SICK
SCHOOL
LOANED
SCHED. OFF
DBLD. UP
EVE MAN

LET COIN DROP
For your convenience

21:viii:74

HOW TO BE SUCCESSFUL & HAPPY

WITHOUT ANYBODY ELSE FINDING OUT ABOUT IT

I was falling asleep in my chair
Now I lie on the floor, ruminating ideas of life's brevity
The feeble intensity of enormous ambition
Hasleton Brasler said he'd be over
He had to pick up his car and take a haircut
You understand what I'm talking about . . .
          "including the power tools"
There's no excuse for an imitation of Billie Holiday.

Think of grass, a half acre of weeds, lawn, eucalyptus trees
Pink lilies on leafless thick red stems, all in a row
Appearing "spontaneously" (not from a regular bed or trench
Of specially cultivated earth. You remember what I'm talking
About, you've been there, but maybe not in lily season)

706

A freezing cold morning, throat and sinuses "burning"
Hasleton Brasler was uncertain: Thursday or Saturday.
He didn't want tea or whiskey. He had forgotten why he
    wanted to see me.

My sleep wrecked with difficult dreams,
Managing crowds of friends, trying to organize them
Interrupted (wakened) by scene with (who?) again
Persuade, explain, hopeless
The lilies shove right up out of the grass
Where one expects flat ground, these big
Vegetable telephone rockets, their irregular line
Fat rutabaga bulbs clearing the surface of the ground
Swelling and subdividing

Probably listening to Hasleton Brasler last night
Trying to come up with helpful suggestions for "coping" with
    his difficulties.
With so little rain the lilies will be late this year.
Why don't I go home to Oregon?
Seventy or eighty feet of "naked ladies" all in a row: Amaryllis

            ". . . brought the apples you wanted . . .
                    . . . more tomorrow," Theocritus says.

                                            6:ix:74

LOOK AWAY

Can we evade the sugar death in time?
Running is losing
The moment I switched off the radio I was free
Richesses!
            Something is undone, something is
            unfinished; I want

707

I am wanted by a sound a picture
CUT OUT
     CUT OUT
          can I afford purple
          I already have the gold
          Stashed in a broken trunk
             folded
          no thing for sale
                  isn't that nice I can
turn the radio all the way off. INDIGO.
And the moon
Egg laid by what gross bird   (cadenza here, for harp,
                         vibraphone & celeste)
PINK
        the cold foot
        the problems of Tschaikowsky
        the end of the Stock Market as we know it
Joanne told Peter, "*You* bought the moon."
Roasting and winning
Chicken dinner; fifty-one.

29:viii–21:x:74

ORGANIZED CRIME

I looked inside the refrigerator and said, "Credit Lyonnais,"
And shut the insulated door (ga-lunk).
Characters in somebody's novels, people who amounted
To anything at all have big accounts in the Banque de L'Indo- Chine

Let's all try to do better!
  All my incandescent armor
  From invidious glebe ration confusion
  Minshew, Peabody, reach and fine
  Inviolably now.

As the Duchess told the magazine,
"One can never be too thin nor too rich."

October–November 1974

ICE PLANT

  A freezing factory; somebody else's jewels
  Used in an attempt to incriminate

  Fat shaving brush flower

7:xi:74

COMPULSIVE OBLIGATORY PARANOIA FLASHES

While ever at my back I hear Time's winged chariot,
More or less skilfully guided by Henry and Claire Booth Luce
He (Agni, the Hindu god of fire) said,
"Why have ye (Devas) brought me to birth?"
They answered, "To keep watch."

Tomatoes must be gently wrapped in suitable coverings
And shut up in a dark place like mad men
Where they ripen

The world is a willful Idea? I'm after something;
Bright changing shadow
(Everything to eat except desire)

"The last time I saw him his face and head
Were completely depilated and all his features gross
And swollen like Gene Sibelius."
"*Jean*," somebody said. "Or *Jan*?"
"What are you, some kind of intellectual?"

September–December 1974

SATURDAY

Tough
New
      grass & weeds
Replace mud
         beer cans & scraps of paper
Green thick & rough
Surrounded by cement

            while from every window
            of a tiny station wagon
            A great solemn dog looks out
                  (not hanging head over,
                     tongue flapping)
            Sitting upright, calm as bears, the
Ancient hippy long grey hair driving,
Young chick beside him, all excited
            Yakking

16:iii:75

710

CONCLUSIONS

1

". . . and what did they do?
cut the face right off
the front of his head . . ."

2

When the sun and the moon
Fall from her hands
Where shall we run

25:v:75

FOR CLARK COOLIDGE

tick
notch
farandole
A Venetian lantern rhyme
Perfume wild thyme gland of youth
Clara Wilkes Booth, Founderess
Red Cross and Salvation Army
Clara Barton Batten Durstine & Osborn
incunabula tightrope novel of blank mind
born clear and smooth   not a wedge in sight
whelms. qualms. nick.
(*scotch*)

sham

5:vi:75

A CRACKLING

Taken by twos who wrote it all
Frying and twisting finally curly animal crystal
Some kind of grease ghost
Perfectly organized vehicle for squares of salt
And a beer with a secret number of drops of vinegar
       in which red chili peppers lie embalmed
Religiously shaken (aspergill)
Cut-glass cruet from the caster set

     or 220 volts direct current
     (the Outraged Majesty of the Law
     and Public Opinion)
     fries brains and all or pellets of cyanide crystals
     the size of pigeon eggs drop into acid bath
     Medea's fountain of youth
     (Boiled King.)

                                 5:vi:75

WINDOW PEAK

    What was that?

O, that was us then in the Good Old Days.
    What were the Good Old Days.
    When we were young and energetic we
    could work all day and dance all night
    When was that?
    That was a long time ago before you were
    even thought of.

      "what exists now was once only
      imagined" (W.B.?)

it was imagined, it was all "thought of" how else
could it be "now"
       "... but never predictable?"
         "50–40"
           I have to bathe
"... Summer in the Carpathians ...
              high in the Carpathians
"The Corinthian Alps."

5:vi:75

BLOSSOMS OF THE LEMON TREE

Pleasure and all delightful glossy
Lemon tree extravagant pleasure
The ornamental orange
A family name ("here's rue for
      you and some for me")

Tachibana Norimitsu was her husband?
   citrus nobilis
That literary lady
Married to the orange tree
Sei Shonagon
       fretful temper
Lemon all delight
       from the mirroring leaves

22:viii:75

DORJE QUANDARY

When I can't breathe it means the north wind is blowing
When I can't sleep the full moon shines.
While trying to sleep forget what I was trying to remember:
Dreamy search for what isn't lost if it's forgotten
Why it can't be found.

Twenty years from now, should I say the same
(Seven-try-one)
Set five-point vajra in direct sun
Orient north and south: results instantaneously
As it is, it is you.

22:viii:75

THE BOUQUET

Marigolds, having too many edges
Can't be shewn in this forgotten page
Yellow garnished with elegant sprigs of anise
      which can't be pictured without a crow-quill
More delicate than fern or feather
      in a white *sake* jar

The Thirtieth Day of October 1975

PROLEGOMENA
TO A STUDY OF THE UNIVERSE

Creation Myth

Falling through speeding emptiness dark & cold I enter a magnetic field and begin radiating light in various colors and radio waves in the 21 cm band. That I can be Heraclitus or (with no effort) the city of Venice (put it closer to home and say Chichen Itza): disentangle it: a spiral track, incomplete spark-circle, a helix of darkness through a brilliant galaxy, whichever color you prefer, but I remember gassed out of my head on ether, Mid-Columbia Hospital 1929 I was Golden Light Child, smiling bright silence & now a new memory of myself leaving town, walking the highway (hot sun) as slowly as it takes to breathe, sleep the night in roadside ditch and walk some more, beyond the farm towns and the ski-lifts high but under the timberline the neighborhood of a lake and off the trail for keeps to stop under tree, cliff, rock and be still, so quiet maybe a porcupine chews off some of my bark, a mountain lion eats an arm, a foot, then somebody new and different starting much later down the mountain, nobody's face I know.

Again

It was quiet a long time then this man said "Ouch!", he'd a little wart on the edge of his right forefinger—caught it on the sharp edge of something.

To distract him, I asked: "Where's my mother?"

"Over at the Western Union", he said, "Maybe I'll see her tonight."

I went to the telegraph office where I found a lady transcribing a Morse-code message. I asked her, "Where's my father?"

She said, "Don't pester me right now, he's over at the hardware store selling nails & fishing tackle. Maybe he'll come to see me tonight."

I waited.

The man said, "We'll marry in August when I have my vacation."
The woman said, "Yes. We'll marry in August & go to the beach."
I waited.

They climbed onto a big rock to look at the ocean. They sat there a long time, talking. Sometimes they sang.

The woman looked over the edge & was afraid. "The tide has come in—we're marooned!"

The man said, "I can carry you back".

They climbed down the rock, then the man took his wife in his arms and began carrying her towards the beach. A big wave broke over them and they both shouted.

My mother said, "My god, Skeeter, I'm wringing wet—let's run!", but it was too late, I'd caught them.

Walking

It is possible—I found out near the top of Sauk Mountain—to walk. As you lift one foot the earth turns the mountain under you, your foot comes down in a different place. (This law applies only beyond timber-line early summer snow in the North Cascades. In the Sierras, each step must turn the whole earth towards you—the mountain must be trodden downwards—and it is only with the greatest effort that one foot follows the other across the water-bars set into the trail.

But the *idea* of walking—let out on Highway 101 somewhere south of Gilroy 2:30 A.M. I must get to Santa Monica 350 miles down the road nothing moving but fog and it stops in the hairs of my wool jacket—high banks on either side of the highway, no sleeping-bag—a one-way fog leading to Salinas (didn't think, at the time, of returning to San Francisco where E_____ had offered me a place in the basement). Nothing to do, no cars stopping for hitch-hikers, I became FEET and after a time SALINAS. Wet or dry no difference, neither light nor dark, FEET moving producing discontinuous geography (and presently) a town.

In A Movie

a man climbing a mountain, the camera pans from him to look down
a sheer cliff thousands of feet into clouds and trees, pans back to
focus on the man's foot which slips, his hand clamps onto a knob of
rock, his foot gets a new hold, he reaches a wide ledge where he
rests, the camera follows his gaze towards distant mountain peaks
across the valley—the man begins climbing again, face to rock.

Article in a picture magazine shows how it's done—actor clings to
a papier-mache mountain six feet above the studio floor, a safety-net
under him and thick gymnasium mats under the net. A doctor & a
nurse are seen on the sidelines with the technical crew. A stairway
with guard-rails leads from the top of the mountain back down to the
floor.

Everybody else can see that I'm on an artificial rock but I feel my
foot slipping, see the rock crumbling away into blankness below. I
get a solid hand-hold, my foot goes up and strikes a solid step.

I know what I'm doing. I tell myself, "Come on, walk down the
stairs and go home to dinner, the lawn wants mowing, take out the
laundry . . ." My foot slips, the rock was rotten, I hang on with both
hands—

3 Days Ago

It quit raining and I could spend some time on the beach turning
over pebbles, low tide and heavy surf, slow flashes of sun behind
clouds. No translucent agates: jasper, a dark- jasper-flecked carnelian
that'll have to be cut and polished to explain why I picked it up.

I waste all this time proving the splendor of the world, everybody
wants out of it or wants it ugly before they'll believe it's really here

X_____ no longer able to bear his own poetical head hands it to
one analyst after the other; either they drop it on the floor and run or
they spend so much time looking into it they suffer radiation burns
and require long hospitalization. Driven gaga by ugliness, he still
keeps explaining to the doctors that what is ugly *must* be real

Y_____ rhapsodizes at great length about the sad defeat of noble derelicts in scabby Chicago alleys. Crossing Third & Mission in San Francisco I see this old bum on a corner, facing all the traffic in the intersection, one leg and a crutch, maybe 65, pissing a stream all over the rush-hour five o'clock pavement, nobody noticing him and his healthy pink dink, a final reply to failure, despair and death, not to mention the confutation of the Neo-Protestant Kierkegaardian-Marxist Church and its invalid theologians.

Years Ago

I kept trying to avoid this noisy hoorah and pain existence, sulking behind the kitchen door not eating my breakfast (Great-Aunt Marie asked me, "What are you doing back there?" and I replied, "Why don't you go home and do your work?") instead of a pleasant Sunday morning drive to Kings Valley.

Or like this: first, I promulgate the Laws of Gravity, then I kick and scream if I lose my grip on a glass and it (I also, some while beforehand, instituted the friability of glass) shatters.

Much Later

I got my father to go with me to the Museum, we needed a place to kill some time while my stepmother was shopping or seeing the doctor.

We looked at Greek pots. My father read one of the cards: "450 B.C.—why, these jars are older than Jesus Christ! What do you know about that?"

I didn't say anything then, but I could remember buying that pot in the sunshine Corinthian agora, something to hold olive oil . . . my father had forgotten painting Heracles and the lion on it. I remembered all the rest of my lives that day.

5th Position

I came here on purpose. Sea-level is lower now because so much of it is out walking around in the mountains.

Until it is the mind reaching out to pick up the cigaret, the cup of tea
(which are of the same substance as that which grasps them.

[1956?–1976]

THE RADIO AGAIN

It wasn't in the cards
That today should go the way I want
Not in the cards.
I can't complain about the way it went.

"It says right on the box"
as her voice tells us her name is Ethel

Lady, it is what the lawyers call a self-serving document

"Oh yes, I always buy this kind."

Voice, tell us
The name of the earth.

November 1975–January 1976

SOMEBODY ELSE'S PROBLEM BOTHERS ME

Warm sun and chilly air, water is low and the creek is clear
Will I accidentally drop a jade ring in the creek
All the new stones glaring light and airplanes
Shall I drop my gold crown in the pool?
Have I derailed my train of thought?
A rock with an elephant's forehead!
Silver turquoise ring dropped into monk's kimono sleeve
What can we answer?

Yellow tin chimneys.

White-crowned sparrows.

Everything a-tilt.

26:iii:76

BEAD

Aimless
Wet finger no foresight
Small craft warning from Telephone Company
Earth
Bear
     Birth
      O
     Breath
     and
     Bread
(Careless wet finger again)

28:iii:76

BLURB

FOR UC EXTENSION SUMMER POETRY SERIES 1976

Since you didn't see
What I said
I'll tell you again
Listen to me
Raving as the gurney
Wheels through the doors to the operating room
And the ether cone comes down

EVERYTHING MUST GO!

26:iv:76

WHERE OR WHEN

The sidewalk joins the concrete wall around the vacant lot
Wiry single plants of timothy hay spring up
      from the minutest cracks in the cement
No space for them so jammed against the wall
They can't make a shadow
We used to say "fox tails"
      furry green plumes all soft and tickle seed
Hairs watered by fog and smallest rains
Crack all San Francisco into crumbs of gravelly dusty
      minerals and sand that feed these grassy feathers
      primitive oats or wheat
The city running to a weed patch right on time.

17:v:76

Tired of dirt on the floor. Take it away.
Fix the broken water. Tear down crumpled wallpaper.
Clean it up and move out.

I suffer a lot with my skin.
Pour on oil. Go out among the sunshine "Where the people
Really are people." (So unreal in here?)
Out where as right now
Air molecules press down upon us
Fifteen pounds per square inch
Sustains a column of mercury thirty inches above its dish
Real air, true authentic, both sides of any coin
        (Roll away pancake
        Tyche rides the wagon tire
        Cannot stand still
        Cannot stand it, won't put up
        With it
           Out)
              always under ajudication
              always in session
                worth worth worthless
                hate love love hate
                utterly totally hopeless

Why go out when you're already here
Deserting each other in the middle of the air
The last time I felt this way
It carried me six thousand miles

                ✵   ✵   ✵

If you will shift your gaze 37.5 degrees to the west
and stop talking for a second
. . . as you were saying?
Columbus, Ohio sailed through the center of a lemon meringue pie
        a hidden plan gradually revealing itself

powder, apples and grease arranged into a flaky
smoking pie? and a little open face tart just
for you? like a *rakku*-ware tea bowl formed fried
and used for drinking all in a single day
Completely spontaneous,
the low-fired lead glaze gently
dissolving into our tea, into our kidneys and brains
I turned my head to observe the padded earphones
The dragon with goat eyes, brown forward-curling horns
The decaying blotter the boring rattan tabouret
A calm bright oaken floor

                ❉   ❉   ❉

if you will shift your white noise phase
you will observe the destruction of the Ploesti
oil fields and environs all confused

                ❉   ❉   ❉

Go
    single-mindedly
        after flowers
Although soft petal cuts the eye
drink blood in Mazatlan
thin shiny vacant shells
Chitinous eyes waiting for no future tenant
    moved out and left ivory smile
Tall green cactus completely hollowed out by owls

19:vi:76

723

POWELL & MARKET

Fat man waves tiny Bible
Shouting threats about Jesus.
Nearby, a younger, thinner man (high on something else?)
Starts undressing.

20:xii:76

LA JOLLA IN THE MORNING

FOR BILL BERKSON

A mockingbird a swimming pool a tennis court
A minute putting-green an ocean among subtropical flowers
The last of California built for Ginger Rogers
The nineteen-thirties completely restored
Subliminal throb of pool filter pump
Gentle roar of heavy traffic among hibiscus bulldozer

Beige/pink telephone lives with other furniture beside the pool
Lost fountain pen lies on silk upholstered chair that is
Fond of rich tea cakes and chocolate creams
A chair that might live in remotest Connecticut
Limp money death in beautiful clothes
Remote from The Dalles or La Jolla

Top of the yacht's mast connects with sharp
Trolley wire/sea/sky line
The outside of the window frame
Inexplicably adorned with brown wood Della Robbia wreath
Glass reflects a yacht not yet in sight
I must lean forward to see the first one
Making for Scripps Oceanographical Institute

724

Where it'll be wrapped in plastic foam
Then loaded onto the Boston plane with its owner
A regatta this weekend in New London

Imagine how to be free of the thought which is to say
Free from the past free from hankering after some future
Bait (or hooked for a second) actually seeing
Elaborated floral rococo handles on an ordinary
Wooden chest of drawers
                              which become Alex Katz:
Three scallops of green bushes
Flat against the ocean's flat horizon
And happily not exactly joining the same line reflected
In the imperfect window glass wavy and uneven so the boat's
    image
And that compulsively vacant (I mean tyrannical) sky/sea
Nonexistent boundary (tyrannical to our eyes,
Which have been taught to see)
Becomes its imaginary self and we are saved again. Whew!

The benefits of travel are immediate; a battleship or
Minesweeper on the horizon among mockingbirds
    (*Liebestraum*
Or Liederkrantz?) twisted around the window frame
Aimless luxury, swollen details ultimately blank
Cement *putti* not only cold but hollow
To deceive the eye, which pretends to be delighted
For maybe thirty seconds

Here is the world before the war, quite different from
    San Francisco
Where we have another style, young rich and careless
Robbery and murder right out in the street
A city hall where a cardinal-archbishop ought to live
A Custom House and a Federal Court that might house Borgias
Or a pope in armor on horseback.

April 1976–January 1977

BRUTAL LANDSCAPE

O drown minus
        (this doesn't make any sense except in Harlan County
        or a classical dictionary . . . Rhadamanthis/Aides)
Drown bull-headed S.O.B. &c.
Drown Midas
        the Bakeoven Road!
        hot clay walls
        leafless dry weed chasm
        (doesn't make any sense except in Wasco County)
Shaniko to Maupin, there's no creek on the map
Nothing but yellow-orange dirt: very small mountains of
    nowhere
Because of The Pioneers and the trout in Tygh Creek
Beanie and Millard at Wapinitia
And Mrs B in her white satin gown
Leading the Mysteries of the Great White Shrine
        (That road actually a short-cut to Madras
        Where she sold McCormick-Deering combines)
Make a loop from Arlington back to The Dalles
Without going through Madras at all, where *die Aegyptische*   *Helen* . . .
But now sirens under my window stop at nothing
A burning automobile right here in Lily Alley: *Erlkönig*
        (" . . . a woman's body, high concentration of drugs,
        alcohol and radioactive substances . . ." in some other
        state, the radio continues, "unexpected
        outbreak of respiratory arrests")
        "Take, O take them lips AWAY"
        Sunyata, all voided out eyes of Little Orphan Annie

Certain things make a great deal of sense in Topeka. Or else.

7:viii:75–24:i:77

MNEMONOTECHNIQUE

Endless fruitless propinquity
Mr. Michael Wynne assures me that it is
MINOT'S LEDGE, straight out beyond Boston Harbor
For he has sailed and fished those waters many years
He remembers photographs of the lighthouse tower
Attacked by forty-foot waves from the open Atlantic
I wondered about the name fourteen years
Did I have it right
"One, four, three:
I Love You," Olson was saying,
"One, four, three—Minot's Ledge Light . . .
What better way to remember?"
I still haven't forgot

12:ii:77

DEFECTIVE CIRCLES

Electric clock died in the night
Big low-pressure system high winds and rain barge through
Present world, wake up in the dark 12:05
". . . made by magic no handmakers know . . ."
Shall I remember that when I get back from the bathroom?
Lines of groovy poem around me
Did I know who I was where then?
12:05 daylight, don't care much about who I am
What I'm supposed to be doing
Still humming and warm to the touch
Neither of us making any sense.

12:iii:77

THE SIMPLE LIFE

I say "I love" and that's enough
The elephant can guess
I'm infatuated with her
If I feed her a peanut and speak gentle nothings
She'll remember me kindly, perhaps
No embarrassment on either side.

No proof, no justification
Get on with it
        since I can't get along without it
        (some kind of torment?)

Dull smokey agates at Stinson Beach
    whether I love you or not
Only another idea
Maybe nobody loves you or me
        Pellegrini & Cudahy

23–24:vi:77

OBSOLETE MODELS

Now the hours of my life grow small
Shoddy months and threadbare years
A favorite pet universe that ought to be "put to sleep"
By the vet; gracefully relinquished.

I say, "Something eludes me
Something is right over there—someplace."

A drop of mercury slides very smoothly away
A description slightly out of focus

At least there are nasturtiums again
Disc leaves dusty green
More entertaining than many another
Verdigris

What do I want
What am I really after
Sometimes a tree answers.

San Francisco 18–19:iv:77

MANY PAGES MUST BE THROWN AWAY

To talk about the green roof
Next to the silvery blue house—pointless
Because the way the light hits them
There are more colors anyhow—
Porpoise flank, eye of albacore

Air all new and clean
Sharp edges of Berkeley reappear
Among bridge cable web and thrum
Sundown crosslight bird clank
City Hall dome throbs and bulges
Opera House whale eyes look west
Suave white geometry lid of cathedral
Translucent, incandescent

I ascend to the roof to look again
Light as it is at Tangiers, they say,
Straight across walls doors hills

Against which waves flash explode eastward
Ocean rushing toward Donner pass

14–23:iv:77

WILD TALENTS

A great big guy played a guitar held
Flat across his lap,
The right hand precisely plunking a simple bass
While a single finger of his left hand
Hit strings at frets in a coded pattern
"Automatically" producing odd but related
Chords that made a tune.
Then he did it with a table fork
        shoved perpendicular among the strings
        tines against fingerboard . . .
If only I could remember those patterns
        when I wake up

                                                        23:iv:77

THE CONGRESS OF VIENNA

What's happening continues
"All still going on out there"
Last night eclipsed the moon
In order to say "Earth is a celestial disc
Over—not under—the moon"

Let's reconvene the Congress of Vienna
Nasturtiums at Schoenbrunn
Posies for Prince Metternich
Nosegays for Prince Talleyrand

On the floor a platter of chicken,
Thin elegant gravy, all of us eating
Most of us resigned to having a third helping
Long-haired gray cat walks into the dish, lies down
Rolls about in the sauce

Universal horror and chagrin!
We try to clean it with a big bath towel
If it licks up too much gravy the cat will have the gout
Annoyance, mirth, and worry
As long as I do not look out the window,
Great things, weird sounds,
High deeds in Lily Alley:
"You there track book!
Brat work! Dropsy!
Dim attending brunt or charred bird."
"What did you have for dinner?"
"Chard quiche."
"Hey there! 1878!"
"Eighteen seventy ate three, hey? There."
Quick change cymbal
". . . the difference to me!"

What though my eyes are blind with age and simple mindedness?
Death's crumby fingers insinuating fate
Tumescent sentences to say, to want to say,
"Flower: The world here becomes pond lilies
Tall yellow iris and trade for a world of rhododendrons
Total experience of wealth beyond rich and poor
Monterey cypress and black pine cliffs
Birdshadows trill and marble hallelujah
Out beyond the throne of time.

San Francisco 4:iv–11:v:77

731

TO THE MEMORY OF

Mr J who had been poor for years
Inherited all the money in the world
Bought a gun to blow a hole in his head
To let in air and light he said
To let me out

Today, I have my head to shave
There are lights and shadows in it
All too soon empty open ashes
Join mirthfully to earth

19:v:77

LINES FOR A CELEBRATED POET

I go into the closet and shut the door.
I put on mother's clothes; then I can hear her,
Talking to me plain as ever.

My liver trembles on a golden tray
Before the Chief Justice of The United States
My kidneys float in a candy jar with an ornamental top,
Lewis County Fairgrounds, Chehalis, Washington;
Brains under several pounds of mercury in a crock

  "What the fairies talk and murmur
  That we understand though mumbled . . ."

Never in Leadville
Never in Lubbock
Never in Twentynine Palms

27–28:v:77

THE WIND CHIMES

Throw them away
They are summer glass thread tangle
September typhoon wrecks them every time.

Winter wants flashing lights
Shiny globes of colored glass
One bronze bell struck 108 times. Deliberately.

13:vi:77

THAT THE TRUE NATURE OF THE UNIVERSE
MIGHT BE LIKE A VAST KLEIN BOTTLE

Our children summon us out of chaos
That they might be born
Pursue this for 1800 pages of elegant
Thomas Browne prose

$$\left\{ \begin{array}{l} \text{Payable on demand} \\ \textit{au demain,} \text{ i.e.} \\ \text{L A T E R O N} \end{array} \right\}$$

Like W A R & P E A C E

L E N D E M A I N

Playing for power
Playing for keepsies
Intentional risk:

"THE HURRY-UP GETAWAY QUICK MONEY CO."

14:vi:77

733

SONG

Sitting home

✻

Drinking wine

✻

Writing pome

✻

"What do you want
done with all *that*?"

✻

"Put it anywhere"

✻

feeling fine (of course)

22:vi:77

"PAST RUIN'D ILION"

Past ancient dusty Antigua bright blue water above Port Royal
Beyond Terre Haute the legendary city
Abandoned to the winds of moon by Tom Field and Cubby Selby
Olson said that Cubby Selby walked up the road all alone
Wearing a baseball glove, tossing a ball in the air
As he approached the campus of Black Mountain College
Left his luggage at the station to await developments
If it wasn't Cubby Selby it was that guy
Who later wrote his recollections of Franz Kline

So much for reminiscences of the great
  "Tossing a ball in the air and catching it. Beautiful."

It probably was Fielding Dawson
Anyway, somebody burned down Pass Christian, Mississippi
Probably not Hubert Selby, Jr
Past the barriers of time and the ruining of Denver
The demolition of Portland (Oregon)
The voice of Nellie Melba echoing in the Parthenon
Sara Bernhardt at the Erechtheum Judy Garland
At the Orpheum
Viciously entangled; everything deliberately scrambled
There is complete exact beauty and satisfaction
Even the empty shells are beautiful to contemplate,

(DESUNT CETERA)

Port Townsend 11–12 July 1977

GARDEN COTTAGE #1

Chill morning moonlight garden by Douanier Rousseau
Some weird bird or animal cries at 3 A.M.
Lost, meaningless, wild.
Temporarily the moon-window in the sleeping loft
Composes a picture of mountains and tree tops
In the Chinese taste, although an edge of the roof cuts a chord
Out of the circle.
If I should die the picture would decompose
The window just be a hole in a wall
The mountains would be someplace else
This probably is all about a poem I wrote sixteen years ago.

Tassajara September–October 1977

"BACK TO NORMALCY"

My ear stretches out across limitless space and time
To meet the fly's feet coming to walk on it
The cat opens an eye and shuts it
That much meaning, use or significance

Wind chime, hawk's cry
Pounding metal generator
Bell and board rehearsing bluejays
Dana, phoning, shouts "You mean fiberglass?"
Telephone grapeleaves shake together
Dull blond sycamore sunshine
Dana says, "All you guys bliss out
Behind the carrot and raisin salad?"
Brown dumb leaves fall on bright ferns
New and thick since the fire.

Tassajara 8–11:xi:77

FOR A BLUEJAY

You're as smart as I am
I'm as bright as you
Mountain dances in sunlight,

Dissolves in rain
Clouds thin out, become cliffs and pinnacles
Orange leaves, yellow truck remind me of squash flowers
Rainbow striped bath towel melts on the clothesline

12:xi:77

A LITTLE SICKNESS

as if I'd got up hungry
in the middle of the night
& ate a whole bar of Palmolive
unassisted

Philip Whalen
21 XI 77
Tassajara

"I USED TO WORK IN CHICAGO"

In a private collection
Hans Memling or Dierck Bouts:
"Madonna & Child, with Sonny Rollins"
A gloss on the Buddhist Hybrid Sanskrit
Anutpattikadharmksanti
"acquiescence in the principle
That the *dharmas* do not come into being"
(Unless of course there's an acceleration of energy)
Until vast black basalt griffin bull with face of
Beard crown of man steps forward

San Francisco 22:xii:77

MESSAGES

1.

How to open out completely
Without frightening or disgusting
The soft clear edges won't cut.
Rhododendron petal silent brilliance
Only two kinds have perfume.

2.

Final statements about spring this year:
A few perfect magnolias
Two strange white wisteria trees
Total eclipse of the moon
Orange and wonderfully solid
Sphere

[1978]

738

SWITCH

pretty flower wiggles wormy petals
all seductively "seeking whom to devour"
deep in the tide pool

Success transforms it
reveals its true shaman's nature
tough bitter cactus dream

San Francisco
Shakespeare's birthday 1978

TEARS AND RECRIMINATIONS

How charming the sticky sweat
The overheated stove the deranged sensibilities
The lady student suspended from College as
"Morally insensate"
As two lovely oranges in a little basket lined with a folded
Red linen napkin

" . . . but only if it gratifies your inmost wish," I said
And the saltine being smeared with peanut butter
Broke in two

Tassajara 5:ii:78

WASTE. PROFLIGACY. FATUITY.

We get ourselves into a mess when we say
"Thank God that's over," "Never again will I do thus & so."
Nothing is over or under; things is and then change,
We think of ourselves as we used to be
What is we now?
Bright cold moon
Too much dinner
Unlimited cookies
Baked bananas
Booby Pie
Cinnamon infested coffee (blarp)
And a salad full of nasty little surprises
    (Creepy croutons, dead beans,
    Unidentified glips, clots, paps)

    ("To think that anyone could SAY such a thing, much less write it
    down!")

Tassajara 19–20:ii:78

DISCRIMINATIONS

Earliest morning hot moonlight
A catastrophe, the garden too theatrical
Feels wild, unearthly
H. P. Lovecraft could use his favorite adjective:
"Eldritch"

The "shooting-star" flowers that Mama used to call "bird-bills"
Bloom around the Hogback graveyard
Suzuki Roshi's great seamless monument
Wild cyclamen, actually, as in the *Palatine Anthology*
I go home to mend my *rakusu* with golden thread.

Tassajara 24:ii:78

HOMAGE TO ST. PATRICK, GARCÍA LORCA, & THE ITINERANT GROCER

FOR M-D. SCHNEIDER

A big part of this page (a big part of my head)
Is missing. That cabin where I expected to sit in the
Woods and write a novel got sold
       out from under my imagination

I had it all figured out
       in the green filter of a vine-maple shade
The itinerant grocer would arrive every week
There was no doubt in my mind that I'd have money
To trade for cabbages and bread

Where did that vision take place—maybe Arizona
       Or New Mexico, where trees are much appreciated—

I looked forward to having many of my own
Possessed them in a nonexistent future green world of lovely prose
Lost them in actual present poems in Berkeley
All changed, all strange, all new; none green.

Tassajara 17:iii:78

WANDERING OUTSIDE

Purple flags for the luxurious color
Extravagant form; and then I calmly
Empty dead tea leaves into the toilet
I hate the world I hate myself the dragon wind
I allow everything to happen

I want luxury, extravagance, to use
To give to you,
A wild naked leap in moonlight surf
Wildflower meadow, swim in alpine lake
Stand under waterfall

André Gide I always think of as dried salmon
Stringy and smoky, but there he is:

> "going up the bed of a mountain torrent
> to a waterfall under which I rushed
> as soon as I could undress. The icy water,
> falling from a height,
> stung like hail . . . "

In the character of Mongaku Shonin—
High passion, murder, and political intrigue

Tassajara 17:iii:78

742

THE LAUNDRY AREA

Each time I hang up a washboard
The slenderest thread of cold water
Runs down my wrist and into my armpit
Without wetting my clothes.

Tassajara 22:iii:78

SCHUBERT SONATA

Fellow friends we haven't met this day
Nor found a word.   Translation:
      The development of insight consumes
      great quantity of protein

   T R A N S Y L V A N I A

The consumption of human blood

C A L U M N I A

Let us turn to a lighter vein?
Relieve the garden of disdain
(I heard the greater floss complain)

T R A N S L A T I O N is what happened to the bishop,
i. e. no dirty words no politics religion no invidious
remarks . . . a cleaned-up act.

23:iv:78

WHAT ABOUT IT?

When I began to grow old I searched out the Land
Of the Gods in the West, where our people have always said it is.
Once I floated there on the water. Once I flew there.
I heard their music and saw the magic dancing.
They appeared in many shapes; once as *kachina,*
Once I could only see shining feet and radiant clothes
Their houses blend into water, trees and stone.
A curtain moved. Water fell in certain order.
Sometimes there was a great mirror of polished bronze.
Other messages were smell of *hinoki, sugi,* gingko
Newly watered stones.
The land itself delivers a certain intelligence.

How embarrassing to note that four days are gone.
All I can say right now is I can see clouds in the sky
If I stand still and look out the window.
Diane Di Prima came and told me, "If we leave
Two hours of the day open for them
The poems will come in or out or however;
Anyway, to devote time in return for a place
That makes us accessible to them."

San Francisco 17–28:iv:78

CYNICAL SONG

You do what you do
Fucky-ducky
You do it anyhow
People don't like it
Fucky-ducky

744

People like it
Fucky-ducky
You do what you do
Fucky-ducky

San Francisco 29:iv:78

"CAN'T YOU BE A LITTLE MORE SELECTIVE?"

When you break it
Make sure it comes apart
Stop at nothing

Is there something there: a broken egg

> "Adipose muchachos
> Compañeros de ma vida,"

Three months and nearly a fourth are spent
Or lost or otherwise missing
They had no more than a conventional existence?
Fluctuat nec mergitur?
And then
The little boat emerges from the Tunnel of Love
All blush and giggle and sweaty
Into the brilliant day.

San Francisco 3–4:vi:78

THE INSPECTION OF THE MIND IN JUNE

All of me that there is makes a shadow.

San Francisco 14:vi:78

TREADING MORE WATER

It is very hard to understand that
We are where we are at; I am here intentionally
Can you want to do anything
What were you doing. Standing around talking
Greater downtown Chehalis
Night or late-blooming seriously
Let us fall back and regroup (Laocoön)

The mad King of Ireland
Suibhne could fly
That is flying was a symptom of his madness
He lived in a tree; he ate nothing at all.
Crowned.

Start again. Direct the imagination
A knotted mass of grey yarn and very delicate blood vessels
Forward (there's no other direction)
Enclosed please find the pig
"fantastically dressed up with flowers"
"mad, crowned with weeds and flowers"
"mad, bedecked with weeds"
"mad, (fantastically dressed with weeds)"

Seven minutes from now. You hear the words.
"Caught between Sybil and Charisma"
I am grown invisible and very wise

San Francisco 11:vii:78

I CAN LOOK ANY WAY I FEEL LIKE

Unless you have one lifetime friend
Whose business is the production of "lewd shows," for example
A friend you associate with your childhood in a provincial town
A place much different in color and style from what you are seeing now
It would be hard to guess what kind of creature you might be.
If you are very rich you own the building (or the ground under it)
Where the show takes place; if you are very poor, maybe you're
Working for your friend or have declined a job with his troupe

He knows you and knew your folks and you knew his
And sometimes you remember you owe him or he owes you ten dollars

His picture appears on the front page once a decade:

PORN KING ARRAIGNED

or

CONGRESSMAN WINS HEAVY IN WHATCOM COUNTY

People tease you for a few days about "Your friend,
The smut pedlar"
"Your pal, Senator X." They are the friends that you have now.

28:vii:78

insist there be a voice, then listen

❁

X: "You can do everything."
Y: "I'm so glad. One day,
    I shall buy a full gallon of Best Foods Mayonnaise."

❁

Budweiser: used egg
New bicycle. Proudly.
    Who.

❁

X: Wouldn't it be strange
    Never to go back to that building
    Revisit (for example) New Mexico
    Or Kyoto every year, commencing now.
Y: Whatever for? & why "strange"?
    There's no reason to go back—you didn't
    Leave your hat, or lose your watch?
X: Monstrous. Gross. Un-natural.
    Love comes back to dote and sigh,
    "If only . . ."

❁

The orphan scottie didn't quite follow me out the door—whether he's
    getting used to the idea that he shouldn't run out into the street . . .
    was he discouraged by the sight of that steep brick stairway or was
    he resigned to the idea that I (like his recent master) was abandoning
    him—who knows? I worry about that dog, unable to care sincerely
    about little else beyond the pleasure of writing it here.
The dog is helpless, fat, and lost; seemingly aware that he's temporarily
    safe and generally admired, but not particularly loved? no specific (as
    once two) person(s) he must love in return;

X: Where has caring gone.
Y: Back to Montana, in a Volkswagen bug.

I love you very much
But sometimes I love you even more from a distance
Never to the vanishing point

It's true, as Duncan used to say,
We need permission for what we do
Next we must grab permission by the horns & hang on
It isn't just a grant, a gift, a boon, grab it and run
Before they change their minds
            PARCAE
            MOIRA
Hang on while he goes through all
His demonic changes,
Old what's his name, out of the sea
Will be obliged to say what's true
If you can keep hold and listen.
You see only flashing in the air from the jewels
That I'm wearing a bear triangle upside down
Gold and silver sleep; diamonds wake.
I see you in spite of my wrinkled eyes

Now the little dog is attached by his leash to the leg of a yellow
upholstered wing-chair in the Flop Room. He lies on the floor, most of
the time, dejected—and sensible of a general (if gentle) rejection.
Some dog enthusiasts cart him out for a walk but they bring him back too
soon and set him in the corner again like a fern. There he must await
developments. He has clean water in a yellow plastic dish. The dish is
probably clean enough for a dog but it looks dingy and sad. The dog's
various wounds, received in a recent fight, have been treated several
times by a vet and are healing.

There is food and care and endlessly interrupted and scattered attention.
The little dog seems indifferent—doped and sad. Lucy says she's doing
her best to find a home for him. Why does his appearance trouble me.
He's only a dog, and everything that can be done for him is being done.

10:vi–8:viii:78

THE HOLDING PATTERN

Invidious joys all sealed in veins
On top of the mailbox Herman Street; what's more,
Two of the big orchid plants bloom all through May
And this far into June.
One is mostly white with pinky-lavender edge to its lip
Other is off-orange yellow with tawny markings
Later, M. tells me that she gave them to Suzuki Roshi,
"Years ago—cymbidium: They need seven years to grow
Before they'll bloom."

12:vi, 23:viii:78

WHAT? WRITING IN THE DINING ROOM?

One long table supported by three sets of winged lions;
Each lion has a single, enormous clawed foot
Their faces resemble those of American highschool students
Expressing rage, horror, disbelief
Here might be kings and commissars affixing signatures and seals
To important documents of state.

750

I imagine a dream recollection of my father
Telling his mother-in-law a plan of collecting 50¢ per night
From every guest in his house.
Hot northwind flaps my clothes.

Is there a way whereby I can stop stoning myself
Get on with my work? I want to write this
I refuse to do anything else as long as I want to
Write this it is important and horrible and meaningless. . . .

There.
"DON'T MOVE"
i.e. by not moving I lend some shade
make a lap for the baby or for the cat
My shoes are set in a row, not going anywhere
As if I'd gone without them
Carted directly to hospital or morgue
To little magic nonexistent worlds
Pagan Rome
Nothing reappeared; two is lost
"The time has come and went," she said
Unable to keep our engagement for lunch

The little dog has gone to live in Visalia.
Everybody misses him, of course.

15–24:ix:78

751

HOW MANY IS REAL

Whether we intended it or liked it or wanted it
We are part of a circle that stands beyond life and death
Happening whether we will or no
We can't break it, we are seldom aware of it
And it looks clearest to people beyond its edge.
They are included in it
Whether or not they know

11:x:78

LOST FRAGMENT FROM *THE IMPATIENT MONUMENT*

"They're all out there on this island, see, and they're high, see . . ."

☼

"You mean if I went down to that Opera House
And spent a lot of money
The Sugarplum Fairy would do her dance for me?
You must imagine that I'm quite naive . . ."

☼

A species of pumpkin or a yellow melon?
Gourd? Cucurbit?
Anise flowers, their suspended
Bursts of yellow plinks . . .

☼

Loud buds in bird tree
Unreliable deities flung
One specific light-point
Beside the turret roof
The morning star

☼

In the picture
The road is a tree
Branching and leaving.

San Francisco August–November 1978

RODOMONTADE

Did you sleep. Did the same person wake.
"I CAN HEAR SOMEBODY BREATHING."
The day swells and contracts tidally
With the sun.

While not able to go ahead I divide
Spread out from ears east and west parallel
To the wall, sometimes far above and beyond it
I don't care about time, either

Each page of the book splits along the edge
To reveal many thin sheets inside:
Color reproductions, drawings, more and newer messages
Brighter words

San Francisco 15:xi:78

WHAT'S NEW?

We keep forgetting the world is alive
Being the same as we
The coathanger and kimono leap off the rail
Hurl themselves to the floor
Instead of the usual instant anger
I pause to admire this prodigy of nature
The kimono flowing in strange billows and festoons
Falling timelessly (if I say so) to the closet floor.

A couple weeks later I'm flailing about
The rug rippled and ruched, table cockeyed
Something tips over, I (furious) grab, rush,
Breathless dark living room
Why can't you, what's to stop your doing
Whatever you want to do—collect SOMETHING
Fill in the blanks later, unexpected brilliant excursions
And back again to the central trunk or channel

Watching the "waterfall" (more accurately, "water curtain")
In Beale St. PGE has done something to my head
I see myself, all persons, animals, trees &c
FALLING through space, dividing and disintegrating
Halfway down, some are shattered on the first step of the "fall"
Fragments thrown into the narrow pool next below "inevitably"
And then pumped, I suppose, to some tank or pool (roof garden?)
Above.

I like to think there's a garden and pond,
Plain green shrubs, maybe azaleas or camellias in tubs
Doors from the company restraurant open onto it
The pond a formal baroque design as at Inoda Coffee Shop in Kyoto
White smooth concrete framing it, mechanical but pleasing
("Grooming displacement behavior"?)

After murdering Kesa Gozen—by his own mistake
But her design—Endo Morito stood under the waterfall
Three weeks in a row, invoking Fudo Myo-o
And came out as Mongaku Shonin the famous monk
Who went really crazy with political intrigue
Lost everything at last and died in exile,
Sado Island, 1193.

4, 27:xii:78

SONGS

1.

Eat a little now
Eat a little later
Eat a little alligator
     Now

2.

Sing Galveston
Sing Amarillo
Your Daddy was
An armadillo

Sing Coeur D'Alene
Sing Pocatello
Your Mother played
A mouldy Cello

3.

You pleaded
          on your bended knee
You spoke as handsome
          as could be
You was wearing your
          very best Brooks Brothers Suit
When you biodegraded me

I really believed
          everything you said
I probably wasn't quite
          right in the head
Now you've left
          town and I
          wish I was dead
'Cause you biodegraded me, &c. &c.

[1979]

LA CONDITION HUMAINE

makes Friedrich Schiller, his personal
Oeconomy almost overrun by tubercle baccilli
Proclaim joy out of Elysium
Joy and brotherhood also drive Schopenhauer,
And Nietzsche, to suicide
Sparks Wagner's megalomaniac theatricals
With humanity as "given"
Expect nothing but trouble: No omelet from rotten eggs
4:31 A.M. war, murder, misery,
But somebody recently arranged eggs without cholesterol
("O King, live forever!")
To take care of your plugged-up veins

Gibbon says " . . . the wisdom and authority of the
Legislator are seldom victorious in a contest
With the vigilant dexterity of private interest."

San Francisco 6:i:79

WELCOME BACK TO THE MONASTERY

A wildly crowded noisy breakfast
Sixty people sounding like 7500 in the highschool gymnasium
A small town in Arkansas where the people haven't seen each other
In a long time
"Just lucky enough to have thought about bringing this little bit of
lunch with us—few scraps of fried chicken, 3 or 4 pounds of potato
salad, salami sandwiches, potato chips, dill pickles and some chocolate
chip cookies, in case the dinner was late or they wasn't anything
planned . . ."

I wished for nasturtium seeds
They appear spontaneously *via* interoffice mail
Neurotic smoke alarm gibbers in the zendo
Its batteries going stale
Every morning cold air on my shaved head
Wakes me before the alarm clock
Can you hear the echo? Do you see the reflection?

Tassajara 13–15:i:79

VIOLINS IN CHAOS?

Yes, now I go ahead,
Words appear and all a living world beside:
Not exactly a peak-out but a distinct blip
On an otherwise flat curve
Knobby leaf mud curtain grows on steep rock
Then lichens, moss, ferns, in Darwinian succession
A tough wide-leaved succulent lays down on top
To hide the details

OLDE SONG: "I went &
$\begin{cases} \text{closed the window} \\ \text{pulled the curtain} \\ \text{put out the light} \end{cases}$

So he shouldn't see my Fancy"

I didn't remember to say, that
The most brilliant white light sounds
Like the shattering of a huge pane of glass
Water makes neat crystal helmet over the rock

Tassajara 20–22:i:79

LITANY OF THE CANDY INFANT OF GENEVA

Sweet jewel baby
Darling candy crown
Sticky luscious orb
Sparkly scepter
Golden bib of holiness pray for us
Chocolate baby pray for us
Tears of KARO pray for us
Crème Yvette wee-wee pray for us
Fondant fundament pray for us

Rum slobber pray for us
Snot of slivovitz pray for us
White crème de menthe sweat pray for us
Yummy baby pray for us
Gown of marzipan shelter us
While we suck you forever!

Tassajara 27:i:79

EXTRAVAGANCE (COMMA,)

as the song of the K A L A V I N K A
produces almost unendurable sensations
of pleasure & delight,
So much that the listener, afterwards,
can scarcely recollect
the experience which aroused them
                on this Thirtieth Day of January, 1979
Possessors of keen memory & more highly developed
Mental Powers are susceptible
Of falling into swoon of pleasure
When remembering the song
An extravagance, too much small wood in the stove
make it take off like a rocket missile
An extravagance of jasper agate color
Exaggerated notions of celebrity and fame
Let it stand there. The explanation is worthless.

31:i:79

HOMAGE TO SOSA-NO-WO-NO-OMIKOTO

My left thumb is cut and sore today so that
I found myself peeling an orange with my right hand
West to east around the globe
Seeing that great Kami-samma "flaying a piebald
Colt of heaven with the backward flaying,"
Just as the *Nihongi* says.

31:i:79

THE BAY TREES WERE ABOUT TO BLOOM

For each of us there is a place
Wherein we will tolerate no disorder.
We habitually clean and reorder it,
But we allow many other surfaces and regions
To grow dusty, rank and wild.

So I walk as far as a clump of bay trees
Beside the creek's milky sunshine
To hunt for words under the stones
Blessing the demons also that they may be freed
From Hell and demonic being
As I might be a cop, "Awright, move it along, folks,
It's all over, now, nothing more to see, just keep
Moving right along"

I can move along also
"Bring your little self and come on"
What I wanted to see was a section of creek
Where the west bank is a smooth basalt cliff

Huge tilted slab sticking out of the mountain
Rocks on the opposite side channel all the water
Which moves fast, not more than a foot deep,
Without sloshing or foaming.

Tassajara 11:ii:79

DYING TOOTH SONG

Now flesh and bones burn inside my mouth
Ganges gushes from under my tongue
To fall in Siva's hair
Tooth temple of Kali
Skull dance place of Siva

Becoming Yama god of death
I become Yamantaka slayer of death
Endless wheel of waterbuckets turns
Through Babylon zodiac

I stays here turning through life and death
Offering up all this flesh and bones
Round and round

Grass greener than yellower
More birds than bluejays
Railway roar of creek
Not going to Chicago

North mountain peak
A pile of patriarchs' bones
Nyogen, Shunryu, host and guest all one heap

Tassajara 28:ii:79

RICH INTERIOR, AFTER THOMAS MANN

Why, as I was walking up the hill,
All in spring light and air
Keep seeing a glass of water standing
On a polished wooden tabletop in a big house at twilight?
As the air warms, flies and bugs hatch out
Come to sit on top of this page, O.K.?

-2-

Yesterday's glass of water:
Standing on bare wood—surely
This was carelessly done!
There'll be a ring.
Of course, rubbing it with lemon oil will remove the mark?
This house is one cared for by "a lady who comes in" daily.
Presently it is her hand which conveys the glass
Through the next couple of handsomely furnished rooms
To the kitchen; the same hand will bring the lemon oil.
An imperfect white ring about 3/8ths of an inch wide
And almost the exact diameter of the glass
Shows where it stood. A stain.

Tassajara 3–4:iii:79

TREADING WATER. BACKING & FILLING.

Here beyond the Hogback I fling myself into the creek
Water not quite chest high, cold and fast
I let the breeze dry me and all of you on this page
Written in the sun where big spiders play on the rocks
Big black butterfly with cream edged wings investigates
What is the justice of any claim? Which Real, which "allowable"?
What I want is to get loose; not to claim or be claimed,

Falling elegantly over the rocks into the creek and gone
Silent, living, moving; sometimes roar, bubble, splash
White, clear, dark smooth, move.
I said once before, "Wet is comfort."
Probably I'm too fishy to be a seagull;
More likely a walrus or sealion.

Here is one specific contentment: shade beside a rapids
A little fall cascading down the opposite rocky bank
Fountains of the Boboli Gardens I doubt that I'll ever visit.
This leaves all Italian gardens wonderful imaginary elegance:
What the designer imagined but didn't get.

How to explain that everything is unimaginably splendid
And horrible? Or that my life at this moment is enormously
Satisfying and dreadful?
Who can resist replying, "So what else is new you got flowers
In the ass?" (O Spring, &c &c!)
& I, "Why ain't you glad I should be feeling wonderful?"
& you, exasperated, "NATURALLY you're happy—you are heartless
And haven't a single brain in your head!"

I grow fatter and fatter and fatter, like the ox who wanted
To be a frog. He bought a tight green suit and went to sit
On a lilypad. One croak and the buttons flew off; two croaks
And the trousers burst; three croaks and the lilypad sank
The whole project a failure

What does the naked man say. Hot and cold, wet and dry, rough and
Smooth. Things are variously colored but that seems an impertinent
Fact. The wind is warm and dry. Lots of my skin
Is still wet.

The shadow of the naked man says, "You are too fat, even if you
Stand with both hands on top of your head." The shadow of a
Young man with a round head and big ears; it doesn't know
How old it is.

In order to be calm and mellow
One must take time to find out what it is and practice it
So that when the atmosphere become busy and buggy, everybody
Rushing about, seeking who to blame for the confusion
They are so industriously creating. . . .
Calm mellowness may not be necessary to me
But will be there for other folks to enjoy—supposing anybody
In all the world is interested in these commodities.
The noisy creek reminds me of silk weaving looms in Kyoto.

Tassajara 6–7:iii:79

CHANSON D'OUTRE TOMBE

They said we was nowhere
Actually we are beautifully embalmed
        in Pennsylvania
They said we wanted too much.
Gave too little, a swift hand-job
        no vaseline.
We were geniuses with all kinds
        embarrassing limitations
O if only we would realize our potential
O if only that awful self-indulgence
& that shoddy politics of irresponsibility
O if only we would grow up, shut up, die
& so we did & do & chant beyond
        the cut-rate grave digged by
            indignant reviewers
O if we would only lay down & stay
        THERE—In California, Pennsylvania
Where we keep leaking our nasty radioactive
    waste like old plutonium factory
Wrecking your white expensive world

Tassajara 27:iii:1979

AND THEN . . .

Everything else begins or stops
Talking into sleepy ears of night
Coals far down are bright red universe of another size
Only a few square inches but still hot as ever, all connected
All perfectly understandable, all night. Go home by moonlight.
Beyond that the molecules divide it up among themselves.
Whether we walk or stand still, very tiny threads provide us
With news of moonlight or we are paralyzed and forget
The multiplication table.

When they are awake they don't remember having listened all night.
Do you follow my drift (I think all that part is about
A gold mine)
A veritable treasure underground
Out to lunch, off the wall, down the tubes
The sun is in Chicago.

Tassajara 29 or 30:iv:79

THE GHOSTS

Of people dead fifty years and not only people—
Theaters and streetcars and large hotels follow me
Into this dusty little gully. None of them ever liked California
Why don't they stay in Portland where they belong.
I'm tired of them.

A new ghost in this morning's dream,
Beautiful and young and still alive
How far will that one follow me? I'm not chasing any,
Any more.

Tassajara 14:vii:79

THE PHANTOM OF DELIGHT

The candy glass taking shape and color
Of brown soup to remind us
That part is all we know about the whole thing
And IS the whole thing
The "beauty" or aesthetic shock
Points at that or nothing

The glass mug shines
Brown and colorless
Exquisite; complete.

Tassajara 10:viii:79

DIVINE POISONS

Do something else. Change everything
Today begins the new life. Today went away.
Change continues.   Radioactive Materials.

What does anybody know about Hawaii?

✸

It's all
PSYCHOLOGICAL

✸

The corners of this room open out
Into infinite space if I look into them
Crosseyed.

766

watch it!

Tassajara 23 or 24:viii:79

LABOR DAY AGAIN, 1979 AT SAN FRANCISCO

News and music all day long.
The great black cat is fatter and older, just like me.
Firecrackers.
Breaking bottles, windows, cars, brains, airplanes
All crumbling back into original plywood, cardboard, baling wire
Threats, menaces, tears and recriminations:

The President rides a steam calliope
Up and down the Mississippi River
"Keeping in touch" with everybody through music, television,
Steam power

A young person fluttering on the streetcorner told me,
"You're so false!", teetering on a pair of high wooden *cothurni*
"Don't fall down," I replied, as it wavered down Laguna St
Repeating, "You're so false!"

San Francisco 3:ix:79

Examine a big stone across the creek outside the kitchen window
Instead of walking out to coffee? Saved by the real world again!
Walk.
Get away from here? Go read thermometer in the garden;
Fingernails unaccountably dirty.

hummingbird

I gross and unwieldy, torpid and silent
I must begin to flap new plumes, great wings
And sing a one-eyed song of Halicarnassus in the spring
Old and immense and hastening to die
Clutch wildly at any spark of life

hummingbird

Yellow anemone
Purple morning Glory
Four nasturtiums (O R A N G E)

Tassajara 5:x:79

768

HOMAGE TO HART CRANE

As golden yellow as possible
The rocks blue-green as T'ang Dynasty
Clothing colors mudded out—red, yellow, blue, green, black
Animals, imaginary lions, elephants and tigers
Realistic birds. I need a big collection of Crayolas.

Image flowers in mirror landscape sexier
Under glass, poem or picture
Reflection statuary reflecting lights and images
Are there many places.
Only by looking at small details of moss or flower centers
Through a magnifying glass

"uncathected Oedipal backlash; schizoid mirror worlds of brilliant silence"

Now I find I've skipped all carelessly onto this page
Leaving the opening preceding this one blank
Fetch the colors! Summon the genius!

Restriction of the view by round window frame
Lends something of the thick
Unobtainable silence of mirrors
When looking at a distant landscape from a great height
Something of the same feeling occurs
The part of the world "over there," mountains &c
Is absolutely silent
While the place where one stands is nearly still.
Hell yes.
A distinct blue line. The thread of the discourse
Tightens up too much; puckers the fabric.

Tassajara 23–26:x:79

769

WHAT ARE YOU STUDYING, THESE DAYS?

The electronic watch runs backwards to five A.M.
At night I read with broken eyes
How to control the Universe: compel with mantra, mandala, vision—
Summon, seal, dissolve, bind, subjugate & destroy &c
Powers to do what is already being done anyway
"Power to do good," or "Sufficient unto the day is the evil thereof"
"Sweet Analytics, 'tis thou hast ravish'd me"

The Merry-go-round, the Ferris Wheel
The shoot-the-chutes

Your trouble is you're not very real, are you.
Hallucinatory fountain pens, eh?
Skin chips and flaky on the outside
Internal organs all blackened and shriveled
What do you expect with too much in mind
Too busy to see or hear a single particular?
I have put on a gown of power I didn't know I had—
Or wanted.

Tassajara 20:xi:79

MAMA

There you are, home from
your trombone lesson
carrying a violin case

Aren't you.
Where did you get it.
Take it right straight

back

[1980?]

THE ROAST IS LOST

(desunt ceterae)

"Sugar, you talk too loud!"

C O M B U S T I O N

everything weighs less, afterwards.

Henry Ford burst in upon the scene!
"Please try to modulate your voice.
We have trained Dinah to respond
to the gentler tones."
(Burn down Priestly's house, burn down Cavendish
witchcraft & sorcery)

P H L O G I S T O N

(desunt ceterae)

[1980?]

THE CRITIC

The trouble with you, Mr Brahms,
are not as crazy as your friend
          Bob Schumann
whose head spun tighter circles
wheels that didn't roll quite
          so far

23:x:80

DEFINITION

          It glows in the dark
          Like the willow tree hangs
     (Frail tapestry!)
     "Nirvana"—"bathing,
               specifically the bathing
               of elephants" {Ingalls}

     "one whose essence has become
          Intelligence,
                    The symbol of the state
                    Elephant fording a river"
                                        {Legge}

          Joy & high finance. The police ran out
               gross philosophical denial
                              gross stress
                    high degree of gross stress
               Q U A L I T Y
          (The price of the voice of the
                         prophet)

29:x:80

EPIGRAMS & IMITATIONS

I
Actions of Buddha

Clip cuticle; drink orange juice
"be confirmed by 10,000 things"
(the next line after that is delinquent)
                    turtles

II
Upon the Poet's Photograph

This printed face doesn't see
A curious looking in;
Big map of nothing.

III
From the Japanese of Kakinomoto Hitomaro

What though my shorts are threadbare
I deserve all your love

IV
False *Senryū*

A cough
waits for the bus.

V

Perpetuum Mobile

Everybody has a car
But something's wrong with it
We are going very fast—
Have you noticed
The driver is a headless corpse

VI

The Concealed Phoenix
Treasure Jewel Terrace,
After Li Ho

Mountains dream tigers and monkeys
The sea imagines dragons
Monstrous birds trouble the air.
The moon bothers all & sundry,
with or without reflection.

1981

DHARMAKAYA

The real thing is always an imitation
Consider new plum blossoms behind the zendō

20:i:81

THE FIRST OF 20 NEW POEMS

While fire engines & ambulances perform
               acts of cormorant grace
Where have you been all this time, Honeybunch
          I don't even remember your face
               or what your name was then
Far away in crystal vaults (I didn't say
               "ice palaces")
Where did you stay?
The expensive Swiss hotel with the pre-war food
Before the war before the big Revolution
       (Dolder Grand in Zurich)

20:i:81

NORMALLY

I sneezed about eleven times
          all over everything
The winter weather
          entering my bones
              along with the often good
         {orphan hood?}

      {N O R W E G I A N W O O D ?}

"Normally I wouldn't say 'No'."
        Too much dust
        Too much incense
        Too much cat dander
        Too many nerves
        Not enough love for all sentient beings

"Have you tried a drier climate have you tried
Arizona?"
I love Arizona but there isn't any seafood there.

26:i:81

SOMEWHERE ELSE

What is not there that one is missing
What is the pitted viper hissing
     "Health & money. Rice & beans"
   Kiss me quick.
        ✿
      ✿ ✿

Now everything is completed, quite
Suddenly. The supper is washed & set away
But this music is called "Dinner Jazz"
I call myself no body replies.
The high pressure ridge has broke. Tremendous
Winds crash in. The piano turns to stone.
        ✿
      ✿ ✿

"I cannot hear of it without tears. {R.I.P.}"
        ✿
      ✿ ✿

"What a sensitive darling you are!"
        ✿
      ✿ ✿

27:i:81

SOME OF THESE DAYS

I And This That is Wednesday

Rain greases all false lips. Earth quacks
       in Hollister & Watsonville
     {"Ducky falls, lips"}
         30 miles south of San Jose
          {"Poor Joseph!"}

Where am I at. "Depend on the kindness
         of strangers."
            ✿
          ✿   ✿

Dumb fatality!
            ✿
          ✿   ✿

How much trouble would it take in order
to gain civil *or* military control over San Francisco?
            ✿
          ✿   ✿

Downtown rain dim lonesome bar no music yet
(what it means is my life as a young soldier)
Steak dinner, drunk hotel room,
        free doughnut & coffee breakfast
        South Dakota
        too far from the ocean
           ✿
         ✿   ✿

28:i:81

II More Wednesday

     Thursday's insistences press
          Wednesday inside a sausage casing

Be very careful with any given moment, e.g.
"What did I tell you. Tie the string
around your overcoat button . . ."

Expensive Balloon already sailing above the department store

S C R E E C H !
✿
✿ ✿

Now a giant kettle of irresistible soup
One dish of good soup deserves another.
Red wine.
✿ ✿
✿

28:i:81

III Thursday

What machine am I talking to
{A D D R E S S O G R A P H }

Thursday major
Thursday of the Chaldees

Utterly hopeless little sounds of chaos & dismay
{". . . The number you have reached is out of
service at this time . . . this is a recording."}
honey-crazed melopath
✿
✿ ✿

The arms of Morpheus: Proper closed eyes
sable or.

✿
✿   ✿

who's been swimming
    in the olive oil?   did that spoil anything?

      {soothe}   {grimace}

✿
✿   ✿

L O S S
✿ ✿
✿

    "Swivel", I thought, forgetting the tears
the painful contretemps, the savage recriminations,

29:i:81

IV THURSDAY, TOO

    There are more days than usual in January
    There are fewer days in old Thibet

W A L T Z   ⎰ can you fry a clam, bake an egg, tap a
S O N G   ⎱ lamb, grope a leg / can you bounce a duck
M A U R I C E ⎱ slice a corn, roll a drunk, die forlorn?
R A V E L

    More days than enough in Cincinnatti
    What do you do with all your time
    What's your story
    February is too short to explain
    Let us cart you off to Egypt
        all time lives there

ditto { groom your brain, sort your wits,
prop your smile, miss your plane, smooth your head
shave your pits, work with guile, don't complain

✿

swift spoilage due to refrigeration failure

✿

L O S S

✿

"Now my days are swifter than a post"

✿

a relapse.

29:i:81

V THURSDAY, THREE

We dream of our ancestors, then it rains
Your ancestors are books or museum exhibits
      protected by mechanical weather
I can't imagine dreaming of the 11th volume
      of Plutarch's *Moralia*—

A Greek vase, a Sumerian seal,
      a carved jade might appear
Hand-made objects with something alive
      about them
      But no rain

Only seagull grandpa can find it
      I see him

✿
✿   ✿

And we are sorry for you.

   INTERNATIONAL SOCIETY OF
   SHAMANS, WARLOCKS & INDE-
   PENDENT TRIBESMEN OF THE
   PAGAN OR HEATHEN KIND, INC.
             ✢   ✢
                ✢

29:i:81

QUACK

   Where's my rubber ducky?

QUARK

   Where are my Elementary Particles?

QUAKE

   O California!

All my life stole away by Time & Death,

   SWOMP

   too much undistinguished music,

   {whose eye is that?}

and the movies?
and eyebrows

{somebody that's eye is too close
to their nose.}

18:x:81

SPLENDORS

as of the Sublime

P O R T E

no outward sign of
any problem
        you may never want to get out
Right before your eyes
except in Nebraska

Spring 1982

THE ELIZABETHAN PHRASE

". . . so the world runs on wheels," they used to say
One of which, I think, has a flat side
Thus accounting for such anomalies as these
Yellow avalanche lilies blooming in
And through the snowfield on Sourdough Mountain
Their color burns the ice away
Big floppy tulip leaves   the ears of deer
Deer lilies probably poison to any other belly.

25:viii:82

FOR SHUNKO ENJO

                            Don't
Slobber on the paper. And then it was

Lunch time. Let us eat sandwiches:
A solo for fluglhorn.
Abysmal Dante, rise again!
The stream flows between rocks or over them.
Natural History doesn't hold the answer.
Molecular theory of recombinative RNA and

              Didn't I tell you Not
              to dribble on the paper?
              Now it will all commence to
              dissociate. Can I say that.
              Why don't you dry your fingers
              after they have been playing in the water,

It is impatience fleeing from Incapacity, as
WM Blake might have said, or the towel didn't per-
form its proper nature, its little fibres being
clogged with silt, soap, tiny flakes of dead skin—
the towel must be restored by the laundry.
TIGERBALM GARDEN
Tromba marina

                                              23:i:83

"SILENCE IN THE MIDDLE OF TRAFFIC"

Silence in the middle of traffic
Men's heads explode in Beirut
Men's hearts explode in the zendō
Who's going to pick up the pieces?
Your finger's on the detonator button.

Zenshin 29:x:83
(last night of 7-day
sesshin, Hosshinji)

NATURALLY MUSEUM

Chunks of plaster
tesserae fallen part of Angelface
glass duckies perfectly preserved among the bullrushes,
flowers of the swamp, stoned water
Grey Lady nose eye mouth hair jewel
Part of her painted house inside the museum/bath/basilica
growing up around it, sealing it in

✿

SUNSET ON STRAITS OF JUAN DE FUCA

✿

variegated marble sky   (travertine
fire sliced showing bright yellow)

21:xi:83

PARTITION

WALLS {WALTZ}

"fallink in loff agayn . . .   { a quote
 . . . I kahnt hellp eat."   { from Eugene
                                    { Berman

Walls knocked to rubble
A swinging ball of solid iron smashes everything
While at Rome they're slowly rising out of the earth
Growing into vaults & colonnades & porticoes
Bursting thin layers of bitumen paving
Scatter of square cobblestones
"Relics from the ruins of New York", Clellon Holmes
Examining bits of carved marble picked up in the street
Kept on his mantle-piece

21:xi:83

SNOW JOB

ATTRITION

Slowly or ablation, swift & invisible
bearing away

CARMINA MUNDI

La Revolution Mondiale in 1 minute, .4 of a second
to none. ("hardly any".)

23:xi:83

THE KENWOOD HOTEL 1928

Percolator fountain thick dome of glass.
Why does it do that. The percolator, the toaster &
the hotplate all running from one extension cord
plugged into a double socket in light fixture overhead
from which clear glass light (200 w) big as a fishbowl.
The fuse never blew. Was there a penny behind it.
The toast is done but them eggs is never going to boil,
aluminum saucepan just big enough to hold them
the electric hotplate doing all that it can.
Rain & wind so nasty.

24:xi:83

THANKSGIVENING

A perfect day to read Emily Dickenson
        and Dostoevsky
wet & dark, to rush off towards
        the Nevsky Prospekt
or an Amherst funeral

$$\left\{ \begin{array}{l} \text{Lambert, Hendricks \& Ross} \\ \text{gym shoes shorts and accessories} \end{array} \right\}$$

Did you ever read
      L I T T L E   D O R R I T ?
Corinthians, Ionians, Dorians, Ephesions
        cuts & bruises.
I see you've got the gas turned on again.

November the 24TH, 1983
D I S M A L   W A W A   ("C H L O E")
Some trumpeter with Duke Ellington
S Q U A W K !

"THE DILEMMA OF THE OCCASION IS"

She says she's funny-looking
She can't decide on hair nor clothes.
There are too many shoes to wear.
Almost every downtown corner
Displays crippled, sick and dirty people
Beat and tromped on. Others look
For what to look at, watch to see
If they are noticed
Where to spend all this money.

"THAT GUY WAS CHECKING ME OUT!"

"SO MUCH FOR YOU, MR BUMFUCK"

Too many shoes
Those are not the ones.

25:xi:83

787

FOR ALLEN, ON HIS 60TH BIRTHDAY

Having been mellow & wonderful so many years
What's left but doting & rage?
Yet the balance of birthing & dying
Keeps a level sight: Emptiness, not
Vacancy, has room for all departure &
Arrival; I don't even know what
Day it is.

28:viii:85

GAMBOGE

{"You've changed!"}. . . . . {"you're *different!*"}

          my eyes, my dirty eyes . . .
             not that it matters

"You better smile when you say that, Stranger."

                  "did I run, & was I tired!"

the demise of the shuttle

23:ii:86

PATHOGENESIS

". . . out where the West begins . . ."

{Scranton?}

{virgin birth?}

is "the beginning of suffering"
                which ends temporarily at death

29 or 30:vi:86

MAPS AND MOUNTAINS

California topo maps all rolled up
("Roll up the sky like a hide")
Shall I ever be in those bright mountains, ever again?

26:vii:86

AT DHARMA SANGHA

We open the zendō at six p.m.
Sometimes people come.
Here we are stillness parked in silence
Great big nothing happens in imaginary void.

In the morning, old paving blocks tip
    as I circumambulate the chörten
Climbing to Forester Pass, under my boots
Upstairs in the Villa Borghese
Tippy marble floor slab (clank)

                      26:vii, 3:viii:86

ON THE WAY TO THE ZENDŌ

A reverse wind blows freeway sounds up-canyon
    through yellow leaves
Ducks quack and cluck flying to Bosque del Apache
SOME VERSIONS OF THE PASTORAL whistle in one ear,
    out the other.
Christopher Robin, Pooh and Piglet
Stomping through the Hundred Acre Wood.

                      18:ix:86

GOURMETS

The moth wishes for a two-pants suit.
His wife wants a fur coat:
"Don't bother to wrap it;
I'll eat it here."

                      14:x:86

"MY FELLOW AMERICANS,"

the president used to call us,
all of them, all of us, all of me
   "a day late & a dollar short"
The black lady in the TV interview said
"all these Americans red, white, & blue—
rednecks, blue collars & white trash
all that's left is to start over—
Overcoming, all over, "We the people of the United States . . ."
You bet we shall.

Santa Fe 19:vi:87

ACTION TRACTION SATISFACTION

I just don't think my blood circulates good any more.
Let sleeping minds lie. Let the old man go, git away!
    Fly to Oxnard or to heaven, whichever soonest,
        Moving right along.
"I could just cry."

Part 2

The unrefrigerated cheese grew a rind;
It did not become soft & manageable, as I had planned.
I don't cry but I like to get my own way.
    "DIE, DIE, DIE, DIE, DIE!"

Boulder 23:vi:87

BY ACCIDENT OR DESIGN

Pinecones and seashells talk in Fibonacci Numbers
Snowflakes are endlessly different
The stars revolve in Platonic music

"What do women want?"

Every now and then I remember the names
      of Cecil Staples Creacy's "lovely artists"
         Ruth Lorraine Close
         Margaret Notz Steinmetz
         Sylvia Weinstein Margolis
         Edwin Beach

When the moon transits the lunar nodes?
      The Dragon's head
      The Dragon's tail
        ?

2:vii:87

FOR ROBERT WINSON

Dr Washbear comes to watch the raccoons.
There's no law against it.
He won't write a book about them; his specialty
is Chinese food plants & where they come from;
Some are indigenous.
He knows all about bronze chimes, Roman glass
      and "classic" automobiles.

Maybe there ought to be a law.
Raccoons tipped over the garbage can—what a mess.
They don't care whether the garden lights are on.
Dr Washbear is very pleased. He never pulls on his beard.
He knows all about the geology of the ocean basins.
The Law of Falling Bodies does not in this case apply.

11:vii:87

GRIEVANCES

Tears & recriminations don't cut no ice
Constantly the Northern Star bewilders the astrolabe
You can't get a fix on what's constantly moving
Not without instant electronics, can you.
Oh, and if, and if, and if, and if, and if!

Boulder 21:vii:87

NEVER AGAIN

Hot this morning, long before sunrise
All my bones ache and Rilke's ghost
Titters in the closet, Frailing
His clanky lyre. The summer grasshopper plague
May now be over.

10:viii:87
14:viii:87

THE EXPENSIVE LIFE

Tying up my plastic shoes
I realize I'm outside, this is the park & I am free
From whatever pack of nonsense & old tape loops
Play with the Ayer's dogs, Barney & Daphne
They don't ask me why I shave my head
"Cut the word lines," Burroughs recommends
Daphne & Barney fatter than ever & only I am dieting
(Crease along the dotted lines)
Loops of tacky thinking fall unloosed. The sun
Getting hotter than my flannel shirt requires
What about THE BUDDHIST REVIVAL IN CHINA?
Won't read it now . . . too blind to see it
Almost too blind to write this, in my room no flowers
The service station wants four bits for compressed air
At only 16 pounds per square inch
I can see the farthest mountain.

29:viii:87

OYSTER MUSIC: ROBERT SCHUMANN

C R Y S T A L with whiskey in it
expensive candy juice from Scotland
grampa's nerve medicine? Not to be
confused with hexagonal prisms trans-
parent chunks of Arkansas
where did I get this garnet
that yesterday or the day before
". . . stand idly by
while *I* . . ."
yuzuriha
". . . a drifting crowd . . ."

4:x:87

794

AFFLICTION

much intolerable suffering rabbit:
alchemical transformation into hasenpfeffer
This is all that happens; you get your name on a list. Then
the junk mail begins to arrive. {Imagine being invited to be-
come a member of the Republican National Committee!}
Jugged hare a la Perpignan. Rabbit stew.
There is no escape: Transformation, change, impermanence.
Tiny soft furry warm horrified bunny. Happy Easter,
Rabbit. Actually, I prefer candied fishes in the Japanese style.
       What did you say?
       Affectionately.
       "It sounds like Cannibalism, so it must be all right."

Santa Fe 17:xi:87

JACK'S HOUSE

 a kite
a window in the front door
a clown's eye
a piece of baclava
the Ace of Diamonds
"diaper" design
tile

8 minutes past 3 pm—somebody's fiddle sounds
like the chanter of a bagpipe.
I've been on my feet most of the day.
There's an opposite to anything? Aren't there
               more possibilities?
Why shouldn't my neck & shoulders ache? It is
               a mechanical problem.
Fake onion broth consoles the vacant belly
I need advice. And soy sauce.

Maybe diamonds. ◇◇◇◇◇ Large ones.
Maybe the dog is asleep. (Wrong.)
Maybe one ought note grope the plaster cupids.
Maybe that's one letter too many. Can you tell
                the difference.
Maybe they was marble once.

II

Where there is not yet a place to live:
There's shelter. temporarily. Enough.
Here's food, warmth, sunshine & music.
"to begin with, there's the English Language"
Palm trees and Norfolk Island pines
Bougainvillea. Henry James.
I'm trying to live some other place & time:
            can't be done; lunch
        is not the answer. And whisky?
Pasta: contrary to all reason. Happy Thanks-
        giving. Positively.
This is different from out on the street
            & a ten mile breeze.
            S C H E H E R E Z A D E
            S H E H E R A Z A D E
            pronounced "sherazahd"
            not unlike "terrist" (a kind of politician)
much more elegant in the original script, all
        flat & curly: strapwork

III

The dog knows & wants W I T H, O U T D O O R S,
        and I N D O O R S, most of all it wants

        W I T H

even if I step on it once per minute
Chickens are all right, liking T O G E T H E R.
     Do the weak & sick
      mind being pecked to death?
Being Orientals they have more class than any dog

    ✿   ✿   ✿

28:xi:87

POETA NASCITUR...

Somebody complained & I
(quick as usual) jumped in with
"I was happy in my dream", supposing
I was quoting something, but couldn't
   find it in any book
"Maybe you said it yourself," she said,
So I guess I'm stuck with it, now.
Joy Joy Joy out of Elysium – I know
That's Schiller & Beethoven
Not a moment too soon.

Philip Whalen
18: IX : 84
16: V : 88

FRIDAY

Fried-A! and why not
Wake up in the middle of the night, enraged
From a dream of simple anger & annoyance
To this absurd & baseless ire (as in a crossword puzzle)
& hasten to remind myself I'm a lot more complicated
Than just "mad"—I'm also "interesting", "silly", "peculiar", "fat"
only one flat spot on one of my wheels ka-blunk ka-blunk ka-blunk

8:vii:88

THE IMPERFECT SONNET

"The person of whom you speak is dead."
Where is the second crystal?
One came in last night & took it; this one
Held the papers on the table
Now I want topaze.

In the middle of the night—
The glass doors locked, nothing else missing
Worthless Quartz eccentrically shaped gone
As Emperor Nicholas Romanov
As "Bebe" Rebozo

Say that you love me say
That you will bring me
A delicious cup of coffee
A topaze cup! From Silesia—
Property of Hapsburg Emperors
The better crystal is upstairs.

New Smyrna Beach 12:xi:88

NOTHING COMES TO MIND AT THE MOMENT

Spotty old man in the photo is me
Whose true age is 5 or 6
The stewardess asks, "Is there a problem?"
(I'm in the wrong seat)

But always new

New Smyrna Beach
12:xi:88

UNAGI-DON

FOR ROBERT WINSON

They've got donburi at the Sushi Hole now
A mound of rice with whatever decorations right on the plank beside the sushi
      hard to scoop up with chopsticks
We always think of you when we go there to eat.

[1997]

APPENDIX A

Contents of Whalen Books in Their First Book Publication

THE CALENDAR, A BOOK OF POEMS, 1951

"The Shock of Recognition"
The Engineer
The Sealion
In the Palace of the Heart
The Great Instauration
The Road-Runner
The Rose Festival Parade
Meta

Theory
Three Satires
"A Country Without Ruins"
Two Miracles
"Of Course," She Said
Song
The Five Queens

LIKE I SAY

"Plus Ça Change . . ."
The Road-Runner
If You're So Smart, Why
    Ain't You Rich?
The Slop Barrel: Slices of
    the Paideuma for All
    Sentient Beings
Homage to Robert Creeley
Scholiast
The Same Old Jazz
from Three Variations, All
    About Love
Invocation to the Muse
Small Tantric Sermon
Invocation & Dark Sayings,
    in the Tibetan Style
Takeout, 15:iv:57

Harangue from Newport, to
    John Wieners, 21:ix:57
4:2:59 Take 1
LETTER, to Mme. E. T. S.,
    2:i:58
For C.
Soufflé
10:X:57, 45 Years Since the
    Fall of the Ch'ing Dynasty
Letter to Charles Olson
Newport North-Window View
Take #4, 15:viii:57
Denunciation, or, Unfrock'd
    Again
Unfinished, 3:xii:55
Further Notice
Sourdough Mountain Lookout

MEMOIRS OF AN INTERGLACIAL AGE

Address to the Boobus, with her Hieratic Formulas in reply
Boobus Hierophante, Her Incantations
Metaphysical Insomnia Jazz. Mumonkan xxix.
20:vii:58, On Which I Renounce the Notion of Social Responsibility
Unsuccessful Spring Poem
Trying Too Hard to Write a Poem Sitting on the Beach
Hymnus Ad Patrem Sinensis
Prose Take-Out, Portland 13:ix:58
From a Letter to Ron Loewinsohn, 19:xi:58
Complaint: To the Muse

A Reply
Something Nice About Myself
A Distraction Fit
With Compliments to E. H.
Poem for a Blonde Lady
"Everywhere I Wander"
A Reflection on My Own Times
Haiku for Mike
Self-Portrait, from Another Direction
Delights of Winter at the Shore
Self-Portrait Sad, 22:ix:58
I Return to San Francisco
All About Art & Life
Since You Ask Me
Awake a moment

EVERY DAY

The Preface

THE DAYS

March 1964
Corinthian Columns
Mexico
Chagrin
Composition
The Lotus Sutra, Naturalized
Early Spring
The Mystery
The Problem
The Metaphysical Town Hall and Bookshop

Hope for the Best
Absolute Realty Co.: Two Views
15:v:64
Tommy's Birthday
Caption for a Picture
Magical Incantation
Goddess
Buck Rogers
The Chain of Lakes
True Confessions
Dying Again
The Ode to Music
I:ii:59 a very complicated way of saying "appearances deceive"?
The Best of It

HIGHGRADE

Preface
[The end of a month of Sundays]
[Take dandelions first salad.]

[A Beautiful Page]
[Requiescat]
[Try doing a small thing well.]

ON BEAR'S HEAD

Like I Say

Soufflé
10:X:57, 45 Years Since the Fall of the
    Ch'ing Dynasty
Letter to Charles Olson
Newport North-Window View

Take #4, 15:viii:57
Denunciation, or, Unfrock'd Again
Unfinished, 3:xii:55
Further Notice
Sourdough Mountain Lookout

Memoirs of an Interglacial Age

Address to the Boobus, with her Hier-
    atic Formulas in reply
Boobus Hierophante, Her Incantations
Metaphysical Insomnia Jazz. Mumon-
    kan xxix.
20:vii:58, On Which I Renounce the
    Notion of Social Responsibility
Unsuccessful Spring Poem
Trying Too Hard to Write a Poem
    Sitting on the Beach
Hymnus Ad Patrem Sinensis
Prose Take-Out, Portland 13:ix:58
From a Letter to Ron Loewinsohn,
    19:xi:58
Complaint: To the Muse

A Reply
Something Nice About Myself
A Distraction Fit
With Compliments to E. H.
Poem for a Blonde Lady
"Everywhere I Wander"
A Reflection on My Own Times
Haiku for Mike
Self-Portrait, from Another Direction
Delights of Winter at the Shore
Self-Portrait Sad 22:ix:58
I Return to San Francisco
All About Art & Life
Since You Ask Me
Awake a moment

Brain Candy

Late Afternoon
Bleakness, Farewell
The Great Beyond Denver
Clean Song
A Botanickal Phrenzy
Papyrus Catalogue
Theophany
Winter Jelly
Some Kind of Theory
Re-Take 20:xii:63 from 7:iii:63
Last Part of an Illustrated Children's
    Book in a Fever Dream
Whistler's Mother
How Was Your Trip to L.A.?

The Walkers' Patio: Giant Plant
A Recall
Salamander
Homage to WBY
Breughel: "The Fall of Icarus" 20:ix:63
The Double Take
To a Nervous Man
St. Francis Lobbies Allen G.
Native Speech
Roxie Powell
My Songs Induce Prophetic Dreams
Inside Stuff
Native Speech
Gradus ad Parnassum

Somebody Else's Aesthetic
Illness
The Fourth of October, 1963
Song
Mystery Poem, for a birthday present
Social Graces
Raging Desire &c.
That Dream
Golden Gate Park
Vancouver
Oh Yes. Vancouver
Where Was I
Letter, to Michael McClure, 11:iii:63
To the Muse
Three Mornings
Invocation and Theophany

Epigram
Tennis Shoes
Friday Already Half-
Plums, Metaphysics, an Investigation, a
    Visit, and a Short Funeral Ode
Life and Death and a Letter to My
    Mother Beyond Them Both
World Out of Control
PW His Recantation
How Beautiful
For Brother Antoninus
Spring Poem to the Memory of Jane
    Ellen Harrison (1850–1928)
Spring Musick
The Coordinates

THE ART OF LITERATURE 1961–1963

The Art of Literature
The Saturday Visitations
Sunday Afternoon Dinner Fung Loy
    Restaurant San Francisco 25:xi:62
Hello to All the Folks Back Home
The Art of Literature, 2nd Part
Heigh-Ho, Nobody's at Home
Ignorantaccio
The Art of Literature, #3, A Total
    Explanation

There It Goes
Saturday 15:ix:62
Fillmore Hob Nob Carburetor
Art of Literature, Part 4th
The Gallery, Mill Valley
Applegravy
The Professor Comes to Call
How We Live the More Abundant Life
    in America
The Art of Literature, Concluded

Minor Moralia

Minor Moralia
Song to Begin *Rōhatsu*
A Short History of the Second
    Millennium B.C.
The Prophecy
Technicalities for Jack Spicer
To the Muse
The Admonitions
The Chariot
The Idol
Mysteries of 1961

Early Autumn in Upper Noe Valley
The Poor
B. C.
Statement of Condition
Easy Living
The Revolutionaries
Saturday Morning
Friendship Greetings
One of My Favorite Songs Is Stormy
    Weather

MONDAY IN THE EVENING

Every Day

Vanilla

Doukhobor Proverb
Priapic Hymn
Grand Historical Ode
Fragment of Great Beauty & Stillness

Homage to William Seward Burroughs
skoolie-bau
Night and Morning Michaelangelo

The Winter

Opening Rainy-Season Sesshin
Eikei Soji
Ginkakuji Michi
"The Flexible Mind"
The Judgment
Synesthesia
Sanjusangendo
Crowded
White River Ode
A Revolution
A Platonic Variation
Above the Shrine
The Trolley
The War Poem for Diane di Prima
Some Places
Ten Titanic Etudes
Ushi Matsuri
The Grand Design
Waiting for Claude
Champ Clair Modern Jazz Coffee
Demachi
A Romantic & Beautiful Poem Inspired
   by the Recollection of William But-
   ler Yeats, His Life & Work 27:i:67

Poem
George Washington
The Dharma Youth League
To Henrik Ibsen
We Sing in Our Sleep. We Converse
   with the Dead in Our Dreams
Failing
The Encore
Confession and Penance
"Sheep May Safely Graze"
Success Is Failure
The Winter
The Garden
The Winter
12:xi:66
Another Blank Discovery!
"Nefas"
All of it went on the wrong page
All of it came to nothing
Winter money gloom
Pet Shop
18:xii:66
Outside

SEVERANCE PAY

"Never Apologize; Never Explain"
7:III:67
Something Childish but Completely
   Classical
Regalia in Immediate Demand!
Grace before Meat

A Wedding Journey, an Opera
Ultimate Frivolous Necessities
Dewey Swanson
The Apparition
The War
October Food

KINDNESS OF STRANGERS, POEMS 1969–1974

"Many Happy Returns"

DECOMPRESSIONS, SELECTED POEMS

ENOUGH SAID, POEMS 1974–1979

HEAVY BREATHING

[A collection of four previous books.—Ed. note]

Severance Pay

Scenes of Life at the Capital

The Kindness of Strangers

Enough Said

CANOEING UP CABARGA CREEK

Unfinished, 3:XII:55

Sourdough Mountain Lookout

Metaphysical Insomnia Jazz.
    Mumonkan XXIX

Hymnus Ad Patrem Sinensis

I Think of Mountains

"Awake a moment"

Haiku, for Gary Snyder

A Vision of the Bodhisattvas

Phillipic, Against Whitehead and a
    Friend

Song to Begin Rōhatsu

Winter Jelly

The Lotus Sutra, Naturalized

Japanese Tea Garden Golden Gate
    Park in Spring

Mahayana

Tara

White River Ode

Above the Shrine

The War Poem for Diane di Prima

Ushi Matsuri

Success is Failure

The Dharma Youth League

Grace before Meat

Walking beside the Kamogawa,
    Remembering Nansen and Fudō
    and Gary's Poem

Tassajara

Kitchen Practice

The Sesshin Epigram

Zenshinji

Somebody Else's Problem Bothers me

"Back to Normalcy"

Discriminations

What's New?

Welcome Back to the Monastery

The Bay Trees Were About to Bloom

Treading Water. Backing & Filling.
    And Then . . .

The Ghosts

Hot Springs Infernal in the Human Beast

Homage to Hart Crane

Preface from Heavy Breathing

Epigrams & Imitations

Dharmakaya

"Silence in the middle of traffic"

At Dharma Sangha

On the Way to the Zendō

What Are You Studying, These Days?

MARK OTHER PLACE

Rome

To The Memory Of

For A Bluejay

The Critic

"The Dilemma Of The Occasion Is"

Gourmets

Maps and Mountains

"My Fellow Americans,"

What About It?
Treading More Water
Treading Water
What? Writing in the Dining Room?
What's New?
Violins in Chaos?
The Bay Trees Were About to Bloom
Dying Tooth Song
Rich Interior, After Thomas Mann

Chanson d'Outre Tombe
*Hot Springs Infernal in the Human
    Beast*
Homage to Hart Crane
What Are You Studying, These Days?
Dharmakaya
Some of These Days
Epigrams & Imitations
For Allen, On His 60th Birthday

The Art of Literature Sequence

The Art of Literature
The Saturday Visitations
Sunday Afternoon Dinner Fung Loy
    Restaurant San Francisco 25:xi:62
Hello to All the Folks Back Home
The Art of Literature, 2nd Part
Heigh-Ho, Nobody's at Home
Ignorantaccio
The Art of Literature, # 3, A Total
    Explanation

There It Goes
Saturday 15:ix:62
Fillmore Hob Nob Carburetor
Art of Literature, Part 4th
The Gallery, Mill Valley
Applegravy
The Professor Comes to Call
How We Live the More Abundant Life
    in America
The Art of Literature, Concluded

APPENDIX B

Calendar:
Notes and Appendices

NOTES

Each of my poems had its beginning in one of the lines of the old Welsh "Song of Amergin," as translated and interpreted by Mr. Robert Graves.[1] According to Graves' analysis, each of the symbols and images in the "Song" represented a letter of the Ogham alphabet, and also one of the months in the ceremonial calendar of the Druids.

The poems I have written commemorate the months of the old ceremonial year, and, taken in the context of "The Song of Amergin," they form a calendar. In some instances it was possible to incorporate a line from Graves' translation; in others, a strictly personal or classical frame of reference was employed; however, the connection between each poem and its corresponding line in "The Song of Amergin" has been retained one way or another.[2] Needless to say, the poems finally stand as interpretations of experience, real or imaginary. The following notes give the sources of quotations and of other background material.

Reed College
September–April
1950–1951

---

1. Robert Graves, *The White Goddess, A historical grammar of poetic myth.* Creative Age Press, New York, 1948.

2. See Appendix II.

"THE SHOCK OF RECOGNITION"

This is the title of a book by Edmund Wilson—a book I have never read.

Line 3—"Only seven have returned"—see Graves' translation of the Welsh "Preiddeu Annwm" (The Spoils of Annwm) in *The White Goddess,* pp. 86–87: "Except seven none returned from Caer Sidi." The "Preiddeu Annwm" is one of the many items of folk literature concerned with the harrowing of Hell.

Graves connects Caer Sidi with the Bronze Age Irish monument at New Grange:

> The castle they entered—revolving,
> remote, royal, gloomy, lofty, cold . . .
> entered by a dark door on the shelving
> side of a hill—was the Castle of
> Death . . . This description fits the New
> Grange burial cave. . . .

He suggests that the seven who returned might refer to such Sacred Kings of Celtic legend as Arthur, Cuchulain, Finn Mac Cumhail, et al.

Line 4—"Striding antlered"—Graves, op. cit., p. 180:

> The antlers found in the burial at New
> Grange suggest that the stag was the
> royal beast of the Irish Danaans, and
> the stag figures prominently in Irish
> myth . . .

Line 8—"seven-score knobs"—Reference to another line of the "Preiddeu Annwm": "They know not the brindled ox, with his thick head band, / And the seven-score knobs in his collar." On p. 210, Graves has: "the ox is the first flight of five months, consisting of 140 days." Also, there were seven vowels in the Ogham alphabet. They could be represented in inscriptions and elsewhere by an arrangement of dots or raised "knobs." See David Diringer's *The Alphabet, A Key To The History of Mankind.* Philosophical Library, New York, 1948: the section on "Oghamic Scripts," pp. 528–529, and Figure 236 on p. 526.

THE ENGINEER

Lines 14 *ff.*—cf. the Indian myth of "Bhagiratha and Agastya" in Heinrich Zimmer's *Myths and Symbols in Indian Art and Civilization,* edited by Joseph Campbell. The Bollingen Series VI, Pantheon Books, New York (n.d.), pp. 113–115.

THE SEALION

Line 3 in "The Song of Amergin" reads "I am a wind on the deep waters." I interpret this to be a symbol of power over the sea. The sealion I saw on the occasion which suggested the poem recalled to my mind the Greek legend of Proteus, who sometimes appeared as a sea-beast.

IN THE PALACE OF THE HEART

The title is rearranged from the Eighth Prapathaka, First Khanda, of the Chhandogya Upanishad in the *Hindu Scriptures,* edited by Nicol Macnicol. Everyman's Library, Vol. 944, London: J. M. Dent & Sons Ltd. New York: E. P. Dutton & Co., "last reprinted 1943," pp. 184–185:

> 1. Hari, Om. There is this city of Brahman
> (the body), and in it the palace, the small
> lotus (of the heart), and in that small ether.

Line 1—"A shining tear of the sun"—quoted from the fourth line of "The Song of Amergin." Graves, in *The White Goddess,* p. 174, interprets this to mean "dew." Dew suggested to me the "jewel in the heart of the lotus" and the line which I quoted from the Upanishad in the preceding note.

THE GREAT INSTAURATION

This is the title of Francis Bacon's annoucement of his forthcoming *Novum Organum.* The poem I wrote marks the Vernal Equinox.

II, line 3—"Boas and Jachin"—These were the names of the two brass pillars set up at the door of Solomon's temple. See I *Kings,* 7, 14–22.

III—The vegetables and the sea urchins I refer to were considered aphrodisiacs by the Romans, according to the authority of Robert Burton (in *The Anatomy of Melancholy*).

THE ROAD-RUNNER

The symbol in "The Song of Amergin" is "a hawk on a cliff"; I have written about a bird no less royal and, to me, both more dynamic and significant.

THE ROSE FESTIVAL PARADE

I have extended and concretized the original figure in "The Song of Amergin," which was more abstract; "I am fair among flowers."

META

The title is the Latin word for one of the turning points on the race course in the Circus Maximus. The poem marks the Summer Solstice, the midpoint of the ceremonial year.

I, line 2—The reference is to the shadow cast on the altar stone at Stonehenge on the morning of the Summer Solstice.

II, line 3—The English peasantry believed, even in comparatively modern times, that on the night of the Summer Solstice the standing stones at Stonehenge (and those of the other stone circles in Britain) had the power of independent motion.

III, lines 2 and 3—cf. line 7 of "The Song of Amergin": "I am a god who sets the head afire with smoke."

III, lines 5 *ff.*—A rearrangement of David's lament over Saul. See II *Samuel*, 1, 20.

THEORY

This poem is based on my memories of the military mentality—the "I" of the poem. "The Song of Amergin" has "I am a battle-waging spear."

THREE SATIRES

According to Graves' interpretation in *The White Goddess,* pp. 151–152, the month whose symbol is the salmon (in "The Song of Amergin": "I am a salmon in the pool") was dedicated to wisdom and satire. Above the pool where the salmon, symbol of wisdom, swims, there grows the hazel, the Celtic Tree of Knowledge, on whose fallen nuts the salmon feeds. But the hazel leaves drip a deadly poison—symbolical of the destructive use of wisdom: satire.

I, line 5, *ff.*—This is all I can remember of a song I learned when I was very young.

II, line 2—*The Tibetan Book of the Dead* Or The AfterDeath Experiences on the *Bardo* Plane, according to Lama Kazi Dawa-Samdup's English Rendering, by W. Y. Evans-Wentz, M.A., D.Sc., Second Edition; Geoffrey Cumberlege, Oxford University Press, London, New York, Toronto, 1949. Introduction, p. 55:

> Let us take, for example, the animal
> thrones of the Five Dhyani Buddhas as it
> describes them, in harmony with Northern
> Buddhist symbology. . . . the Peacock,
> beauty and power of transmutation, because
> in popular belief it is credited with the
> power of eating poisons and transforming
> them into the beauty of its feathers.

III—"Tradition and the Individual Talent"—The title of one of T. S. Eliot's essays.

Line 1, *ff.*—"jade bell," &c.—Ceremonial objects mentioned in the *Analects* of Confucius. They were symbols of order and authority. The bathtub to which I refer was the property of King Wen, who was one of Confucius' models of conduct. The inscription, "Every day a clean start," is quoted as I remember it; more recently I have seen it rendered by Ezra Pound as "Make it new."

"A COUNTRY WITHOUT RUINS"

For the title, see *The Notebooks of Henry James*, edited by F. O. Matthiessen and Kenneth B. Murdock. Oxford University Press, New York, 1947, p. 14:

> In a story, someone says—'Oh yes, the
> United States—a country. . . . without
> palaces, or castles, or country seats or ruins,
> without a literature, without novels.

Line 16—"Where has not Artemis danced?"—quoted by Martin Nilsson in his *The Minoan-Mycenaean Religion, and its Survival in Greek Religion.* C. W. K. Gleerup, Lund, 1927. From the *Proverbia Aesopi*, No. 9, *Corpus paroemiogr. graec.*, II, p. 229.

TWO MIRACLES

Both of these poems are based upon material taken from Heinrich Zimmer's *Myths and Symbols in Indian Art and Civilization:* the first, from the Vishnu Purana (the line "Every time I carry you this way" is a direct quote from the Purana), and the second from the myth of "The Origin of the Lingam"—pp. 17–18, and pp. 128–130 ,respectively. Taken together, the poem marks the autumnal equinox. Cf. particularly the following lines from "The Song of Amergin":

> "I am a ruthless boar,
> "I am a threatning noise of the sea. . . .

I, line 1—"Dark sleep . . ."—The god Vishnu asleep on the waters of nonexistence (the snake of line 4).

I, line 3—"Eight-Eyes"—The god Brahma, who has four heads.

I, line 6—"You've skipped a breath. . . ."—The cycles of universal existence and nonexistence are symbolized in some Indian myths as the in-breathings and out-breathings of Brahma.

I, lines 10–11—The Gander is an animal *avatar* of Brahma, while the Boar is Vishnu's.

I, line 14, *ff.*—The speaker is Shiva, in the guise of the Lord of the Lingam. Shiva, traditionally represented in Indian art as a dancer, is believed by his devotees to regulate the rhythms of the universe in his dance—the rise and fall of Creation, and of all life within it. Cf. W. B. Yeats' poem "Among School Children," last verse:

> O body swayed to music, O brightening glance,
> How can we know the dancer from the dance?

II, line 5, *ff.*—The speaker is the Earth-goddess, rescued once more from the water-snake of dim chaos and old night by Vishnu in his Boar-avatar.

"OF COURSE," SHE SAID

The last month of the year, the death of the year by water—"I am a wave of the sea" in "The Song of Amergin."

SONG

This poem marks the extra day of the year—the day of the incarnation of the new year—the day of the Winter Solstice.

Line 12- "Hagia Sophia"—The Second Person of the Gnostic Trinity: The Father, Creator; Holy Wisdom, the Mother; and Jesus the Son. I am indebted to Kurt Seligmann for his explanation of Gnosticism in *The Mirror of Magic.* Pantheon Books, New York (n. d.), pp. 98–106.

THE FIVE QUEENS

I. Victoria seems to me to be as good a symbol as any for the Magna Mater—the Mother of the World.

II. This was suggested by the paintings I have seen on the subject of the Mystic Marriage of S. Catherine.

III. There is a popular saying—"The best wives come out of the whorehouse."

IV. Graves, *The White Goddess,* p. 182: "Aega who was the human double of the goat Amalthea . . ." and Amalthea was the goat who suckled the infant Zeus. The Aegis was made of her skin.

V. Artemisia was the wife of King Mausolus of Caria (d. 353 B.C.). After Mausolus' death, Artemisia built an elaborate tomb for him, which became known as the Mausoleum—one of the Wonders of the Ancient World.

Line 1—A direct quote from *The Oxford Companion to Classical Literature*, compiled and edited by Sir Paul Harvey. Oxford at the Clarendon Press, 1946, p. 263.

APPENDIX I

Mr. Robert Graves' translation and rearrangement of "The Song of Amergin" and its five-line "pendant" as it appears on pages 173–174 and 180 of his book *The White Goddess:*

God speaks and says:

I am a stag of seven tines,
or   an ox of seven fights,

I am a wide flood on a plain,

I am a wind on the deep waters

I am a shining tear of the sun,

I am a hawk on a cliff,

I am fair among flowers,

I am a god who sets the head
afire with smoke,

I am a battle-waging spear,

I am a salmon in the pool,

I am a hill of poetry,

I am a ruthless boar,

I am a threatning noise of the
sea,

I am a wave of the sea,
Who but I know the secrets of
    the unhewn dolmen?

I am the womb of every holt,
I am the blaze of every hill,
I am the queen of every hive,
I am the shield to every head,
I am the tomb of every hope.

APPENDIX II

The following table collates the lines of "The Song of Amergin" with
the months of the year and with the titles of my poems.

"The Song of Amergin"	Month of The Ceremonial Year	Poem Titles
I am a stag of seven tines *or* an ox of seven fights	Dec. 24–Jan. 21	"The Shock of Recognition"
I am a wide flood on a plain,	Jan. 22–Feb. 18	"The Engineer"
I am a wind on the deep waters,	Feb. 19–Mar. 18	"The Sealion"
I am a shining tear of the sun,	Mar. 19–Apr. 15	"In the Palace of the Heart" "The Great Instauration"
I am a hawk on a cliff,	Apr. 16–May 13	"The Road-Runner"
I am fair among flowers,	May 14–June 10	"The Rose Festival Parade"
I am a god who sets the head afire with smoke,	June 11–July 8	"*Meta*"
I am a battle-waging spear,	July 9–Aug. 5	"Theory"
I am a salmon in the pool,	Aug. 6–Sept. 2	"Three Satires"
I am a hill of poetry,	Sept. 3–Sept. 30	"A Country Without Ruins"
I am a ruthless boar,	Oct. 1–Oct. 28	"Two Miracles"
I am a threatning noise of the sea,	Oct. 29–Nov. 25	
I am a wave of the sea, Who but I know the secrets of the unhewn dolmen?	Nov. 26–Dec. 22	"'Of Course,' She Said"
	Dec. 23	"Song"

I am the womb of every holt,
I am the blaze of every hill,
I am the queen of every hive,
I am the shield to every head,
I am the tomb of every hope.

"V.R."
"S. Catherine"
"Theodora"
"Aega"
"Artemisia"

APPENDIX C

Essays and Prefaces by Philip Whalen

"GOLDBERRY IS WAITING"; OR, P.W.,
HIS MAGIC EDUCATION AS A POET
from *The Poetics of The New American Poetry*

When I was in highschool I wrote for the fun and excitement of writing. Later on—after I learned that I couldn't go to college and learn medicine—I seriously tried to make myself into a writer, a professional novelist. I believed that I could write fairly correctly; I had learned a great deal about English grammar and composition by studying French and Latin and doing lots of translations, dramatic adaptations, parodies, poems, essays and stories. I supposed that the next thing I must do was to acquire a sparkling and witty style which the editors of magazines should find irresistible. I spent more time reading and working as an office boy than I did at writing, however.

Then I went into the Army Air Corps. While I sloppily soldiered along, I continued to write poems and stories. My comrades in arms (recruited from various colleges and universities) set me to reading Joyce, Faulkner, Proust, Huxley and Thomas Wolfe. Reading Wolfe encouraged me immensely. I, too, came from a poor family; we lived in a remote and beautiful section of the country, far from the intellectual life of New York and Paris. And my family and their friends had a fine salty way of speaking . . . I began writing page after page of romantic description and farm gossip and native folk speech. I discovered that I was a sensitive genius from the Oregon woods whose beautiful writings would bring immortal fame and lots of money.

I wrote lots of unfinished (and almost illegible) manuscript, hundreds of letters to my family and friends, long intellectually searching journals and worries and recollections, but no novels. I wrote poems from time to time, using every technique I had seen other poets use. I played with words and experimented with them, trying to find out what they would do and what they would let me say. At this time (1943), a friend of mine sent me a copy of Gertrude Stein's *Narration*. Reading the book gave me great encouragement and pleasure. I read as many of her books as I could find.

I wanted style, I wanted a theory of writing, I wanted to be able to explain, to whoever asked me, how come I should be a writer and why writing was so important to me. I also wanted a completely believable philosophy of life. I was having trouble interpreting my religious feelings—if that's what they were; perhaps they were only some kind of Druid backlash from all my antique Irish genes, I didn't know. I thought of myself as a "modern" agnostic rationalist: Were not all religions merely a confection of superstition and lies which were imposed upon the ignorant in order to make them obedient to authority? On the other hand, music and poetry and pictures and novels could move me profoundly. I would experience exaltations, "highs," and strange knowledges which seemed to correspond with what I had read about in the *Upanishads* and the *Bhagavad Gita*.

After the war I met a number of people at Reed College who were interested in writing and who were producing the school literary magazine. They persuaded me that it was no longer possible for anyone to seriously write poetry. Yeats and Eliot, Rilke and Pound had said all there was to say, quite perfectly. There was no more poetry to be had. There was no more in the well.

I was, as I say, persuaded—but from time to time I'd forget my despair and sophistication and write a poem. I found that I could at least finish poems, whether they were any good or not, whereas I seemed unable to invent a solid prose style. (I was continuing to work at making myself into a novelist.) Professor Lloyd Reynolds was most encouraging. I took his classes in creative writing. He taught us by using great examples: Joyce, Blake & Williams—and by his great enthusiasm for good writing in every genre. He succeeded in changing my mind about the hopelessness of writing poems or anything else in this late and decadent period of the world; his encouragement and advice and friendship cut through all the fogs and megrims which I had contracted from reading the "New Criticism" and *The Partisan Review*.

It was towards the end of this period that William Carlos Williams arrived—in person—to dispel what remained of those brumes and mists. He was interested in what we had to say. He made us feel like poets, not students any more; he talked to us as if we were his equals. It was at that point, I think, that I really could begin to take myself seriously as a writer.

Being an American, I imagined that life was a matter of owning things, having things. I wanted a family and a house and many books and musical instruments and cars and boats and a little place in the mountains and a small shack near the ocean. I suppose I was remembering all the *Esquire* magazines I had read back in 1937 and 1938. I thought that if I could just write a fine big novel and send it off to Harpers or Scribners in New York, they could not fail to accept it and print it and so my fortune (in the shape of this extravagant *Esquire* life) should be made.

Having all these illusions made it difficult for me to work at an ordinary job for any length of time. After working for a few months, I'd quit and spend perhaps a week buying books and squandering what money I had made, then I'd write for a few days but no novel came of it all. Soon I would be penniless and begging all my friends for help. I needed time to write. The time seemed only to be had for money. I had no money; therefore I couldn't write anything so I had better move out of my friend's attic (or basement or guest room or garage or backyard or living room) and get another job and make some money . . . there was usually someplace I wanted to go, someplace where I thought that I could live quietly alone and write . . . and there were usually some books I had to have very soon.

If my friends had not helped me, I should have starved or gone, at last, to the nuthouse. They fed and clothed and housed me, arranged poetry readings for me, got my work published and reviewed, made other people buy my books, and now they faithfully write letters to me, which I answer promptly. These experiences made me realize that I didn't need money in order to write: what I needed was love and poetry and pictures and music in order to live. This knowledge not only freed me from a lot of old hangups, it also changed my feeling towards poetry and all the other arts. I saw that poetry didn't belong to me, it wasn't my province; it was older and larger and more powerful than I, and it would exist beyond my life-span. And it was, in turn, only one of the means of communicating with those worlds of imagination and vision and magical and religious knowledge which all painters and musicians and inventors and saints and shamans and lunatics and yogis and dope fiends and novelists heard and saw and "tuned in" on. Poetry was not a communication from ME to ALL THOSE OTHERS, but from the invisible magical worlds to me . . . everybody else, ALL THOSE OTHERS, "my" audience, don't need what I say; they already know.

I had been very worried about theories and philosophies and orthodoxies; I now perceived that I had had far too many; so many, that I had been separated from my own senses, my own real experience of the natural world. (It took a great deal of experimentation and study and thought to find out the true nature and function of my various senses and faculties.) The impulse to write had overthrown all my theories as well as the question of "Where does it come from?"

People tell me that it must be very difficult to write, to be a writer. I no longer argue the point with them. I can only say here that I like doing it. I also enjoy cutting and revising what I've written, for in the midst of those processes I often discover images and visions and ideas which I hadn't been conscious of before, and these add thickness and depth and solidity to the final draft, not simply polish alone. In the act of revision and complication and turmoil, a funky nowhere piece of writing can suddenly pick up and become an extraordinary, independent creature. It escapes from my too certain, too expert control. It frees itself not only from my grasp but also from my ego, my ambition, my megalomania . . . simultaneously, the liberation of a piece of writing liberates myself from these delusionary systems. Ideally, the writing will give the reader that same feeling of release, freedom and exaltation: a leap, a laugh, a high.

"How long does it take you to write a poem," people often ask. "How much revising do you go through before you consider a poem finished? How many drafts?" No matter how I answer these questions, the inquirers always look disappointed afterwards. It is impossible to describe how poems begin. Some are simply imagined immediately, are "heard," quite as if I were hearing a real voice speaking the words. Sometimes I "hear" a poem in this way and it is a complete statement, a complete verbal or literary entity. Sometimes the same imagination provides me with single lines or with a cluster of lines which is obviously incomplete. I write them down and put them away. Maybe a few hours later I'll "receive" more lines. Perhaps they won't arrive until weeks or months go by. Some of my long poems took years to come, and then it took a few days or weeks in which to revise and fit all their pieces together.

Some poems arrive as dreams. Others begin from memories. Some start out of the middle of a conversation I'm involved in or words that I overhear other people speaking. An imagination of the life of some historical person may occur to me: I may suddenly suppose I understand what it felt like to be Johannes Brahms on a particular morning of his life. A landscape, a cat, a relative, a friend, a letter (or the act of answering a letter), walking, the unexpected receipt of a new poetry magazine full of work by new young writers, the arrival of a new book of poems by a friend or somebody I don't know personally; re-reading Shakespeare or reading Emily Dickinson on the streetcar and suddenly moved to tears; shopping for vegetables, making love, looking at pictures, taking dope, sitting still and looking at whatever is happening in front of me, getting a haircut, being afraid of everybody and everything, hating everybody, playing music, going to parties, visiting relatives, riding in trains, buses, taxis, steamboats, riding horses, getting drunk, dancing, praying, practicing meditation, singing, rolling on the floor, losing my temper, looking for agates, arguing, washing sox, teaching, sweeping the floor, operating this typewriter right now (bought in Berkeley 12 years ago and wrote ten books on it) while the cicadas and taxis all sing in ravening hot Japanese summer 1967 . . . all this is how to write, all this is where poems are to be found. Writing them is a delight.

People tell me, "Of course, writing prose is a great deal different, isn't it." I don't think so. I finally found the novel, *You Didn't Even Try*, while I was walking in the woods in Mill Valley. First I had a page of dialog between some man and his wife—they had no names then. For a number of weeks it went no further; I wasn't thinking of writing a novel; I was worried about too many other things. Then one day as I walked along through the woods I recalled that scrap of imaginary conversation. I began to see who the speakers were, where they were, and I could see or feel what they would do, and I suddenly knew that it could all be arranged in three sections, three blocks of prose. The "blocks of prose" would each have a specific weight and shape and color. I wrote many independent sections and paragraphs in the succeeding days. The book wasn't written in sequence: I didn't start with the first sentence and end with the final one. Instead I wrote a great deal of material and then fitted it together to form the first section of the book. The same technique was used to write the other two sections. The whole manuscript was typed and revised, then I could do no more with it until it had to be prepared for the press. At that time, my friend, Zoe Brown, went through the manuscript and pointed out places in which the language or the sense appeared to break down. I repaired them as best I could. The result is, I think, not a very good book, but sort of an interesting one.

At one point a friend of mind read the incomplete manuscript and asked me a question about how did one of the characters find the money to do something. The result of this question was my invention of a new character and a couple new scenes for the book, none of which I had planned on, and I was surprised to find the character already there in my mind, I had no trouble writing about her or the scenes in which she appears.

The novel which I completed earlier this year (1967), *Imaginary Speeches for a Brazen Head*, began to be written while I was sitting in a small bar in Kyoto. The place has a large and powerful stereophonic phonograph on which they play recordings of new American jazz. I sat listening and feeling homesick and so I began writing about an American couple in a hotel room in London. They weren't feeling homesick, but they were having lots of other feelings. Later I began trying to figure out how they got to London and where were they going next and what was their life like before and after, and who did they know and how. I had no architectural plan this time, I didn't know how long it would take—either in time of composition or in number of pages of writing—to tell all about these people. And did I want to tell all. And what, after all, did I really know. I had to invent London and Vienna and Katmandu and someplace in Ceylon and some places in Oregon and California and Massachusetts and Colorado, and that was difficult. But finally I wrote it all, then I typed and corrected it all, and then, to my horror, I found that I had to correct and retype it all again, although I very nearly couldn't, I hated typing and thinking and keeping the whole story in my head continuously. Maybe some day it will be printed.°

Writing this present essay or message or *cri de coeur* began several weeks ago. On July 9th I began writing what has become 48 pages of longhand notes, in reply to the request of Mr. Donald M. Allen that I write something about writing. I selected and condensed some of this material into three and a half typewritten pages on the 17th of July, but this typewritten version only suggested more ideas, recollections and fancies. This morning, 23 July, I wrote the final longhand notes and then began this typescript, adding and cutting as I went along. The idea of telling about the novels and the writing of this present essay occurred to me after I had typed five and a half pages. I must correct all of this and recopy it. Did I say that I did it by asking myself, "How do you do it?"

[23:vii:67}

°Published in 1972. Ed.

PREFACE

I write everything with a fountain pen that must be coaxed and warmed before it will work properly. The following pages were written more for the pen's benefit and instruction than they were for mine or for that of the public.

A few of these sheets have appeared in magazines and elsewhere. When Coyote Books offered to print a whole book of them, I felt dubious about the project, but I was too vain to refuse.

P.W.
San Francisco
January 1966

THE PREFACE
(from *Every Day*)

A continuous fabric (nerve movie?) exactly as wide as these lines—
"continuous" within a certain time-limit, say a few hours of total at-
tention and pleasure: to move smoothly past the reader's eyes, across
his brain: the moving sheet has shaped holes in it which trip the
synapse finger-levers of reader's brain causing great sections of his
nervous system—distant galaxies hitherto unsuspected (now added
to International Galactic Catalog)—to LIGHT UP. Bring out new
masses, maps old happy memory.

12:viii:64
7:xi:64

AUTHOR'S NOTE
(from *On Bear's Head*)

I don't like the idea of a volume of collected poems; I'm still writing
more and I'm not really satisfied with the ones which appear here.
Nevertheless, here are most of the ones I've written *"ad interim."*

It's necessary to acknowledge here the love and patience and help
which my family and friends have put into the production of this
work. I must also thank several institutions: Reed College, San Fran-
cisco State College and the University of California: at different times
they paid me money to read my poems to them and made it possible
for people to hear me. Quite unexpectedly the Poets Foundation
gave me a prize one year, and the American Academy of Arts and Let-
ters gave me a grant-in-aid which made it possible for me to travel to
Japan, where friends had set up a part-time job for me. And last, or
first, I must mention my great debts to the "underground" press: the
little magazines where most of this material first appeared, and the
individual publishers and printers who had to scrimp and borrow and

blarney their way into money enough to print my first books: LeRoi Jones's Totem Press, Dave Haselwood's Auerhahn Press, Bill Thomas's Toad Press, and the Coyote Books firm's Bill and Zoe Brown and James Koller. (I must add here the fact that one magazine, *Northwest Review,* and its editor, Mr. Edward Van Aelstyn, were suppressed, censured, fired, and investigated by the authorities of the University of Oregon, the Oregon Board of Higher Education, and the Oregon State Legislature because some of my work was published there. It was this trouble and bother that resulted in the founding of *Coyote's Journal,* and, later, of Coyote Books.) Without the continued interest and encouragement of the private publisher and the little magazine it would have been much harder for me to find out how my writing looked in print and, incidentally, whether anybody could get any good out of it. I'm always flattered when somebody tells me that they did.

PREFACE

(from *Decompressions*)

I don't believe that poets ought to write prefaces to their own work. Readers imagine that they can understand anything written in prose. The misinterpretations of the famous Preface to Wordsworth's *Lyrical Ballads* continue and their baleful effects on young scholars and writers persist. Nobody reads the Prefaces that Whitman made for the several editions of his *Leaves of Grass;* they are the natural corrective to those of Wordsworth. People who are afraid to tell me that they don't like my poetry are absolutely confident when it comes to saying that they don't like one of my novels or other prose. With prose, anybody can see what is there; poetry is supposed to be complex and high class and to knock poetry means that one is a Philistine—who wants to be counted among the uncircumcised? It would be like saying that Beethoven is boring, or that Matisse was a pipsqueak.

Jean Cocteau was a pipsqueak, but he said something important, once: "Please don't understand me too quickly." This is important because it gives the whole show away. On one hand, if a poem doesn't work immediately, the reader is probably better off without it. He is free to shop around for one that gets to him right away. On the other hand, a poem that has instant charm has very little else to offer—it will move the reader from A to B and then stop, which is all right if that's all you know about the alphabet (the Roman alphabet—please remember the Cyrillic, the Greek, the Phoenician &c.). On the third hand, poems were made for the pleasure of making them, not for the purpose of being merely "understood" by the literary scholars and bluestockings who edify themselves with the "study" of poetry. I suspect that even Milton, one of the most "committed" of writers, got a lot of fun out of making up speeches for God and Jesus and the Angels and Adam & Eve. Had he only been expressing his commitment, *Paradise Lost* would not be so much fun to read.

This leads us into the problem created by our feelings of exuberance joy ecstasy satori, whatever. These are basically antisocial feelings. When expressed in other modes than artistic ones, something is likely to get broken, somebody might get hurt, quite accidentally. We should, after all, take great care not to harm ourselves or others. We can put our exuberance into poetry or piano playing or dancing or teaching or cooking or making love. The effects of our delight will become broadcast the more we concentrate them in acts of creation. I don't mean, "I feel really good today, I think that I shall write a poem," the poem is going to precede the thinking; it is going to think itself, in addition to ripping the poet out of his head—think of light wave/particle/bundles being slowly emitted in a pattern from the surface of somebody's face and traveling very slowly through space to mingle with the chemicals of a photographic film and slowly change them so that they in their turn remember the pattern and can reproduce it whenever called upon. Those wave/particle/bundles and their combinations are words for a poet and his mind is at once their source and the pattern of their intensities. Gertrude Stein said it more exactly:

> If you exist any day you are not the same as any other day no nor any minute of the day because you have inside you being existing. Anybody who is existing and anybody really anybody is existing anybody really is that.

But anything happening well the inside and the outside are not the inside and the outside inside.

Let me do that again. The inside and the outside, the outside which is outside and the inside which is inside are not when they are inside and outside are not inside in short they are not existing, that is inside, and when the outside is entirely outside that is it is not at all inside then it is not at all inside and so it is not existing. Do you not see what a newspaper is and perhaps history.

(*Narration*, 1935)

By strict attention to (and application of) a version of logic and empiricism and the experimental method, we have been able to create a luxurious life for a certain number of people in the United States. That number of people is sufficient to keep voting into office a kind of government which is able to control any combination of those elements who, for whatever reason, are unable to afford the luxuries enjoyed by several millions of white lower-middle-class Americans (not to mention a few millions of middle-middle and upper-middle-class Americans and—Heaven forbid that we should neglect them!—the twenty-five upper-class Americans who, because of their good luck and personal beauty, inherited possession and control of the money machine).

We have a feeling that not only the physical world but that our minds and bodies as well are designed to operate according to the same kind of linear logic. Close inspection proves that this isn't so. Any poem here means something quite exact, but not everything that it means could be expressed in prose. It would have changed, the thing it is describing would have changed, and the reader would have changed from the time he started reading the explanation until he finished reading. The poem doesn't exist on account of its meaning. It takes an apparent course, now, from start to finish, but it wasn't composed to fit a plan.

I only regret the topical political poems; I haven't removed them or suppressed them: I take full responsibility for them. The regret comes from looking at them now and feeling that their very urgency and topicality has made them dustier and duller than cold oatmeal. Much of it is stuff that I felt I *ought* to write. Various teachers and friends had sold me the idea that it was the poet's duty to speak out in behalf of the oppressed masses bleeding under tyrannical heels &c. I know now that imagining myself to be a responsible intellectual and a revolutionary was nonsense. Today, it is very clear to me that the *Palatine Anthology* and the poems of Frank O'Hara are greater revolutionary documents than the entire literary production of N. Lenin or Chairman Mao.

The necessity for complete political revolution is very clear to me. The economic system of finance capitalism and international monopoly is manifestly evil. It is killing us all with wars and machines and is swiftly burying the surface of the world in slag and garbage and poison. The governments whose job it is to protect us from the depredations of these monopolies have simply become instruments of the industries they were supposed to control. So of course the big government big monopoly combine must be dismantled very soon. It will be necessary to hang an "out to lunch" sign over Washington DC and sit down together and figure out a different way of managing our affairs. The answer certainly does not involve the manufacture of oatmeal poetry, unless perhaps, one were to take the quality of the poetry for a symptom of the truly desperate necessity for effecting the kind of changes I've been talking about.

I have a hunch that if I write a really good poem today about the weather, about a flower or any other apparently "irrelevant" (I suppose the proper word, now, is "nonrelevant," if we are to be understood) subject, that the revolution will be hastened considerably more than if I composed a pamphlet attacking the government and the capitalist system. If you think about it a moment, the reason becomes obvious.

So now I have done with it. The reasons for not writing a preface are manifold; the chief one is that I do not write as well as the late Bernard Shaw, that virtuoso of the preface. Furthermore, I have tried to defend what nobody has taken the trouble to read, much less to attack.

People have been pleased to describe my book, *On Bear's Head,* as "the collected poems of PW." I wish that they'd stop. It may be possible for me, next year or so, to consider making up a volume of "all the poems that Mr W. sees fit to release to the printer." *On Bear's Head* wasn't such a book. This present volume, arranged by & at the instance of my friend Don Allen, must not be construed as such a volume. Later.

PW

ABOUT WRITING AND MEDITATION

(from *Beneath a Single Moon,* ed. Kent Johnson and Craig Paulenich, Shambhala, 1991)

I thought that I'd write books and make money enough from them to travel abroad and to have a private life of reading and study and music. I developed a habit of writing and I've written a great deal, but I've got very little money for it.

With meditation I supposed that one could acquire magical powers. Then I learned that it would produce enlightenment. Much later, I found out that Dogen is somewhere on the right track when he tells us that the practice of zazen is the practice of enlightenment. Certainly there's no money in it. Now I have a meditation habit.

Jack Kerouac said that writing is a habit like taking dope. It's a pleasure to write. I usually write everything in longhand. I like the feel of the pen working on the paper.

In my experience these two habits are at once mutually destructive and yet similar in kind. I write for the excitement of doing it. I don't think of an audience; I think of the words that I'm using, trying to select the right ones. In zazen I sit to satisfy my sitting habit. It does no more than that. But while sitting, I don't grab onto ideas or memories or verbal phrases. I simply watch them all go by. They don't get written; they don't (or anyway, very seldom) trip the relay on my writing machinery. Considering that I've spent more days in the past fifteen years sitting zazen than I have spent in writing, it's little wonder that I've produced few books during that time.

I became a poet by accident. I never intended to be a poet. I still don't know what it's all about. If I wrote poetry at all, it's because I could finish it at the end of the page. Maybe it would run halfway down the next page, but it would come to a stop. What I wanted to do with writing was to write novels and make money like anybody else. And now I find myself in this ridiculous industry of writing these incomprehensible doodles, and why anybody's reading them I can't understand.

As far as meditation is concerned I'm a professional. I've been a professional since 1973. And that's my job. I find it very difficult to sell. And that's interesting; that's another job I have, to sell you on this idea that it's good to sit. Maybe that's where the poetry comes into all this, that it has to be an articulation of my practice and an encouragement to you to enter into Buddhist practice. To get yourselves trapped into it I hope. And then try to figure out how to get out of it. It's harder to get out of Buddhist practice than it is to get out of writing poetry.

I write very little nowadays. There is a journal in which I write things like "the sun is shining" or "Michael McClure was in town and we had a nice time" or "the flowers are blooming." And so I don't have much to say because I talk all the time. I have to give lectures, I participate in seminars, and I have not much chance to wander up and down a hillside picking flowers and picking my nose and scratching my balls and whatnot. And thinking of hearing, having a chance to hear what's going on around me, or hearing people in restaurants or on a bus. There are no restaurants in Santa Fe worth sitting in, there are no buses at all. So I don't hear anymore, hardly at all, unless I travel. I was recently in New York and around, and now I'm here at Green Gulch Farm, and it's interesting to hear what's going on outside. While somebody was talking there was a robin outside raising hell. But that doesn't mean anything. I mean I'm not about to write a poem on the subject of so-and-so talking, while a robin outside was raising hell.

And so I'm here under false pretenses. You must deal with that however you can. I'm quite willing to talk to people and explain things to them if they have questions. Or I might be sitting doltishly looking out the window. So it will be necessary for you, if you want something from me, to try to get it by asking questions. I'm not about to offer anything, I don't have anything to offer. I'm sorry—that's the "emptiness" part.

I think there's a great deal of misunderstanding about what emptiness is, the idea that emptiness is something that happens under a bell jar when you exhaust all the air from it. That's not quite where it's at as far as I understand it. The emptiness is the thing we're full of, and everything that you're seeing here is empty. Literally the word is *shunya*, something that's swollen up; it's not, as often translated, "void." It's packed, it's full of everything. Just as in Shingon Buddhism, the theory that everything we see and experience is Mahavairochana Buddha, the great unmanifest is what we're actually living and seeing in. Wallace Stevens said, "We live in an old chaos of the sun." Well we're living in a live chaos of Mahavairochana Buddha. What are you gonna do with it? How are you gonna handle that?

My Buddhist name is Zenshin Ryufu, which is very impressive. The reason that you have a name like that is that you keep forgetting it and it makes you wonder about why you got it and why it's for you, because it's a very exalted idea. *Zenshin* means "meditation mind" and it's also a Japanese pun. It means something like "complete mind." There's also a zenshin essay by Dogen. *Ryufu* is two Chinese characters that literally mean "dragon wind," but in Chinese literature I found out it means "imperial influence" (the dragon stands for the Chinese emperor). It's pretty complicated, and you wonder, well what does that have to do with me? Four words—Zen-Mind-Dragon-Wind. What in the world, what connection does that have with this individual who has received this name and is ordained as a monk? So that is a problem that becomes more or less clear as you continue being a monk—what your name is. And of course names and poetry all come together. Gertrude Stein says poetry is calling the name of something. That's what we do all the time, actually—call ourselves. There's the story of the Zen master who every day would call his own name. He'd say, "Zuigan!" And he'd say, "Yes!" "Zuigan! Don't be misled by other people!" Of course the other people were Zuigan too.

I like the idea somebody mentioned of erratic practice. It immediately reminded me of rocks that were left around when the glaciers receded. A lot of times setting out in a field there are no other rocks. It's a very strange appearance. You can't account for the rock's position unless you remember the glacier that carried the rock there and then went away. Zazen is slow but leaves erratic boulders.

I have a number of fancy titles at the Dharmasangha in Santa Fe. But when push comes to shove it means that I'm the person who goes down and does the opening ceremony in the zendo every morning and sits two periods. And then I go down again at 5:30 in the evening and sit again with whoever shows up. And the rest of the time I study. We have two seminars a week with Baker Roshi on the koans in the *Shoyoruko* as translated by Thomas Cleary. I've also been studying with Baker Roshi closely for the last three years with the intention at last of trying to become a Buddhist teacher, to help get this show on the road, which is still very precarious in this country. The chances as I see it of Buddhism simply becoming something that people do on Sunday just like Methodism or Catholicism are very strong. But I hope that there will continue to be centers in the country like Tassajara, or Shasta Abbey, or Mt. Baldy. There will be these hidden spots around the country where people can hide out and do more serious, concentrated practice, to keep the door open for everybody to get the chance to try it out, find out what it's like to not do anything except follow a particular schedule and do a lot of sitting and a lot of physical work. This is something that I think is necessary in order for human beings to go on being human beings. So far all we've been able to invent in the United States is the business of building small cabins in the woods and going there to hide out, then come back and write a book about it.

That practice, that sort of individual, hermit, erratic practice, is something that's really important. The danger of Zen Centers or monasteries is that people will take them seriously as being real. We should find our own practice; we might start out in an official place, but we should discover somehow that we don't need official institutions. It's exactly like Lew Welch says in his poem about the rock out there, the Wobbly Rock, "Somebody showed it to me and I found it myself." The quote isn't exact. Lew was an erratic Zen practitioner who was a great poet.

The real tension, I think, is between official poetry, the kind that we're taught in school and is kept in libraries, and the kind we really believe in—what we are writing and what our friends write. The same thing holds for meditation; what we discover for ourselves and learn. At some point you can forget it and go off and make a pot of spaghetti. We used to go down to Muir Beach years ago to gather mussels off the rocks. We'd build a bonfire, put seaweed on the fire to steam the mussels. We'd eat them, then jump up and down in the waves and have fun. That was . . . enough. Probably enough. Or too much. Oh, I guess Blake said it, "Enough, or too much." That's all.

PREFACE
(from *Enough Said*)

The most interesting thing about this book is that it was written under ideal conditions. The author was living a life of elegant retirement in the character of a Zen Buddhist priest at the Hossen Temple in San Francisco and at the monastery of Zenshinji at Tassajara Springs, far in the mountains east of Big Sur. Given ideal conditions, how could life be anything but a joyous round of pleasure. What could possibly go wrong.

At the top of the hill above the Third Culvert (counting from the first one over Cabarga Creek as one ascends the road to and from Tassajara) I sat down for a minute to consider what's possible. A sentence, a word, a monkey flower. Sun heats; wind cools, simultaneously. What am I after. From this point the road is uphill and downhill. The flowers are too pale to be monkey flowers. They aren't the exact color of wild azaleas. My ears fry in the sunlight. There are monkey flowers no matter what I say, just as K. M. still has a terrible cough this morning. Wild larkspurs have three different shades of blue.

Early the next morning I find that my brains have come loose and are floating up against the skull bones, gently bumping and knocking with the motions of the tide. I used to believe that I could do anything so long as I really understood that there'd be consequences, whether pleasant or unpleasant, consequences of specific size, shape, color and duration. They were to be accepted and digested. (People used to say, "Never buy anything you can't eat.") Now I'm uncertain whether all the consequences of any—even the simplest—action can be known immediately; I fear that some of the smaller details which one may have overlooked may bring about a disaster which will arrive at the door on some innocently beautiful Sunday morning. Why not.

At the turnout above the Third Culvert I found a set of *juzu* beads which I hadn't realized leaving or losing. There they were drying in the sun beside variegated lupine flowers. At sundown that day I noted that a great wind was blowing lumps and sheets of cloud across the narrow sky; maybe that's all that was scheduled to happen that day. Later the air was fresh and still. The full moon appeared.

Returned to the city after many months I find too many things in my rooms and not enough air. What can be is a slice of Nob Hill in the distance. Radio delivers KJAZ without hesitation. No ideas or anything; imported beer. There was a visit to the rhododendrons blooming in the Park. In Stockton Street, Gregory Corso hollers to me from the window of his mother-in-law's blue station wagon, also blooming. (Max doesn't say hello but appears and disappears, grinning, from under an Army blanket on the floor of the car behind his father's seat.) Ideal conditions prevail in the city and in the country. I continue, after all; and the consequences.

Tassajara/San Francisco, 1980

APPENDIX D

Biography and Bibliography

SHORT BIOGRAPHY

Philip Whalen was born on October 20, 1923, in Portland, Oregon. Shortly thereafter, his family moved to The Dalles, a small town on the Columbia River. Graduating from high school in 1941, he did odd jobs and then joined the armed forces before attending Reed College on the GI Bill from 1946 to 1951. It was at Reed that he met fellow poets Gary Snyder and Lew Welch and came under the influence of Lloyd Reynolds, professor of literature and creative writing, whose course on calligraphy contributed to Whalen's interest in the way poems appear as visual statements on the page. During this time he also met William Carlos Williams, who had come to Reed on a college reading tour, an experience that would prove to be one of the turning points in Whalen's poetic career. After graduation, Whalen traveled the West Coast, staying with friends and working summers as a fire lookout. One of his most famous poems, "Sourdough Mountain Lookout," reflects this experience. In 1955, at Snyder's suggestion, he took part in the Six Gallery reading in San Francisco where he met East Coast Beat writers Allen Ginsberg and Jack Kerouac, with whom he shared a common outlook. He was also part of the San Francisco Renaissance scene, associating with such poets as Joanne Kyger, Michael McClure, and Kenneth Rexroth. In 1960, he was included in Donald Allen's seminal *New American Poetry* anthology, and his first two poetry collections, *Like I Say* and *Memoirs of an Interglacial Age*, were published. In the 1960s, Whalen wrote three novels: *You Didn't Even Try, Imaginary Speeches for a Brazen Head,* and *Diamond Noodle.* And *Highgrade,* a unique blend of Whalen's calligraphy and doodling, also appeared in the 1960s. In 1967, he traveled to Japan to teach English, where his previous interest in Zen Buddhism turned into a more serious commitment. Whalen lived in Japan off and on until 1971, returning briefly to the United States in 1969 to oversee the publication of his major poetry collection, *On Bear's Head.* On his eventual return to the Bay Area, he moved to the San Francisco Zen Center at the invitation of Richard Baker Roshi and was ordained as a monk in 1973. During the 1970s several volumes of his poetry were published, later collected in 1980 in *Heavy Breathing,* along with a shorter selected volume of poems, *Decompressions.* In the 1990s several new collections appeared: *Some of These Days,* a volume of Buddhist poems, *Canoeing Up Cabarga Creek,* and *Overtime,* a major selected volume of verse. During this time, Whalen deepened his commitment to Zen Buddhism. In 1987 he was given dharma transmission, and in 1991 he was made abbot of San Francisco's Hartford Street Zen Center. Due to failing health, Whalen retired from this position in 1996, but remained as a teacher until his death on June 26, 2002. Whalen's unique contribution to American letters may be seen in his commitment both to the practice of poetry and to that of Zen Buddhism, merging traditions of West and East.

—Jane Falk

BIBLIOGRAPHY

The Calendar, a Book of Poems, Portland, Ore.: Reed College, thesis (B.A.), 1951.
Three Satires. Portland, Ore.: Privately published, 1951.
    Wrappers. 13 copies.
Song. Portland, Ore.: Privately published, 1951.
Self-Portrait from Another Direction. San Francisco: Auerhahn Press, 1959.
The End, of a Month of Sundays. San Francisco: Auerhahn Press, 1959.
    Wrappers.
NOTE: 1. Cover title of only "Auerhahn Press" for this folded broadside, which is also encountered with wrappers.
    2. John Wieners, Philip Lamantia and Michael McClure.
    3. Commonly referred to by Wieners's title, "Bag Dad by the Bay."
Memoirs of an Interglacial Age. San Francisco: Auerhahn Press, 1960. 51 pp.
    Two issues, no priority:
    1. Hardcover, no priority:
    a. 60 copies.
    b. 25 copies, with an original drawing and holograph poem by the author.
    c. 15 copies, signed by the author.
From Memoirs of an Interglacial Age. Cambridge, Mass. Paterson, ca. 1960.
    Mimeographed sheet.

Like I Say. New York: Totem Press/Corinth Books, 1960. 47 pp.
　　Gray wrappers.
　　Publishers' names on copyright page.
Hymnus Ad Patrem Sinensis. San Francisco: San Francisco Arts Festival Commission, 1963.
　　Broadside.
　　300 copies, most of which were signed by the author.
NOTE: Laid in portfolio entitled "San Francisco Arts Festival: A Poetry Folio: 1963."
Three Mornings. San Francisco: Four Seasons Foundation, 1964.
　　Broadside.
Monday, in the Evening, 21:vii:61. Milan: Privately published, 1964.
　　Wrappers, no priority:
　　1. 291 copies, numbered.
　　2. 18 copies, hors commerce.
Goddess. San Francisco: Don Carpenter, 1964.
　　Broadside, no priority:
　　1. 100 copies.
　　2. 25 copies without colophon, for the use of the author.
Dear Mr. President. San Francisco: Impressions Production, 1965.
　　Broadside.
　　1. 500 copies.
Every Day. Eugene, Ore.: Coyote's Journal, 1965.
　　Wrappers.
　　Coyote Book #1.
　　1. 500 copies.
　　Second Printing: Ann Arbor, 1965. 5 1/2 x 8.
Nobody Listening to You? San Francisco: Philip Whalen, 1965.
　　Broadside.
NOTE: Issued to celebrate "Gentle Thursday" and often listed by that title.
Highgrade: Doodles, Poems. San Francisco: Coyote's Journal, 1966.
　　Wrappers.
You Didn't Even Try. San Francisco: *Coyote's Journal,* 1967.
　　Wrappers.
The Invention of the Letter: A Beastly Morality (Being Illuminated Moral History for the Edification of Younger Readers). New York: Irving Rosenthal, 1967.
　　Hardcover, ring-bound.
Intransit: The Education Continues Along Including Voyages, a TransPacific Journal. Eugene, Ore.: Toad Press, 1967. 61 pp.
T/O. San Francisco: David Haselwood, 1967.
　　Wrappers.
　　80 copies.
Winning His Way or The Rise of William Johnson. Kyoto, Japan: Irving Rosenthal, 1967. 26 pp.
　　Wrappers.
On Bear's Head. New York: Harcourt, Brace & World/*Coyote's Journal,* 1969.
　　Two issues, no priority:
　　1. Hardcover, dust wrapper. 406 pp.

2. Wrappers.

"First edition."

Severance Pay. San Francisco: Four Seasons Foundation, 1970.

Two issues, no priority:

1. Hardcover, no priority:

a. Trade edition. 51 pp.

b. 50 copies, signed by the author. 51 pp.

2. Wrappers.

Writing 24.

Scenes of Life at the Capital. San Francisco: Maya, 1970.

Wrappers, no priority:

1. 250 copies. 74 pp.

2. 50 copies, numbered, signed by the author.

Maya Quarto Ten.

Also: Bolinas, Calif.: Grey Fox Press, 1971.

Wrappers.

"First edition."

NOTE: Expanded edition.

Imaginary Speeches for a Brazen Head. Los Angeles: Black Sparrow Press, 1972.

Two issues, no priority:

1. Hardcover, acetate dust wrapper; no priority:

a. 200 copies, numbered, signed by the author. 156 pp.

b. 26 copies, lettered, signed by the author.

2. Wrappers.

1,500 copies.

Looking for Help. San Francisco: Panjandrum Press, 1972.

Broadside.

In the Night. Privately published, ca. 1972.

Broadside.

100 signed copies.

On Bread & Poetry: A Panel Discussion with Gary Snyder, Lew Welch & Philip Whalen. Berkeley, Calif.: Grey Fox Press, 1973. 48 pp.

The Kindness of Strangers: Poems 1969–1974. Bolinas, Calif.: Four Seasons Foundation, 1976. (Listed as New Departures in Four Seasons Paperback book list at back of this edition.)

Wrappers. Writing 33. 59 pp.

Prolegomena to a Study of the Universe. Berkeley: Poltroon Press, 1976. Introduction by Kevin Powers.

290 copies.

Zenshinji. Port Townsend: Copper Canyon Press, ca. 1977.

Prose Take. Bancroft Library, 1977.

Broadside.

Two editions.

26 lettered and signed.

50 numbered copies signed.

Anchor Steam Beer, for Michael McClure, unspeakable visions of the individual. Arthur and Kit Knight Production. 1978.

Decompressions. Bolinas, Calif.: Grey Fox Press, 1978.
   Wrappers. 86 pp.
Off the Wall, Interviews with Philip Whalen. Bolinas, Calif.: Grey Fox Press, 1978.
   Wrappers.
The Diamond Noodle. Berkeley, Calif.: Poltroon Press, 1980.
   Two issues:
   1. 100 copies, signed and sealed by the author.
   2. Wrappers.
Enough Said: Fluctuat Nec Mergitur: Poems 1974–1979. San Francisco: Grey Fox
   Press, 1980.
   Two issues:
   1. 56 hardcover copies, numbered, signed by the author. 75 pp.
   2. Wrappers.
The Wind Chimes. Arif Press, 1980.
   Broadside.
Tara. San Francisco: Black Stone Press, 1981.
   Broadside.
   100 copies.
In Takagamine, from *Scenes of Life at the Capital.* San Francisco: Black Stone Press,
   1981.
   Broadside.
   99 copies.
Heavy Breathing. San Francisco: Grey Fox Press, 1983. 207 pp.
   Wrappers.
Two Variations: All About Love. San Francisco: Arif Press, 1983. Wesley Tanner.
   Broadside.
   19 copies.
A Vision of the Bodhisattvas. Albuquerque, N.M.: Living Batch Bookstore, 1984.
   Illustration by Jeff Bryan.
   Broadside.
   100 copies.
For C. San Francisco: Arion Press, 1984.
   First appeared in *Like I Say,* then again in *Temple of Flora.*
   With illustrations by Jim Dine.
The Elizabethan Phrase. Santa Barbara Calif.: Designed & printed by David Dahl
   for Table-Talk Press, 1985.
   Broadside.
Two Novels. Somerville, Mass.: Zephyr Press, 1985. 250 pp.
   Two editions:
   1. Hardcover, dust wrapper.
      a. Trade edition. 300 copies.
      b. 50 copies signed and numbered by the author.
   2. Wrappers. 1,200 copies.
Window Peak. Santa Fe, N.M.: Casa Sin Nombre, 1986. Photographs by Annie
   Liebowitz.
   Broadside.
   500 copies.

Driving Immediately Past. Berkeley, Calif.: Poltroon Press, 1989.
> First appeared in *A Bibliography of the Auerhahn Press & Its Successor Dave Haselwood Books,* compiled by a printer, Poltroon Press, 1976.
> Broadside.

Canoeing Up Cabarga Creek: Buddhist Poems 1955–1986. Introduction by Richard Baker. Foreword by Allen Ginsberg. Berkeley, Calif.: Parallax Press, 1996. 68 pp.

Mark Other Place. Pacifica, Calif.: Big Bridge Press, 1997.
> First appeared in Big Bridge online chapbook issue January 1997.

Japanese Tea Garden Golden Gate Park in Spring. Boulder, Colo.: Kavyay
> The Naropa Institute 1998.
> Broadside.

Some of These Days. San Jose, N.M.: Desert Rose Press, 1999.
> Two editions:
> 1. 50 copies hardbound, signed by the poet.
> 2. 250 copies sewn in wrappers.

Goofbook for Jack Kerouac. Poem by Philip Whalen. Edited by Michael Rothenberg. Pacifica, Calif: Big Bridge Press, 2001. 32 pp.

Prose [Out]Takes. Philip Whalen. Edited by Alastair Johnston. Berkeley, Calif: Poltroon Press, August 2002. 20 pp.

The Unidentified Accomplice or, The Transmissions of C. W. Moss. ©1968 Philip Whalen. © 2005 Philip Whalen Estate. Brunswick, Maine: Coyote Books, 2006.

INDEX OF TITLES

INDEX OF FIRST LINES